Wildlife Travel

wi

| Foreword by Kate Humble

For Sally,
Joseph & Eleanor

All photographs
by the author except
where stated

Foreword

I have been lucky enough to lead a pretty wild life; not in the Rolling Stones sense of 'wild', you understand, but in the amount of time I've spent with some of the world's most engaging inhabitants. An encounter with a truly wild animal is an unforgettable experience, one that will make your heart race and put a great big, unashamed grin all over your face.

I was diving in California for work one year, lying on the seabed talking about seastars, when the cameraman pointed behind me. Very slowly I turned round and came nose to nose with a young sea lion, fascinated by this strange-looking creature who had turned up in her patch. We regarded each other for a minute or more before she spun away in one effortlessly balletic move and left me gazing at a trail of bubbles with a smile so wide I nearly lost my regulator.

We share our planet with an extraordinary array of other creatures, yet the hurly burly of modern urban life can make us feel ever-more detached from the natural world. Science tells us time spent with nature is good for us and from personal experience I can absolutely vouch for that. The magical moment of catching sight of a barn owl swooping over a field at dusk, the heart-stopping anticipation of seeing a big cat stalking its prey, the joy of spotting dolphins from a boat, all these are experiences I cherish.

So what better way to spend a well-earned holiday than in the company of some of our world's wildest inhabitants? It will be good for you, and if you follow the advice and guidance offered in this excellent book, it will be good for the world's wildlife and the communities that support it too.

Kate

Kate Humble

Kate Humble and Badger

Television presenter Kate Humble fronts the BBC's *Springwatch* and *Autumnwatch* programmes with Chris Packham. She is also president of the Royal Society for the Protection of Birds and founded the innovative Stuff Your Rucksack scheme (page 15).

What better way to spend a well-earned holiday than in the company of some of our world's wildest inhabitants. It will be good for you, and if you follow the advice in this excellent book, it will be good for the world's wildlife

Contents

Introduction 6

Essentials 10

Encounters 44

2   **Foreword by Kate Humble**

6   **Introduction**
9   About the book
9   About the author

12   Where the wild things are
14   Responsible wildlife travel
18   Anatomy of an ecolodge
20   Planning a trip
22   Wildlife travel year planner
24   Choosing an operator
30   What to take
34   Wildlife photography
38   Wildlife journals & sketchbooks
40   Staying healthy

46   Best of: birdwatching to small wonders
56   Safaris
72   Primate watching
86   Brief encounters: snow leopard
88   Brief encounters: wolf
90   Bear watching
98   Whale watching
112   Wildlife cruises
124   Wilderness trips
128   Conservation trips

Tales from the wild

50 Swimming with whale sharks
Ningaloo Reef, Western Australia

52 The wonderful thing about tigers
Corbett National Park, India

64 Tracking the Great Migration
Serengeti-Mara, Tanzania & Kenya

68 A short walk in the Okavango Delta
Botswana

80 In the midst of mountain gorillas
Volcanoes National Park, Rwanda

82 Making contact with the cousins
Semliki Valley, Uganda

94 Eye to eye with the ice bear
Churchill, Canada

96 Hiking in bear country
Olympic National Park, USA

106 The Pacific lagoons of Baja
Baja California, Mexico

110 The smile on the face of a dolphin
North Bimini, Bahamas

120 Setting sail for an Arctic wilderness
Svalbard

122 Exploring the Enchanted Isles
Galápagos Islands, Ecuador

Destinations

132

136 North America
140 Alaska
144 Western United States
148 Eastern United States
150 Florida
152 Western Canada
154 Eastern Canada
156 Wild nights out

158 South & Central America
162 Mexico
164 Caribbean
164 Belize
165 Honduras
166 Costa Rica
168 Venezuela
169 Guyana
170 Brazil
172 Ecuador & the Galápagos Islands
178 Peru
180 Bolivia, Argentina & Chile
184 Wild nights out

186 Europe
190 Britain
192 France
194 Spain

197 The Azores & Canary Islands
198 Italy
200 Eastern Europe
202 Scandinavia
203 Iceland
204 Wild nights out

206 Africa
210 Gabon & West Africa
212 Kenya
216 Tanzania
221 Uganda, Rwanda & Ethiopia
222 Zambia
226 Zimbabwe, Malawi & Mozambique
228 Botswana
230 Namibia
232 South Africa
236 Madagascar
238 Wild nights out
243 Seychelles

244 Asia
248 India
251 Sri Lanka, Nepal & China
252 Malaysian Borneo
256 Indonesia
258 Wild nights out

260 Australasia
264 Australia
270 New Zealand
272 Papua New Guinea
274 Wild nights out

278 Polar regions
284 Svalbard
286 Antarctica
288 Falkland Islands
290 South Georgia
292 Wild nights out

294 Directory
298 Index
303 Photography credits
304 Acknowledgements
304 Publishing credits

Introduction

I will never forget my first encounter with a basking shark. It emerged from the planktonic murk of the Irish Sea and swam straight under my legs – as silent and unswerving as a nuclear submarine. First came its cavernous mouth and then, nine metres later, a great scything tail that left me and the jellyfish swirling in its wake.

Nor will I forget the moment when, paddling through Florida Bay's Ten Thousand Islands, a group of manatees surfaced alongside my canoe. Or the time I glimpsed chimpanzees in a Ugandan rainforest, polar bears on the Canadian tundra and hawksbill turtles in an Indian Ocean lagoon.

Each of these encounters only lasted a few seconds, but that was more than enough time to sear indelible memories on my mind.

That's the thrill of wildlife travel. You can never predict what, if anything, is going to happen. Whether you're slip-sliding through a Rwandan jungle in search of gorillas or staking out a salmon-choked stream in Alaska waiting for a hungry grizzly bear, there's no guarantee you'll see either.

Wildlife travel is supercharged with anticipation. It can also inspire a spectacular array of experiences, from kayaking with whales and tracking big game on foot to scaling a canopy walkway in a tropical rainforest. Deciding where to go and what to see can be a real dilemma.

Of course, some people have firm ideas of what makes a dream wildlife trip. It often revolves around a single charismatic species, like a big cat, whale, ape or bear. But if you don't have an urgent desire to see a tiger or polar bear you could instead join a more general natural history tour that encompasses several habitats and a rich diversity of wildlife. A journey across the Andes, for example, could include everything from alpine desert and cloud forest to river and jungle – each with their unique cast of creatures.

Alternatively, you could time your trip to coincide with a wildlife spectacle, such as the Serengeti-Masai Mara wildebeest migration in Kenya and Tanzania or the mass arrival of monarch butterflies in central Mexico. At the other extreme, a fleeting glimpse of a lone orang-utan, jaguar or other rarity can be just as riveting. And for the ultimate adrenaline rush, there are plenty of opportunities for coming face-to-face with some of nature's top predators, like great white sharks and saltwater crocodiles.

There is no doubt that wildlife holidays can sometimes prove frustrating – disappointing even. But more often than not, you will return home feeling enlightened and humbled. Don't worry too much if the tigers, whales or gorillas elude you. An awareness of the beauty and importance of a wild place can be just as rewarding.

Wildlife travel offers a privileged opportunity to immerse yourself in some of the world's last remaining wildernesses. And, perhaps most important of all, it can provide a lifeline to the creatures themselves.

By supporting responsible tourism projects that not only have minimal environmental impact, but also put funds back into conservation and benefit local communities, your wildlife holiday can (and should) make a positive contribution. Whether we like the idea or not, wildlife increasingly needs to pay its way in order to survive. Visionary, sustainable tourism can transform a poacher into a wildlife ranger, a dynamite fisherman into a turtle-watching guide. It can be the catalyst for community-run lodges and a cornerstone of local employment. Responsible wildlife travel could hold the key to survival for some of our most endangered species.

Gilded hunter – an adult female cheetah scours a dusk-washed Serengeti for prey

Southern Plains, Serengeti National Park, Tanzania

Clocked at 105km/h, cheetahs have the run of the plains in the Serengeti and neighbouring Masai Mara where their preferred prey are gazelles. They hunt by day, however, so be careful not to cramp their style. Ask your driver to keep a respectful distance.

Wildlife travel offers a privileged opportunity to immerse yourself in some of the world's last remaining wildernesses. And it can also provide a lifeline to the creatures themselves

Wildlife Travel | wishlist

A straw poll of tour operators revealed the following top 10 favourite wildlife destinations. Although dominated by Africa, other close contenders included the Great Bear Rainforest ❶, Churchill (for polar bears) ❷, Baja California ❸, Costa Rica ❹, Svalbard ❺, Madagascar ❻, Sabah ❼, Kimberley ❽, Papua New Guinea ❾ and Kamchatka ❿.

❶ Galápagos Islands, Ecuador
Wildlife bonanza above and below the waves. Seabirds, sea lions, giant tortoises and marine iguanas are unfazed by humans. Visit year round. Cruises from 3-10 days are available. Some boats offer diving.

❷ Serengeti/Masai Mara, Tanzania/Kenya
Vast plains teeming with game. Witness the epic migration of wildebeest, zebra and gazelle as they struggle across rivers and run the gauntlet of crocs and big cats.

❸ South Luangwa, Zambia
Mosaic of woodland, grassland and wetland oozing wildlife and perfect for exploring on foot. Visit June to October and enjoy some of Africa's finest camps and most knowledgeable safari guides.

❹ Okavango Delta, Botswana
Watery wilderness on the edge of the Kalahari offering an exciting range of game-viewing options, including 4WD vehicle, dugout canoe, horse riding and elephant-back safaris. Visit year round.

❺ Antarctica
Take a peek at life in the freezer during the Austral Summer from November to March. Spot whales from the deck of a cruise ship and goggle at crowded seal and penguin colonies.

❻ India's tiger reserves
Join a big game safari Asia-style with chances of spotting gazelles, monkeys, sloth bears and tigers. Prime time for big cat watching is February to April when vegetation withers at the end of the dry season.

❼ The Peruvian Amazon
Tambopata and Manu Reserves protect vast areas of virgin jungle. Visit June to August and venture from your lodge on foot or by canoe in search of giant otters, freshwater dolphins and scarlet macaws.

❽ The Pantanal, Brazil
Huge seasonal wetland (about half the size of France) with superb birdlife, giant anteaters, anacondas, howler monkeys, capybaras, caimans and even jaguars. Visit July to September.

❾ Volcanoes National Park, Rwanda
Track rare golden monkeys and mountain gorillas in their rainforest stronghold. Other good spots to meet your distant hairy cousins include Bwindi in Uganda.

❿ Alaska
From tundra to temperate rainforest, Alaska is varied and vast – with wildlife to match. Bears, whales, eagles and wolves can all be found. Visit June to September, taking in Denali and Kenai Fjords.

The ultimate global safari

January Watch the courtship dance of blue-footed boobies in the Galápagos Islands.

February See grey whales and their calves in the Pacific lagoons of Baja California, Mexico.

March Track tigers in Satpura National Park, India, on a walking safari.

April Paddle a dugout past browsing elephants in the Okavango Delta.

May Snorkel with whale sharks off Ningaloo Reef, Western Australia.

June Trek through a Rwandan jungle in search of mountain gorillas.

July Explore the rainforest of Manu Biosphere Reserve, Peru.

August Watch migrating wildebeest and zebra cross the Mara River.

September Walk to a carmine bee-eater colony in Zambia's South Luangwa Valley.

October Watch polar bears gathering on the shores of Hudson Bay.

November Observe turtles coming ashore to nest on Costa Rica's Pacific coast.

December Lose count of penguins on a cruise to the Antarctic Peninsula.

About the author

Leaving Durham University with a zoology degree, Will's writing career began during a six-week stint of voluntary work surveying birds on Heron Island, a coral cay on the Great Barrier Reef. It was here that he had the idea for his first book, *Coral Reefs & Islands – The Natural History of a Threatened Paradise*, published in 1993 (at the age of 23) and commended in the Conservation Book Prize.

A prolific period of wildlife and adventure travel writing and photography followed, during which Will contributed to publications ranging from *The Sunday Times* to *National Geographic Traveler*. In 2002, he was voted Travel Writer of the Year.

When twins, Joe and Ellie, arrived they instantly became mini globetrotters, joining Will and his wife, Sally, on numerous assignments for magazines, newspapers and the BBC's *Holiday* programme.

Will's series of family travel guides for Footprint includes the award-winning *Travel with Kids* – the definitive guide to family holidays worldwide – and follow-up titles *Europe with Kids*, *Britain with Kids* and *Cornwall with Kids*. His Family Man blog appears monthly on the *Wanderlust* website (wanderlust.co.uk) and he's a regular contributor of wildlife travel features to the magazine. William and Sally are also editors of the family travel website, 101familyholidays.co.uk.

In 2009, Will scooped both Travel Photographer of the Year and runner-up Travel Writer of the Year at the British Guild of Travel Writers' Awards, and the following year he was voted fourth in the *Press Gazette's* Top 50 Travel Journalists. His images are represented by several photographic libraries, including AWL Images (awl-images.com).

william-gray.co.uk

About the book

A guide to the ultimate global safari, *Wildlife Travel* is packed with all the information and inspiration you need to start planning your own dream wildlife trip, whether it's an African safari, a voyage around the Galápagos Islands, birdwatching in Europe or bear watching in Alaska. The book is divided into three main sections – Essentials, Encounters and Destinations.

Essentials
This is where you will find background information, such as how to choose a travel operator, stay healthy and pack the right gear. Responsible travel is a theme that underlies the entire book and you'll find an introduction to this important subject on page 14.

Encounters
This section of the book covers various types of wildlife travel, including safaris, primate watching, bear watching, whale watching and wildlife cruises. As well as providing practical information, Encounters aims to inspire through a series of 'Tales from the Wild' – firsthand accounts of the author's wildlife travels.

Destinations
Top wildlife travel locations are covered continent-by-continent in the Destinations section. This isn't intended to be an exhaustive directory, but it will give you plenty to start thinking about. Sidebars entitled 'Making tracks' provide background on travel practicalities, while 'Wild nights out' highlight some of the best (and most ecofriendly) camps and lodges for each region.

Also look out for...
Leading wildlife experts reveal their all-time favourite wildlife encounters in 'It's a wild life', while top guides share their experiences in 'Guiding stars'.

Key to symbols

Greatest ticks
- Distribution
- Habitat
- Diet
- Size
- Population

Making tracks
- Wildlife travel operators
- Getting there
- Accommodation
- Time difference
- Climate & seasons
- Warnings
- Currency
- Tourist information
- Conservation groups

Wild nights out
- Guided wildlife watching activities
- Walks & treks
- Mountain biking
- Horse riding
- Swimming
- Snorkelling & diving
- Canoeing & kayaking
- Sailing
- Fishing
- Hot-air ballooning

12 Where the wild things are

14 Responsible travel
14 10-point plan
16 Code green
18 Anatomy of an ecolodge

20 Planning a trip
20 Checklist
21 Eight classic books
22 Wildlife travel year planner

24 Choosing an operator
24 What to look for
25 Guiding stars
26 Directory

30 What to take
30 Travel gear
32 Binoculars
33 Field guides

34 Wildlife photography
34 Equipment
36 Technique

38 Wildlife journals & sketchbooks

40 Staying healthy
40 First-aid
41 Vaccinations
43 Dangerous animals

Making tracks – a flap-neck chameleon hits the road

Chamaeleo dilepis
Bushmanland, Northeast Namibia.

Essentials

Where the wild things are | biodiversity hotspots

Of an estimated 10 to 30 million species on this remarkable planet, we're the only ones able to appreciate the role of these myriad lifeforms in maintaining the balance of life on Earth. Humans are also the only species capable of travelling to every environment, visiting the most far-flung places and celebrating biodiversity. That's a special gift, but with it comes a responsibility to travel in a way that preserves the world's wildlife – whichever of the 4,800 known mammal species, 10,000 birds, 8,000 reptiles, 5,500 amphibians, 26,000 fish or one million insects you happen to be seeking.

Two thirds of all animal species are thought to live in tropical forests, while coral reefs are home to a quarter of all varieties of marine life. Areas rich in endemic species also fall under the spotlight when it comes to biodiversity. Only 18 countries support more than 100 endemics and, of these, several – including Australia, Mexico and South Africa – have more species threatened with extinction than anywhere else.

The current annual extinction rate on Earth is thought to be 10,000 times higher than the background rate over the past 60 million years. Habitat loss, climate change, pollution and over hunting are just some of the threats facing wildlife. Creating protected areas will not only safeguard species, but also provide people with ecological services (clean air and water, medicines, recreation, natural flood prevention etc) worth an estimated US$35 trillion per year. Tourism has its role to play in this. Carried out responsibly, it can benefit both wildlife and local people.

Canadian tundra

North America boreal forest

Pacific Northwest temperate rainforest

Rocky Mountains

North American prairie

Sonoran Desert

Sea of Cortez

Everglades

Caribbean coral reefs

Central American rainforest

Llanos

Amazon Rainforest

Atacama Desert

Pantanal

South American pampas

Andes

Antarctic Peninsula

Greenland Icecap

American alligator
(Aptenodytes patagonicus) Endemic to the southeastern United States, gators can grow to a length of 4.4 m.

Monarch butterfly
(Danaus plexippus) The flightiest of the butterflies, monarchs migrate between Mexico and southeast Canada.

Going up in the world
A journey from equator to pole passes through the same sequence of biomes (rainforest, deciduous forest, conifer forest, tundra and permanent ice) as you'd encounter climbing a mountain from near sea level to its summit at 3,500 m.

King penguin *(Aptenodytes patagonicus)* After emperors, kings are the second largest of the world's 17 species of penguin.

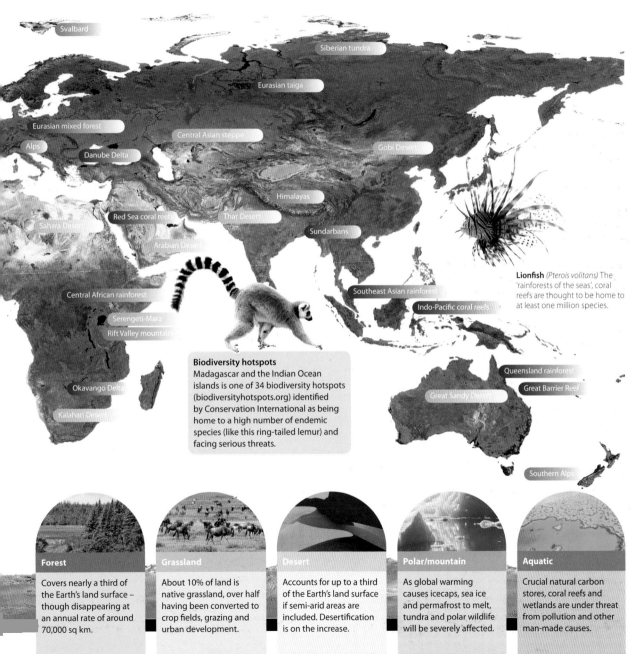

Svalbard

Siberian tundra

Eurasian taiga

Eurasian mixed forest

Central Asian steppe

Alps

Gobi Desert

Danube Delta

Himalayas

Red Sea coral reefs

Thar Desert

Sahara Desert

Sundarbans

Arabian Desert

Lionfish (*Pterois volitans*) The 'rainforests of the seas', coral reefs are thought to be home to at least one million species.

Central African rainforest

Southeast Asian rainforest

Indo-Pacific coral reefs

Serengeti-Mara

Rift Valley mountains

Biodiversity hotspots
Madagascar and the Indian Ocean islands is one of 34 biodiversity hotspots (biodiversityhotspots.org) identified by Conservation International as being home to a high number of endemic species (like this ring-tailed lemur) and facing serious threats.

Okavango Delta

Queensland rainforest

Great Barrier Reef

Great Sandy Desert

Kalahari Desert

Southern Alps

Forest

Covers nearly a third of the Earth's land surface – though disappearing at an annual rate of around 70,000 sq km.

Grassland

About 10% of land is native grassland, over half having been converted to crop fields, grazing and urban development.

Desert

Accounts for up to a third of the Earth's land surface if semi-arid areas are included. Desertification is on the increase.

Polar/mountain

As global warming causes icecaps, sea ice and permafrost to melt, tundra and polar wildlife will be severely affected.

Aquatic

Crucial natural carbon stores, coral reefs and wetlands are under threat from pollution and other man-made causes.

Responsible wildlife travel | 10-point plan

The sea was so placid when guide Matt McFadyen and I launched our two-person kayak that we could hear the sighs of breath from a sea lion surfacing 200 m away. Paddling out from the coastal hamlet of Portobello on New Zealand's Otago Peninsula we were surrounded by white-fronted terns plunge-diving for fish, each splash carrying clearly, like pebbles tossed in a pond. "It doesn't get much better than this," said Matt as we settled into an easy rhythm, wavelets chuckling beneath our bows. "You get such a great perspective of marine life from a sea kayak."

He was right. Rounding Taiaroa Heads, we confronted a brisk southwesterly, strong enough for the albatrosses that nest on the clifftop above to get airborne. As they soared overhead, cradling the wind on 3-m wingspans, fur seals cavorted amongst writhing arms of honey-coloured kelp or preened their glistening pelts on rocky haul-outs. Stewart Island shags streamed from their nests like the opening salvo of arrows in a medieval battle, while yellow-eyed penguins huddled nearby.

Experiencing wildlife – not just looking at it, but immersing yourself in it, hearing it, smelling it, feeling it – has been one of the greatest pleasures of researching this book. It could so easily have been a whirlwind tour: filling a ticklist, but depriving the soul.

Wildlife travel is much more than simply seeing animals. It's about slowing down to the natural ebb and flow of a wild place, taking time to understand what makes it tick. It's about the small wonders that stop you in your tracks and the mighty landscapes that leave you feeling humbled. It's about making a connection. And that, in essence, is what responsible travel is all about.

Only by bonding with the environment you're visiting will you appreciate the importance of treading lightly and minimizing your impact. You will also better understand how to make a positive contribution to wildlife conservation.

But this isn't an isolated experience: just you and the great outdoors. Responsible travel is as deeply rooted in culture as it is in nature. Making a connection with local people, learning and sharing information, will not only enhance your wildlife

A census of mountain gorillas conducted in March and April 2010 revealed 480 mountain gorillas in the Virunga Massif of DRC, Rwanda and Uganda which, along with a further 302 individuals in Uganda's Bwindi Impenetrable National Park, put the world population of this critically endangered species at 786 – an annual population increase of around 4%.

holiday, but can also strengthen the vital links between community and conservation.

Throughout this book there are numerous examples of how community-run lodges and other sustainable tourism projects not only support conservation efforts, but also give local people a financial incentive for safeguarding wildlife.

Nowhere is this more clearly demonstrated than in Rwanda where mountain gorilla tourism has made a huge difference to people living near Volcanoes National Park. Part of the revenue from gorilla tracking permits (a chest-pounding US$500 each) has been channelled into community projects ranging from education to sanitation. Poachers now find employment as trackers, local livelihoods have diversified into everything from craft making to tour guiding, while lodges recruit staff from nearby villages.

There's an enormous sense of pride in the gorillas. Enough money spent by travellers remains in the pockets of local people for them to view the apes' mountain stronghold as a wild refuge to be treasured and cared for – rather than something to be dug up and converted to farmland.

Without tourism, mountain gorillas would still be on a slippery slope towards extinction, rather than climbing steadily (around 4% annually) to the 786 individuals recorded during the 2010 census.

> **"The privilege of visiting wild places and enjoying the world's spectacular natural history comes with a responsibility, and that is for each of us to play our part in its conservation. Choose your tour operator, guide or accommodation owner based on their responsible tourism policy, and ensure local communities benefit directly from your visit – in a crowded planet our wildlife's future is in their hands"**

Justin Francis, MD and co-founder of responsibletravel.com

There are countless other cases – from rhinos and tigers to whales and coral reefs – where tourism is joining the battle for conservation, if not being the ultimate guarantor of survival for an endangered species or habitat.

When it comes to wildlife holidays, responsible tourism is not just an option – it should be considered an intrinsic part of the whole process.

10 ways to be a responsible wildlife traveller

There are some aspects of travel that you have to accept are going to have an impact, but try to balance the negatives with positives by following these guidelines to responsible travel.

➼ Cut your emissions
Plan an itinerary that minimizes carbon emissions whenever possible. This might involve travelling by train, hiring a bike or booking a walking or canoeing tour rather than one that relies on vehicle transport. See page 16 for details of carbon offset programmes.

ⓘ Visit seat61.com for worldwide train travel.

➼ Check the small print
Choose wildlife travel operators that abide by a responsible travel policy (if they have one it will usually be posted on their website). See page 18 for further information on how to pick a responsible travel operator, and visit responsibletravel.com.

➼ Keep it local
If travelling independently, try to use public transport, stay in locally owned accommodation, eat in local restaurants, buy local produce and hire local guides.

➼ Cut out waste
Take biodegradable soap and shampoo and leave excess packaging, particularly plastics, at home. The countries you are visiting may not have the waste collection or recycling facilities to deal with it.

➼ Get in touch
Find out if there are any local schools, charities or voluntary conservation organizations that you could include in your itinerary. If appropriate, take along some useful gifts or supplies.

ⓘ stuffyourrucksack.com has a list of projects that could benefit from your support.

➼ Learn the lingo
Practice some local words, even if it's just to say 'hello', 'thank you' and 'goodbye'. Respect local customs and dress codes and always ask permission before photographing people – including your wildlife tour guide. Once you get home, remember to honour any promises you've made to send photographs.

➼ Avoid the crowds
Consider travelling out of season to relieve pressure on popular destinations, or visit a lesser-known alternative. For example, rather than cruising around the Galápagos Islands (where tourism has increased dramatically in recent years) head instead for Isla de la Plata where you'll find many similar species – such as the blue-footed booby (right) – an hour's boat ride off the Ecuador coast (see page 172).

➼ Take only photos
Resist the temptation to buy souvenirs made from animals or plants. Not only is it illegal to import or

What not to pack

According to the European Commission (eu-wildlifetrade.org), the most commonly seized wildlife souvenirs are alligator and crocodile products, queen conch shells, coral jewellery and ornaments, boots, bags, belts, shoes and watchstraps made from snake and lizard skins, traditional Asian medicines containing tiger bone, rhino horn, bear bile and musk, live plants such as cacti and orchids, shawls of shahtoosh (from the Tibetan antelope), turtles and tortoiseshell, elephant ivory, caviar, live or dead specimens of parrots, scorpions and reptiles and woodcarvings made from rare timber species.

Blue-footed booby

Sula nebouxii
Isla de la Plata, Ecuador

Responsible travel | code green

export many wildlife souvenirs, but their uncontrolled collection supports poaching and can have a devastating impact on local populations, upsetting the natural balance of entire ecosystems.

ⓘ CITES, the Convention on International Trade in Endangered Species (cites.org) bans international trade in around 900 species of animals and plants, and controls trade in a further 33,000 species. Several organizations, including WWF, TRAFFIC and the Smithsonian Institution have formed the Coalition Against Wildlife Trafficking (cawtglobal.org).

▸▸ Use water wisely
Water is a precious commodity in many countries. Treating your own water avoids the need to buy bottled water which can contribute to the build-up of litter.

▸▸ Don't interfere
Avoid disturbing wildlife, damaging habitats or interfering with natural behaviour by feeding wild animals, getting too close or being too noisy. Leave plants and shells where you find them.

Code green for hikers
• Take biodegradable soap, shampoo and toilet paper, long-lasting lithium batteries and plastic bags for packing out all rubbish.
• Use a water filter instead of buying bottled water and save fuel at remote lodges by ordering the same food at the same time. Only take a hot shower if the water has been heated by solar power.
• If no toilet facilities are available, make sure you are at least 30 m from any water source.
• Keep to trails to avoid erosion and trampling vegetation. Don't take short cuts, especially at high altitude where plants may take years to recover.

Code green for divers and snorkellers
• Help conserve underwater environments by taking part in local cleanups or collecting data for Project AWARE (projectaware.org).
• Choose resorts that properly treat sewage and wastewater and support marine protected areas.
• Choose operators that use mooring buoys or drift

How should I offset my carbon emissions?

According to the Intergovernmental Panel on Climate Change (ipcc.ch), 'global atmospheric concentrations of carbon dioxide, methane and nitrous oxide have increased markedly as a result of human activities since 1750'. Carbon offsetting schemes allow you to offset greenhouse gas emissions by donating to various projects, from tree planting to renewable energy schemes. Although some conservation groups are concerned that carbon offsetting is being used as a smoke-screen to delay the urgent action needed to cut emissions and develop alternative energy solutions, it remains an important way of counterbalancing your carbon footprint.

How does carbon offsetting work?
For every tonne of CO_2 you generate through a fossil fuel-burning activity such as flying, you pay for an equivalent tonne to be removed elsewhere through a 'green' initiative. There are numerous online carbon footprint calculators (such as carbonfootprint.com). Alternatively, book with a travel operator that supports a carbon offset provider like TICOS (ticos.co.uk) or Reduce my Footprint (reducemyfootprint.travel).

Where does my money go?
Tree planting schemes used to swallow most of the funds from carbon offsetting programmes, but many have been discredited on the basis that fast-growing monoculture plantations require high inputs of fertiliser and energy. Support now goes to a far wider range of climate-friendly technology projects, ranging from the provision of energy-efficient light bulbs and cookers in the developing world to large-scale renewable energy schemes such as wind farms.

Keep your distance

Diving and snorkelling are 'hands off' activities in fragile environments like coral reefs.

diving techniques, rather than anchors that can damage fragile marine habitats like coral reefs.
• Never touch coral. Practice buoyancy control skills in a pool or sandy area before diving around coral reefs, and tuck away trailing equipment.
• Avoid handling, feeding or riding on marine life.
• Never purchase marine souvenirs.
• Don't order seafood caught using destructive or unsustainable practices like dynamite fishing.

Avoid disturbing wildlife, damaging habitats or interfering with natural behaviour by feeding wild animals, getting too close or being too noisy

Should I swim with wild dolphins?

The Whale and Dolphin Conservation Society (wdcs.org) doesn't recommend wild dolphin swims. According to the charity, 'it is very difficult to ensure that the encounter takes place on the dolphins' terms and is not an intrusive or stressful experience.' Reputable operators, however, insist that they do nothing to alter the cetacean's natural behaviour and that it's up to the dolphins if they want to approach and interact with people in the water. You should enter the water in a quiet, relaxed manner. Sound plays a crucial role in a cetacean's life, so do not add your own noises to the complex medley of squeaks, clicks and whirrs that dolphins use during hunting and socializing. Snorkel at the surface, finning slowly and gently with your arms at your sides. Let the dolphins approach you. Never chase them or try to reach out and touch them. When free-diving, keep your actions smooth, slow and relaxed to avoid startling these powerful creatures. See also pages 106-111.

Should I drive off-road?

All off-road drivers have a responsibility to choose routes with care. Not only is 4WD access to many national parks and conservation areas controlled by strict regulations, but some particularly fragile habitats, such as vegetated dunes, alpine meadows, wetlands, seasonal nesting areas and cryptobiotic soils (which form a living crust of lichen, moss, algae and micro organisms in some desert and tundra regions) are easily scarred by vehicle tracks and should be given a wide berth. The slower you drive the less environmental impact you'll create in the form of erosion, dust and potential damage through accidents. Engage 4WD and use your low-range gearbox to maximize control. Stop frequently and scout ahead on foot for potential hazards. Where possible try to avoid mud where wheel spins can cause rutting. Ford rivers at designated points, make sure your vehicle is mechanically sound and check regularly for any leaks of oil, fuel or hydraulic fluids.

Should wilderness be sacred?

Purists would argue that wilderness areas should, by their very nature, be inviolate. Although no one in their right mind would advocate mass tourism to the world's last wild frontiers, even the most eco-sensitive, small-scale tours leave human impressions. The fragile tundra of Arctic islands, for example, can become pockmarked with footprints by even a small cruiseship landing party, while some deserts have a similarly fragile crust. Any activity that potentially jeopardises the wilderness value of a region should be avoided. Needless to say, it doesn't require much thought or effort to pack out refuse, stick to trails to minimize erosion and avoid contaminating water sources with waste. You can also choose a responsible operator. If Antarctica, the world's greatest wilderness, is in your sights, be sure to book a trip with a member of the International Association of Antarctic Tour Operators (IAATO) which adheres to a strict environmental code. See also pages 126-129.

Code green for sailors
• Avoid anchoring on fragile marine habitats.
• Never dump waste or rubbish overboard and dispose of unwanted or tangled fishing line properly.
• Avoid disturbing turtle- or seabird-nesting sites.

Code green for canoeists
• Remote beaches and islands are often used by birds, turtles and other species for roosting or nesting. Take care to avoid disturbing wildlife and practice minimum-impact camping (see opposite).
• Use biodegradable toilet paper (or burn it) and always use the intertidal zone where the sea can wash the beach clean. Use biodegradable and phosphate-free shampoo and soap if washing in the sea.
• Do not collect shells or other natural souvenirs.
• Abide by all whale watching guidelines. Do not pursue, feed, touch or disturb cetaceans, manatees, dugongs or whale sharks.
• Pack out all garbage.

Code green for campers
See page 205.

Gently does it – treating the natural world with respect ∧

Swimming with spotted dolphins in the waters off Bimini, the Bahamas; a Land Rover safari in the Valley of 10,000 Dunes, Namib Desert; hiking in the High Arctic archipelago of Svalbard.

Backcountry camping >

Ten Thousand Islands, Everglades National Park, Florida

Named after a traditional Indian shelter-on-stilts, chickees have been built in sheltered bays of the Everglades to enable canoeists to pitch their tents away from fragile, wildlife-rich (and mosquito-ridden) mangrove habitats. Elsewhere, sandy beaches offer low-impact wilderness camping.

Chumbe Island, Tanzania

Following centuries of cultivation (largely for the island's spice plantations), only fragments of Zanzibar's original vegetation remain. One such vestige is 16-ha Chumbe Island, where a world-renowned ecolodge sets the benchmark for low-impact, sustainable tourism that benefits both the environment and local people. Chumbe's forest is a refuge for Aders' duiker, a small antelope that is running out of places to hide elsewhere in Zanzibar. The island's coral reef is also a crucial sanctuary. As many reefs in the Zanzibar archipelago continue to suffer from overfishing and the impact of coastal development, Chumbe's reef still supports some 200 species of hard coral – 90% of the total ever recorded in this part of the Indian Ocean.

In addition to the bungalows, Chumbe Island has a striking education and dining area (resembling a miniature thatched version of Sydney's Opera House) where local school children can learn about the importance of coral reefs and forests. The only other constructions on the island are the ruins of a small mosque and an intact stone lighthouse which was built by the British in 1904. From the blustery balcony that encircles the lighthouse's original lamp, the green mantle of Chumbe Island's forest provides a unique glimpse of what the entire Zanzibar archipelago must have been like before humans arrived.

Education matters
Local school students regularly visit Chumbe Island to learn about marine biology, forest ecology and environmental protection.

Eco toilets
Composting toilets need no water and prevent sewage from seeping through the porous groundrock into the Reef Sanctuary by rapidly composting human waste. Wind powered vent pipes minimize odours.

Wildlife sanctuary
One of the rarest antelope in the world, the shy Ader's duiker (*Cephalophus adersi*), is endemic to Zanzibar, where less than 500 individuals remain. A translocation project has enabled Chumbe to become a special sanctuary for this endangered species.

Waste treatment
Wherever possible, non-organic products are avoided, but any waste that can't be composted or recycled is incinerated in a special facility constructed by the project on Zanzibar.

Plant power
To ensure that no pollution enters the sea, used water from showers and basins is filtered before being passed through plant beds that absorb nitrates and phosphates.

Keeping it local
Local people are employed as park rangers, maintenance staff, cooks, housekeepers, waiters and administrators. Many come from rural fishing communities along the coast of Zanzibar and have little formal education prior to working at Chumbe. Training and language development are key parts of their professional development. Chumbe also encourages the employment of under-educated women who, in the local Islamic culture, often have difficulty finding work.

Tourism is key
Chumbe Island Coral Park is a financially self-sustaining, non-profit organization with funding provided by visitors.

Reef relief
Since the creation of Chumbe's Reef Sanctuary, fishing and unauthorised anchoring have been banned.

Natural cooling
Cooling sea breezes flow through the open-designed bungalows, creating natural air conditioning. Louvres can be lowered or closed to modulate the temperature.

Bright ideas
To protect the natural feeding and breeding behaviour of the island's nocturnal wildlife (especially its rare coconut crabs), the walkways, nature trails and beach areas on Chumbe are not artificially illuminated at night. Solar-powered torches are provided for guests each night.

Safe water
Advanced filters clean readily available tap water from Zanzibar to provide perfectly safe drinking water, avoiding the need for mineral water in plastic bottles.

Supporting local business
Bathrooms are supplied with organic soaps produced by a local women's co-operative in Zanzibar.

Catching every drop
The roof of each bungalow is specially designed to maximize rainwater catchment. Water is stored in underground cisterns from where it is hand-pumped through solar-powered heating systems for shower and hand basins.

Grand designs
Each bungalow is constructed entirely of sustainably harvested mangrove poles and thatch.

Green energy
Solar panels generate eco-friendly 12V energy.

Planning a trip | checklist

Tiger, gorilla, bear, lemur, cheetah, whale, rhino... wildlife travel has no shortage of must-see A-List celebrities, but the inspiration for your trip could equally be a wildlife spectacle or remote wilderness. Planning a wildlife holiday is like grappling with your very own theory of natural selection. As your plans evolve, certain things will inevitably fall by the wayside (dismissed perhaps by budget restraints or seasonal factors) – but at the same time, fresh ideas will emerge that lead you to exciting new possibilities.

The wishlist

This is the fun part of planning a wildlife trip. The Encounters section of this book explores the diverse range of wildlife holidays available, from safaris and bear-watching trips to expedition cruises and conservation volunteering, while the Destinations section delves into the world's wildlife hotspots. You'll also find a tour operators' Wildlife Wishlist on page 8.

As you compile a shortlist of wildlife you hope to see, places you'd like to visit and activities you want to try, give some thought to what else you may want to do, whether it's a few days flopping on a beach or some city sightseeing.

ⓘ Check whether a travel advisory has been issued by your government warning against visiting an unsafe country by checking fco.gov.uk/travel (for UK citizens) and travel.state.gov/travel (for US citizens).

The reality check

Once you've compiled a wishlist, it's time to apply logistics to weed out the trips that are non-feasible.

Timing is everything. There is little point, for example, in planning the trip of a lifetime to see penguins in South Georgia if you can only travel in August. A quick glance at the Wildlife Travel Year Planner on pages 22-23, will reveal that Antarctica has a brief window of opportunity for viewing wildlife during the austral summer (from around November to February).

Although some wildlife is relatively static and present year round (mountain gorillas for example), many species respond to seasonal changes in their environment or life cycle and travel great distances.

Ask yourself this...

• Is there a particular species, habitat or natural event that I want to see?
• Where can I see it?
• When is the best time to see it?
• When can I go?
• How long can I go for?
• How much can I spend?
• Do I want to travel alone or as part of a group?
• How can I get there?
• Is the trip suitable for everyone in the group (children etc)?
• Are the right activities included in the trip?
• How will my trip benefit the environment and local communities?
• Do I have adequate travel insurance?
• Are my vaccinations up to date?
• Do I need anti-malarials?

To maximize your chances of a sighting you need to synchronise with the migration of humpback whales; you have to understand how the post-monsoon flush of vegetation can make tiger spotting in India almost impossible, or how the annual spawning of salmon along the coast of British Columbia and Southeast Alaska can bring a bumper crop of bear sightings.

It's also important to consider the **length of your trip.** Trying to shoehorn a wildlife holiday into too few days cannot only be impractical, but it can also mean you spend most of your trip travelling.

Budget is likely to reap the most casualties on your wishlist. That dream trip traversing Ecuador, from the coast (or Galápagos Islands) to the Amazon Basin might become prohibitively expensive once you've thoroughly researched hidden costs, like internal flights, visas, national park fees and non-inclusive activities. Many wildlife destinations, however, have a range of options when it comes to cost. In Namibia, for example, you could book a top-end safari, zipping along the Skeleton Coast in a chartered Cessna and dropping in at luxury tented camps, or, for a fraction of the cost, you could join an overland camping safari where you pitch your own tent and help cook meals.

The nitty gritty

Once you have decided on the theme and highlights of your wildlife trip and allocated an appropriate budget and time frame, it's time to start tackling the paperwork and practicalities.

Now is the time to decide **how you want to travel** – whether you'd prefer to join an organised group tour, ask an operator to tailor-make a trip for you or plan everything independently. As well as cutting costs, going solo can offer the freedom to travel at your own pace and the flexibility to adapt your travel plans – handy, for instance, if wildlife viewing proves particularly rewarding in one area and you want to extend your stay. Independent travellers can also make responsible travel decisions such as staying in locally owned accommodation and hiring local guides.

However, be sure to check whether an organised tour doesn't, in fact, offer better value once you've taken into account the discounts that operators can pass on to their clients from block bookings. Remember, too, that bonded operators guarantee financial security, high standards of service and a commitment to responsible travel through their membership of ATOL, IATA, AITO and other organizations. Perhaps most crucial of all, it is only by arranging your travels through a specialised operator that you can gain access to locations like Antarctica. Good wildlife travel companies (like the ones listed on pages 26-29) will also have intimate knowledge of the places you're interested in visiting. They'll be passionate about wildlife and keen to share their personal recommendations.

Once you've booked your trip, make sure that your **passport** is in date for at least six months beyond your period of travel and apply well in advance for any **visas** that you might need. Check that your **vaccinations** are up to date (see page 41) and find out if you need to start a course of anti-malarials. Arrange **travel insurance** that is comprehensive enough to cover the activities you'll be doing. Most operators will require this as part of the conditions for booking a trip.

As far as **money** is concerned, traveller's cheques are the safest way to carry money, but it's also a good idea to take some cash in either local currency or US dollars. Many camps and lodges accept credit cards which are also useful for security deposits (against car rental etc), cash advances at ATMs or in emergency situations when you might need to replace stolen gear or purchase an air ticket at short notice.

Although international **flights** are usually included as part of a tour package, some operators offer 'land only' rates, leaving you to make your own travel arrangements. Searching online for bargain flights is one option, but you could also consider travelling by train, overland truck or ferry to reduce your carbon footprint.

Just as you need to plan well in advance for obtaining visas and vaccinations, it's important to include a **training and fitness** regime on your countdown-to-departure calendar. A typical African safari doesn't demand athletic levels of fitness, but you'll appreciate some pre-trip toning if you're planning to track mountain gorillas or paddle a canoe along the Zambezi. Some wildlife trips involve simple-to-learn **activities** like sea kayaking, while others require more demanding skills such as scuba diving.

I've been addicted to natural history books for as long as I can remember. My well-thumbed copy of David Attenborough's *Life on Earth* has an inscription in the front wishing me a happy tenth birthday. This definitive, eloquent classic opened my eyes not only to the diversity of life, but also to the sense of wonder that accompanies all wildlife travel. 'It is not difficult to discover an unknown animal,' writes Attenborough in the book's opening lines. 'Spend a day in the tropical forest of South America, turning over logs, looking beneath bark [and] sifting through the moist litter of leaves...' With this simple description, Attenborough plunges us into an Amazonian bug-hunting expedition. That's the thing about good natural history writing. It makes you feel like you're there, a natural accomplice, delving into the same environment, sharing the revelations. The best wildlife books inform and inspire, and *Life on Earth* (Collins, 1979) definitely belongs in my top eight. Picking the others, however, was no easy task. Some are there for their riveting travelogues, others for their groundbreaking revelations, passionate voice, eye-watering humour or breathtaking photography and art.

The Voyage of the Beagle
Wordsworth Editions, 1997
Charles Darwin's wonderfully observed, revelatory voyage to South America and the South Pacific.

The Wild Places
Granta Books, 2007
Robert MacFarlane's eloquent portrait of Britain's last wild places.

The Diversity of Life
Belknap Press, 1992
Edward O Wilson's definitive essay on the importance of biodiversity.

The Snow Leopard
Vintage Classics, 2010
Peter Mathiesson's evocative account of mountains and mysticism.

Into the Heart of Borneo
Penguin, 2005
Redmond O'Hanlon's keenly described and often hilarious jungle adventure.

Eye to Eye
Taschen, 2009
Incredible images by Frans Lanting, one of the world's greatest wildlife photographers.

One Man's Island
HarperCollins, 1984
A wildlife artist's year on Scotland's Isle of May, revealed through beautiful sketches and watercolour paintings. Keith Brockie's work is a celebration of the art of natural history observation.

Planning a trip | wildlife travel year planner

January	February	March	April	May	June
	River safaris, South Luangwa NP, Zambia	→	Birdwatching in Bangweulu Wetlands, Zambia	→	Dry season; camps open, Zambia
			Lemur courtship season, Madagascar		
Wildebeest calving in southern plains (Ndutu) of Serengeti, Tanzania	→	→		Migration in Western Corridor of Serengeti, Tanzania	→
	Leatherback and loggerhead turtles nesting on beaches of KwaZulu Natal, S Africa	→	Kalahari Desert teems with game following rains	→	
				Botswana's Okavango Delta in full flood	→
Big game viewing in Kgalagadi, South Africa	→	→			
	Wolf tracking season, Romania	→	Good birdwatching in Danube Delta until October	→	→
				Bear watching season until August in Finland	→
	Bird migration passes through Coto Doñana, Spain	→		Nesting ducks, Lake Myvatn, Iceland	→
			Whale watching season, Iceland	→	
	Best time to spot tigers, India	→			
	Snow leopards descend Ladakh's mountains in search of prey, India	→	Best time for panda tracking in Qinling Mountains, China	Rhododendrons and other flowering shrubs bloom on the slopes of the Himalayas	→	Wildflowers bloom in Denali National Park, Alaska until September
Bull elephant seals fight for dominance, Piedras Blancas Beach, San Simeon, California	→	Blue whales off the south coast of Sri Lanka	→		
				Grey whales head north past Vancouver Island, British Columbia	
	Monarch butterflies overwintering in Mexico	→		Grizzlies and black bears emerge from hibernation, Canada	Dry season starts in Brazil's Pantanal, a good time for mammal sightings
Whale watching season in Baja California, Mexico	→	→			
Grey whales migrate along Pacific coast of Baja California, Mexico	→	→	→	Best season for jaguar sightings until August, Guyana	→
	Orcas off the coast of Valdés Peninsula, Argentina	→	→		
Green turtles arrive to nest, Galápagos Islands	Flamingos nesting, Galápagos Islands	Waved albatross arrive, Galápagos Islands	→	Marine iguanas hatch, Galápagos Islands	Humpback whales, Galápagos Islands
Seal pups, Falklands & South Georgia	Penguin chicks fledge and adults moult, Antarctica		Beluga and narwhal gather in Davis Strait and off Baffin Island		Seabirds nest during Svalbard's brief summer, until July
	Best time for sighting orca and minke whale, Antarctica	→	Bowhead and beluga whales follow open leads in Arctic pack ice	→	→
Alpine flowers bloom in Southern Alps, New Zealand				Waterbirds concentrated in dry-season wetlands, Kakadu, Australia, until September	→
			Whale sharks feed on plankton off Ningaloo Reef, Western Australia	→	Wildflowers in bloom, Western Australia

July	August	September	October	November	December
Good time for gorilla tracking, Rwanda	Carmine bee-eaters nesting, South Luangwa, Zambia				Green season begins in Zambia
Humpback whales congregate off northeast coast to give birth , Madagascar					
Wildebeest cross Grumeti River, Tanzania	Wildebeest cross Mara River, Tanzania & Kenya		Elephants move into mopane woodland north of Okavango Delta, Botswana	Wildebeest return south into Serengeti , Tanzania	
	Wildebeest in Masai Mara, Kenya				
Best time for big game viewing in southern Tanzania					
Southern right whales arrive in bays along South Africa's Cape coast to give birth					
		Namaqualand in flower, South Africa			
Best time for wildlife watching in Etosha National Park, Namibia					
		Bird migration passes through Coto Doñana, Spain			
Whale watching season, Iceland				Birdwatching in Bharatpur , India, until February	
			India's national parks open until April		
Caribou migration, northern Alaska					Wetland birds nesting in Everglades, Florida, until April
	Humpback whales bubble-net feeding in Chatham Strait and Frederick Sound, Alaska		Polar bears gather near Churchill, Manitoba		
Orcas along Pacific west coast, Alaska & British Columbia				Clear post-monsoon skies make this a good time for Himalayan trekking, Nepal	
Beluga whales gather to calve in Churchill River, Manitoba	Bay of Fundy whale watching				
Brown bears feed on salmon, Alaska & British Columbia			Migrating cranes at Hortobágy National Park, Hungary		Humpback and sperm whales off the coast of Corcovado National Park, Costa Rica
Green, leatherback and hawksbill turtles nest Tortuguero National Park, Costa Rica			North American migrants arrive in Ecuador and Venezuela		
Southern right whales off Argentina's Valdés Peninsula					
Breeding seabirds Galápagos Islands	Galápagos hawk courtship	Sea lions active Galápagos Islands	Blue-footed boobies with chicks, Galápagos	Good time to snorkel, Galápagos Islands	Giant tortoises hatch, Galápagos Islands
Prime month for spotting polar bears, Svalbard			Spring wildflowers on the Falklands and South Georgia	Austral summer – visit Antarctica between now and March	
			Height of penguin and seabird courtship, Antarctica		
Dry season in the rainforests of northern Queensland, Australia			Turtles nesting on islands of the Great Barrier Reef , until February		

Choosing an operator | what to look for

There's no doubt that with thorough planning and careful research, independent travel can offer freedom and choice of budget. However, by arranging your wildlife trip through a specialist travel operator, you'll receive the benefit of first-hand knowledge of your chosen area, as well as an itinerary that includes everything from transport and accommodation to national park entry fees and the services of a professional guide. There is also a lot to be said for travelling with like-minded people on an organised trip.

Track record, accommodation, quality of guides, group size and responsible travel should all be taken into consideration when selecting a wildlife tour operator. Before making a reservation, use the following checklist to help you decide whether a company comes up to scratch.

Business matters
How long has the travel operator been in business? Is it affiliated to a professional association which provides a quality charter and financial security? In the UK, for example, the Association of Independent Tour Operators (aito.co.uk) not only provides high levels of consumer protection should one of its members go out of business, but it also awards travel companies a star rating for meeting high standards of responsible travel (see below).

Responsible travel
Does the operator have a responsible travel policy? Is it something that lies at the heart of the business or is it merely greenwash? Test an operator's eco-credentials by asking the following questions:
• How do you minimize the environmental and cultural impact of your tours and can you provide me with information on travelling responsibly?
• How do your trips benefit local communities?
• Do you employ local guides and leaders and are they trained in responsible tourism practices, such as how to avoid disturbance to wildlife?
• What systems do you have in place to minimize pollution, both at home and abroad? Do you support a carbon offset programme (see page 16)?
• Which conservation charities do you support? Can

you tell me about any successful environmental projects you've been involved with?
• How much produce is sourced locally on your trips?
• Can I stay in community-run or family-owned accommodation? What environmentally sustainable camps and lodges can you recommend?

Wild nights out
Accommodation is largely down to personal choice and budget, but think hard about the options. Mobile camping may enable you to reach remote, wildlife-rich areas, but if you'd prefer four solid walls and a roof between your bed and the wild unknown there is a plethora of lodges to choose from. Try to judge accommodation not just by whether it has a swimming pool and air-con, but also on its environmental credentials (see pages 18-19).

ⓘ Throughout this book, there are recommendations for places to stay that benefit local communities and respect the environment.

Game plan
Look carefully at your itinerary. Are enough days allocated to exploring national parks or is too much time spent travelling between too many highlights? If you're a keen photographer or interested in animal behaviour, concentrating on one area may prove more satisfying than flitting from one to another. Is the timing right? Bargain deals might conceal unfavourable conditions for viewing wildlife – it could be the wet season when access is difficult or simply the 'off season' when wildlife has migrated elsewhere.

Group size & guide-wise
Two final aspects to bear in mind when choosing an operator are group size and the quality of your guide. Small groups of a dozen people are quiet and unobtrusive, and an expert guide who can communicate with a genuine passion for the natural world will elevate a wildlife holiday to the trip-of-a-lifetime – whether you're searching for butterflies in the Alps or blue whales off California.

ⓘ For complete freedom and flexibility, tailor-made wildlife trips are available from numerous operators.

Jackson Looseyia
Nomadic Encounters, Kenya
nomadicencounters.com

Number of years as a guide 24

Most memorable wildlife encounter
I was on a walking safari with my late father when a bull buffalo charged and separated us. The buffalo singled out the old man and I watched helplessly as it tossed him up in the air. At the age of 16 this left me with a permanent fear and respect for these bull buffaloes, also known as brigadiers.

Favourite animal
Leopards, because they are beautiful, shrewd, elusive, scary and powerful. I have seen a young giraffe kill up a tree. Just imagine how a leopard, weighing half the weight, could have carried it there.

Top tip for travellers
Bring a good pair of binoculars. Safaris in Africa are life-changing experiences and some of the sights you will see can only be watched through binoculars. While you are on safari remember to drink a lot of water during the day. Apply sun cream before you leave your tent and remember that to be up early with the eagle you don't stay up late with the owls.

Responsible travel
It's important to me because it's about caring for the wildlife and not pushing for a close-up photograph that changes its natural behaviour. Responsible travellers are ready to listen, learn and help whenever necessary. Our company contributes a lot to the development of schools and cultural visits whereby tourists can exchange ideas with the local people. The contribution to the local economy of my camp has stopped deforestation in the area, saving the habitat for wildlife and microorganisms.

Derrick Nabaala
Basecamp Explorer, Kenya
basecampexplorer.com

Number of years as a guide 4

Most memorable wildlife encounter
When I was herding cattle as a boy, a buffalo ran out from where he was hiding in the bushes and charged me. Luckily I was able to lie down amongst the cattle so he couldn't see or smell me and eventually he went away. Buffalo are one of the most dangerous animals in Africa and are responsible for many deaths.

Favourite animal
Elephants, because of their social and family structure. They always look after the elderly, similar to our own Maasai culture. They have incredible memories, a complex communication system (part of which is unable to be heard by the human ear) and a strength second to none.

Favourite place
The Masai Mara is one of the best wildlife viewing areas in Africa where you can see many species and almost be guaranteed to have close encounters with big cats like lion and cheetah. As you drive around the reserve, the spectacular scenery is constantly changing.

Top tip for travellers
Always carry extra batteries and memory cards for your camera, bring a pair of binoculars and a notebook and pen to record all the species you see.

Funniest thing a client has said on safari
How many kilograms of meat does an elephant eat?

Responsible travel
Responsible travel is important so that there is no negative impact on the land, the wildlife and the people. Responsible tourists care about the environment.

Ralph Bousfield
Jack's Camp, Uncharted Africa Safari Co, Botswana, unchartedafrica.com

Number of years as a guide 34

Most memorable wildlife encounter
I was on safari with a blind man and I wanted him to experience the zebra migration. We walked towards a herd of 5,000 zebra, crouched down and managed to make our way to the centre. We both felt part of the herd and were able to substitute sight with the smell of the animals and the sound of thousands of hooves. The encounter was unbelievable for both of us and my guest was so moved by the experience that he had tears in his eyes.

Favourite animal
I've always aimed to be as cooperative, tough and gentle as the brown hyena. Its superb adaptation to the Kalahari, loner behaviour and supportive pack interaction makes it the ideal team member.

Top tip for travellers
Come with an open mind and heart; expect the unexpected and be prepared for something life-changing.

Responsible travel
Our work gives value to traditional ways of life – and traditional knowledge of botany and wildlife. We aim to help preserve the old ways, saying to the Bushmen: "Your knowledge is worth something." I was discussing our safaris with some Bushmen, and they said to me: "We would like to do exactly what you do." I said: "What do you think I do?" And they replied: "You use the knowledge that you inherited from your father. People pay you to do what he taught you. We want to do the same thing with what we know." The guys were totally getting it. Rather than looking into the past, they were looking to the future and finding a way to mutually benefit.

Choosing an operator | directory

❀ Check out the responsible travel credentials of each operator by looking for this symbol.

The Adventure Company
adventurecompany.co.uk

Over 80 trips focus on wildlife in the Adventure Company's worldwide portfolio, which includes treks, family adventures and The Collection (for added style and comfort). Wildlife destinations include Africa, Costa Rica, India and the Galápagos Islands.

❀ A foundation supports grassroots projects, while Hands-On Adventures allow you to spend time helping local communities as part of your holiday.

Exodus
exodus.co.uk

Exodus offers everything from polar expeditions and wilderness trips to African safaris, tiger watching, Galápagos cruises and Amazon tours.

❀ Responsible travel has a strong presence on this website. Exodus supports various community-based projects in partnership with Friends of Conservation. All of its polar expeditions 'apply the most stringent rules of minimum impact travel'.

Bridge & Wickers
bridgeandwickers.co.uk

Click on 'Wildlife and Safari' and this well-written, stylish website delivers a sumptuous feast of luxury, tailor-made options in Africa, Asia, Canada, Australia and New Zealand.

❀ Bridge & Wickers' commitment to responsible travel includes pioneering tourism in post-conflict destinations like Rwanda as a means of protecting their natural heritage and contributing to growth and stability.

Explore
explore.co.uk

African and Indian safaris, Galápagos cruises, polar voyages and gorilla, bear and whale watching all feature in this extensive, worldwide collection of adventure tours. There are also sections on treks, boat and rail journeys.

❀ An industry leader in responsible travel, Explore has a 5-star responsible tourism rating from AITO and was voted Best Tour Operator in the Virgin Holidays Responsible Tourism Awards.

Discover the World
discover-the-world.co.uk

'Wildlife and Nature Holidays' can be found under 'Holiday Types' on this comprehensive site by one of the UK's leading specialist tour operators. Its collection includes tailor-made or group trips to Iceland, Scandinavia, the Arctic, Antarctica, New Zealand and Canada.

❀ Holds AITO's 3-star responsible travel award and raises funds for the Born Free Foundation, Scott Polar Research Institute and other organizations.

Journey Latin America
journeylatinamerica.co.uk

A great selection of wildlife holidays, with old favourites like Costa Rica and the Galápagos Islands embellished with more off-beat destinations such as Guyana and Nicaragua. Antarctica and the Falkland Islands also feature.

❀ A strong sustainable travel policy underlies all Journey Latin America trips. The operator supports local charities in Latin America and offsets all staff travel through the TICOS scheme.

❝ ❞ **All too often these days, tour operators are trying to cut costs which often means cutting service and quality. Look for value, not the lowest price, and never underestimate the difference a good travel specialist can make in planning the perfect holiday**

Clive Stacey, Managing Director, Discover the World (discover-the-world.co.uk)

★ Wildlife Worldwide
wildlifeworldwide.com

Part of the Chameleon Worldwide group, which includes Oceans Worldwide (expedition voyages and whale watching) and Dive Worldwide (a breathtaking range of dive trips), Wildlife Worldwide offers the definitive collection of wildlife holidays. Using hand-picked, tried and trusted lodges, cruise vessels and guides, its tailor-made and group tours range from natural history odysseys in Costa Rica and Borneo to bear watching in Finland and tracking leopards in Zambia's Luangwa Valley. Its range of Galápagos and polar cruises is second to none. Keen photographers will find dedicated tours led by professionals, while the annual Festival of Wildlife (held in a different wildlife hotspot each year) offers masterclasses, workshops and presentations with well-known wildlife experts, such as Jonathan Scott and Mark Carwardine.

✿ Responsible travel has been at the heart of Wildlife Worldwide since its inception in 1992. As well as a comprehensive policy 'to preserve the natural environment and minimize any negative impact on local cultures', the company supports several conservation organizations and community-based projects. These include the David Shepherd Wildlife Foundation, The Galápagos Conservation Trust, Horny@50 (working to conserve critically endangered rhino populations) and Raincoast Conservation (raising awareness of the plight of British Columbia's Great Bear Rainforest). Wildlife Worldwide also supports two schools in Zambia's Luangwa Valley and offers carbon offset through Climate Care.

Naturetrek
naturetrek.co.uk

For total immersion in wildlife, this widely respected operator offers the world's largest selection of expert-led small-group tours. Birdwatchers in particular will find the detail on its website invaluable. You can search by species, destination or tour focus.

✿ Naturetrek's sustainable tourism policy includes guidelines for clients, donations to wildlife charities and partnerships with local communities.

Reef & Rainforest Tours
reefandrainforest.co.uk

Tailor-made holidays, escorted group tours, cruises and family adventures all feature on this superb site which includes an exotic round-up of some of the world's finest natural history locations – from Ecuador and Madagascar to Papua New Guinea.

✿ 'Preservation through Visitation' involves support for local communities and donations to charities such as the Durrel Wildlife Conservation Trust.

Rainbow Tours
rainbowtours.co.uk

A specialist in tailor-made travel to Africa and the Indian Ocean, Rainbow Tours offers a colourful kaleidoscope of safaris. Search under 'Family', 'Luxury' and 'Adventure' or click on 'Eco' for a list of lodges that have made a significant contribution to sustainability.

✿ Rainbow Tours follows a responsible travel Code of Practice which includes supporting community tourism and using locally owned accommodation.

Steppes Discovery
steppesdiscovery.co.uk

Take your pick from expert-guided, small-group tours, cruises and photo expeditions to the world's premier wildlife locations. This clear, well-designed website allows you to search by destination, wildlife or holiday type and includes a useful year planner.

✿ Big on responsible travel, Steppes Discovery underpins all of its trips with sustainable ethics and supports a wide range of conservation charities.

Also try the following operators

Acacia Africa | acacia-africa.com
Africa in Focus | africa-in-focus.com
Aqua-Firma | aqua-firma.co.uk
Art Safari | artsafari.co.uk

Audley Travel | audleytravel.com
Busanga Safaris | busangasafari.co.uk
Classic Journeys | classicjourneys.co.uk
Cox & Kings | coxandkings.co.uk

Freeman Safaris | freemansafaris.com
Gecko's Adventures | geckosadventures.co
Great Glen Wildlife | greatglenwildlife.co.uk
Greentours | greentours.co.uk

Choosing an operator | directory

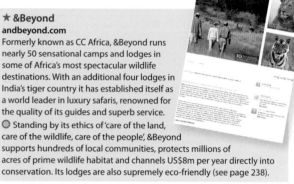

Tribes Travel
tribes.co.uk

Pioneers of responsible travel, Tribes offers tailor-made holidays in Africa, Asia and South America. Its wildlife options include a tempting line-up of community-run camps and lodges.
🌐 Global winner of both the Responsible Tourism and Tourism for Tomorrow Awards, Tribes is at the forefront of sustainable travel. Its code of eco and ethical practices has made it a role model for other small operators.

★ &Beyond
andbeyond.com

Formerly known as CC Africa, &Beyond runs nearly 50 sensational camps and lodges in some of Africa's most spectacular wildlife destinations. With an additional four lodges in India's tiger country it has established itself as a world leader in luxury safaris, renowned for the quality of its guides and superb service.
🌐 Standing by its ethics of 'care of the land, care of the wildlife, care of the people', &Beyond supports hundreds of local communities, protects millions of acres of prime wildlife habitat and channels US$8m per year directly into conservation. Its lodges are also supremely eco-friendly (see page 238).

WWF Travel
worldwildlife.org/travel

Each year, the Worldwide Fund for Nature organises a select range of tours led by expert naturalists and WWF staff. Amazon river voyages regularly feature, as do expedition cruises in Alaska and trips to Churchill, Namibia, Borneo and the Galápagos Islands.
🌐 Up to 10% of your tour cost goes to WWF's conservation work. Trips support community tourism, eco-friendly lodges and small, low-impact ships.

Wilderness Travel
wildernesstravel.com

The photography on the website of this premier adventure tour operator is in a class of its own. Look beyond the pretty pictures, though, and you'll discover a wealth of holiday ideas, grouped under small-group adventures, private journeys and one-off expeditions.
🌐 With 30 years' experience, US-based Wilderness Travel is deeply committed to responsible tourism and is a founding member of several conservation groups.

Wild Ambitions
wildambitions.co.uk

A sister company to the ever-popular group tours run by The Travelling Naturalist, Wild Ambitions offers a tailor made service for independent wildlife holidays worldwide. Canada, Antarctica and Australia are the pick of the bunch.
🌐 Holder of a 5-star responsible travel rating from AITO, Wild Ambitions operates to a strict ecotourism code and supports conservation work by the RSPB and other environmental charities.

Wildland Adventures
wildland.com

Based in Seattle, Wildland Adventures offers small-group and tailor-made holidays worldwide. Pick of the wildlife destinations include Alaska, Costa Rica, Panama, Argentina, Galápagos, Botswana, Kenya and Tanzania.
🌐 A leader in ecotravel, Wildlands supports local conservation groups and community development projects co-sponsored by its non-profit Travelers Conservation Trust.

> ❝❞ **Bridge & Wickers promotes camps and lodges that strive to reduce their carbon footprint, celebrate the wilderness and its inhabitants with excellent guiding and appropriate infrastructure, and work in just and genuine partnership with local communities**
>
> David Wickers, Co-Founder, Bridge & Wickers (bridgeandwickers.co.uk)

Wildlife & Wilderness
wildlifewilderness.com

This simple, stylish website showcases a good selection of quality, bespoke wildlife holidays grouped not only by destination but also by special interest (birdwatching, bears, whales, primates and big cats).

❁ Wildlife & Wilderness publishes its sustainable tourism policy on its website and offers tips for responsible travel. Carbon emissions are offset with Climate Care and the World Land Trust.

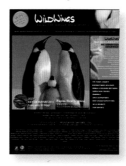

Wildwings
wildwings.co.uk

Taking travel to extremes, Wildwings not only runs an extensive collection of birdwatching tours, whale and dolphin watching trips and expedition cruises, but also delves into space and deep ocean adventures.

❁ As well as supporting frontline conservation projects, such as Save the Albatross, Wildwings uses local businesses and guides on each of its tours and holidays.

Wildlife Trails
wildlifetrails.co.uk

Starting with Tiger Trails in 1999, this tailor-made wildlife specialist now features bears, gorillas and wolves, as well as rhinos in Nepal and leopards in Sri Lanka. The emphasis is very much on providing unique, intimate and personal wildlife experiences.

❁ Awarded a 5-star responsible travel rating by AITO, Wildlife Trails' ecotourism initiatives include setting up a community tourism camp in India.

World Primate Safaris
worldprimatesafaris.com

If gorillas or orang-utans are on your wishlist, World Primate Safaris offers a tailor-made service for safaris to Rwanda, Uganda and Borneo. Sister companies include World Big Cat Safaris and World Bear Safaris.

❁ A percentage of each safari sold goes towards to the conservation of endangered primates. World Primate Safaris also encourages the use of local guides and accommodation.

★ Expert Africa
expertafrica.com

Expert Africa's chunky, beautifully designed and award-winning brochure is available to download from the company's equally comprehensive website. Browse through either and you quickly realise where Expert Africa gets its name from. Search for holiday ideas by destination, special interest or by clicking on annotated maps and you access a wealth of information on key locations, places to stay and more than 100 safari recommendations. Expert Africa covers Botswana, Malawi, Mozambique, Namibia, Rwanda, Seychelles, South Africa, Tanzania, Zambia, Zanzibar and Zimbabwe. Note that Kenya isn't featured. 'We only offer trips to areas that we know inside-out,' claims the operator, and this refreshing honesty is also reflected in the unedited trip feedback reports posted on the website. Carefully crafted tailor made trips are the cornerstone of Expert Africa's trips, but it also offers small-group guided safaris to Botswana, Namibia, Tanzania and Zambia through its Wild about Africa programme (wildaboutafrica.com).

❁ Holder of a 5-star AITO award for responsible travel, Expert Africa supports local community-based projects and small-scale businesses to help them secure a fair share of the benefits from carefully managed tourism.

Also try the following operators

Island Ventures | islandventures.co.uk
Jetwing Eco Holidays | jetwingeco.com
Jungle Guru | jungleguru.com
KE Adventure Travel | keadventure.com

Kumuka Worldwide | kumuka.com
Last Frontiers | lastfrontiers.com
Motmot Travel | motmottravel.com
Mountain Travel Sobek | mtsobek.com

Peregrine | peregrineadventures.com
Pioneer Expeditions | pioneerexpeditions.com
Tracks Safaris | trackssafaris.co.uk
Windows on the Wild | windowsonthewild.com

What to take | travel gear

polar & mountain

1 Jacket (rohan.co.uk) Choose an outer shell that's windproof, waterproof and breathable like this Rohan Mountain Guide Jacket. For polar expeditions, consider a mid-thigh length down parka **2** Fleece (thenorthface.com) Essential mid layer **3** Gloves and socks (terra-nova.co.uk) Keep hands snug with thick waterproof mitts. Wear a pair of thin socks beneath thick wool outer socks **4** Warm hat (berghaus.com) Minimize heat-loss through your head **5** Sunglasses (julbo-eyewear.com) Protect your eyes from glare with wrap-around sunglasses and apply sun screen to face and lips (minimum SPF 30) **6** Wellington boots Useful on cruises when shore excursions may involve paddling ashore

jungle

1 Poncho (travelproof.co.uk) Less clammy than a jacket and can also be opened out to use as a shelter or groundsheet **2** Jungle boots (jungleboots.com) Quick-drying, breathable canvas uppers, anti-clogging soles and high lace-ups to keep ants and leeches out **3** Work gloves (petzl.com) Protect your hands from thorns, ants and stinging nettles **4** Head torch (petzl.com) Essential jungle kit, along with whistle, compass and knife. A bandana is useful as a sweat rag **5** Long-sleeve shirt (craghoppers.com) Impregnated with insect repellent; long trousers also essential **6** Mosquito net (nomadtravel.co.uk) Nets treated with permethrin deter biting insects **7** Backpack (lowealpine.com) Choose a lightweight pack, like this Zepton 50, with an airflow back system to reduce moisture build-up **8** Insect repellent (mosi-guard.com) Natural repellents available as roll-ons, sprays and creams **9** Clothing treatment (nomadtravel.co.uk) Treat socks with 100% DEET or buy leech-proof socks

desert

1 Shirt (rohan.co.uk) Long sleeves are best. This Rohan Expedition Shirt is breathable, loose fitting and UV resistant, with under-arm vents for keeping cool **2** Desert boots (desertboots.us) High-sided boots, with breathable canvas or suede uppers, guard against rocks and thorns **3** Hat (tilley.com) A wide-brimmed sunhat is essential. The T5MO Tilley Hat is made from organic cotton and has an airflow mesh to keep your head cool. Don't forget sunglasses with full UV protection and side shields **4** Daypack (camelbak.com) Combat dehydration by taking a daypack with built-in water reservoir. The CamelBak Mule is ideal **5** Drywash (lifeventure.co.uk) When water is scarce, keep your hands clean using an antibacterial drywash **6** First aid Make sure you keep a first-aid kit handy with rehydration sachets, skin moisturiser, lip balm and eyewash. A compass and whistle could be life-savers if you get lost in the desert **7** Jacket Temperatures can plummet at night in the desert, so remember to pack a lightweight, windproof fleece jacket **8** Sandals Give your feet a breather around camp during the evenings, but never wear sandals during the day – you can easily burn the tops of your feet

① Holdall (eaglecreek.com) Far more flexible than a rigid suitcase, a holdall can be easily stowed in a safari vehicle and is essential if you're using light aircraft (with limited cargo space) to reach your destination. Remember to pack light – some flights have a baggage allowance of just 12-15 kg **② Shirt** (thesafaristore.co.uk and regatta.com) Choose clothing with neutral tones to help you blend in – particularly important on walking safaris. Avoid blue or black as these colours can attract tsetse flies. Long-sleeve shirts will protect you from sunburn and biting insects, while a technical fibre, such as polyamide, will not only keep you cooler than cotton, but will also wick moisture away from your body and be easier to wash and dry. Other features to look for include built-in UV protection (SPF 30+) and insect repellent. As well as the shirts shown here from The Safari Store and Regatta, try Rohan and Páramo **③ Trousers** (craghoppers.com) Long trousers provide protection against the sun, thorns and biting insects, but these NosiLife Duo Convertibles from Craghoppers have the added versatility of zip-off legs when you want to be cooler **④ Safari vest** (rohan.co.uk) Particularly useful if you're a photographer and need lots of pockets for storing spare memory cards, lens cleaning gear etc, a safari vest is also extremely handy for everyday bits and pieces, such as notebooks, field guides, binoculars, snacks, suncream, insect repellent and cash **⑤ Daypack** (thenorthface.com) This 30-litre Jester Backpack from The North Face has useful mesh side pockets for holding water bottles, while the removable hipbelt and moulded shoulder strap provide added comfort **⑥ Binoculars** (zeiss.com) Essential for all wildlife travel. These all-purpose Zeiss binoculars have a large field of view, good light transmission, weather-proofing and 10x magnification. See pages 32-33 for more information on choosing binoculars **⑦ Field guides** A good field guide will greatly enhance your wildlife trip. Recommended guides for birds, mammals and other wildlife are given throughout this book **⑧ Sunhat** (rohan.co.uk) A wide-brimmed hat provides the best protection from the sun, but choose one with neck cords to stop it blowing off your head when you're travelling in an open vehicle or boat **⑨ Suncream** (garnier.co.uk) Keep high-factor suncream and lip balm handy at all times and remember to reapply frequently **⑩ Water bottle** (snugpak.com) Bottled water can contribute to the build-up of plastic waste, so consider taking a sturdy aluminium bottle to fill with treated water each morning **⑪ Insect repellent** (jungleformula.co.uk) Cover up at dawn and dusk when mosquitoes are most active and apply repellent to any exposed skin **⑫ Camera** (canon.com) See pages 34-37 for advice on photographic equipment and techniques **⑬ Walking shoes** Lightweight walking boots are best. Make sure they have good ankle support and breathable uppers to help keep your feet cool **⑭ Accessories** Extras to pack include a mini first-aid kit and malaria prophylaxis (see pages 40-41), sunglasses, battery charger, adaptor plugs and a torch.

What to take | binoculars

Agood pair of binoculars is your window on the natural world. Going on a wildlife trip without them is like snorkelling without a mask or skiing without goggles. Binoculars are essential for spotting wildlife and making those crucial calls on identification, but they also bring a whole new dimension (and vivid detail) to up-close and personal encounters. You haven't really seen a lion properly until you've honed in on the scars on his nose or the tick clinging to his mane...

What to look for

For wildlife travel, binoculars need to have a decent magnification, brightness and field of view, and be tough, compact and not too heavy or fiddly to use.

ⓘ Binoculars are classified by two numbers. The first denotes the magnification, while the second indicates the diameter of the objective (or light-gathering) lens. A pair of 10x42 binoculars, therefore, will magnify the subject 10 times more than the naked eye sees it, and will have a 42 mm lens.

A magnification of 10 is ideal for most wildlife travel, especially if you are a keen birdwatcher. Remember, however, that the higher the magnification the more prone the binoculars are to hand-shake. Brightness, field of view and depth of field also diminish as magnification increases. You can boost the brightness of the image by choosing a pair with a large objective lens – although this, of course, may increase overall weight and size. The exit pupil, a measurement of brightness, is calculated by dividing the diameter of the objective lens by the magnification, so a pair of 8x32 binoculars will have an exit pupil of four – the minimum you should look for.

Ultimately, the best way to choose a pair of binoculars is to try before you buy. Do they feel comfortable in your hands and against your eyes? Does the focusing wheel fall naturally under your thumb? Is the image sharp right to the edges of your field of view? Do they feel durable and not too heavy?

Choosing binoculars is all about making compromises and, inevitably with optics, you get what you pay for. An expensive, high-quality pair of binoculars, however, is a life-long investment.

Cock-of-the-rock

Rupicola peruvianus
Manu Biosphere Reserve, Peru

Getting an eyeful of this Andean cloud forest beauty requires binoculars with good light-gathering qualities.

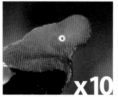

Opticron Explorer BGA	Nikon Monarch DCF	Bushnell Legend Ultra HD
An excellent compromise between price and quality, the Opticron Explorers deliver good resolution, brightness and contrast with very little edge distortion. Fairly compact and lightweight, they have very smooth focusing, bringing infinity down to 2 m in just a half-turn of the chunky focus wheel.	Lightweight, waterproof (up to 1 m for 10 minutes) and encased in rubber armour, these well-made Nikon binoculars are designed to withstand the rough-and-tumble of travelling life. They provide a solid hand grip and the lenses and prism are multilayer coated for bright, sharp images. Great value for money.	The build quality of these lightweight, rubber-coated binoculars is outstanding. A waterproof and fogproof construction combined with rain-repellent lens coating makes them ready for any situation. Optics are excellent too, thanks to the use of premium ED glass for maximising brightness, light transmission and contrast.
Models 8x42, 10x42	**Models** 8x42, 10x42, 12x42	**Models** 8x36, 8x42, 10x42
Weight 743-757 g	**Weight** 610-620 g	**Weight** 638 g
Dimensions 155x132 mm	**Dimensions** 146x129 mm	**Dimensions** 130x145 mm
Field of view 106-117 m	**Field of view** 87-110 m	**Field of view** 113 m
Minimum focus 1.5 m	**Minimum focus** 2.5 m	**Minimum focus** 1.9 m
Price guide £200	**Price guide** £350	**Price guide** £400
Contact opticron.co.uk	**Contact** nikon.com The	**Contact** bushnell.com

Going hand in hand with your binoculars, a field guide will not only help you with identification, but will also provide information on behaviour, habitats and distribution. Regional field guides are available that cover birds and mammals in most parts of the world, but there are also some excellent global titles. The following five set the benchmark.

Raptors of the World
Helm Field Guides, 2005
Get to grips with all 340 of the world's raptor species, from mighty eagles to diminutive falcons. The superb artwork in this field guide will help you identify birds of prey roosting and in flight. There's also information on subspecies and juveniles.

Parrots of the World
Helm Field Guides, 2006
Joseph M Forshaw is a world authority on parrots and this dazzling volume features illustrations of every species in glorious detail, along with distribution maps and introductory sections on taxonomy, evolution, breeding biology, behaviour and conservation.

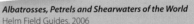

Whales, Dolphins and Seals
A&C Black, 2006
A field guide to the marine mammals of the world, this stunning guide is a must for anyone embarking on a polar voyage. It covers every species of cetacean, pinniped and sirenian in the world, along with the sea otters and the polar bear.

Albatrosses, Petrels and Shearwaters of the World
Helm Field Guides, 2006
Not always easy to identify – particularly when you're on the pitching deck of a ship – these magnificent pelagic seabirds are described in vivid detail in this book, which includes clear illustrations of each species in flight, as well as distribution maps.

Coral Reef Fishes
Princeton University Press, 2001
No less than 2,118 species of marine fish from both the Indo-Pacific and Caribbean regions are illustrated and described in this definitive guide. An essential companion for anyone interested in snorkelling or diving on the world's coral reefs.

How to be a Bad Birdwatcher
Short Books, 2004
Not so much a guide as a celebration of birds and the pleasure that comes from simply observing them, Simon Barnes dismisses the popular myth that you need expensive binoculars and an anorak to enjoy birdwatching.

Swarovski SLC 42

The high performance HD fluoride lenses in these binoculars guarantee sharp images, even in low light. Compact and rugged, this continuously refined classic has a lightweight but tough magnesium body, comfortable wide-angle eyepieces for a large field of view and an ultra-smooth focusing mechanism.
Models 8x42, 10x42
Weight 790-810 g
Dimensions 149x120 mm
Field of view 110-136 m
Minimum focus 1.9 m
Price guide £1,450
Contact swarovskioptik.com

Leica Ultravid HD

Designed to fit snugly in your hands, these stylish binoculars have a large focusing wheel that feels smooth and natural. As you would expect for the price, optics are sharp and bright with a coating to repel dirt and water, while build quality is second to none. Ultravids are watertight to a depth of 5 m.
Models 7x42, 8x42, 10x42
Weight 750-790 g
Dimensions 120x147 mm
Field of view 112-140 m
Minimum focus 2.9-3.3 m
Price guide £1,600
Contact leica.com

Wildlife photography | equipment

With their interchangeable lenses, Digital Single Lens Reflex cameras (DSLRs) are the most versatile option for wildlife photography. Digital technology is evolving at such a rate, however, that choosing the right camera can quickly lead to jargon-overload. Cut through the techno-babble by focusing on a few key features.

Making sense of sensors

There are two things you need to know. Firstly, more megapixels (MP) means better quality images. A camera with an 8MP sensor will enable you to print sharp A3 prints. Secondly, sensors come in different sizes. Full-frame sensors cover the same area as a piece of 35 mm film and have no effect on the focal length of lenses. Most DSLRs, however, have smaller sensors which typically crop the picture area by a factor of 1.6, multiplying the focal length of lenses by the same amount. A 300 mm lens, therefore, becomes a 480 mm lens – great news for animal snappers!

Ready for action

Wildlife rarely poses for the camera, so maximize your chances of capturing fleeting moments by selecting a DSLR that has quick and responsive autofocus (including servo AF which tracks moving subjects) and a good rate of fire – ideally a minimum of five frames per second.

Useful extras

A depth of field preview button allows you to assess the zone of focus and adjust the aperture accordingly (see page 36). Reviewing your pictures for correct exposure, meanwhile, is made much easier if the LCD screen on the back of the camera includes a histogram display. Basically, this shows, at a glance, whether an image is over exposed, under exposed or spot on. Additional features worth adding to your wish list include robust build, dust and moisture resistant buttons and switches, and a built-in sensor-cleaning device.

It just feels right

Don't rush out and buy a new camera the day before you leave. The best camera to use is the one you know so well you can adjust any control without taking your

Unpacked: the author's kit

❶ **Digital SLR** The Canon EOS 5D has a full-frame sensor, while the Canon EOS 7D has an 18MP, 1.6x sensor, fast autofocus and eight frames per second continuous shooting, making it perfect for high-speed telephoto action ❷ **Telephoto zoom lens** This 100-400 mm zoom is a good all-rounder for wildlife photography. Image stabilisation reduces camera shake. A fast maximum aperture 70-200 mm f2.8 lens (not shown) is useful for low-light shooting, while a 500 mm f4 has the pulling power for bird photography ❸ **Extender** Boost lens focal length by 1.4x or 2x ❹ **Macro lens** A 100 mm or 180 mm macro allows you to get close-ups of insects without having to get too close ❺ **Wideangle zoom lens** A 17-35 mm zoom can be used for landscapes, dramatic close-ups and for showing wildlife in its habitat ❻ **Flash** Useful when used off-camera to add highlights, but take care not to startle wildlife ❼ **Cleaning gear** Blower brush, lens cloth and sensor cleaning brush ❽ **Spare lens caps and batteries** ❾ **Memory cards** Bring several and ensure that they have fast write speeds ❿ **Downloader** Back up, view and even edit your images on a portable hard drive ⓫ **Cable release** Use with a tripod to minimize camera shake ⓬ **Beanbag** Useful camera support for times (ie in a vehicle) when a tripod is impractical.

A maintenance kit should contain a jeweller's screwdriver, duct tape (for emergency repairs), pencil eraser (for cleaning battery contacts), cotton buds (for cleaning hard-to-reach places) and zip-lock plastic bags with silica desiccant sachets (for absorbing moisture from rain- or wave-soaked gear.

Protect the front element of your lenses against scratches and dust, with a UV or skylight filter. Lens hoods provide additional protection and help to eliminate flare.

As well as an important back-up device, portable downloaders allow you to preview and edit your images.

Wildlife photography | equipment & technique

eye from the viewfinder. It feels right in your hands and you're not afraid of getting it scratched.

Through the looking glass

A DSLR has all the fancy buttons, light-up screens and gadget appeal, but it's lenses that wildlife photographers ultimately rely on. If you're on a limited budget, invest in the best lenses you can afford, rather than splurging out on a flashy camera body. Zoom lenses are a flexible option for wildlife trips where fast-changing situations call for rapid shifts in focal length. They also help to minimize lens changes – a boon for digital users who need to keep dust away from delicate sensors. An ideal zoom for general wildlife photography is the 100-400 mm (see page 34 for other wildlife lenses). Features to consider when buying lenses are maximum aperture (lenses with large maximum apertures of f2.8 let in more light, but are heavy and expensive) and image stabilisation (very useful for hand-holding telephoto lenses or shooting in low light).

Carrying it off

Don't skimp on the camera bag. Saving a few pounds may prove to be a false economy. There are several excellent ranges for wildlife photography, including photo-backpacks, waist pouches and hybrid backpacks where you can store personal belongings above a dedicated camera compartment. An ideal bag should have comfortable shoulder straps and waist belt, ease-of-access, good quality zips and seams as well as a slip-on waterproof cover. Steer clear of traditional shoulder bags – they're cumbersome and pull you off balance.

Need something smaller and lighter?

Digital compacts are getting ever more advanced. This Canon SX30 IS weighs just 600 g, but has a whopping 35x optical zoom, 14.1 megapixel sensor, image stabiliser and servo AF. Everything, in fact, that you need for shooting wildlife.

The right exposure
Modern DSLRs have very sophisticated metering systems, but you still need to be wary of situations when they are prone to under- or over-expose a subject. For a bird with white plumage, such as this albatross for example, accurate exposure is required to avoid the white plumage from 'burning out' and losing detail.

Black-browed albatross
ISO rating 200
Shutter speed 1/800s
Aperture f5.6
Focal length 370 mm

Narrow depth of field
Adjust the aperture setting on your camera to control how much of the image is in focus. A wide aperture (around f2.8-4.5) creates a narrow depth of field and can be used to isolate a subject from its background. Here, a single nesting gentoo is picked out from a crowded penguin colony that's been thrown out of focus.

Gentoo penguin
ISO rating 320
Shutter speed 1/250s
Aperture f3.5
Focal length 300 mm

Maximum depth of field
To get everything in focus, from the foreground to the background, select a small aperture (around f16 and above). Here, the sand ripples, penguins and distant waves are all sharp. The compromise of a small aperture is that shutter speeds drop, so be sure to use a tripod to avoid any camera shake.

Gentoo penguin
ISO rating 50
Shutter speed 1/40s
Aperture f18
Focal length 120 mm

Silhouettes
Under-exposing a subject to form a silhouette against a dramatic sunset or pre-dawn sky certainly conveys atmosphere. DSLRs, however, will often try to find detail in the subject. Ensure it stays a silhouette by taking a meter reading from the brighter background or setting exposure compensation to -1 or -2 stops.

Striated caracara
ISO rating 200
Shutter speed 1/80s
Aperture f5.6
Focal length 300 mm

Low light
A big advantage of digital cameras over film ones is that sensors are much more sensitive to light, meaning you can continue shooting even when conditions are getting pretty murky. Long after the sun had set, this trio of gentoo penguins could be photographed simply by pushing the camera's ISO setting to 600.

Gentoo penguin
ISO rating 600
Shutter speed 1/60s
Aperture f4.5
Focal length 150 mm

Keep it simple
Simple and uncluttered compositions tend to make more striking images. By taking a low viewpoint and filling the frame with the head of this elephant seal, all attention is focused on his bulbous nose. A telephoto lens provides a tight crop – and keeps you a safe distance from potentially dangerous animals!

Elephant seal
ISO rating 50
Shutter speed 1/125s
Aperture f5.6
Focal length 400 mm

Demonstrating 16 key aspects of wildlife photography, these pictures were all taken within a few days of each other during a trip to the Falkland Islands (see pages 288-289). For more tips on wildlife photography, look out for the ⊙ symbol.

Sharp focus
The general rule is to always focus on the eyes. DSLRs have lots of tricks to help you keep a subject in focus. You can activate various focus points to cover different areas of the viewfinder and you can also select different autofocus modes. Predictive autofocus locks onto a subject and keeps it in focus when it moves.

Black-browed albatross
ISO rating 200
Shutter speed 1/600s
Aperture f4.5
Focal length 400 mm

Freezing the action
Porpoising penguins move at an incredible rate and you need a very fast shutter speed to stand any chance of capturing the moment they burst above the surface. Keep shutter speeds high by boosting the ISO rating. Also remember to set your camera to continuous shooting and use servo or predictive autofocus.

Gentoo penguin
ISO rating 400
Shutter speed 1/2000s
Aperture f4.5
Focal length 300 mm

Going with the flow
Experimenting with slow shutter speeds inevitably means you lose detail, but the fluidity of images like this gentoo striding along a beach conveys the motion of wildlife far better than a freeze-frame approach using a high shutter speed. Pan the camera with your moving subject and fire a sequence of shots.

Gentoo penguin
ISO rating 50
Shutter speed 1/8s
Aperture f36
Focal length 400 mm

Golden hours
As with all photography, light is the key to successful images. Early morning and late afternoon are not only characterised by warm, saturated light and rich textures, but they are also the times when many wild animals are at their most active. This king penguin was returning to its rookery at dusk.

King penguin
ISO rating 50
Shutter speed 1/30s
Aperture f5.6
Focal length 350 mm

Backlight
Keeping the sun behind you, with light falling directly on your subject is all well and good, but take a risk occasionally and shoot into the light. You'll find that backlighting gives added mood and 'zing' to many wildlife images, accentuating textures, such as the punky head feathers on this rockhopper penguin.

Rockhopper penguin
ISO rating 200
Shutter speed 1/400s
Aperture f5.6
Focal length 200 mm

Leave some space
By positioning your subject off-centre, you create space that it can either look into or, in the case of a moving animal, walk or fly into. This makes a far more pleasing composition than keeping everything dead centre. Although not shown here, a portrait format can also form a strong composition – particularly with birds.

Gentoo penguin
ISO rating 80
Shutter speed 1/500s
Aperture f8
Focal length 24 mm

Take a wider view
Shooting wildlife with a wideangle lens is both challenging and liberating. It's a great way of showing animals in their natural habitat. If you can get close enough, wideangle photography can also lead to some dramatic close-ups, but you may have to set your camera up on a tripod and use a remote trigger device.

Black-browed albatross
ISO rating 300
Shutter speed 1/200s
Aperture f16
Focal length 17 mm

Look for details
Good photography is about telling a story. Once you've taken the obvious shots, like groups and portraits, try to focus on interesting details, abstracts and various aspects of behaviour that say more about the subject. In this way, you'll develop a varied portfolio. On these pages, for example, you can see gentoo penguins in many guises!

Gentoo penguin
ISO rating 160
Shutter speed 1/6400s
Aperture f5.6
Focal length 100 mm

Know your subject
Don't spend every minute with your eye glued to the viewfinder. Wildlife photography is as much about being a naturalist, observing behaviour and natural rhythms, as it is about taking pictures. This caracara had been prowling around a gentoo penguin colony for some time – interaction was inevitable.

Gentoo and striated caracara
ISO rating 400
Shutter speed 1/1600s
Aperture f4.5
Focal length 300 mm

Keep your distance
If your wildlife photography affects the natural behaviour of your subject, you are too close. No photograph is important enough to jeopardise the breeding or hunting success of a wild animal. Nor is any picture worth the degradation of the environment. Tread carefully, respect wildlife and know when to leave it in peace.

Black-browed albatross
ISO rating 200
Shutter speed 1/160s
Aperture f9
Focal length 85 mm

Wildlife journals & sketchbooks | keeping a record

Sketches from the author's notebooks

Territorial coots in the East of England (pencil, watercolour and gouache); anatomical study of a female swift-footed crab found on Heron Island, Great Barrier Reef (ink and watercolour); quick sketch of hippos and oxpeckers on the banks of the Luangwa River, Zambia (pencil).
Far left: A brush with nature – all you need to get started is a set of watercolours, some sketching pencils, paper and the time to sit and observe.

In a world of smartphone cameras and digital SLRs it's all too easy to let your wildlife travels become blinkered by viewfinders and LCD screens. Keeping a written record of your experiences and trying your hand at sketching some of the wildlife you encounter is not only incredibly rewarding, but it can also make you slow down and appreciate things in more detail.

Call me old fashioned, but I still use a notebook and pencil to record my travels. It's simple, quick and puts the smallest of barriers between you and what you're experiencing. Scribble something down, there and then. If you wait until the evening when you're back at your camp or lodge, you'll rarely remember exactly what was seen or said.

Sketching wildlife should be equally relaxed and spontaneous. Don't expect to rattle off a masterpiece every time you put pencil to paper. A few responsive strokes can be enough to capture the graceful curve of a giraffe's neck or the wheeling flight of a gannet. Keep it simple and try to focus on your subject, glancing only occasionally at your drawing.

One of the biggest challenges with sketching wildlife, of course, is that it tends to move. Don't get frustrated. Keep several sketches on the go at once, developing earlier ones if you get the chance. Vary the weight of your lines and practice tonal drawing to indicate light and shade. Think about light and how it affects shadows and the texture of fur or feathers. An understanding of basic anatomy is also invaluable to the wildlife artist.

Practise sketching animals at a zoo or farm before you go on your travels – and if you're particularly keen on getting creative in the wild, join a dedicated wildlife art trip (see page 62). For budding journalists, travel magazines such as *Wanderlust* (wanderlust.co.uk) run regular overseas workshops.

Take note – simple is best

The legendary Moleskine notebooks (moleskine. co.uk) have been used by travellers for decades. Sketchbook and watercolour versions are also available.

it's a wild life

Bruce Pearson | Wildlife artist | brucepearson.net

↘ My big five

① North Norfolk coast, England I spend a lot of time working here, especially during winter when the landscape is full of wildfowl and waders.

② Luangwa Valley, Zambia After a number of visits over many years the smells and colours of Africa have become addictive.

③ South Georgia Living for six months each austral summer for three years on remote Bird Island was hugely formative – a young man set loose among countless penguins, albatrosses and fur seals.

④ Extremadura, Spain So exotic, so accessible and so beautiful.

⑤ Svalbard Painting in the low sunshine of midnight is a particularly memorable experience.

❝ ❞ I was on a ship ploughing through the long swell and strong winds of the South Atlantic with scores of oceanic seabirds in our wake. Writing notes in my cabin one morning a non-birding shipmate suddenly put his head round the door and excalimed, "There's a bloomin' great chicken outside!" And there it was – my first wandering albatross, the largest flying bird in the world effortlessly riding the wind in long sweeps and rising arcs. It was breathtaking, the whole oceanic vista forming a powerful image and excitement about the rhythm and restlessness of the natural world that has lasted with me for 36 years since.

Staying healthy | first aid

Travelling in search of wildlife might, by its very nature, seem like a dangerous undertaking. Most wild animals, however, do their utmost to avoid human contact and will only attack people if they feel threatened. There are a few exceptions – polar bears, for example, are formidable predators and pose a real danger when they come into contact with human settlements, while crocodiles are opportunistic ambush hunters more than capable of snatching people who approach within range. Understand what's out there and take heed of your guide's advice and you should remain perfectly safe. Far more serious are the potentially fatal diseases transmitted by biting insects and contaminated water. As well as taking precautions against contracting these, you should also be aware of the dangers posed by extreme cold and heat, intense sun and high altitude.

Altitude sickness

Climb to altitudes of 3,000 m and above too quickly and you may start to develop early symptoms of Acute Mountain Sickness (AMS) such as headache, nausea and disorientation. Ignore these warning signs and push on higher and you may develop a life-threatening pulmonary or cerebral oedema. Always build acclimatisation days into your schedule, climb slowly and drink plenty of fluids. The best cure for AMS is to descend as quickly as possible, rather than resorting to drugs such as diamox. Seek urgent medical help if symptoms persist.

Bites – insects

In addition to malaria (see table opposite), other diseases spread by biting insects include dengue fever (mosquito), leishmaniasis (sandfly), river blindness (blackfly), sleeping sickness (tsetse fly) and tick-borne encephalitis. Try to avoid being bitten by wearing long-sleeved shirts and long trousers pretreated with insect repellent and always sleep under a mosquito net in malaria zones. Apply repellents to exposed skin, particularly between dusk and dawn when many mosquitoes are active. Avoid wearing blue or black clothing which can attract tsetse flies, and tuck trousers into socks (or wear gaiters) when walking through grassy areas that may be infested with ticks.

Bites – snakes

In the event of a venomous snake bite try to keep the victim calm – panic increases the heartbeat which will spread venom around the body more quickly. Clean and bandage the wound and lay the casualty down with the injury below heart level. Do not cut the wound, try to suck out the venom or apply a tourniquet. If possible, take a photograph of the snake responsible for the bite – this will help medical experts administer the correct anti-venom.

Bites – other animals

Clean the wound thoroughly, apply a sterile dressing (adding pressure to stop blood flow if necessary), bandage securely and keep the injury above heart level. Rabies and tetanus vaccinations may be required – if in doubt, seek medical advice.

Bleeding

Clean and dress even minor cuts to avoid infection. Use sterile tweezers to remove small foreign bodies, like thorns, but never attempt to dislodge large or deeply embedded objects. For severe external bleeding, perform ABC if necessary (see page 42), press a clean dressing to the wound and apply pressure to stop blood flow. Bandage firmly but not too tightly. Monitor patient until medical help arrives.

Blisters

Bursting a blister increases the risk of infection, so leave it intact, clean thoroughly and apply blister pad.

Burns and scalds

Flood the injury with cold water for at least 10 minutes to relieve pain, then cover with a non-adhesive dressing and bandage. Do not apply creams or ointments. Prevent infection by wrapping a clean polythene bag around the damaged skin.

Dangerous animals

See page 43.

Diseases

Well before departure, seek medical advice on which of the vaccinations, opposite, you may require for the areas you're visiting.

	symptoms	causes	prevention	vaccine
Cholera	Nausea, diarrhoea, vomiting, cramps and dehydration	Bacterial infection from contaminated water and food	Treat drinking water, avoid undercooked food	Recommended for high-risk areas
Diptheria, tetanus & polio	Diptheria: sore throat, swollen neck, skin ulcers. Tetanus: fever, muscle spasms, difficulty swallowing. Polio: fever, sore throat, nausea, headache and, in extreme cases, paralysis	Diptheria: bacterial infection spread through contact. Tetanus: bacterial infection from spores entering cuts. Polio: viral infection from contaminated food or drink	Diptheria: Avoid contact with carriers. Tetanus: Clean all wounds thoroughly. Polio: treat drinking water, avoid undercooked food	Combined vaccine; part of childhood immunisation programme with booster every 10 years for travel
Hepatitis A	Chills, fever, loss of appetitive, nausea, lethargy, jaundice, dark urine, pale faeces	Viral liver disease from faecally contaminated food and drinking water	Treat drinking water, avoid undercooked food, maintain high levels of hygiene	Vaccination plus booster provides immunity for 20 years or more
Hepatitis B	Nausea, vomiting, jaundice, pale urine. Infected people may not develop symptoms	Viral infection transmitted through sexual contact or contact with contaminated blood, needles etc	Carry a sterile kit, avoid unprotected sex	Recommended for people spending long periods in endemic areas
HIV	No specific symptoms	Viral infection that can lead to AIDS. Transmitted through sexual contact or contact with contaminated blood etc	Carry a sterile kit, avoid unprotected sex	Currently no vaccine or cure, although anti-viral drugs can delay the progress of the disease
Japanese encephalitis	Severe flu-like symptoms, including headache, stiff neck, confusion and eventually coma. Fatal in around 30% of untreated cases	Viral disease from night time-biting mosquitoes in areas of Indian Subcontinent and South East Asia	Take precautions against being bitten. Avoid rice fields at night where this type of mosquito is known to breed	Recommended for stays of one month or more in rural areas. A course of three vaccines should be started six weeks before travel
Malaria	Fever, chills, shivering, headache, lethargy. In worst cases, a life-threatening coma can develop within 24 hours of first symptoms developing	Parasitic disease transmitted by mosquito bite	Take precautions against being bitten. Seek advice on the best course of anti-malarial tablets for your destination. Seek urgent medical attention if you develop a temperature of 38°C or more after entering a risk area	None currently available. Medication is effective if given early enough. Self-treatment kits are available for those travelling for long periods in remote locations
Rabies	Fever, headache, aggression, loss of appetite, thirst, inability to drink, tingling around wound, paralysis	Viral disease transmitted through the bite of an infected mammal. Often fatal once symptoms develop	Never approach or handle animals you don't know. Clean and sterilise wounds thoroughly. Seek vaccination without delay	Recommended for travellers who are more than 24 hours away from medical facilities. One-month course of vaccines
Typhoid	Headache, fever, delirium, lethargy, abdominal pain, constipation	Bacterial infection from faecally contaminated water and food. Highest risk area is the Indian Subcontinent	Treat drinking water, avoid undercooked food. Antibiotics provide effective treatment	Provides 80% protection for three years. Available as combined vaccine with hepatitis A. Recommended for travellers visiting areas with poor hygiene
Yellow fever	Severe flu-like symptoms, jaundice	Viral disease spread by daytime-biting mosquitoes in parts of Africa and Central and South America	Take precautions against being bitten	Certificate of vaccination mandatory for entry to certain countries. Vaccine effective for 10 years

Diarrhoea & vomiting

Ward off dehydration by encouraging the patient to drink plenty of fluids, including rehydration solutions.

Eye injury

Wash out foreign bodies with plenty of clean water or a moist swab, but never try to remove an object that has penetrated or adhered to the eyeball. In this situation, lay the casualty down, lightly bandage a dressing pad over the eye to protect it and seek medical help.

Fractures

Immobilise the fracture and the joints above and below with a sling, splint or padding. Treat for shock and monitor patient until help arrives.

Frostbite

First, treat for symptoms of hypothermia (see below). Remove gloves or socks and boots carefully. Warm affected areas in your lap, under your armpits or in luke-warm water – but do not rub.

Heat exhaustion

Typical symptoms include headache, dizziness, nausea, cramps and rapid breathing. Lay the casualty in a cool, shady place with feet raised to improve blood circulation to the brain. Administer sips of a weak saline solution to replace lost fluids and salts.

Heatstroke

A potentially fatal condition where the body temperature soars to over 40°C, symptoms of heatstroke include headache, dizziness, hot and flushed skin, rapid pulse and delirium, followed by unconsciousness. Reduce the body temperature as quickly as possible, covering the casualty in cold soaked clothing. Monitor the patient carefully in case resuscitation is required. Contact emergency services.

Hypothermia

A dangerous condition caused when the body temperature drops to below 35°C, hypothermia victims should be wrapped in warm dry clothing and helped into a sleeping bag or survival blanket. Offer a warm drink and be ready to resuscitate if necessary.

✚ The ABC of resuscitation

Airway Check patient's mouth and remove any obstruction. Tilt head back by lifting chin and pressing gently on forehead.
Breathing Place your cheek next to patient's mouth and nose for up to 10 seconds to detect breathing. Watch for movement of chest.
Circulation Check the patient's pulse. If necessary, begin artificial ventilation and/or cardiopulmonary resuscitation (CPR).

Natural hazards

Always be prepared for extremes of weather by packing appropriate clothing and equipment. Seek local advice before swimming or bathing in areas that might be affected by offshore rip-currents.

Shock

A reduction of blood flow around the body can lead to organ failure and death. Treat shock by lying the victim down with legs raised above head level. Loosen clothing, monitor pulse and breathing and offer reassurance. Keep the patient warm with a sleeping bag or coat until medical help arrives.

Stings

Remove bee stings, wash affected area and apply sting relief cream. Check whether patient is susceptible to anaphylactic shock.

Sunburn

Always protect your skin by wearing a hat, sunglasses and long-sleeved clothing and regularly apply high-factor suncream and lip balm. Treat sunburn by laying a cold soaked cloth over affected area. Apply calamine lotion or after-sun cream.

Water

Contaminated water is the cause of several serious diseases. The best way to ensure that water is safe to drink is to boil it for several minutes. Water filters containing sterilising chemicals such as iodine are also effective. If using bottled water, always check that the seal around the cap is unbroken before consuming. Avoid ice and washed vegetables and salads if you are in any doubt as to whether the local water is safe.

It only takes a single, isolated shark or bear attack to whip the media into a frenzy of 'deadly creature' statistics. The reality is that very few, if any, animals are actually out to get us

Deserving your respect

Clockwise from top left: mosquito, black widow spider, poison dart frog, African elephant, box jellyfish, polar bear, moose, Nile crocodile and puff adder.

Dangerous animals

From grizzlies to great whites, black mambas to black widows, the world seems full of creatures hell-bent on killing people. That, at least, is what the press would have you believe. It only takes a single, isolated shark or bear attack to whip the media into a frenzy of 'deadly creature' statistics. The reality is that very few, if any, animals are actually out to get us.

Certain venomous spiders and snakes are dangerous to humans because we inadvertently invade their space or fail to recognize their camouflage or warning markings. Some find man-made habitats, like crop fields, woodpiles or even houses, just as good as natural ones. Other species mistake us for their natural prey (a great white shark, for example, confusing a human swimmer for a seal), while some, like the Nile and estuarine crocodile, see people as fair prey if they come within range.

Then there are the opportunists – elephants, buffalo, big cats, grizzly bears etc – which raid crops, kill domestic cattle or associate hikers with a free lunch. Confrontation inevitably leads to casualties – on both sides. Occasionally, human and animal worlds simply collide – a territorial hippo, for example, finding someone between it and the river, or a bull moose stepping onto a highway at the wrong moment.

Some innocuous looking creatures (like the box jellyfish and poison dart frog) produce venoms and toxins that are lethal enough to kill a human several times over – but remember that they evolved these substances long before people arrived on the scene. Monkeys, racoons, bats and even domestic animals can all be rabies carriers, while mosquitoes, of course, are responsible for transmitting malaria – a disease that claims around two million human lives every year.

Stay safe by following these rules:

❶ **Observe warning signs** Beaches in northern Australia, for example, will have signs warning if box jellyfish or crocodiles are present.

❷ **Heed expert advice** Local guides and national park wardens will brief you on what to do in the event of a potentially dangerous encounter.

❸ **Don't go looking for trouble** Respect the territories of wild animals and never interfere with their feeding or courtship behaviour, threaten their young, attempt to feed them or get too close for a photograph.

❹ **Take precautions** Reduce risk by taking anti-malarials and properly equipping yourself, ie: wearing stinger suits if swimming in seas where jellyfish may be present, or tying bear bells to your pack if hiking in grizzly country.

STINGER

46 7 of the best birdwatching trips
47 6 of the best riding trips
48 7 of the best snorkelling & diving trips
49 6 of the best small wonders trips
50 Swimming with whale sharks
52 The wonderful thing about tigers

56 Safaris
64 Tracking the Great Migration
68 A short walk in the Okavango Delta

72 Primate watching
80 In the midst of mountain gorillas
82 Making contact with the cousins

86 Brief encounters: snow leopard
88 Brief encounters: wolf

90 Bear watching
94 Eye to eye with the ice bear
96 Hiking in bear country

98 Whale watching
106 The Pacific lagoons of Baja
108 The smile on the face of a dolphin

112 Wildlife cruises
120 Setting sail for an Arctic wilderness
122 Exploring the Enchanted Isles

124 Wilderness trips
128 Conservation volunteering

Land blubbers – sea lions on a beach in the Galápagos Islands

Zalophus wollebaeki
Gardner Bay, Española Island,
Galápagos Islands

Totally unfazed by humans,
Galápagos sea lions allow
remarkably close encounters.
Snorkelling is equally captivating
as these agile swimmers will often
pass within a whisker of your
goggle-eyed face (see p49).

① Hummingbird heaven
Bellavista cloud forest, Ecuador
Just 90 minutes' drive from chaotic Quito, the
Bellavista Cloud Forest Reserve is a peaceful green
oasis in the Andean foothills where the only sounds
you're likely to hear are the buzz of hummingbird wings (from
jewelled beauties like this buff-tailed coronet) and the ratchet cry of
rare plate-billed mountain toucans. Some 400 species of birds inhabit
the cloud forest, while an ecolodge provides an excellent base from
which to explore a network of trails (bellavistacloudforest.com).

7 of the best | birdwatching trips

② Noddy land
Heron Island, Great Barrier Reef, Australia
A sliver of coral sand 89 km off the Queensland coast,
this forested gem is home to thousands of black
noddies, wedge-tailed shearwaters (Oct-Apr) and reef
herons. Check into the luxury resort (heronisland.
com) for a few days of birding paradise.

③ Flamingo free-for-all
Great Rift Valley, Kenya & Tanzania
Even a lone flamingo is a head-turner. Just imagine
over a million of them strutting their stuff, flushing
pink the soda lakes of Bogoria, Nakuru, Magadi
and Natron. The hubbub is extraordinary, the smell
unforgettable. Breeding occurs on Natron Oct-Dec.

④ Wetland wonders
Everglades, Florida, USA
Roseate spoonbill, purple gallinule, osprey, black
skimmer, short-tailed hawk and great white egret
(left) are just a few birdwatching highlights in this
water-wonderland. The nearby Corkscrew Swamp
Sanctuary is a good spot for wood storks.

⑤ Macaws enmasse
Manu & Tambopata, Peruvian Amazon
Stake out a clay lick (early morning is best) and you
may be treated to a multicoloured melée of macaws
as hundreds flock to the riverbank for their daily
nibble of mineral salts. Scarlet, blue-and-yellow and
red-and-green species are often seen.

⑥ Penguin spectacular
Antarctica and the sub-Antarctic islands
Head south for huge colonies of emperor penguins
on the Ross Ice Shelf (trekking back to sea Dec-Jan)
and equally impressive gatherings of kings on South
Georgia, Adélies on the Antarctic Peninsula and
gentoos (left) in the Falkland Islands.

⑦ Seabird cities
St Kilda, Orkney and Shetland Islands, Scotland
Nothing raises the spirits (or binoculars) more than a
seacliff crammed with nesting guillemots, kittiwakes
and gannets, with puffins (left) adding to the avian
extravaganza with their airborne sorties from clifftop
nesting burrows. Catch the action Apr-Jun.

6 of the best | riding trips

❶ Elephants on parade
Abu Camp, Okavango Delta, Botswana
Whether you're walking alongside them or sitting atop one, the elephants at Abu Camp (abucamp.com) make you an honorary member of the herd, roaming the Okavango, mingling with other wildlife and getting on intimate terms with pachyderm behaviour.

❷ Wild West wildlife
Chilcotin Mountains, British Columbia, Canada
Saddle up on sure-footed Cayuse horses, following game trails in search of bighorn sheep (left) and mule deer. Camping out in the mountains, you may also glimpse black bear. Horse pack adventures (chilcotinholidays.com) are available mid-May-Oct.

❸ Ride the high plains
Lanin National Park, Argentina
Ride through forests of indigenous monkey puzzle trees and high into the Andes on a horse pack trip, keeping an eye open for condors (left), armadillos and guanacos. Estancias like Huechahue (huechahue.com) offer multi-day rides, camping in the Andes.

❹ Spot rhinos from the back of an elephant
Kaziranga National Park, India
Around 80% of the world's population of Indian one-horned rhinoceros is found in this rich stew of swamp, reedbed and forest, along with good numbers of elephant and buffalo. Explore on an elephant-back safari and keep watch for tigers.

❺ Camel trek in the Outback
Simpson Desert, Northern Territory, Australia
Walk through the arid heart of the Outback with a camel train carrying everything you need for an intimate encounter with life in the Australian desert (cameltreks.com.au). Following good rains, dry river beds spring to life, rejuvenating seasonal wetlands.

❻ Mush through the Arctic
Kuhmo, Eastern Finland
Ride a dog sled through silent, snowclad taiga forest, staying overnight in wilderness cabins (taigaspirit.com). You'll see tracks of winter wildlife and, with luck, glimpse species like the great grey owl, forest reindeer, elk, wolverine and even wolves.

From the back of an elephant you can see more of Africa. You can feel his spine dip and flex, smell his tangy bovine scent and run your fingers across the wrinkled maze of his skin. You can hear the vacuum rush of air in his probing trunk, the deep, resonating rumble of his cavernous stomach and the rhythmic grinding of fist-sized molars (see 1, Abu Camp)

7 of the best | snorkelling & diving trips

❶ Drifting along with manatees
Crystal River National Wildlife Refuge, Florida, USA
Endangered West Indian manatees migrate to this refuge each winter – the best time to snorkel with them is Dec-Mar when the weather is at its coolest and manatees are concentrated around warm-water springs (fws.gov/crystalriver).

❷ Swept away at Sipadan
Sipadan Island, Sabah, Eastern Malaysia
Barely a stone's throw from the beach, the coral reef at Sipadan, off northeast Borneo, plunges 600 m to the ocean floor – the setting for large gatherings of pelagic species, including sharks, barracuda (left), turtles and manta rays (sipadan-kapalai.com).

❸ Marvelling at mantas
Maldives
A necklace of coral atolls unravelled across 868 km of the Indian Ocean, the Maldives are a diver's mecca. Island resorts provide easy access to reefs, but head for the deepwater channels between atolls for the best chances of seeing whale sharks and manta rays.

❹ Diving the wall
Belize Barrier Reef
The world's second longest barrier reef supports habitats ranging from mangrove forests and coral islands to drop-offs and blue holes. Turneffe Atoll is renowned for eagle rays, turtles, sharks (including whale sharks) and large schools of snapper.

❺ Eye-balling great whites
Gansbaii, Western Cape, South Africa
Getting up-close and personal with one of the ocean's top predators is to witness the embodiment of power, grace and menace. Cage diving is available year round, but is best Apr-Sep when the sharks are particularly active feeding.

❻ Jumping in with the jellies
Jellyfish Lake, Palau, Micronesia
Eil Malk Island in the Micronesian archipelago of Palau has a landlocked lake brimming with the Mastigias jellyfish. Isolated from predators, they have lost the ability to sting so you can immerse yourself in jellyfish soup without a fear in the world.

Like an aquatic Peter Pan I am swept along the reef. At least half a dozen turtles are riding the ocean surge; some are feeding amongst thickets of coral sprouting from the drop-off, while another is asleep inside a giant sponge. And there are sharks, too. Not distant, fleeting shadows, but groups of two or three up-close – their slender bodies twisting gracefully, mocking the current (see 2, Sipadan Island)

6 of the best | small wonders trips

❶ Walking safari
East & Southern Africa
It doesn't matter where you set out on foot. Take any area of African bush and a good guide will soon have you marvelling at the architectural achievements of termites, deciphering animal tracks and luring baboon spiders (far left) from their burrows.

❷ The little things in life
Madagascar
Small is beautiful on Madagascar where the high level of endemism has given rise to the diminutive mouse lemurs (left), the Madagascar pygmy kingfisher and the dwarf chameleon (*Brookesia minima*) – little bigger than a human fingernail.

❸ Treasures of the wetlands
La Brenne Regional Nature Park, Central France
A mosaic of some 2000 lakes, La Brenne, near Poitiers, is brimming with wildlife. Waterbirds may rule the roost, but equally eye-catching are the 36 species of orchids, 97 varieties of butterflies and dozens of dragonflies, including the southern darter (left).

❹ Flower power
Namaqualand, Northern Cape, South Africa
Little daisies make a big impact when the mass flowering of Namaqualand transforms a chunk of desert twice the size of Wales into a petal patchwork. Although influenced by rainfall in preceding winter months, the best flowering season is usually Aug-Sep.

❺ Winged wonders
Michoacán, Central Mexico
Each year, between 250 and 600 million monarch butterflies stream southwards from North America to over-winter in a few groves of Mexican pine forest, smothering branches in shimmering golden cloaks. See them at the butterfly reserve of El Chincua.

❻ Batty in Borneo
Mulu National Park, Sarawak, Eastern Malaysia
The world's largest cave passage (4 km long and up to 148 m high), Deer Cave is a fitting backdrop to the nightly exodus of several million wrinkle-lipped bats leaving their roost to feed over the rainforest. The beating of their wings sounds like distant surf.

❼ Frolicking with sea lions
Galápagos Islands, Ecuador
Few underwater escapades are more exhilarating than snorkelling with sea lions. At first, all you see is silvery strings of bubbles and distant fleeting shadows. Then, without warning, sea lions are hurtling towards you – all puppy-dog eyes and whiskers – twisting and pirouetting through the shallows in an unabashed display of exuberance. You duck-dive and they follow you down; you raise your head above the surface and they are porpoising around you. Los Islotes in the Sea of Cortez, Baja California, is a fine spot to take the plunge, but Champion Islet, off Floreana in the Galápagos Islands, tops the podium for sea lion shenanigans.

Ningaloo Marine Park, Australia

Visibility underwater was poor – like trying to peer through a blizzard. Diced into flickering shards, sunlight probed the plankton-rich seas off Western Australia's 260-km-long Ningaloo Reef, transforming jellyfish into glowing orbs and igniting the fizzing turmoil of the swell. I felt powerless – my strength sapped by the rollercoaster sea. There was little I could do but tread water.

The 10-m shark appeared right in front of me, its letterbox mouth agape, ploughing through the turbulent water. Its skin was a beautiful mélange of stripes and spots, caressed by a lacework of sunlight. The effect was ethereal. Despite its bulk, the shark blended seamlessly with its surroundings – as unobtrusive, it seemed, as the translucent jellyfish. Entranced, I almost forgot the 3-m exclusion zone and began frantically back-pedalling. But it was obvious that the shark was well aware of me. With little discernible movement of its great tail or splayed pectoral fins, it banked into a graceful turn, an entourage of tiny yellow fish following in its wake.

> With no discernible movement of its great tail or splayed pectoral fins, it banked into a graceful turn, an entourage of tiny yellow fish following in its wake

Of the handful of whale shark hotspots (such as Honduras, Mexico, South Africa and the Galápagos Islands), Australia's Ningaloo Marine Park is one of the best placed. Not only do sharks congregate here in good numbers between March and June, but they are easily accessible – usually cruising just beyond the reef which is only 100 m offshore at its nearest point.

My base was Coral Bay, a one-street cluster of caravan parks, a hotel and backpackers, plus a few shops and restaurants at the southern gateway to the marine park. It had a barefoot, frontier feel; a branch of the Perth-Exmouth road fizzling out on its beach.

Whale sharks are not the only marine heavyweights to lure snorkellers to Coral Bay. Measuring up to 7 m across and weighing two tonnes, manta rays congregate in the shallower, calmer lagoons. Gliding like gigantic aquatic bats over the sandy seabed, they are easy to spot.

It's a different story, however, in the open ocean beyond the reef. An hour had passed since our first whale shark encounter and all eyes were turned skyward, tracing the white speck of the spotter plane circling overhead. "From up there, even a 10-m shark looks like a tadpole," the pilot had told me earlier.

Although whale sharks are the world's largest fish, aerial reconnaissance is still the best way to spot them. There is never any guarantee you'll see, let alone swim with one. Whale sharks are shrouded in mystery. No one knows how many there are or what triggers their trans-oceanic migrations. These enigmatic creatures can dive to depths of 700 m, yet feed on surface plankton. They can reach 18 m in length, but how long they live is unknown.

The IUCN lists the whale shark as 'vulnerable to extinction'. Apart from orcas, humans are their greatest threat – a single Indian fishery is believed to have killed over 1,000 between 1999 and 2000. Shark fin soup commands a high price – but so too should the privilege of swimming with these gentle giants. Ecotourism could provide an economically viable alternative to hunting, as long as it is properly managed to minimize disturbance. "This is a 'hands-off' experience," our guide had warned us. "If you get too close, I'll tug your fin – three tugs is a red card offence and you're back on the boat."

Suddenly, the radio crackled into life and minutes later we were back in the water alongside another whale shark. Steadily, it pulled ahead, then began to dive. I watched the spots on its back turn luminous blue – pulsing like fireflies. Snatching a breath of air, I folded at the waist and dived after the strange lights. But after a few seconds, my sinuses protested and I spun upright, groping for the surface. As the others clambered aboard the launch, I lingered off the stern, sneaking glances underwater. But it was wishful thinking. The whale shark had gone and the only lights in the sea were the flecks of plankton shimmering in columns of early evening sunshine.

Going overboard for whale sharks – Ningaloo Reef is the setting for the ultimate 'big fish' story

Rhincodon typus
Ningaloo, Western Australia

Whale shark ecotourism is worth an estimated US$47.5 million a year, but swimmers must remember to maintain a minimum distance of 3 m and avoid using flash photography and underwater motorised diver propulsions.

Making tracks

⬤ **Coral Bay Adventures** (coralbayadventures.com) run shark tours, diving trips, scenic flights and whalewatching tours. UK-based **Dive Worldwide** (diveworldwide.com) offer dive and safari packages.
✈ **Skywest** (skywest.com.au) has regular flights between Perth and Exmouth, 140 km north of Coral Bay.
🏕 **Sal Salis** (salsalis.com.au) offers eco-friendly bush luxury in safari tents pitched metres from the Ningaloo shore.
🕐 GMT+8
☀ Whale sharks March-June, humpback whales June-November, manta rays year round.
ⓘ westernaustralia.com
⬤ whalesharkproject.org

Tales from the wild | the wonderful thing about tigers

Corbett National Park, India

It was almost as if the tiger had flicked a switch in the forest. One moment it was quiet and calm – the trees swathed in webs of early morning mist – the next it was charged with tension. Gomati had heard the distant alarm calls – the shrill snort of a spotted deer, the indignant bark of a langur monkey – and her mood suddenly changed. She blasted a trunkful of dust up between her front legs, then shook her head so vigorously that I had to clutch the padded saddle to keep my balance. Gomati's mahout, sitting astride her neck, issued a terse reprimand before urging the elephant into the tangled forest.

There was no path. Gomati made her own. Soon the air was infused with the pungent aroma of crushed herbs and freshly bled sap. Spiders and beetles drizzled from shaken trees; our clothing became wet with dew and stained by moss and lichen. We sounded like a forest fire – crackling, snapping, trailblazing. But through all the noise came a single piercing cry. Gomati stopped and we heard it again – the telltale alarm call of a spotted deer.

Manoj Sharma, my guide, leaned towards me. "When the tiger moves, the deer calls," he murmured. "We must be close." I nodded slowly, my eyes chasing around the shadows of the forest. Sunlight sparked through chinks in the canopy, but the understorey was still a diffuse patchwork of muted greens and shadows-within-shadows – the perfect foil for tiger stripes. Apart from an occasional rumble from Gomati's stomach, the forest was silent. No one spoke or moved.

A minute passed, perhaps two. Then we heard a woodpecker hammering against a dead tree. I glanced at Manoj, but he shook his head. The woodpecker was not one our forest spies. "Scimitar babbler, laughing thrush, green magpie." Manoj's voice was barely a whisper. "They will tell you if a tiger is near." So we waited. And we listened.

Gradually, the tension slipped from our bodies. The woodpecker stopped drumming and Gomati grabbed a branch and stuffed it into her mouth. I reached forward to stroke the elephant's neck. There was a soft patch, free of bristles, behind her ear.

Over 1,300 sq km of forest and grassland tucked into the Himalayan foothills, Corbett National Park is home to about 140 tigers – but they are shy and elusive. "People have been coming here for years and never seen a tiger," Manoj had told me earlier. To expect to see one on my first elephant ride in Corbett was perhaps asking too much. Still, I was happy enough tickling Gomati behind the ear. And at that moment, none of us realised just how close the tigress – or her cubs – really were.

They say tigers make the orchestra of the jungle play and, suddenly, spotted deer began whistling to our left, while langur, babblers and others pitched in with well-rehearsed repertoire of grunts and chatters.

Guided by the commotion, Gomati waded, once more, into the undergrowth. After 50 m or so, the alarm calls ceased, but now Gomati's trunk was raised and she began to hesitate. The mahout dug his heels in, but she shuffled to a halt. For the first time that morning, the elephant let out a deep, resonating rumble. Clearly, Gomati was going no further.

Moments later we saw why. Less than a dozen metres ahead, the vegetation thrashed from side to side as three tigers burst from cover. The two cubs kept low to the ground, melting into the forest like wisps of smoke. But the tigress paused to glance over her shoulder. For a second or two, she stared straight at us – her eyes locked on ours with the intense scrutiny of a supreme predator. Then she turned and vanished.

It was the briefest of encounters – an exchange of glances that jolted the senses; seared the mind. "You are very lucky," Manoj told me as Gomati trundled back to the rest house. "Not one tiger, but three!" Somehow, though, numbers seemed irrelevant. It wasn't the glimpse of the tigers that had moved me, so much as the supercharged atmosphere of their native forest stronghold. Spotting the tigers had merely reaffirmed their beauty; tracking them had revealed their spirit.

Later, during our afternoon elephant ride, we heard and saw nothing – no alarm calls pulsing through the forest, no pug marks on the sandy tracks that led from the rest house. The following dawn, Manoj took me out in a jeep to explore a wider a area of the reserve. But again, no tigers. The forest seemed to be guarding their whereabouts; a silent reminder of their secrecy and rarity.

Tiger, tiger, burning brighter – a recent survey revealed an increase in the Indian population of Bengal tigers

Panthera tigris tigris
Ranthambhore National Park, India

In 2010, a census carried out in India (home to half the world's wild tigers), revealed a population increase from 1,411 individuals (in 2007) to 1,706. Despite the encouraging news, the census also noted an alarming decline in the numbers of tigers outside protected areas and an increase in human-tiger conflict in places such as Corbett, Ranthambhore and Bandhavgarh.

It wasn't the glimpse of the tigers that moved me, so much as the supercharged atmosphere of their native forest stronghold. Spotting the tigers merely reaffirmed their beauty; tracking them revealed their spirit

Tales from the wild | the wonderful thing about tigers

Leaving the forest, we drove out on to the floodplain of the Ramganga River where tendrils of mist squirmed in the gathering heat of mid-morning. A large herd of spotted deer, perhaps 200-strong, grazed peacefully, while families of wild boar snuffled amongst them. It was a scene more reminiscent of Africa – a tawny grassland peppered with game; vultures wheeling overhead; a pair of jackals on the lookout for an easy meal. There were even wild elephants, far across the plain, looking for all the world like giant river boulders, except for the occasional puff of dust that rose above them.

Quietly and methodically, like a holy man reciting a mantra, Manoj totted up a list of nearly 100 bird species that he had either seen or heard that morning. A huge variety were concentrated around a lake at the heart of the reserve. Herons tip-toed around basking gharial crocodiles, while pied kingfishers hovered overhead.

If anything, my next destination should have provided an even greater avian spectacle. Travelling overnight on the sleeper train to Agra, I hired a car and driver to take me the short distance to Bharatpur Bird Sanctuary – a former royal hunting estate. During the breeding season, Bharatpur is usually throbbing with painted storks, ducks, pelicans and other waterbirds, but the monsoon had failed and the network of lagoons had all but dried up.

The Rajasthan countryside on the drive between Bharatpur and Ranthambhore was equally arid. Cattle-drawn ploughs struggled through the hard-baked soil, while women, balancing copper *colloshes* on their heads, queued at every village water pump

Ranthambhore had not escaped the drought either. In the 300 sq km national park (at the core of the tiger reserve), the lakes were dry and the dhok forest – usually lush after a monsoon soaking – was scantily clad with brittle, golden leaves.

There are no elephant-back safaris in Ranthambhore. Instead, a controlled number of vehicles is granted access to specific routes on the park's 300-km network of tracks. We had a wonderful encounter with a lolloping sloth bear, glimpsed a rare wild dog and witnessed sambar deer stags lock antlers in a rutting contest. On my fifth, and final, drive I also saw a tiger – lying up in the shade of a narrow gully.

Ultimately, however, the most thrilling tiger encounter of my safari was not actually an encounter at all. It took place several days earlier when Manoj and I were leaving Corbett National Park. It was a quiet morning. The sal forest had shrugged off its blanket of morning mist and Manoj was happily scanning the trees for tawny fish owls

When a jeep approached us from the opposite direction, we paused to chat to the driver, but he hadn't seen the owls either – so we headed on towards the park gates. A short distance further, Manoj suddenly stiffened and pointed to the dirt track ahead. "Tigers."

With one word, he transformed our laid-back birding ramble into an edge-of-seat drama. There, clearly imprinted over the tyre marks of the jeep we had just passed, were the pug marks of a tigress and her three young cubs. Less than five minutes had elapsed since we saw the other vehicle and, in that time, the cats must have emerged from the forest, strolled along the road a short distance and disappeared into the trees again.

We took a long, hard look around us. A rustle of leaves spun our heads, but it was just a pheasant scrabbling about on the forest floor. Manoj thought he heard the alarm call of a babbler, but whatever it was stopped almost immediately. He signalled to our driver to reverse up the track. A hundred metres beyond a sharp bend, we found more tiger prints – this time overlaying our own tyre tracks! Again, we stopped and listened. Somewhere, very close, a family of tigers was probably doing the same.

We never did see them. And, yet, it felt as though we had been directly interacting – pitting our wits and senses against each other. It had been an exhilarating experience – a moment of heightened awareness that stirred some primordial human instinct; part fear, part respect. I had discovered how it feels to fall under the spell of the tiger.

> **We found more tiger prints – this time overlaying our own tyre tracks. Again, we stopped and listened. Somewhere, very close, a family of tigers was probably doing the same**

Tiger country, Corbett National Park (from top, left to right) – Indian elephant on the floodplain, elephant safari in the forest, tiger tracks, langur on the lookout, tiger on the prowl, Corbett landscape

Originally established in 1936 as Hailey National Park, Corbett was renamed in 1955-56 after the legendary hunter-turned-conservationist, Jim Corbett.

Making tracks

⤴ Numerous operators offer tiger safaris in India; see p26-29 for details.

✈ The headquarters for Corbett NP, Ramnagar has a direct train from New Delhi (cleartrip.com). Alternatively, it's a 240-km road journey.

🛏 Dhikala Forest Rest House overlooks Patli Dun valley and offers no-frills accommodation in the heart of the national park. Lodges and hotels are located outside the park.

🕐 GMT+5.5

☀ Corbett NP is open November to mid June, although October to April is best for wildlife watching as this is when leaves fall and grasses wither, improving visibility.

ⓘ corbettnationalpark.in

Safaris

Dawn sunlight seeped through the bush, a glowing tangerine tide that gilded the acacia trees and sparkled through dew-laden grasses. When it reached the lions, huddled together in a clearing, they responded instantly to its warmth. One of the males stood and stretched, while the rest of the pride rolled in the grass, pawing and flirting in a tangle of tawny-gold limbs and black-tipped tails. They barely glanced in the direction of our Landcruiser. We were parked just a few metres away, yet the big cats seemed completely unfazed by our presence. They briefly contemplated a distant herd of impala, then sauntered off, single-file, into the dense scrub. The softly berating call of a turtle dove infiltrated the silence that followed the lions' departure. Then somewhere close by we heard the sound of branches snapping and splintering. Lions and elephants in a single morning's game drive... and the sun was only just clear of the horizon.

Considering our mutual bond with their domestic cousins, it's little wonder that so many people yearn to see Africa's big cats. Nothing gets the spine tingling more than the smouldering gaze of a lioness.

Safaris have become hugely popular, but planning one can leave you wallowing in logistics like a proverbial hippo. Will you opt for the big skies and big game of the Serengeti, take a walk on the wild side in Zambia's Luangwa Valley, paddle a canoe along the Zambezi or drive yourself to Etosha or Kruger? Are you looking for 'safari chic' at an upmarket lodge, or is roughing it with a tent and some fire sticks more your kind of thing?

Then there are the seasons to consider, what gear to take, the costs, modes of transport, independent trip versus package or tailor-made and whether you really need to pack one of those multi-pocketed khaki waistcoats.

Still keen I hope? After all, compared to a century ago, planning a safari is a breeze. In 1892 Lord Randolph Churchill advanced into the bush with 30 staff and seven wagons laden with 20 tons of supplies, including two-dozen rifles, a piano and a generous quantity of eau-de-cologne. Small wonder that he never made his mark as a great hunter.

Thankfully, safaris are now more subtle affairs with the emphasis on blending with nature, rather than blasting it with a 10-bore Holland & Holland. Armed with just your senses and a pair of binoculars, you'll return home intoxicated with vivid sights, sounds and smells. You'll have heard the bewitching 'whoop' of a hyena, studied the grafitti of tracks around a waterhole, and felt the electric anticipation of a big cat sighting. The names of hundreds of birds will be fresh in your mind, while the pepper-sweet tang of the bush will linger in your nose for days.

But having said all that, let's not forget the dust, the pre-dawn wake-up calls and those buttock-numbing, three-hour game drives when all you see is the retreating posterior of a lone warthog, its perky tail held aloft like a defiant flag of victory. Safaris are not for everyone, but then again, those who have 'gone bush' in Africa invariably come back for more.

> Considering our mutual bond with their domestic cousins, it's little wonder that so many people yearn to see Africa's big cats. Nothing gets the spine tingling more than the smouldering gaze of a lioness

Forget the Big Five – spot Africa's Super Seven

If you find the whole concept of the Big Five outdated, think 'Super Seven' instead. In addition to elephant, rhino, lion, leopard and buffalo, South Africa's Greater Addo Elephant National Park, near Port Elizabeth, offers the chance to spot great white sharks and southern right whales off its Eastern Cape coastline. Kenya also mixes big game with big fish thanks to the arrival of whale sharks between November and March. For a totally marine twist on the Super Seven, Rocktail Bay in KwaZulu-Natal offers encounters with manta rays, whale sharks, leatherback turtles, bottlenose dolphins, great hammerhead and ragged-tooth sharks, as well as migrating humpback whales. If small is beautiful, try tracking down Africa's Small Five: elephant-nose shrew, rhinoceros beetle, ant lion, leopard tortoise and buffalo weaver.

Bored of the flies – a yawning lioness displays her killer canines

Panthera leo
Masai Mara National Reserve, Kenya

On a typical safari you would be unlucky not to see Africa's iconic predator – lions are still widespread, despite their numbers plummeting from around 200,000 in the 1980s to less than 25,000 today. Cheetahs are also having a hard time – their population has crashed to just 10,000, a quarter of which survive in their stronghold of Namibia.

Safaris | inspiration

❶ Glimpse geladas in the Great Rift
Simien Mountains, Ethiopia
Along with large troops of gelada baboon, the dramatic Rift Valley escarpments of the 4,000-m Simien Mountains are inhabited by walia ibex, Ethiopian wolf and lammergeier vulture.
▸▸ October to March for trekking

❷ Stroll out with the Samburu
Laikipia Plateau, Kenya
Camel trekking with Samburu warriors provides an intimate, low-impact way to explore the arid frontier land of Laikipia – home to Grevy's zebra, reticulated giraffe, black rhino and gerenuk.
▸▸ January to March, July to October

❸ Rise above it all in a hot-air balloon
Kenya, Tanzania, Namibia & South Africa
Dawn balloon flights are available from camps in the Masai Mara and Serengeti, as well as Loisaba in northern Kenya. You can also get aloft above the Namib Desert and several locations in South Africa.
▸▸ Year round

❹ Experience nature's greatest show
Serengeti-Mara ecosystem, Kenya & Tanzania
The perpetual pilgrimage of 1.5 million wildebeest, 500,000 Thomson's gazelle and 200,000 plain's zebra is punctuated by the dramatic crossings of the Grumeti and Mara Rivers.
▸▸ Year round, see pages 64-65 and 218-219

❺ Fly-camp in the wilderness
The Selous, Tanzania
Walk in one of Africa's greatest wildlife reserves, sleeping out in the bush at small, temporary camps where dinner is cooked over an open fire, the sounds of the African night all around.
▸▸ July to October

❻ Follow in Livingstone's footsteps
Kasanka and Bangweulu, Zambia
North of the Luangwa Valley, the little-visited papyrus swamps, floodplains and moist forests of Kasanka National Park and the Bangweulu Wetlands are rich in big game and birdlife.
▸▸ November to March for birdwatching

❼ Take a walk on the wild side
Luangwa Valley, Zambia
South Luangwa National Park has long been renowned as *the* place in Africa for walking safaris. Its lavish spread of dappled woodlands, rivers and lily-covered lagoons is perfect for exploring on foot.
▸▸ June to late October (Nov-May for birdwatching)

❽ Canoe along the Zambezi
Mana Pools, Zimbabwe
Launch a canoe on the River Zambezi, paddle silently past hippos and herds of browsing elephant, drift within a few feet of bee-eater colonies and camp out on remote islands.
▸▸ April to November

❾ Witness the rebirth of a park
Gorongosa, Mozambique
Following a devastating civil war from the late 1970s to 1990s, this diverse national park is being restocked and now offers an exciting safari experience in a little-visited corner of Africa.
▸▸ April to November

❿ Get carried away in the Delta
Okavango Delta, Botswana
This extraordinary wetland is home to an amazing variety of wildlife, from frogs and fish eagles to elephants and wild dog. Drift along the waterways in a *mokoro* (dugout canoe).
▸▸ March to November

⓫ Track wildlife with Kalahari Bushmen
Tsumkwe, Namibia
No one knows the Kalahari better than the Bushmen. Joining Ju/'hoansi hunters in Bushmanland as they track game, set traps and gather wild food is a unique privilege.
▸▸ Year round

⓬ Drive yourself on safari
Damaraland & Etosha, Namibia
Namibia makes an excellent self-drive destination – the roads are quiet, it's safe and places like Damaraland and Etosha National Park have plenty of camps and lodges for independent travellers.
▸▸ Year round

⓭ Go 'safari chic' in a private game reserve
Kruger, South Africa
One of Africa's finest national parks, Kruger is ideal for self-drive, but for those in search of a spot of pampering, private game reserves, like Sabi Sands, offer opulent accommodation and fine cuisine.
▸▸ Year round

⓮ Island safari
Madagascar
Lemurs (see pages 236-237) may be the stars of this evolutionary treasure chest, but Madagascar also boats many other unique, often bizarre, creatures, including a dazzling variety of chameleons.
▸▸ April to November

Safaris in India
See pages 248-250

Best for first-timers | Kenya
Why? Long-established safari scene, superb wildlife and plenty of options for all budgets.
How? For the best introduction, book a safari that combines the Masai Mara and Lake Nakuru with somewhere more off-the-beaten track like Laikipia.
When? Avoid the rains by travelling July to October or January to March.
Also consider: Tanzania's northern circuit or South Africa's Kruger National Park.

Best for diversity | Tanzania
Why? Tanzania has it all, from wildlife-rich game reserves to the snow-capped peak of Kilimanjaro and the coral reefs of Zanzibar.
How? In just two weeks you can combine Serengeti National Park, Ngorongoro Conservation Area, Lake Manyara and Tarangire National Parks in the celebrated 'northern safari circuit'.
When? The southern Serengeti is teeming with game from December to March, while the wildebeest migration heads west and north between April and July and returns to the Serengeti around October.
Also consider: Botswana for the verdant waterways of the Okavango and the stark Kalahari saltpans.

Best for photographers | Namibia
Why? Pixel-popping desert scenery, one of Africa's premier national parks and natural wonders galore.
How? Rent a car (you don't need 4WD) and combine a few days in Etosha National Park with a visit to the giant red dunes at Sossusvlei and Cape Cross seal colony on the Skeleton Coast.
When? Year round, but July to late October is best for game viewing.
Also consider: Ethiopia's Simien Mountains for rare wildlife in dramatic Rift Valley scenery.

Best for adventurers | Zambia
Why? Walking safaris were pioneered in the Luangwa Valley, while offbeat Liuwa Plain requires a mini expedition just to reach.
How? Join a walking safari linking bushcamps in Luangwa, or plan a 4WD trip to Liuwa.
When? June to October.
Also consider: The Selous in Tanzania, canoeing on the Zambezi or tracking wildlife with the San in Namibia's Bushmanland.

Best for families | South Africa
Why? Malaria-free and family-friendly game reserves of the Cape.
How? Drive along the Garden Route towards game reserves like Kwandwe.
When? Year round. November to March is the hottest, sunniest period.
Also consider: South Africa's Madikwe and Ngala Game Reserves.

Gorillas, chimps and lemurs
See pages 72-85

Safaris | fieldcraft

You are likely to see more species of large mammal on an African safari than any other wildlife trip. You don't want to become too obsessed with ticking off the cast of *The Lion King*, but some basic bushlore will help you track down the following key species.

Big cats

To boost your chances of a wild cat encounter, set off early in the morning or late in the afternoon when these predators are more likely to be active. With the exception of cheetahs, most are nocturnal hunters, spending the middle part of the day resting. Their superb camouflage can render them almost invisible, so look for other tell-tale clues, such as fresh tracks or alarm signals from nearby wildlife. **Lions** are relatively common and it's unusual not to see at least one pride during a week's safari. Good spots include the Masai Mara and Serengeti. Although widespread, **leopards** are nocturnal and elusive, so night drives offer the best chances of seeing them. Try South Luangwa and Lower Zambezi National Parks in Zambia and the game reserves in northern Botswana and South Africa. **Cheetah** prefer the wide-open wilderness areas like Tanzania's Serengeti and Ruaha, the Busanga Plains of Zambia's Kafue National Park and the Kgalagadi Transfrontier Park in South Africa and Botswana. For guaranteed sightings, visit Okonjima in Namibia, home of the AfriCat Foundation.

Wild dogs

Highly endangered after decades of persecution and habitat loss, wild dogs are making a stand in a few remote parts of Africa, notably Tanzania's Selous, northern Botswana, Zimbabwe's Hwange National Park and Zambia's Busanga Plains. Sighting this enigmatic pack hunter, however, is not easy. Lying up during the heat of the day their beautiful camouflage can render them almost invisible. They can also cover vast distances at a ground-swallowing trot, often moving through impenetrable bush. There will be times, though, when they use vehicle tracks, so always keep an eye out for fresh pugmarks in the sand.

Elephants

Despite terrible losses during the height of poaching in the 1980s, elephants are still widespread in all of the main African safari destinations. Key areas include Chobe National Park and the Tuli Block in Botswana, Addo Elephant National Park in South Africa, Zambia's Lower Zambezi National Park and Tanzania's Ngorongoro Crater – home to some big tuskers.

Rhinos

Saved from the brink of extinction, Africa's rhinos are still uncommon. For **black rhino**, head to Tanzania's Ngorongoro Crater and Namibia's Etosha National Park and Damaraland. The slightly larger, less aggressive **white rhino** can also be found in Etosha, as well as game reserves in South Africa's Cape and Kenya's Lake Nakuru National Park.

Tracks and scats

Studying animal tracks is a valuable skill, especially if you come across fresh prints like this jackal pugmark. Animal droppings can also tell you what animals are about – and reveal what they're eating. This leopard scat, picked up in South Luangwa, Zambia, contains undigested hooves of a puku fawn. Chris and Tilde Stuart's *Field Guide to the Tracks and Signs of Southern and East African Wildlife* (Struik, 2003) will have you scrabbling in the dust for hours on end.

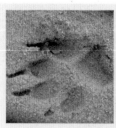

Watching the dust fly

Loxodonta africana
Mashatu Game Reserve, Tuli Block, Botswana

Stake out a pachyderm-pampering hotspot like this favourite dust bath and you'll increase your chances of an intimate elephant encounter.

guiding star

Shabani Omary

Serengeti Under Canvas, Serengeti NP, Tanzania
&Beyond (andbeyond.com)
Favourite animal Lion.
Favourite place Ndutu Plains of the southern Serengeti in February and March when the wildebeest are giving birth.
What does it take to become a guide? Four months at &Beyond's training school at Klein's Camp, spending most of the time out in the bush.

African wild dog
Lycaon pictus
Packs run down prey; dominant female in clan society
- Patchy, south of Sahara
- Savannah, woodland
- Mainly antelope

Bat-eared fox
Otocyon megalotis
Enormous ears detect prey; burrow-dwelling; forefeet good for digging
- Ethiopia to South Africa
- Mainly grassland
- Termites and beetles

Lion
Panthera leo
Length up to 3.3 m; weight up to 260 kg; the only truly sociable cats
- Sub-Saharan Africa
- Savannah, woodland
- Porcupines to giraffes

Cheetah
Acinonyx jubatus
Daytime hunter, capable of sprinting at 112 kph over short distances
- Widespread, also in Iran
- Open savannah
- Small mammals, gazelles

Leopard
Panthera pardus
Solitary, adaptable predator; caches kills in trees out of reach of lions and hyenas
- Widespread
- Exploits all, except desert
- Hares to antelopes

Serval
Felis serval
Uses large ears like antennae to locate prey and long legs for pouncing
- Sub-Saharan Africa
- Savannah, woodland
- Rodents, birds

Brown hyena
Hyaena brunnea
Less predatory than spotted hyena, clans roam large territories
- Southern Africa
- Arid grassland, desert
- Rodents, fruit, carrion

Meerkat
Suricata suricata
Mobs number up to 30 individuals; sentries keep a lookout for predators
- Southern Africa
- Dry, open country
- Insects, scorpions etc

Aardvark
Orycteropus afer
Nocturnal, solitary and rarely seen; superb burrowers; 30 cm-long sticky tongue
- Sub-Saharan Africa
- Savannah to semi-desert
- Termites

African elephant
Loxodonta Africana
Weight up to 5,000 kg for savannah elephant; forest elephant smaller
- Sub-Saharan Africa
- Desert, savannah, forest
- Grass, leaves, bark, fruit

Grevy's zebra
Equus grevyi
Largest member of Equid family; narrower stripes than more common plains zebra
- S Ethiopia and N Kenya
- Arid savannah
- Grass

Black rhino
Diceros bicornis
Weight to 1,400 kg; upper lip hooked, in contrast to wide-mouthed white rhino
- Very rare outside reserves
- Woodland, savannah
- Leaves, herbs

Common eland
Tragelaphus oryx
Massive, ox-like antelope; males weigh up to 950 kg and have large dewlap
- East Africa south to Natal
- Savannah, woodland
- Grass, leaves

Sable
Hippotragus niger
Males darker and with horns up to 170 cm long
- Various subspecies south from Kenya's Shimba Hills
- Woodland, grassland
- Grazers

Gerenuk
Litocranius walleri
Also known as 'giraffe antelope'; can stand erect on hindlegs 2 m high
- Ethiopia to N Tanzania
- Semi-arid thornbush
- Leaves

Kirk's dik-dik
Madoqua kirkii
Tiny, standing only 35-45 cm in height; trunk-like snout; large glands near eyes
- Somalia south to Namibia
- Arid thornbush
- Leaves, shoots, berries

Cape buffalo
Syncerus caffer caffer
Males' horns can reach a spread of 1 m tip to tip; forms herds thousands strong
- Sub-Saharan Africa
- Savannah, near water
- Grass

Giraffe
Giraffa camelopardalis
Males can reach height of 5.5 m and have more horns and bumps on their heads
- Various subspecies
- Savannah with acacias
- Acacia leaves

Hippopotamus
Hippopotamus amphibious
Lower canines can reach 45 cm in length; males can weigh up 3,200 kg
- Sub-Saharan Africa
- Rivers, lakes, swamps
- Nocturnal grazer

Warthog
Phacochoerus africanus
Both sexes have curved upper tusks; warts behind eyes are prominent in males
- Sub-Saharan Africa
- Savannah, woodland
- Rhizomes, roots, seeds

Safaris | game plan

A typical day on safari usually starts with an early wake-up call. You'll need to be up and about when it's cool and the wildlife is most active. Game drives generally last around three to four hours. There will be lots of bumping around on rutted tracks and perhaps some frustrating periods when you see very little. But this will be far outweighed by the excitement of your first encounter or the tidbits of bushlore that you glean from a good guide. You may well stake out favoured wildlife haunts, like waterholes or fruiting trees, or, if regulations allow, take a short walk in the company of an armed scout. Back at your lodge or camp, a large breakfast or brunch will be waiting. Then you have a few hours to lie low during the hottest part of the day when much of the wildlife has also retreated to the shade. By late afternoon it's time for another game drive. At dusk, you might stop for a sundowner, before continuing your safari on into the night when a new cast of nocturnal creatures emerges. Dinner may well be served around an open fire – perfect for stargazing.

Game, but not drive

Driving around in a 4WD vehicle certainly allows you to get close to wildlife, but it's not the only way to go on safari. Instead, you could canoe down the Zambezi, ride an elephant or horse through the Okavango Delta (see page 47), float above the Serengeti in a hot-air balloon or fly a microlight over Kwa Madwala Private Game Reserve in South Africa.

ⓘ Some operators, such as Wildlife Worldwide (wildlifeworldwide.com) offer special photographic safaris accompanied by experts. If you prefer to deal with paint rather than pixels, Art Safari (artsafari. co.uk) and Art Safari Africa (artsafariafrica.com) offer a brush with the wild.

One of the best modes of transport when it comes to safaris, however, is your own feet. Nothing beats the sense of freedom or 'oneness with nature' of walking in the wilds of Africa (see pages 68-71). Although some national parks and game reserves don't allow walking, you may well find it's possible from camps and lodges in adjacent private concessions or buffer zones. Good

Plain cruising

Toyota Land Cruisers (above) and Land Rovers are the vehicles of choice for most safaris. They either have open sides or pop-up roofs. Safari minibuses are commonly used in East Africa, particularly Kenya, but they are not as comfortable and can't be driven as reliably off-road.

> **Camps in Zambia's Luangwa Valley pioneered foot safaris in the 1960s and offer various single- and multi-day options, walking between bush camps in the company of expert guides and trackers**

spots for a walk on the wild side include northern Kenya (where you can trek with camels and Samburu guides), Tanzania's Selous Game Reserve, Mana Pools National Park in Zimbabwe, Mundulea Nature Reserve in Namibia and Linyanti in Botswana. A step above the rest, however, camps in Zambia's Luangwa Valley pioneered foot safaris in the 1960s and offer various single- and multi-day options, walking between bush camps in the company of expert guides and trackers.

ⓘ While the diversity of wildlife on an African safari is something to be marvelled at, it's worth slowing down, or staying put, for a morning or afternoon and observing a single group of animals. After several hours in the company of a herd of zebra or a family of cheetah you'll observe all kinds of behaviour and begin to synch with their natural rhythms – something that's all too often missed on safari.

Package versus tailor-made

Tailor-made safaris are obviously more expensive than package trips, but they do allow you full control of your plans. If you opt for a package safari, be sure to find out what's included. A 'bargain' safari may conceal hidden extras, such as national park fees. On cheap safaris you could also be fighting for a window seat in a crowded vehicle or be frustrated by a driver-guide who is more 'driver' than 'guide'. Good guides will take you away from big groups of other vehicles. They'll also know the best spots for wildlife and be able to tell you more about what you're seeing.

Where to stay

Accommodation is largely a matter of personal preference and budget. Lower cost camping safaris, in which you take an active role in pitching tents, cooking etc, are excellent value and can be great fun – particularly if you're travelling alone. Lodges and camps often have swimming pools and offer night drives and other activities. Generally, the smaller, more intimate and remote the lodge or camp is, the higher the rates.

ⓘ If you fancy the challenge of a self-drive safari, renting a 4WD vehicle and camping in the bush, contact a specialist like Safari Drive (safaridrive.com).

Big game might be foremost in your sights on safari, but birds are a wonderful distraction wherever you go in Africa. The moment you touch down at the airport in Nairobi or Johannesburg you'll start spotting plovers and egrets on grassy areas next to the runway. But it's out in the bush that the continent's head-spinng avian diversity really shines. Whether you're watching weaverbirds plaiting their nests or white-backed vultures pillaging a wildebeest carcass, birds are as captivating on safari as any big cat or rhino encounter. Keen birders can join specialised safaris where expert guides will know the best spots for getting ticks on life-lists. Africa's best birdwatching sites include:

Okavango Delta, Botswana
A mosaic of habitats, from Kalahari thorn scrub to reed-fringed lagoon, the Okavango supports a huge variety of resident birds, boosted by migrants in September.

Kruger National Park, South Africa
No less than 507 bird species can be found in this prime birding spot.

South Luangwa, Zambia
Carmine bee-eaters nest in riverbanks (September to December), while vast flocks of red-billed queleas wheel over rivers in the dry season.

Bangweulu Wetlands, Zambia
Waterbirds galore, with the shoebill stork top of most people's wishlist.

Rift Valley Lakes, Kenya & Tanzania
Pretty in pink thanks to flamingos, Nakuru, Natron and freshwater lakes like Naivasha also attract pelicans, cormorants, fish eagles, plovers and herons.

Safari cynic clinic

Aren't safaris really expensive?
Not when you consider the logistics of maintaining a camp in an area of remote wilderness. Some camps are seasonal and have to be dismantled and reassembled each year. Then there are the high standards of accommodation, food and guiding, the high staff-to-guest ratio, inclusive activities and – for top-end camps – the inevitable price of exclusivity.

Am I going to wake up every morning to find an aardvark in the shower and one of those big hairy spiders in the toilet?
An aardvark is unlikely, but I did once share a bush shower with a tree frog – and I've watched elephants dangle their trunks into the toilet of my open-air en suite for a quick drink. There are plenty of creepy-crawlies in Africa, but the vast majority will give you a wide berth. Having said that, however, you must take every precaution against being bitten by mosquitoes.

I never get any decent photos.
Most of the dramatic close-up shots of African wildlife you see are the result of hours spent in the bush and a good pinch of luck. Give your photography a boost by spending longer on safari, ideally in a single location to become familiar with the wildlife, or shoot less demanding subjects like landscapes, camp life and lodge interiors.

Someone suggested a safari for our honeymoon, but those early mornings are a complete turn-off.
A safari is an ideal choice for a honeymoon, particularly if you splash out on one of the more exclusive camps or lodges. And you can always catch up on sleep by combining a safari with a week in the Seychelles or Mauritius.

Khaki is so 1990s. Can't I wear something brighter?
Not if you want to maximize your chances of seeing wildlife. Earthy colours really are *de rigueur*, particularly if you are joining a walking safari.

Black-shouldered kite ∧

Elanus caeruleus
Serengeti National Park, Tanzania

Kids can come too ∨

Numerous camps are child-friendly, while operators like Exodus run family safaris. For ultimate luxury, Safari Houses (safarihouses.com) offer exclusive, fully staffed family properties with private guides.

Serengeti National Park, Tanzania & Masai Mara National Reserve, Kenya

Mid-August in the Masai Mara. Our Land Cruiser is parked beside a river, no more than 100 m wide and flowing in shallow rapids between low banks of crumbling sand. At any other time of year, we'd barely have given it a second glance – pausing only, perhaps, to look for hippo or the iridescent flash of a kingfisher. Today, however, the Mara River has us transfixed. The reason is overwhelmingly clear: we have a front-row seat for one of the most spectacular wildlife events on earth: the Great Migration.

Milling around in restless herds to our left are several thousand wildebeest and zebra – a fraction of the two million-plus animals that take part in the annual trek through the plains of the Serengeti and Masai Mara. To our right, hundreds of vultures crowd the riverbanks like rows of leering, hunchbacked fans at some macabre gladiatorial show.

It's hardly surprising the wildebeest and zebra are reluctant to cross the river – it's littered with carcasses. Bloated wildebeest, legs protruding like cocktail sticks in fat party sausages, are strewn across the rapids – casualties from earlier river crossings. Marabou storks pace between the vultures, while enormous Nile crocodiles lie motionless in the shallows, watching and waiting.

The wildebeest and zebra gradually swell in number as more animals drift in from the plains. There isn't a purposeful surge towards the river – it's more of a slow, irresistible massing, like a kettle building a head of steam. Sooner or later, something has to give.

A few dozen wildebeest turn tail and walk away from the river in single file – a loose thread unravelling from the main ball. Then a lone zebra stallion cautiously makes his way to the water's edge, ears pricked forward; his entire body rigid with concentration. Others jostle behind him; a frisky, jittery mass of black and white stripes. Water starts

to froth beneath their hooves and there's an almost unbearable sense of anticipation as vulture, crocodile and camera-toting tourist wait with baited breath...

Several months later and it's a quite different scene in the southern Serengeti. Our camp, Serengeti Under Canvas, has been pitched in shady grove of acacias a short distance from the Ndutu Plains where, from January to March, the wildebeest gather to give birth.

The first coral-streaks of dawn have barely permeated the copse before we are driving out onto the savannah for a bush breakfast. Wildebeest and zebra are everywhere, peppering the grassland in their tens and hundreds of thousands. As the engine noise of our Land Cruiser dies, all we can hear is the grunting of the gnus and the whisper of wind over endless seas of grass.

We sip fresh coffee as mini-dramas unfold around us: a newly born wildebeest calf, still wet, tottering beside its mother; hitchhiking oxpecker birds fussing over zebra manes; swallows weaving dizzy paths through the herds, picking at insects disturbed by the scuffing of a million hooves.

Later, we find a female cheetah with three almost fully grown cubs lying up in asparagus scrub on the edge of the plains. A herd of skittish Thompson's gazelle wanders past and the cats are instantly alert, four spotted heads turning in unison to follow their progress. But the gazelles are wary; they sense danger and keep their distance.

We join the cheetah's vigil, watching them and their prey from a respectful few hundred metres. An afternoon passes. The cheetah never get quite close enough to launch an attack, but it's still a privilege to spend five or so hours in their company, synching with the natural rhythms of the Serengeti: shadows of clouds passing over the plains; wildebeest trailing past, head to tail, like columns of ants...

From adrenaline-charged river crossings in the Masai Mara to lazy days in the Serengeti, the Great Migration is the ultimate natural history blockbuster – an epic story full of action, intrigue and drama.

> **A lone zebra stallion cautiously makes his way to the water's edge, ears pricked forward, his entire body rigid with concentration. Others jostle behind him**

A moving story (from top, left to right) – catching up with the migration in the Serengeti's southern plains; newborn wildebeest; Serengeti Under Canvas; wildebeest stampede; lions on a kill; grazing wildebeest; vultures squabbling over a carcass in the Mara River

Kenya or Tanzania? Both countries play host to the Great Migration. See pages 218-219 to find out what's happening, when and where.

Making tracks

⟲ Numerous operators offer safaris, including **Expert Africa** (expertafrica.com) and the **Zambezi Safari & Travel Co** (zambezi.com).
✈ Travel by road to the Masai Mara (5 hrs from Nairobi) or take a light aircraft flight. From Kilimanjaro airport, fly or drive to the Serengeti.
🛏 **&Beyond** (andbeyond.com) moves its low-impact, luxury Serengeti Under Canvas camp to prime migration spots throughout the year.
🕐 GMT+3
☽ See the migration calendar on page 219.
⚕ A yellow fever vaccination certificate is required for all travellers visiting Tanzania.

**Leap of faith – Wildebeest
brave rapids and crocodiles
in the Mara River to satisfy
their urge to migrate in
search of fresh pasture**

*Connochaetes taurinus,
Masai Mara National Reserve,
Kenya*

Andy Rouse | Photographer, author & presenter | andyrouse.co.uk

↘ My big five

❶ Svalbard

One of the most beautiful places on earth – and superb for polar bear sightings.

❷ Rwanda

An encounter with mountain gorillas strikes right to your heart. There is nothing quite like watching a playful youngster in its mother's arms, under the watchful gaze of the powerful yet gentle silverback.

❸ Alaska

Rugged and wild, Alaska is home to so much cool wildlife. I always go there for my grizzly bear experiences, but Alaska is also a great place for whales, moose and wolves – all surrounded by incredible scenery.

❹ Galápagos Islands

Galápagos wildlife is unique and completely unafraid of tourists. For me, the real reward is below the waves, snorkelling with turtles, fur seals and penguins.

❺ Bosque del Apache, New Mexico, USA

Every year the migration of the snow geese ends at Bosque del Apache in New Mexico. Seeing these beautiful white birds erupt into crystal clear blue skies in their thousands is one of nature's most awesome spectacles – and an unexpected treat.

66 99 **If you only ever see one wildlife spectacle in the world, go and see the annual wildebeest migration as it crosses the Talek and Mara Rivers in the Masai Mara. Thousands of wildebeest make the long trek from Tanzania, forming huge lines which can be seen from space. As they reach these two mighty rivers they start to bunch up until the plains are literally alive with the sights, sounds and smell of wildebeest. The river crossings are incredible to watch as thousands upon thousands of wildebeest leap into the swirling waters and try to evade the waiting jaws of huge Nile crocodiles. Get there in September to guarantee a decent crossing.**

Andy Rouse, one of the world's leading wildlife photographers, took the polar bear image on the cover of *Wildlife Travel,* as well as the wildebeest image, left

Ursus maritimus
Svalbard

Tales from the wild | a short walk in the Okavango Delta

Okavango Delta, Botswana

The hyena dropping was white and brittle and after a gentle squeeze it exploded in a puff of chalky dust, just like the meringues my grandmother used to make. "Hyenas aren't fussy," Adrian explained as he picked out slivers of bone, beetle wing-cases and tangled fur balls from the powdery remains in his hand. "They'll eat anything. They're survivors."

Adrian Dandridge knew about survival. A life spent roaming Botswana's bushveld, living off the land, he was Africa's answer to Huckleberry Finn. "Heading north?" He glanced at White, his Bushman tracker, who was crouching nearby looking for tell-tale signs in the sand. "North." White nodded, pointing to a hyena paw print, half obscured by tracks dimpling the game trail.

Adrian shouldered his rifle and, with White casting ahead for spoor, we started walking. Our boots scuffed clouds of bicarbonate-of-soda on the parched, sun-cracked skin of an empty waterhole. The land felt desiccated; stunned by the dry, breathless torpor of winter. Tall grasses bowed under full heads of seed and the air was thick with the heady aroma of wild thyme and basil. Far to the east a bush fire raged, gasping pallid blue smoke high into the sky.

This wasn't the Okavango I had anticipated. Not the verdant gem of Africa, the teeming Kalahari oasis. But there was an expectant air about the still and arid land, as if it was holding its breath, waiting for change.

We took refuge from the noon sun in the shade of a giant marula tree. "The water's close now," Adrian told me. "We could meet the flood any day now."

Several months earlier, good rains had fallen on the Angolan highlands 1,000 km to the northwest. Dwindling streams had become gushing torrents, feeding the rivers that flow south towards Botswana. The Okavango Delta's life-line had been recharged. Like a pulsing umbilical cord the Okavango River was swelling the delta into full flood.

From the vantage of a termite mound I stared north. It seemed inconceivable that a tide was flowing towards us through those dusty grasslands.

This was only the first morning of our four-day walking safari, but already my senses thrilled to the adrenaline surge of exploring the bush on foot. As the sun dipped from its zenith and we began walking again, I felt the primeval tingle of being part of the food chain. There were shadows in the tawny grass like lions crouching in ambush. Far ahead a small herd of zebra cantered into the heat haze like a line of melting bar codes and a ground hornbill called once, a remote booming, like wind lost in a labyrinth.

This was a safari of the senses. An intimate affair with wild Africa. No noisy safari vehicles or mad chases to see the big five. There was not a tick list between us. Instead we walked slowly, stopping often to marvel at small wonders.

"Watch this," Adrian said quietly, plucking a feathery seed from a tall grass stem. He wetted his finger, gently dabbed the seed and placed it carefully on the ground. Slowly the seed began to rotate, stirring to life, and within seconds it had drilled itself into the sand ready to germinate. "The magic of water."

Dusk flushed the sky as we reached our first camp. The cricket chorus beat its soft staccato rhythm and a barred owl purred from a nearby leadwood tree. Somewhere far away jackals yelped. Then, much closer, the long 'whoop' of a hyena rose and fell; the mournful herald of the African night.

Early the following morning, Adrian and White read the sands, firing vivid episodes of bush life through my mind. A zebra rolling in a clearing, compressing the sand and scuffing deep gashes with its flaying hooves. A python meandering across the oval craters stamped in the ground by a bull elephant.

Later that afternoon, as we walked to our second camp, Adrian noticed a strange object lying half buried in the sand. It was smooth and dome-shaped, the size of a football. When he stooped to pick it up, I noticed that there were others scattered about the pan. Terrapin shells. Dozens of them, lying bleached and broken. And in amongst them, jaws gaping as if fixed in its final gasp for water, the hideous skull of a catfish lay shattered in the hot sands. The last time the Okavango flooded, this dusty clearing was the bed of a lake.

We started walking at dawn the next day while dew still glistened on the feathery plumes of silky Bushman grass and the land was burnished in gold. I was hardly aware of the breeze that came sighing through the grasses. It was only when Adrian turned to

Delta force – when the Okavango floods, dry grasslands spring to life

Dragonfly
Odonata sp

The Okavango supports an incredible diversity of life, including 122 mammal species, over 440 different birds, 100 reptiles and amphibians, 70 fish and 5,000 insects.

This was a safari of the senses. An intimate affair with wild Africa. No noisy safari vehicles or mad chases to see the big five. There was not a tick list between us. Instead we walked slowly, stopping often to marvel at small wonders

me and whispered, "Can you smell it?" that I detected the strange odour. It was the scent of freshly dug soil, sweet and moist after the dry tang of the bush. "Listen!" I tilted my head, but heard nothing but the distant churring of a dove. Then for a brief moment the breeze stiffened, carrying with it a strange fizzing sound. "The water's close!" Adrian's eyes were wide with excitement.

Skirting a patch of mopane scrub, we turned briskly to the north. Adrian knew a short-cut through a stand of marula trees and it wasn't long before we broke into a wide corridor of grassland. We stopped and stared across the plain, squinting into the low rays of sunlight.

They came in a long line, low over the tree tops; a wide V-shaped skein, their wings thudding the air like the steady pulsing of a heart. "Wattled cranes," Adrian smiled from beneath his binoculars. "Sixty five of them. I've never seen such a large flock." As we watched, the huge birds with gangly necks, long trailing legs and finger-tipped wings changed their flight pattern. The orderly line began to break up and one by one, they tumbled and twisted out of the sky, their legs hanging down, braced for landing.

The woodland blocked the birds from our view and it was several hours before we spotted them again in another large wedge of grassland. Obscured by distance and the wavering heat haze they resembled gnarled fence posts strung across the plain.

We set off towards them, eager to discover what had lured so many wading birds to one spot. But we'd hardly walked a few paces before White signalled urgently for us to stop.

A large male baboon swaggered into a clearing barely 100 m ahead, his fur ignited into a golden halo by the low afternoon sun. Behind him, a rabble of skinny youngsters cavorted through the grass, pouncing and somersaulting like puppets on elastic strings. We crouched down. The baboons were moving slowly towards us, pausing to winkle buried morsels from the dry crust of the pan. A warthog trotted to the edge of the clearing, its tail erect like a flag of truce.

Electric blue flared nearby as a glorious lilac-breasted roller fanned its wings to land.

Then, slowly, smoothly, like the shadow of a passing cloud, a dark stain began spreading across the clearing towards us. I watched, captivated, as it grew long probing tendrils which slithered forward as they found a way through the scuffed surface of the sand. Water was consuming the clearing. It formed shallow, glistening puddles in platter-sized elephant tracks and bubbled and frothed as it flooded a network of gerbil burrows. In minutes the water was running in eager rivulets around our feet. After drinking their fill, the baboons moved to a small wooded copse sprouting from the phallic tower of a termite hill which was fast becoming an island.

Water was consuming the clearing. It formed shallow, glistening puddles in platter-sized elephant tracks and bubbled and frothed as it flooded a network of gerbil burrows

We backed off slightly from the leading edge of water, hurriedly removing our boots and socks. The water was cool on our bare feet and beneath the light film of surface dust it was the colour of well-brewed tea. In awed silence we waded into the flood. Stalking to within 100 m of the wattled cranes, the water was still no higher than our ankles.

At this closer range we could see other birds mingled with the cranes. Pacing the shallows like beaters at a pheasant shoot, marabou storks struck hammer blows at desperate rodents evicted from their flooded burrows. I watched as gerbil after gerbil was plucked, sodden from the water, thrown in the air and swallowed whole. Hundreds of saddlebilled storks, cattle egrets, herons and hammerkops joined the feeding frenzy while a pair of African fish eagles wheeled overhead.

All around us, clouds of dragonflies drifted amongst the stems of grasses that still protruded above the surface. A herd of lechwe, the aquatic, splayed-hoofed antelope of the delta, scattered as we approached, kicking sparkling arcs of water behind them. Then, as dusk approached, a chorus of frogs and toads rose from the water, filling the air with the clatter of a million castanets as if they were celebrating the miracle of the Okavango in flood.

Going with the flow (from top, left to right) – when the floods arrive, saddlebilled storks and other waders patrol the shallows hunting frogs, lizards and rodents; small wooded termite mounds are destined to become islands; guide Adrian Dandridge with flood-victim gerbil; wattled crane; a paddle in the shallows

Summer rains in Angola take six months to flow 1,000 km to quench the Okavango Delta.

Making tracks

🚶 Two of the best options for walking safaris in the Okavango are **Footsteps across the Delta** in Shinde concession and **Linyanti Walking Safaris** in the Chobe Enclave (kerdowneybotswana.com). Either can be combined with safaris by vehicle, motorboat or mokoro.
✈️ Light aircraft, often single-propeller Cessnas, serve camps in the Delta from Maun.
⛺ Camps cater for around 6-8 guests in simple, twin-bedded tents with bucket showers and long-drop toilets.
🕐 GMT+2
🚶 Walking safaris operate May-November.
ⓘ botswanatourism.co.bw

Primate watching

Ever since David Attenborough's escapades with mountain gorillas in *Life on Earth*, people have been fascinated by the prospect of an intimate get-together with our distant hairy cousins. A primate watching holiday, however, is no chimps' tea party. Physical contact is forbidden in order to minimize the risk of passing on our germs. Then there's the sad reality that, following years of persecution, most wild primates are extremely wary of humans. Couple this with the fact that they often inhabit thick forests and you'll begin to wonder why primate watching has become so popular.

The reason, of course, is that few other animals display such a captivating and familiar range of behaviour and expressions. Make brief eye contact with an orang-utan or a gorilla and you are connecting with another mind. It's a sobering and privileged moment that we're more than happy to slog for hours through humid, muddy jungles for a chance to experience.

Remove humans from the picture and primates are mostly found in tropical and subtropical forest and woodland throughout Latin America, Africa and Asia – the introduced Barbary macaques of Gibraltar being their only toehold in Europe.

The prime sites for mountain gorilla watching are Bwindi and Mgahinga in Uganda and Volcanoes National Park in Rwanda where several families have been habituated. Chimpanzees can be spotted in forest reserves throughout East and West Africa, including Kibale in Uganda and Mahale Mountains in Tanzania. Africa is also home to common primates like baboons and vervet monkeys, which you'll more than likely see on a typical safari (see pages 56-63). For lemurs, however, you will need to plan a trip to the island of Madagascar.

The world-renowned Kabili-Sepilok Forest Reserve in Sabah, Borneo, provides an opportunity for close encounters with orang-utans, while a boat trip on the Kinabatangan River often reveals proboscis monkeys. New World primates, which include the diminutive marmosets and tamarins, are perhaps more elusive, although you can't fail to miss the cry of a howler monkey.

There are thought to be around 634 species of primates – a precise figure is surprisingly elusive, partly due to taxonomists being undecided as to whether certain closely related varieties should be considered separate species, and partly due to the fact that new species are discovered all the time. Since 2010, the primate family tree has blossomed with discoveries of a new snub-nose monkey in Myanmar and a fork-marked lemur in Madagascar. Our knowledge of lemurs has grown in leaps and bounds over the past 20 years, with the number of species known to science climbing from around 30 to over 80.

Sadly, however, time is running out for our closest living relatives. Around 48% of all primates are classified as threatened with extinction on the IUCN Red List of Threatened Species (iucn.org/species). Major threats include habitat destruction and hunting – both for food and the illegal wildlife trade. Urgent conservation measures are crucial, but carefully managed responsible tourism projects could also throw many primate species a lifeline.

> **Make brief eye contact with an orang-utan or a gorilla and you are connecting with another mind. It's a sobering and privileged moment**

Primates in peril

According to a report published by the Primate Specialist Group of IUCN's Species Survival Commission, the world's 25 most endangered primates include the greater bamboo lemur (*Prolemur simus*), grey-headed lemur (*Eulemur cinereiceps*), northern sportive lemur (*Lepilemur septentrionalis*), silky sifaka (*Propithecus candidus*), Tana River red colobus (*Procolobus rufomitratus*), Niger Delta red colobus (*Procolobus epieni*), Cross River gorilla (*Gorilla gorilla diehli*), golden-headed langur (*Trachypithecus p. poliocephalus*), Tonkin snub-nosed monkey (*Rhinopithecus avunculus*), eastern black crested gibbon (*Nomascus nasutus*), Sumatran orang-utan (*Pongo abelii*), cotton-top tamarin (*Saguinus oedipus*) and brown spider monkey (*Ateles hybridus*).

King of the swingers – a juvenile mountain gorilla hangs on in Rwanda

Gorilla beringei beringei
Volcanoes National Park, Rwanda

Despite encouraging signs of recovery, the world population of mountain gorillas (restricted to a narrow chain of volcanoes in East Africa) hangs in the balance. Climate change may affect the specialised vegetation zones on which they depend, while careless contact with a virus-carrying tourist could trigger an epidemic.

Primate watching | inspiration

South & Central America

① Corcovado National Park, Costa Rica
Lush tropical rainforest rucked up against a wild stretch of Pacific coast, this biodiverse hotspot is home to all four species of monkey found in Costa Rica: Central American squirrel monkey, Geoffroy's spider monkey, mantled howler and white-headed capuchin. Costa Rica's Manuel Antonio National Park is also prime territory for primates.
» December to April

② Mamiraua Sustainable Development Reserve, Brazil
Travel by boat from Manaus to reach Mamiraua where a floating lodge offers forays into the flooded forest of the Amazon in search of white uakari and other primates.
» Year round

③ Manu National Park, Peru
Vast tract of pristine tropical rainforest with 13 species of primate, including capuchin, common squirrel monkey, red howler, two varieties of spider monkey, emperor tamarin, Goeldi's monkey and pygmy marmoset.
» Year round, but driest May to October

④ Poco das Antas Biological Reserve, Brazil
A two-hour drive from Rio de Janeiro, this rare piece of Atlantic coast rainforest provides a refuge for the equally vulnerable golden lion tamarin. Nearly a quarter of the 1,000 individuals remaining in the wild are found here.
» May to September

Europe

⑤ Gibraltar
Introduced colony of Barbary macaques are Europe's only non-human primates living wild. They can also be found roaming the cedar forests of Morocco and Algeria.
» Year round

Africa

⑥ Simien Mountains National Park, Ethiopia
Large troops of Gelada baboon can be seen on the plateaux and escarpments of this rugged national park.
» October to March

⑦ Kibale Forest National Park, Uganda
Home to no less than 13 primate species, including chimpanzee which can be tracked through the forest. Also try Kyambura Gorge, Ngamba Island Chimp Sanctuary and Semliki Valley Wildlife Reserve.
» Year round

⑧ Bwindi Impenetrable National Park, Uganda
Mountain gorilla stronghold. Track one of three habituated troops in steep, often challenging terrain. Mgahinga National Park in southern Uganda has one habituated gorilla family.
» Year round

⑨ Volcanoes National Park, Rwanda
Seven mountain gorilla families have been habituated in the mountains where Dian Fossey worked, along with two troops of the endemic golden monkey.
» Year round

⑩ Nyungwe National Park, Rwanda
Located in southern Rwanda, Nyungwe is prime habitat for chimps (habituation is ongoing), as well as large troops of black and white colobus, blue monkey and grey-cheeked mangabey.
» Year round

⑪ Nouabalé-Ndoki National Park, Congo
A natural jungle clearing, Mbeli Bai provides an opportunity to watch lowland gorilla and forest elephant. Dzanga-Ndoki National Park (Central African Republic) has the world's only other group of habituated lowland gorillas.
» Year round

⑫ Lopé National Park, Gabon
Western lowland gorilla and chimpanzee are found here, but none are habituated. The best chance of a sighting is at Langoue Bai. Lopé also has large troops of mandrill, plus a variety of other primates.
» July to August for mandrill

⑬ Mahale Mountains and Gombe Stream National Parks, Tanzania
With forested mountains rearing above sandy beaches on Lake Tanganyika, Mahale offers a beautiful setting for tracking chimpanzees. Alternatively, try picking up the trail of the Gombe Stream chimps of Jane Goodall fame.
» May to November

⑭ Montagne D'Ambre National Park, Madagascar
Mountain rainforest and waterfalls provide a stunning backdrop for walks in search of crowned lemur.
» April to November

⑮ Andasibe-Mantadia National Park, Madagascar
One of Madagascar's most popular parks and the best

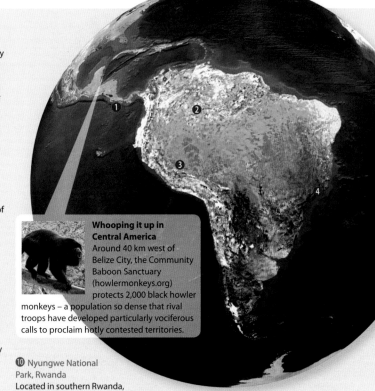

Whooping it up in Central America
Around 40 km west of Belize City, the Community Baboon Sanctuary (howlermonkeys.org) protects 2,000 black howler monkeys – a population so dense that rival troops have developed particularly vociferous calls to proclaim hotly contested territories.

Out of bounds in the Congo Basin
An hour's drive from Kinshasa, the Lola ya Bonobo sanctuary (friendsofbonobos.org) is home to 52 bonobos and offers a wonderful opportunity for observing what is perhaps our closest wild cousins. Check government travel advisories before visiting the DRC.

Chilling out in Japan
Better known as snow monkeys, the Japanese macaques of Jigokudani Monkey Park (jigokudani-yaenkoen.co.jp) are partial to hot-tubbing in the thermal springs of this mountainous region to the northwest of Tokyo. The behaviour was started by a plucky female in 1963 and now all 270-odd monkeys are at it.

place to see the indri.
➤➤ April to November

16 Ranomafana National Park, Madagascar
Ranomafana has at least 12 species, including the rare golden bamboo lemur.
➤➤ April to November

17 Berenty Private Reserve, Madagascar
Best known of the island's reserves, Berenty offers relaxed walking in gallery forest where ring-tailed lemur and Verreaux's sifaka are seen at close range.
➤➤ April to November

18 Periyar National Park, Kerala, India
Periyar National Park is home to four species of primates – lion-tailed macaque, bonnet macaque, common langur and Nilgiri Langur.
➤➤ September to May

Asia

19 Horton Plains National Park, Sri Lanka
Montane cloud forest supports toque macaque, purple faced langur and an endemic slender loris.
➤➤ December to March

20 Baima Snow Mountain Reserve, Yunnan, China
Snub-nosed monkeys in remote conifer forests.
➤➤ June to September

21 Taman Negara National Park, Malaysia
Lowland rainforest with macaques, leaf monkeys and white-handed gibbons.
➤➤ February to September

22 Bako National Park, Sarawak, Malaysian Borneo
Small rainforest reserve, with trails into proboscis monkey territory.
➤➤ March to December

23 Kinabatangan River, Sabah, Malaysian Borneo
Boat trips to see proboscis monkey, orang-utan, gibbons and macaques.
➤➤ March to October

24 Kabili-Sepilok Reserve, Sabah, Malaysian Borneo
Rehabilitation centre for orang-utans rescued from logging, hunting and the pet trade.
➤➤ March to October

25 Mentawai Islands, Sumatra, Indonesia
Seven endemic primates can be found here,

including Kloss's Gibbon and Mentawai macaque.
➤➤ May to September

26 Gunung Leuser National Park, Sumatra, Indonesia
The Bohorok Orang-Utan Sanctuary is near Bukit Lawang, the main access point for treks in Gunung Leuser – home to wild orangs, tigers and rhinos.
➤➤ April to September

27 Tanjung Puting National Park, Kalimantan, Indonesia
Orang-utan, proboscis monkey and macaques.
➤➤ April to September

Primate watching | fieldcraft

When it comes to fieldcraft, primates can be split into two main camps: those that are habituated and those that aren't. Habituated primates have been acclimatized to the presence of humans; they are often the subject of scientific field research and offer some of the closest and most rewarding encounters. Tracking them usually relies on following a guide who is in radio contact with scouts that have kept a close watch over your target primates since daybreak. Unhabituated apes or monkeys, on the other hand, present a far greater challenge. To catch even a fleeting glimpse of them you'll need to pit your wits against some of the smartest minds in the animal kingdom. There are exceptions, of course – savannah-dwelling baboons are not exactly shy, while some species of langur and macaque have adapted to urban areas, becoming streetwise monkeys ever on the lookout for free food. India's temple monkeys and Gibraltar's rock apes will probably find you long before you find them.

Shining eyes
Not all primates are diurnal. Take a walk at night in the forests of Africa, India or South East Asia, cast a torch beam into the trees and you could well find a pair of round eyes shining back at you. Largely nocturnal, prosimians are the oldest members of the primate family and include lorises, pottos, bushbabies, lemurs, tarsiers and the aye-aye. Holed up in trees by day, these goggle-eyed gremlins only emerge to feed under cover of darkness. In Latin America, the nightshift is filled by owl monkeys which not only resemble owls with their huge, disc-shaped eyes, but also sound like them, uttering low-frequency hoots.

Howlers and cry babies
Listening out for their calls can be a good way to track down nocturnal primates. Bushbabies, in particular, have a loud shriek that has an unnerving resemblance to a crying human infant. Some diurnal lemurs kick up a racket during the day. One of the most haunting calls in nature, the song of the indri can carry for around 3 km, adults joining in duets to proclaim their territories. For forest dwellers this is an effective way to declare their location to other primates. Other species are equally vocal, from bellowing howler monkeys and pant-hooting chimpanzees to the wonderful whooping of gibbons. In many forests, the dawn chorus of primates rivals anything that birds can offer.

In addition to marking territory, primates make a song and dance over predators. Alarm calls could be anything from baboons barking at a leopard slinking from its daytime cover to langurs grunting indignantly at a tiger. Keep your ears open and these tell-tale sounds can lead you to all kinds of interesting wildlife.

Sweet something
There's nothing more irresistible to most primates than a tree in flower or fruit. Stake one out, rather than stroll randomly through a forest, and you'll greatly increase your chances of spotting primates – particularly the more elusive canopy-dwelling species. Orang-utans, for example, are notoriously difficult to see in the wild, but they'll travel large distances to gorge themselves on fruit. You will know when there's one feeding in the tree above you when empty fruit husks start raining down.

Other primates frequent particular habitats for feeding – lowland gorillas, for example, are partial to the tubers and shoots of water plants growing in swampy *bais* (or clearings) in the Congo rainforest.

Behaviour
This is what intrigues us most about primates. A mere sighting will always leave us wanting, because it's only through patient and sustained observation that you begin to recognise so much familiar behaviour – playing infants, social dominance, even tool use. Ultimately, it's the experiences of primatologists like Jane Goodall that provide the best lesson in fieldcraft: take your time, sit quietly and simply observe.

Mother's pride – olive baboon with infant

Papio anubis
Ngorongoro Crater, Tanzania

Baby primates rely on their mothers for food, warmth, security and even transport. This young baboon will be carried, jockey-style, on its mother's back.

Primatologists provide the best lesson in fieldcraft: take your time, sit quietly and simply observe

Social grooming
There's nothing like nit-picking to cement relationships between family and friends. Social grooming – seen here in golden monkeys, Rwanda – is the glue that bonds primate communities, and makes fascinating watching.

Bushbaby
Galago sp
Nocturnal tree-dweller with cry like that of a human infant
⊗ East and Southern Africa
◔ Forest, scrub, savannah
❀ Fruit, leaves, seeds, insects, small vertebrates

Ring-tailed lemur
Lemur catta
Spends up to a third of its time on the ground
⊗ Southern Madagascar
◔ Scrub, dry forest
❀ Fruit, leaves, seeds, bamboo, insects

Indri
Indri indri
Distinctive duet can carry for up to 3 km. Known locally as *babakotu* (grandfather)
⊗ Northeast Madagascar
◔ Scrub, dry forest
❀ Fruit, leaves, seeds, bark

Verreaux's sifaka
Propithecus verreauxi
Strong arboreal leaper (up to 9 m in a single jump). On land, bounds along upright
⊗ Western Madagascar
◔ Scrub, forest
❀ Fruit, leaves, seeds, bark

Aye-aye
Daubentönia madagascariensis
Elongated middle finger used for probing for grubs
⊗ Eastern Madagascar
◔ Dry forest, rainforest, spiny desert
❀ Insect larvae, fruit, nectar

Tarsier
Tarsius sp
Nocturnal hunters; powerful leapers with huge eyes
⊗ Malaysia, Indonesia, Philippines
◔ Rainforest, mangrove
❀ Insect, small vertebrates

Golden-headed lion tamarin
Leontopithecus chrysomelas
Live in groups of 5-9, foraging during the day; scent marks its territory
⊗ Southeast Brazil
◔ Atlantic coast forest
❀ Fruit, nectar, insects

Squirrel monkey
Saimiri sp
Social primate living in large groups throughout Amazon
⊗ Brazil, Colombia, Ecuador, Guyana, Venezuela
◔ Tropical rainforest
❀ Fruit, insects

Uakari
Cacajao sp
Bald, red-headed primates with shaggy coats
⊗ Brazil, Colombia, Peru, Venezuela
◔ Tropical rainforest
❀ Fruit, leaves, insects

Howler monkey
Alouatta sp
Dawn chorus of bellows can carry for up to 5 km
⊗ Central, South America
◔ Tropical rainforest, mangrove, savannah
❀ Fruit, leaves, flowers

Macaque
Macaca radiata
India's Bonnet macaque (above) is one of 21 species in this successful group.
⊗ N Africa, India, SE Asia
◔ Wide range of forests
❀ Fruit, leaves, insects

Mandrill
Mandrillus sphinx
Males recognisable by bright blue and red snouts and rumps; weight to 30 kg
⊗ Cameroon, Gabon, Congo
◔ Tropical rainforest
❀ Fruit to small animals

Black and white colobus
Colobus guereza
Often seen grooming or leaping in trees with flowing white fur 'cape' and long tail.
⊗ West, Central, East Africa
◔ Wide range of forests
❀ Leaves, fruits, flowers

Langur
Trachypithecus johnii
Several species including Nilgiri langur (above)
⊗ India, SE Asia
◔ Forest, savannah, scrub, farmland and urban areas
❀ Primarily leaves

Proboscis monkey
Nasalis larvatus
Pink face, pot belly, big nose; readily seen on river trips; can swim to escape danger
⊗ Borneo
◔ Coastal and riverine forest
❀ Leaves, fruit, small animals

White-handed gibbon
Hylobates lar
One of 12 gibbon and siamang species, all fast-swinging, loud-whooping
⊗ Southeast Asia
◔ Tropical forests
❀ Fruit, leaves, insects

Bornean orang-utan
Pongo pygmaeus
Sumatran species has lighter coat and more slender build
⊗ Borneo, Sumatra
◔ Tropical rainforest
❀ Anything from fruit and bark to birds' eggs and honey

Mountain gorilla
Gorilla beringei beringei
Virunga mountain gorillas have hairier brow ridges than Bwindi ones
⊗ DRC, Rwanda, Uganda
◔ Montane tropical forest
❀ Leaves, bark, fruit

Lowland gorilla
Gorilla gorilla
Three subspecies: western lowland, eastern lowland and Cross River
⊗ DRC, CAR, Congo, Gabon
◔ Tropical (swamp) forest
❀ Wide range of vegetation

Chimpanzee
Pan troglodytes
Share 99% of human DNA
⊗ Scattered populations, Senegal to Tanzania
◔ Forest, savannah
❀ Fruit, leaves, insects, other primates (colobus)

Primate watching | game plan

On a typical vehicle safari in Africa you should see common primates like baboons and vervet monkeys (and, with luck, bushbabies on night drives). Similarly, an Indian safari will turn up sightings of grey langur. In Borneo, boat travel is the way to go for spotting proboscis monkeys – trips are available on rivers like the Kinabatangan in Sabah. Getting afloat in the Amazon and parts of Central America, meanwhile, will put you in a good position to observe species such as howler monkeys and uakaris. However, the fact that most primates inhabit dense forest means that, sooner or later, you'll need to put in some footwork.

Guided treks are available to visit habituated chimpanzees and gorillas (see box), while walking in Madagascar's Berenty Reserve often involves close encounters with sifakas and ring-tailed lemurs. Ecolodges in Latin America make ideal bases for jungle walks in search of New World monkeys – best observed from canopy-viewing towers or walkways.

ⓘ Specialist primate watching holidays are available from operators such as World Primate Safaris (worldprimatesafaris.com) which donates a percentage of each safari sold towards the conservation of endangered primates.

Where to stay
In **Belize**, the **Community Baboon Sanctuary** (see also p74) is a model ecotourism project in which some 200 landowners (having volunteered to manage their land to safeguard howler monkey habitat) boost their income through accommodation, guided tours and other visitor services. You can camp at the sanctuary or stay with a community member in a local B&B. There's also a Nature Lodge next to the Sanctuary Museum. Guided walks are the best way to get close to habituated troops.

Accommodation near **Costa Rica's** Tortuguero National Park includes **Pachira Lodge** (pachiralodge.com) and **Mawamba Lodge** (grupomawamba.com), both offering excellent access to the region's forest-fringed lagoons and canals where you should see spider, howler and capuchin monkeys.

The floating **Uakari Lodge** (uakarilodge.com) in

Sepilok Nature Resort

Sabah, Malaysian Borneo

Greystoke Camp perches on the shores of Lake Tanganyika like a miniature thatched version of Sydney Opera House. Fashioned from old dhow timber, it offers a stylish base from which to track chimpanzees in Mahale National Park, Tanzania

Brazil has rainwater collection, solar power and other eco-friendly touches and makes an excellent base for exploring the seasonally flooded forests of the Amazon (May-July). Paddle canoes will get you quietly in range of red howlers, uakaris and spider monkeys. Located in a private reserve in the southern Amazon, **Cristalino Jungle Lodge** (cristalinolodge.com.br) is another low-impact option. Home to the endemic white-whiskered spider monkey and several other primate species, the lodge has a 50-m canopy tower. See page 185 for other Amazonian ecolodges.

Primate-watching accommodation in the **Republic of Congo** is limited to **Mbeli Bai Camp**, a remote outpost with long-drop toilets and bush showers – but just a 40-minute walk from Mbeli Bai and the chance to spot lowland gorillas.

Closed in September 2010 due to an aviation dispute, **Loango Lodge** (africas-eden.com) in **Gabon's** Loango National Park was renowned as a prime location for seeing western lowland gorillas, chimpanzees and a wealth of other wildlife, including the famous 'surfing' hippos along the park's wild coast. Check the lodge's website for the latest news.

In **Rwanda** there's an excellent choice of places to stay near Volcanoes National Park, including the upmarket **Sabinyo Silverback Lodge** (see page 80) and comfortable **Virunga Lodge** (volcanoessafaris. com) – both with breathtaking views of the volcanoes.

With just eight, beautifully furnished stone cottages, **Clouds Mountain Gorilla Lodge** (wildplacesafrica.com) provides easy access to gorilla tracking trails in Bwindi Impenetrable Forest, **Uganda.** Other intimate options (all with views over the forest) include **Buhoma Lodge** (ugandaexclusivecamps.com) and **Bwindi Lodge** (volcanoessafaris.com). For Kibale Forest, try **Primate Lodge** (ugandalodges.com) where you can stay in a cottage or bring your own tent. A sanctuary for orphaned chimpanzees, **Ngama Island** in Lake Victoria has an eco-friendly tented camp (ugandaexclusivecamps.com) sleeping up to eight.

In **Tanzania,** the exotic **Greystoke Camp** (greystoke-mahale.com) perches on the shores of Lake Tanganyika like a miniature thatched version of Sydney Opera House. Fashioned from old dhow timber, it offers a stylish base from which to track chimpanzees in Mahale National Park.

A morning with the mountain gorillas

Madagascar boasts a range of lodges well-placed for ventures into lemur land. In Andasibe-Mantadia National Park, **Vakona Forest Lodge** (hotelvakona.com) has comfortable bungalows overlooking a lake, while **Berenty Lodge** offers chalet accommodation with the added bonus of ring-tailed lemurs and Verreaux's sifakas dropping by on a daily basis. See pages 240-242 for more African ecolodges.

In **Borneo, Sepilok Nature Resort** (sepilok.com) has stunning lakeside gardens and is within easy walking distance of the Kabili-Sepilok Forest Reserve and its orang-utan sanctuary. **Kinabatanagan Riverside Lodge** makes a great base for encounters with proboscis monkeys, while the rustic **Borneo Rainforest Lodge** (borneorainforestlodge.com) lies in the heart of primary rainforest in the Danum Valley and offers treetop safaris and night walks.

For orang-utans in **Sumatra, Bukit Lawang Cottages** is close to a rehabilitation centre for the endangered Sumatran species of the great ape and is well located for hikes in Gunung Leuser National Park.

Primate-watching code of conduct

✅ **Follow the advice of your guides** They're there to keep you and the primates safe.

✅ **Keep your distance** Respect minimum distance rules.

✅ **Speak softly, if at all** Silence is best when in the company of primates, especially the great apes.

✅ **Kneel or sit** You'll appear less intimidating.

✅ **Turn off your camera's flash** Blinding bursts of light will startle animals used to the shadowy world of forests.

✅ **Respect their habitat** Keep to trails, walk single file and remember not to smoke or take food with you.

❌ **Don't stare** Prolonged, direct eye contact with a primate may be mistaken for a challenge. Avoid potential confrontation by glancing sideways.

❌ **Don't pass on your germs** Infectious viruses can be transmitted from humans to primates with lethal consequences. If you have a cold, do the right thing and stay in your lodge rather than go primate watching.

❌ **Don't point** Any sudden movement can be frightening to wild primates, or seen as a threat.

❌ **Don't feed or try to pet them** Giving handouts to primates can adversely affect their health and behaviour, while any attempt to touch them is asking to be bitten. Diseases can also be transmitted through contact.

Too close for comfort? A mountain gorilla passes within a couple of metres of a guide

Gorilla beringei beringei Volcanoes National Park, Rwanda

There's a 7-m limit on how close you are allowed to get to mountain gorillas – but they don't know that. Relaxed individuals may pass right by you. If that happens, it's imperative that you remain calm and quiet, slowly withdrawing to give the gorillas some space.

🔅 **Exposure, camera shake and rain – three things to watch out for when photographing primates in the rainforest**

Your camera may compensate for the dim light (and dark fur) by over-exposing. Try a few test shots and add up to 1+ stop of exposure compensation if necessary. The use of flash or tripods are not allowed, so set a high ISO (400-600), get down on your hands and knees and rest the camera on the ground to help prevent camera shake. Lenses with image stabilisation also help. Remember to protect your camera from rain with a plastic cover and lens hood.

▶▶ **0530** Wake-up call (that's for you, not the gorillas – they're probably still napping in the forest).

▶▶ **0600** Tea and a light snack at your lodge; drive to the national park HQ. Don't forget essential kit: walking boots, waterproof jacket and trousers (or gaiters), gardening-style gloves to protect against stinging nettles, binoculars, camera gear, water bottle and a few US$10 notes for hiring a porter and tipping your guide.

▶▶ **0700** At the park HQ, check that your permits are in order and wait to be assigned your gorilla group (you may be able to choose one depending on your preference for a short or long hike). Maximum of eight people per group.

▶▶ **0730** Briefing at park HQ with your guide in which you'll learn about the family structure of your assigned troop, and some general gorilla facts.

▶▶ **0745** Short drive to the forest access point nearest to your gorilla group.

▶▶ **0800** Meet your porters. They can be hired (usually for around US$10 a trek) to carry your daypack. Walking sticks are often available too.

▶▶ **0815** Start walking. Sometimes you'll hike straight into forest, but more often than not, there will be a short stroll across farmland to the national park boundary.

▶▶ **0845** Before entering the national park your guide will give a second briefing, this time on gorilla etiquette (see left, Primate-watching code of conduct). Now is the time for anyone with a cold to confess and go back – human viruses are potentially lethal to gorillas. Remember, too, that no food must be taken into the forest.

▶▶ **0900** Start hiking single file into the forest, usually following buffalo trails. Keep an eye open for gorilla dung and nest sites.

▶▶ **1100** Meet the scouts that located the gorilla family at daybreak and have been updating your guide by radio on their movements. Speak softly, if at all; leave your daypacks and walking sticks with the scouts; ensure that your camera flash is turned off (set a high ISO speed to compensate), then follow your guide towards the still-hidden gorillas.

▶▶ **1110** Your allotted hour with the gorillas begins. It passes quickly, so be sure to lower your camera occasionally to savour the atmosphere, sounds and smells. Always be alert to your guide's instructions. He or she will be constantly judging the gorillas' mood and behaviour.

▶▶ **1210** Your guide ushers you away; remain silent until you are well clear of the gorillas.

Tales from the wild | in the midst of mountain gorillas

Volcanoes National Park, Rwanda

Meeting mountain gorillas is the main event in Rwanda's Volcanoes National Park, but golden monkeys make an impressive warm-up act. Unique to the foothills of the Virunga Mountains, a population of around 3,700 of these perky primates inhabits the bamboo forest on the lower slopes of the now dormant peaks. A morning spent tracking them before trying your luck with gorillas has its advantages. It not only stretches your legs and introduces you to the tangled chaos of the forest, but it also removes the blinkers and opens your eyes to the wider environment of this spectacular corner of the Great Rift Valley.

I begin my date with the golden monkeys with an early morning briefing at the national park headquarters before being driven to the nearest forest access point. There, we hand daypacks to porters (an important source of local employment) and collect stout, wooden walking sticks. Before setting off, our guide establishes radio contact with trackers who have been in the forest since sunrise, locating the monkeys.

To begin with, we follow paths through farmland where villagers tend fields of potatoes and beans. The transition from patchwork fields to impenetrable forest is abrupt. We thread, single file, into a meshwork of bamboo and after an hour, rendezvous with the trackers. They motion to where the monkeys are and we edge forward, straining for our first glimpse. As it turns out, the golden monkeys are keen to put on a performance for us, leaping and tumbling about in a sunny glade a few metres from where we crouch.

Unlike gorillas, there is no minimum distance for approaching golden monkeys and so, once the rough and tumble of playtime is over, we follow them as they begin dispersing through the forest. At times we are totally surrounded by dozens of curious, bobbing faces, peering at us as they chew on bamboo.

The following morning, cloud is slumped over 3,474-m Gahinga and there is an ominous roll of thunder as we begin walking towards the mountain. Somewhere on the misty slopes above us, trackers have located the Kwitonda troop of mountain gorillas.

It's a slow, stuttering slog up the mountain, pigeon-stepping along elephant and buffalo trails riddled with exposed roots and hemmed in by vines. Mist transforms the forest to a monotone blur of ferns and lichen-clad trees. The plant life is so intense, so pressing, that our first clue as to the apes' presence is a deep, guttural rumbling sound – the unmistakable contact call of a silverback mountain gorilla. He's letting us know that we've been seen. His message is clear – this encounter is entirely on his terms.

Our guide ushers us forwards and there he is… domed head and massive shoulders protruding from under a bush. He hasn't even bothered to turn and look at us, so engrossed is he by the half-shredded branch held in his great, balled fists.

Then, without warning, he rises on all fours and walks towards me, reaching out to pluck a branch that's lying less than a metre from where I'm huddled.

Her infant steals the show, tightrope walking along a vine and repeatedly falling off. Elsewhere, two juveniles lick raindrops off each other's fur

Suddenly, a great mass of black fur is towering over me, brow ridges bunched above amber eyes; bushy sideburns around flared nostrils. Snapping the branch in half, as if he's just partaken of a pretzel, the silverback rocks back onto his haunches and starts chewing. Several seconds pass before I realise there's an unused camera lying in my lap.

Slowly withdrawing from the silverback, our guide continually mimicking his throaty calls to keep the great ape at ease, we edge towards an adult female. Her infant steals the show, tightrope walking along a vine and repeatedly falling off. Elsewhere, two juveniles lick raindrops off each other's fur.

Our allotted hour with the gorillas passes quickly and all too soon we are shuffling back down the mountain. Making eye contact – albeit briefly – is often hyped as the definitive experience of encountering mountain gorillas, and there's no doubt that you do feel as if you're connecting with another mind. But simply seeing them – behaving naturally in their mountain forest stronghold and calmly accepting human visitors – is equally poignant.

From top, left to right – Sabinyo Silverback Lodge; juvenile, adult female and silverback mountain gorilla; golden monkey; Rwenzori chameleon; trekking through montane forest

Mountain gorilla (*Gorilla beringei beringei*) and golden monkey (*Cercopithecus kandti*) Volcanoes National Park, Rwanda

Making tracks

🜨 **Expert Africa** (expertafrica.com) can arrange tailor-made safaris to see mountain gorillas and golden monkeys in Volcanoes National Park.

✈ **Kenya Airways** (kenya-airways.com) has flights from Nairobi to Kigali, from where it's a 2-3 hr drive to Volcanoes National Park.

🛏 **Sabinyo Silverback Lodge** (governorscamp.com) supports various community conservation projects in the area.

🕓 GMT+2

☀ Year round, but July-August is the best time.

ⓘ rwandatourism.com

🌐 **International Gorilla Conservation Programme** (igcp.org)

Tales from the wild | making contact with the cousins

Toro-Semliki Game Reserve, Uganda

They're watching us, I'm sure of it. And laughing, too. Great chesty whoops and high-pitched hysterics echoing through the forest. My guide, Simon, calls it 'pant-hooting' – a common method of communication. But then he would – he's a biologist. My theory is that the chimpanzees are simply enjoying a good joke.

Look at it from their point of view – along come their cousins, showing off on all-twos, way up the evolutionary tree. Then a few steps in the primeval forest and all they seem capable of is tripping over tree stumps, cursing horseflies and falling in streams. I'd laugh if I was a chimp.

Fortunately we humans have also evolved a sense of humour. After insect repellent, it's the most essential thing for tracking our closest relatives through their Ugandan forest home. This is our third dawn trek in search of chimpanzees – and each time they've given us the slip. Our scout, Adolph, isn't surprised. He didn't dream of chimps last night. Until he does, he says we might as well have a lie-in.

"These chimps are wild," Simon explains as we venture back into the forest the next morning. "Habituation takes years – they're still wary of us."

The transition from savanna to forest is abrupt. One moment I am walking tall, wading through chest-high grass, the pepper-sweet tang of Africa spicing my nostrils – the next, I'm bent double beneath a pressing tangle of trees and vines; a twilight world permeated by the loamy odour of decay. We follow a scant path, walking silently in single file. Adolph hunts for clues: a knuckle print or shreds of bark where the chimps have been searching for grubs. Suddenly he freezes. "If it's buffalo, keep calm," whispers Simon. "Look around; find a tree to climb if they charge."

I nod slowly, my eyes flicking through tears of sweat from one tree to the next. Each one is either thinner than my wrist or sprouts its lowest branch 10 yards above my head.

I can hear footsteps now – a rhythmic patter on brittle leaves. Whatever it is, is moving towards us – fast. I focus on a gap in the meshwork of plants. Something dark passes behind it. Surely too small for a chimp, though? I glance at Adolph. The tension has already slipped from his body. Once again the chimps have eluded us. Even as the guineafowl emerge into a clearing ahead of us, we hear a distant outburst of pant-hooting. "You're right, I think they're laughing at us," says Simon. He shakes his head, Adolph shrugs and I slap a horsefly.

At dusk, we hold vigil at the edge of the forest. Chimpanzees are creatures of habit. Each evening they build sleeping nests and call loudly to each other as they settle down – a kind of ape-version of *The Waltons*.

But we hear nothing more than the trill of cicadas. Without some kind of clue, we don't stand a chance of finding them. "Let's give it another 10 minutes," suggests Simon. They call in less than two. Adolph judges their position and soon we are scampering through the forest, sweat slicked across our backs and faces. Then Adolph whistles softly and clenches his fist.

"We're so close!" Simon murmurs. "If only they'd call again, we could pinpoint where they're nesting." But the forest has fallen silent. As bats flicker around our heads in the murky slide towards night we have no choice but to turn back.

Crouching on damp leaf litter the following dawn, we sift the sounds of the forest. A rustle of leaves momentarily lifts our heads and our hopes. But it's a troop of black and white colobus monkeys performing leaps of faith in the canopy. We sit and wait. Twitching in its death throes, a praying mantis is edging towards me, carried aloft on a grisly tide of safari ants. I begin to accept defeat...

Then Adolph tenses and I see the familiar fist signal. He's seen something – a branch moving? We walk a few paces off the trail, then simultaneously freeze and sink to the ground, like balloons deflating. "There!" Simon's voice is hoarse. I follow his stare, but my brain is scrambled by the riot of plants. "They're climbing out of that tree." Eyes bulging, chin straining forwards, he's willing me to spot them.

"Yes!" I breathe. "I see one!"

A hairy shoulder; hands and feet clasped around a trunk – four chimps are shinning down the tree. Briefly, a face appears around the trunk, eyes staring as intently as mine. It's the merest glimpse and then they're gone – moving silently like smoke in the forest. Adolph smiles. "Last night," he whispers, "I dreamed of chimps."

Monkey business – tracking unhabituated chimpanzees in their forest stronghold requires patience, insect repellent and a good sense of humour

Pan troglodytes
Uganda

Semliki Forest forms the easternmost reaches of the Central African rainforest and supports a diverse range of species, including chimpanzee, forest elephant, buffalo, leopard and black and white colobus. At least 30 endemic bird species are also found there.

Toro-Semliki Game Reserve
Uganda
Entebbe
Lake Victoria

Making tracks

↻ Several operators, such as **World Primate Safaris** (worldprimatesafaris.com), can tailor make safaris to Uganda which include chimp tracking in either Semliki or Kibale Forest.

✈ Semliki is a 1 hr drive from Fort Portal, or 1 hr flight from Entebbe.

⌂ With views of the Virungas, **Semliki Lodge** (wildplacesafrica.com) has large, luxurious tents.

🕒 GMT+3

☀ Year round. Main rains April to May and November to December.

ⓘ visituganda.com

● **Ape Alliance** (4apes.com/chimpanzee)

Tales from the wild | making contact with the cousins

> **66 99** They're watching us, I'm sure of it. And laughing, too. Great chesty whoops and high-pitched hysterics echoing through the forest. My guide, Simon, calls it 'pant-hooting' – a common method of communication. But then he would – he's a biologist. My theory is that the chimpanzees are simply enjoying a good joke. Along come their cousins, showing off on all-twos, way up the evolutionary tree. Then a few steps in the primeval forest and all they seem capabable of is tripping over tree stumps, cursing horseflies and falling in streams. I'd laugh if I was a chimp

William Gray

it's a wild life

Amanda Marks | Tribes Travel | tribes.co.uk

My big five
1 **Uganda** for gorilla and chimp trekking.
2 **Galápagos Islands** for incredible bird and marine species.
3 **Botswana** for outstanding wild dog sightings and much more.
4 **South Luangwa**, Zambia, for thrilling walking safaris.
5 **Tanzania** – one of my perennial favourites.

> **66 99** I wasn't expecting my reaction to chimps in the wild to be quite so visceral. Their calls echo through the forest and reverberate through your chest well before you spot them – it's a very primeval experience which makes your body tingle. It's very different from meeting the generally more chilled out gorillas. The chimps move so quickly, they beat tree roots, they're so loud, and seem so much more aggressive that it's altogether a more edgy, thrilling experience. Yet they can also be calm and when you look into their eyes or watch their hands, you absolutely know that this animal is not so very different from us.

Brief encounters | snow leopard

Don't get too excited. Scientists who have dedicated their entire lives to studying these exquisite, endangered big cats in their high mountain strongholds may have only glimpsed them on a few occasions. The snow leopard is the Holy Grail of wildlife encounters. Spot this silver-coated feline slinking along an icy ridge or peering from behind a boulder and you are guaranteed eternal contentment – as long as your heart starts beating again. But where to begin your quest? Probably the best bet is to join a conservation holiday in the remote mountains of Central Asia where you will be assisting local field workers to track and monitor these elusive beasts.

The **Snow Leopard Conservancy** (snowleopard conservancy.org) works on community-based conservation projects to protect the snow leopard and help local farming communities coexist with the big cat. Gathering data on such a secretive, wide-ranging, mountain-dwelling species, however, is no easy task. But by collaborating with conservation holiday operators, the Snow Leopard Conservancy (and other organizations, such as WWF Russia) gets the additional resources and manpower it needs for collecting crucial information for protection plans.

One such partner is California-based **KarmaQuest Adventure Travel** (karmaquests.com). Its snow leopard tracking trips focus on the remote valleys of Hemis National Park in Ladakh, India. Accompanied by local experts, you'll look for signs of snow leopard prey (blue sheep), scent marks, prints and scats. You may not spot the big cat itself, but other wildlife in the area includes brown bear, ibex, wolf, wild yak, golden eagle and bearded vulture.

The Snow Leopard Conservancy also collaborates with **Biosphere Expeditions** (biosphere-expeditions.org) on its snow leopard conservation holidays in the Altai Mountains. Soaring from open steppes this rugged range is an important corridor for snow leopards moving between Mongolia and Russia, but more data is needed before a conservation management plan can drawn up.

Trekking from a base camp at 2,300 m, work centres around locating tracks, scats, kills and, with luck, the cats themselves.

Silver shadow – the snow leopard has an almost ethereal presence in the mountains of Central Asia

Uncia uncia
Ladakh, India

Found in 12 countries across Central Asia, there are an estimated 4,500-7,000 snow leopards left in the wild.

The snow leopard is the Holy Grail of wildlife encounters. Spot this silver-coated feline slinking along an icy ridge or peering from behind a boulder and you are guaranteed eternal contentment

Brief encounters | wolf

Persecuted for centuries, the wolf has been eradicated from much of its original territory. Only recently, with greater tolerance from landowners and a more enlightened conservation policy, have these wonderful animals begun to reclaim their old haunts. Nothing embodies a wild place with more vivacity and spirit than a pack of free-roaming wolves; ancient forests echoing with their haunting cries and every other animal alert to their presence.

Despite being created in 1872 (as the United States' first national park) Yellowstone continued to lose its grey wolves until 1926 when the last one was shot. A reintroduction programme began in 1995 and the park now supports around 100 wolves in 14 packs. Guided wolf-tracking tours, available from **The Wild Side** (wolftracker.com), feature spring-time treks in the Lamar Valley where wolf hotspots include Hellroaring Creek. During winter, the trips are based at Buffalo Ranch, with snowshoe forays to Rose Creek – the original release site for Yellowstone's wolves.

Winter and spring are generally the best times for tracking wolves as you're more likely to find their tracks in the snow. In Scandinavia, **Wild Sweden** (wildsweden.com) offers three-day winter wolf tracking trips in partnership with the Grimso Wildlife Research Station, near Lindesberg. **Wildlife & Wilderness** (wildlifewilderness.com) operate trips to find wolves, bears, European bison and lynx in Poland's Bialoweiza Forest National Park, while **Biosphere Expeditions** (biosphere-expeditions.org) runs a wolf-tracking ecovolunteer project in the Carpathian Mountains of Slovakia.

Perhaps the most remarkable story of wolf revival in Europe in recent years is the species' reclamation of the French Alps (spreading west from a relic population in Italy). The first official sightings of wolves in the Alpes Maritimes were in the early 1990s and it is now thought that there are at least two packs – surviving, no doubt, on the region's healthy numbers of chamois, mouflon, wild boar and deer. **Undiscovered Alps** (undiscoveredalps.com) provides a chance to track these canny predators in the company of a local mountain guide, sleeping in remote winter refuges deep in wolf territory.

Running wild – wolves are making a comeback in much of their former range

Canis lupis lupis
Kuhmo, Finland

The grey wolf and European wolf are the largest members of the Canidae family, which also includes the coyote of North and Central America, the Australian dingo, Ethiopian wolf, South American maned wolf, African wild dog and Arctic fox.

Nothing embodies a wild place with more vivacity and spirit than a pack of free-roaming wolves; ancient forests echoing with their haunting cries and every other animal alert to their presence

Bear watching

The increasing popularity of bear-watching holidays must have something to do with the cute-and-cuddly appeal of the furry family Ursidae. However, you only have to watch sparring 600-kg polar bears cuffing each other on the Arctic tundra or a full-grown grizzly standing 3 m tall on its hind legs to quash any misconceptions that these formidable predators are mere teddy bears.

Bears can be extremely dangerous, particularly when surprised or when they've been encouraged to associate humans with food, and they demand the same high levels of respect and space as any wild animal you might encounter on holiday.

Although the Ursidae family has eight members (including the rare and elusive giant panda, sun bear and spectacled bear), most bear-watching trips focus on three species: brown, black and polar.

Despite the environmental threats facing their Arctic realm, polar bears are still reliably seen near Churchill on the shores of Hudson Bay where, each autumn, tundra buggies provide incredible opportunities for close-up views. Svalbard also supports good numbers of the 'ice bear'.

American black bears can be glimpsed in forests from Vancouver Island to the Appalachian Mountains, but British Columbia is by far the best location for reliable sightings. You can also find white 'spirit bears' here. They're not a separate species – just black bears with a genetic colour variation – but a quest for one of these rare, honey-coloured beauties on Princess Royal Island can almost reach mystical proportions.

The Asiatic black bear is a separate species to its North American cousin. Confined to hilly forests in South Asia it's not often seen. In fact, you are more likely to glimpse the sloth bear, usually as a shaggy-coated blur lolloping through the forests of Indian national parks like Ranthambhore and Satpura.

It's the brown bear, however, that is the most widespread and commonly seen of the family.

Ranging from North America, through Europe to wilderness areas of Russia, *Ursus arctos* is the subject of much head-scratching by taxonomists keen to classify the various subspecies of this archetypal bear.

For the wildlife traveller, there are various honeypot locations, each with their own subspecies of brown bear. The grizzly bear (*Ursus arctos horribilis*) roams the Great Bear Rainforest of British Columbia, as well as Alaska and the Northwest United States. A heavyweight version, known as the Kodiak bear (*Ursus arctos middendorffi*) is found in the Kodiak Archipelago of Southwestern Alaska. For an encounter with Eurasian brown bears (*Ursus arctos arctos*) head for the wild forests of Finland and Romania or, if you're feeling intrepid, track down *Ursus arctos beringianus* on Russia's Kamchatka Peninsula.

Wherever you end up going, you're in for a treat. As the world's largest land predators, bears have an almost regal presence. They are also supremely intelligent and adaptable, displaying a range of behaviour that will have you enthralled – whether you are watching grizzlies fishing for salmon, polar bears swimming along channels in pack ice or black bears ripping at bark on a quest for beetle grubs.

> Bears display a range of behaviour that will have you enthralled – whether you are watching grizzlies fishing for salmon, polar bears swimming along channels in pack ice or black bears ripping at bark on a quest for beetle grubs

On the trail of the giant panda

It might be the most conspicuous-looking of the Ursidae family, but there is nothing black and white about tracking the giant panda (*Ailuropoda melanoleuca*) in its native bamboo forests, high on the slopes of the Qinling Mountains in China's Shaanxi province. Focus your efforts on three nature reserves: Foping, Laoxiancheng and Changqing. All three are centres for giant panda tracking, although sightings are never guaranteed. Giant pandas are masters of evasion, and you'll be hiking through dense vegetation. Simply being in the same habitat as this icon of conservation, however, can be rewarding enough – and there is always the chance you'll spot other rare species, such as golden snub-nosed monkey, takin and clouded leopard. Accommodation is in nearby villages, staying in local guesthouses or hostels.

The one that didn't get away – a grizzly bear grabs a quick bite in Alaska

Ursus arctos horribilis
Brooks River, Katmai National Park, Alaska

Although grizzlies are partial to sushi (gathering at rivers throughout Alaska and British Columbia during salmon spawning season), they are not particularly fussy feeders and will happily eat anything from plants, berries, roots, seaweed and fungi to insects, birds, mammals and carrion.

Bear watching | inspiration

North America

① Kodiak Archipelago, Alaska, USA
Some 3,500 brown bears inhabit these islands. Hiking, kayaking and camping trips are available in Kodiak National Wildlife Refuge.
➤➤ July to September

② Katmai National Park, Alaska, USA
One of the most spectacular bear-viewing locations in the world, Brooks Falls is leaping with salmon each summer, attracting large gatherings of hungry grizzlies.
➤➤ July to August

③ Great Bear Rainforest, British Columbia, Canada
Bella Coola is the gateway to this magestic mosaic of coastal mountains, river valleys and dense forests – home to healthy populations of both grizzly and black bears, as well as the white 'spirit bears' of Princess Royal Island. Further north, Southeast Alaska's Admiralty Island is known by local Tlingit Indians as the 'Fortress of the Bears.'
➤➤ Summer, but aim for late August to September for grizzlies fishing Atnarko River.

④ Yellowstone National Park, Wyoming, USA
Grizzly bears are most often seen in the Hayden and Lamar Valleys and around the Dunraven Pass area.
➤➤ June to September

⑤ Churchill, Manitoba, Canada
Polar bear capital of the world, offering tundra buggy tours along the shores of Hudson Bay.
➤➤ October to November

⑥ Laurentide Wildlife Reserve, Quebec, Canada
Canoe along the Pikauba River, scanning the forested shoreline for black bears.
➤➤ June to August

⑦ Great Smoky Mountains National Park, Tennessee, USA
Around 1,500 black bears inhabit this protected swathe of the Appalachians. Your best chances of spotting one are in open areas like Cataloochee and Cades Cove.
➤➤ May to September

South America

⑧ Northwest Andes
The Andean spectacled bear is notoriously elusive. Try cloud forest reserves in Ecuador or visit the Chaparri Ecological Reserve, a bear rescue centre in Peru.
➤➤ Year round

Europe

⑨ Romania
The Carpathian Mountains are a stronghold for Eurasian brown bears. You can see them in Bulgaria, Slovakia and Ukraine, but Romania's Kingstone Mountain National Park, near Zarnesti, promises some of the best sightings.
➤➤ May to September

⑩ Finland
Deep in the taiga forest of Finland's Kainuu wilderness, the Martinselkosen Eräkeskus wildlife centre is the perfect base for observing brown bears from special hides.
➤➤ June to August

⑪ Svalbard
Travel by expedition ship through the wildlife-rich Svalbard archipelago (see p120-121) for riveting encounters with polar bears and other Arctic species such as walrus and bearded seal.
➤➤ June to October

Asia

⑫ India
Tigers may be foremost in your sights on an Indian safari, but it's worth giving that 'shadow' in the woods a second glance – it could be the secretive sloth bear.
➤➤ November to June

⑬ Southeast Asia
You would be lucky indeed to glimpse a sun bear in the wild. These shy creatures inhabit dense rainforest.
➤➤ Year round

⑭ Kamchatka, Russia
Volcanoes provide a spectacular backdrop to viewing Kamchatka's brown bears. Try a river rafting trip.
➤➤ July to September

Bear watching | game plan

The bear necessities for a good grizzly sighting might simply be a salmon-spawning river and a safe vantage point. For polar bears, make that a tundra buggy with 1.7-m-high wheels or a zodiac launched from an expedition ship. You can also stay overnight in a tundra buggy, sleep on a floating lodge or plan a backcountry camping expedition. Bear-watching holidays are bristling with adventure.

Where to stay

In **Alaska**, **Brooks Falls Lodge** (katmailand.com) in Katmai National Park is a short walk from the famed stretch of river where as many as 50 bears can be viewed fishing during peak salmon season. The lodge's hearty Alaskan fare will ensure that you are also well fed, while timber cabins provide comfortable accommodation. **Alaska Adventures** (alaska-wildlife-cruises.com) gets you afloat in Katmai aboard a 24-m cruiser, while Denali's **Kantishna Roadhouse** (kantishnaroadhouse.com) puts you right in the heart of Alaska's premier national park.

British Columbia has several lodges in prime bear-viewing locations, including **Tweedsmuir Park Lodge** (tweedsmuirparklodge.com) in Bella Coola Valley; the floating **Great Bear Lodge** (greatbeartours.com), **Knight Inlet Lodge** (knightinletlodge.com) in Glendale Cove and the **Spirit Bear Lodge** (spiritbear.com) on Princess Royal Island. See pages 156-157 for details. With eight double cabins, the 21-m ketch **Island Roamer** (bluewateradventures.ca) plies the coastline of the Great Bear Rainforest.

In **Churchill**, the **Tundra Lodge** (greatwhitebeartours.com) sleeps up to 36 people in a static 'train' of wheeled cabins stationed close by the shore of Hudson Bay in the Churchill Wildlife Management Area – a polar bear watcher's dream. The lodge has two sleepers, a lounge car and a dining car.

With room for 26, **Martinselkosen Eräkeskus Wildlife Centre** (martinselkonen.fi) in **Finland** has excellent accommodation, including a sauna, while **Elena Guesthouse** (pensiuneaelena.ro) in Zarnesti, **Romania** sleeps 16 and offers delicious local cooking.

In **Svalbard**, various expedition vessels explore the archipelago's dramatic coastline each summer. See pages 292-293.

Tundra Lodge wake-up call
Polar bear, Churchill

Bear essentials | Staying safe

✅ **Make some noise!** Bears don't like surprises, so make them aware of your presence on trails by clapping, shouting or singing. Don't hike after dark.

❌ **Do not run or climb trees.** You can't outrun a bear and it may elicit a charge. Black bears and some grizzlies are also good climbers. In the event of a mock charge, stand your ground, wave your arms and shout until the bear stops, then slowly back away. In the very rare event of an attack, drop to the ground, lie face down, and clasp your hands behind your neck. Lie still and silent so as not to provoke the bear further.

✅ **Give bears space.** Use telephoto lenses to photograph them.

❌ **Do not leave food out.** Hang food out of reach of bears or use bear-proof containers. Never store food inside your tent and avoid cooking food that can make your clothing smell (ie bacon).

American black bear
Ursus americanus
Highly adaptable, even venturing near cities; cubs leave winter den Apr-May
⊗ Non-Arctic North America
◗ Mainly forest
✽ Vegetation, insects, meat

Brown bear
Ursus arctos
Varies in colour from blond to black; weight up to 450 kg
⊗ NW North America, Europe, Northern Asia
◗ Tundra, boreal forest
✽ Berries, fish, mammals etc

Polar bear
Ursus maritimus
Population estimated at 25,000; good swimmers using webbed front paws
⊗ Coastal Arctic
◗ Tundra, sea ice
✽ Seals, fish, carrion, berries

Sloth bear
Ursus ursinus
Lack of front teeth enables them to suck up insects; cubs ride mother's back
⊗ Indian Subcontinent
◗ Forest, grassland
✽ Termites, honey, fruit

Tales from the wild | eye to eye with the ice bear

Churchill, Manitoba, Canada

Polar bears can weigh 650 kg and sprint at over 40 kph. They are fearless, powerful hunters that can smell you coming from miles off. That's why I'm in a Tundra Buggy – a giant-wheeled 'snow bus' that provides a safe vantage from which to observe these magnificent beasts. Timing is crucial though. Peak period is October-November when they congregate near Churchill, a Canadian frontier town rubbed raw by frigid winds that howl across Hudson Bay.

Our polar bear safari sets off at a glacial pace, the buggy creeping through a tundra landscape of lichen-blotched rocks and wind-pruned shrubs. We splash through shallow lakes and crunch over the shingly ridges of glacial eskers, always following rough tracks so as not to damage this fragile habitat.

It takes a good half hour to reach the shores of Hudson Bay (a mile away) where a northerly wind has white-ribbed the sea and piled spume against huge drifts of kelp heaped along rock-strewn beaches. It's a harsh environment, particularly during late autumn before the first snows have smoothed things over.

Tossed around by the wind like loose refuse sacks, ravens twist and turn; a lone tundra swan hunkers down in a pond and, briefly, we spot a peregrine falcon scything above the tundra, scattering willow ptarmigan through a patch of dwarf birch.

Our first polar bear is dozing on rocks behind the beach. The buggy edges to within 12 m of him, but the bear's not bothered by our presence. He barely glances towards us before turning his attention to a full pedicure of his forepaws. Grooming finished, he yawns, rolls over and goes back to sleep, oblivious, it seems, to the dozen or so pairs of human eyes transfixed by his every move. After all, to him it's just another day waiting for the bay to freeze over.

This ice bear seems particularly chilled, so we leave him in peace and trundle on across the saturated landscape, more water than land it seems (an appropriate haunt of *Ursus maritimus*).

Other wildlife to be found here includes arctic fox, caribou and several species of birds, including gyrfalcons and snowy owls. Apart from a flurry of willow ptarmigans, however, we have a quiet couple of hours – a game drive in slow motion. The tundra yields its natural treasures slowly. This is not a place to be rushed. You have to be patient and look hard.

It helps, of course, if your Tundra Buggy driver knows a particularly good spot for polar bears. An exposed point jutting into the bay has been a favoured haunt for years. Overnight buggies are set up here for the season, both for scientists and tourists.

Soon we have found three bears. The first is sleepy and secretive, barely visible in a birch thicket. But the other two, a young male and an older male with a scar on his right shoulder and a full Roman nose, are out in the open. The youngster is in playful mood and keeps wandering over to the older bear and butting him. No reaction. Still looking for mischief, he ambles towards a Tundra Buggy and gives it a good once-over, gnawing a tyre, checking out the suspension and straining upright on his hindlegs to sniff at the tourists who are craning over the outdoor viewing platform at the rear of the buggy.

> **The youngster is in playful mood and keeps wandering over to the older bear and butting or nudging him. No reaction. Still looking for mischief, he ambles towards a Tundra Buggy and gives it a good once-over**

When this loses its novelty, he returns to the older bear and succeeds in getting him riled enough to have a play fight, both bears taking swipes at each other, standing up in face-offs and baring teeth. The older bear uses his massive weight and height advantage to keep the youngster at arm's length, but after 10 minutes or so he's clearly bored with such juvenile behaviour and finds himself a quiet patch of scrub to hide in.

The younger bear redirects his attention to the tundra buggies, this time ambling over to ours. He rears up and places two massive paws on the side of the viewing platform and, for a brief moment, I am staring into the eyes of a wild polar bear, his black muzzle snuffling a few feet below me.

When push comes to shove – polar bears sparring on the tundra, waiting for Hudson Bay to freeze over so they can move out onto the ice to hunt seals

Ursus maritimus
Churchill, Manitoba

Male polar bears frequently engage in these tests of strength when they congregate along the coast of Hudson Bay. Damage is rarely inflicted.

Hudson Bay
• Churchill
Manitoba
Winnipeg

Making tracks

🌀 The **Great Canadian Travel Company** (greatcanadiantravel.com) offers three- to eight-day itineraries in Churchill, while UK tour operators include **Discover the World** (discover-the-world.co.uk).

✈ Flights with **Calm Air** (calmair.com) connect Winnipeg with Churchill, or take the 43-hr train journey (viarail.com).

🛏 **Lazy Bear Lodge** (lazybearlodge.com)

🕐 GMT-5 (Mar-Nov), GMT-6 (Dec-Feb)

☀ October to November is peak season for bears; see p153 for summer wildlife highlights.

ⓘ churchill.ca

🌐 polarbears international.org

the
**Tundra
Buggy**
ADVENTURE

Tales from the wild | hiking in bear country

Olympic National Park, Washington State, USA

Suddenly, we realise we're totally alone. In the time it has taken to walk a few hundred metres from the visitor centre, the forest has drawn a green veil around us; a silent shroud of moss and leaves strung between soaring trunks of Sitka spruce and western hemlock. Some of the trees are colossal. Their bases must be 10 m around; their crowns 60 m or more above our craning necks. Layer upon layer of branches filter the rays of sun so that by the time they permeate to the forest floor, everything is suffused with a soft, green haze. Even sound is muted. I can hear the Hoh River, but it's a murmur among the trees – as if the forest is guarding its whereabouts.

One of North America's last great wildernesses, Olympic National Park is a primeval realm of mountains and forests – ideal country for backcountry hikes (including the 29-km Hoh River Trail) and perfect territory for numerous black bears.

"Been a problem bear in Elwha Valley," a ranger at the visitor centre confided in us earlier. "When he got a whiff of some hikers' lunch they just upped and went, leaving the food behind. Result: bear associates humans with free food." He went on to describe how such bears have been known to 'ambush' hikers once they'd discovered this association – but armed rangers soon put an end to it. A fed bear is a dead bear.

"You got bells?" the ranger asked us.

We nodded and coyly revealed the two small, silver bells on Velcro wrist straps.

"That's great!" he said. "The most dangerous bear is a surprised bear."

There can be few occasions in the ancient history of North America's most pristine temperate rain forest when its brooding silence has been shattered by sporadic outbursts of singing, accompanied by bear bells and clapping hands on particularly dark and spooky corners. But it seems to work. We meet no bears on our first day's 14-km hike.

We pitch our tent at Olympus Campsite – a grand title for what amounts to a deserted ranger's hut, a long-drop toilet and a few grassy clearings beside the River Hoh. Our next priority is dinner. Setting up our wilderness kitchen on a gravel bar next to the milky, glacial melt-waters of the river, we follow the first basic rule for cooking in bear country – prepare food away from your tent. Dinner-for-two consists of a single foil bag containing the dehydrated ingredients of what is optimistically entitled 'almond chicken'. Simply add boiling water, stand for ten minutes *et voilà!* – a quick and simple meal that is completely odourless and lacking in any flavour; perfect when there might be bears around.

Squatting on stranded logs, we take turns dipping our spoons into the dinner bag. The river valley faces west and we watch the conifer-clad slopes smoulder in the sunset as swarms of lacewings drift above the river, glowing like fairies in the golden evening light.

We linger as long as we dare – but night falls quickly in the forest. Hurrying back to our tent we locate the nearest bear wire, a contraption installed by rangers to enable hikers to store food (and other 'high odour' items) out of reach of bears. Basically, it consists of a system of cables and pulleys tied between two trees that you can use to suspend things about 4 m above ground – which is worryingly the kind of height you need to put something to stop a full-grown black bear reaching it on tiptoes.

Having hoisted our bag of food and cooking equipment, we scurry in to our tent, only to emerge a few minutes later to lower the bag again when we discover what 14 km of trekking has done to our socks. Satisfied that our tent is a 'pong-free' zone, we slip into a fitful sleep – constantly straining to hear noises of creatures that aren't there.

Inconsiderate bladders haul us outside sometime during the night. Like a pair of rabbits caught in the open, we are all ears and eyes. But the night seems calm and peaceful; the river chuckling nearby and a

Whether it's a subtle shift of breeze or a deeper instinct that warns us, I'm not sure. But suddenly, the air is heavy with the unmistakable, cloying odour of an animal

Land of giants – a hiker pauses beside the colossal trunk of a Sitka spruce

Picea sitchensis
Hoh River Trail, Olympic National Park, USA

Offering easy to moderate hiking, the 29-km Hoh River Trail passes through a range of habitats, from temperate rainforest to subalpine meadow.

Making tracks

◗ **Seattle Tours** (seattletours.us) offers guided trips to Olympic National Park.
✈ **Kenmore Air Express** (kenmoreair.com) flies from Seattle to Port Angeles, the park's main access point. You can also catch the **Black Ball Ferry** (cohoferry.com) from Victoria, BC.
▭ Permits can be obtained from Hoh Visitor Center or Port Angeles **Wilderness Information Center** (T360 565-3100) which can also advise on trailhead shuttles.
🕐 GMT-8
☾ Late June to September.
ⓘ nps.gov/olym
⚠ All food, garbage and scented items must be stored in bear canisters.

spattering of stars arching through a gap in the black and silent forest.

At dawn we are sipping coffee on the gravel bar. A light frost glistens on the pebbles while tendrils of mist squirm above the river. By the time the first glancing rays of sunlight have enflamed the riverside maples, resplendent in autumn foliage, we are back on the trail. The valley narrows as it feels the squeeze of 2,428-m Mount Olympus, still hidden from view.

Our progress is slow. There are numerous streams to ford and fallen trees to limbo under. Some of the larger trunks have been sawn through by rangers, creating strange canyons through the hearts of trees that may have germinated nearly three centuries ago. But even when vanquished, these giants act as 'nurse logs' for rows of seedlings which take root in their decaying wood. Olympic's forest is plant growth at its most rampant. Nourished by over 4 m of rain each year, it is said to be the greatest weight of living matter, per area, in the world.

Slowly, imperceptibly, we fall under its spell. Our singing dwindles, while the bear bells seem weak and distant. The forest commands a cathedral hush. By the time we reach the small waterfall, we haven't uttered a word for over an hour.

At first, we fail to realise the significance of the boulder stripped of its moss – or the well-worn path bisecting the main trail. We sit on a tree stump and begin to unwrap our sandwiches.

Whether it's a subtle shift of breeze or a deeper instinct that warns us, I'm not sure. But suddenly, the air is heavy with the unmistakable, cloying odour of an animal. My eyes chase around the shadows of the forest, then come to rest on the bare boulder. I can see the claw marks now – where the bear has been pausing for its daily pedicure. The path nearby is freshly trampled. And the smell…

"This looks fresh," I murmur, prodding a berry-studded pile of droppings with a stick. "It's still warm."

Once more, I take a long hard look around us. But the forest seems to be holding its breath; the trees standing sentinel in the aching silence.

"I think we should go," I whisper and, gathering up our uneaten picnic, we begin walking as the tinkle of bear bells begins to filter once more through Olympic's mighty rainforest.

Whale watching

"**B**ubble net to starboard!" The cry comes from an officer on the fly bridge of the *Matanuska* ferry as she edges through Southeast Alaska's Frederick Sound. I turn just in time to witness at least eight humpback whales burst through the mirror surface of the sea, tiny silver fish leaping from their gaping mouths like shards of broken glass. There is a stunned silence onboard the ferry as we watch the whales wallow in an orgy of feeding before slowly sinking underwater again. The captain stalls the ship's propellers and we drift to a standstill, ferry schedules forgotten as all eyes rove the sea. "There!" Another shout, heads spinning to port as several hundred tons of humpback rear once more from the sound.

To whale watchers, bubble-net feeding is the Holy Grail. "They circle a big shoal of fish, blowing bubbles to form a kind of net; the fish panic, bunch together and then those guys just come up through the middle, mouths open and wham, bam, thank-you ma'am!" A fellow passenger barely has time to gabble his description of the humpbacks' unique feeding method before the spectacle repeated itself – this time barely 10 m off the *Matanuska's* bow.

Gradually, it dawns on us that there are other humpbacks nearby: lone feeders, females with calves and exuberant males breaching in jaw-dropping synchrony – leaping vertically from the sea like a pair of plump exclamation marks.

Humpback whales are undoubtedly the extroverts of the cetacean world – the big show-offs. However, the majority of whale watching experiences (whether they're organised trips or impromptu sightings from a ferry or cliff top) involve little more than tantalizing glimpses – a smoky plume of breath hanging above the sea, a smooth back rolling through the waves, or perhaps a tail fluke arching briefly above the surface, like a giant hand waving goodbye.

Whales are masters of suspense. They have a hypnotic power over humans – show us a flipper, maybe a fluke, then nothing for an hour and we'll still be riveted to the sea. Can you imagine going on a three-hour game drive and being as elated having only glimpsed the left shoulder of an elephant, or the rump of a rhino?

At times, whale watching can almost feel like an attempt to make contact with creatures from another world. The insignificance of our presence – drifting on the surface of their vast oceanic realm – seems entirely appropriate. Responsible whale watching is always on the whales' terms, and has the power both to captivate people and to inspire them to support cetacean conservation projects around the world.

Every year, some 13 million people go whale watching, with activities in 119 countries and overseas territories valued at around US$2.1 billion. Whales are big business. They always have been. The challenge now is to ensure that whale watching never becomes a mindless pursuit for profit, but instead acts as a catalyst for safeguarding these mysterious, mesmerizing creatures and the oceans they roam.

Ocean wanderers

Many species of cetacean migrate during winter months to warmer latitudes where they mate and give birth. One of the most well known leviathan journeys is that of the grey whale, which leaves its feeding grounds in the Bering Sea each October and heads south to Baja California. Humpback whales move between the Caribbean and Greenland, Antarctica and Queensland and Alaska and Hawaii, although a resident population in the Arabian Sea suggests that not all humpbacks have such itchy flukes. Southern right whales spend the austral winter off the coasts of South America, South Africa and Australasia, cruising back to Antarctica for the summer. Orcas, meanwhile, pop up in places where potential prey is abundant. Some trail the salmon runs off the coast of British Columbia, while others snatch seal pups off beaches in the Falklands and Argentina's Valdés Peninsula.

> Whales are masters of suspense. They have a hypnotic power over humans – show us a flipper, maybe a fluke, then nothing for an hour and we'll still be riveted to the sea

Show time – a breaching humpback makes a big splash

Megaptera novaeangliae
South Africa

Why do whales breach? No one knows for certain, but it could be a means of communication or a way of ridding the skin of parasites. Humpbacks are the most exuberant of breachers, particularly at their mating sites, so it may also have something to do with breeding behaviour.

Whale watching | inspiration

North America

① Greenland
Humpbacks, Paamiut.
» June to August

② Southeast Alaska
Humpback whales
bubble-net feeding, killer
whales hunting salmon
and marine mammals.
» June to early September

③ British Columbia
Johnstone Strait and Puget
Sound are two of the world's
best places to see orca, while
grey whales migrate along
the west coast of Vancouver
Island. Humpbacks also seen.
» March/April for grey whales,
May to September for orca

④ California
Grey whales migrate along
the coast, while the food-rich
canyons and banks of
Monterey Bay attract blue,
humpback, grey, fin, minke
and beaked whales.
» Greys arrive late January;
prime time for Monterey Bay
is August to October

⑤ Baja California
Grey whales calve and mate
in Baja's Pacific lagoons,
while the Sea of Cortez is
renowned for blue,
humpback, Bryde's, fin,
sperm and minke whales.
» January to April for grey
whales; year round for the
Sea of Cortez

⑥ Hawaii
Humpbacks migrate to a
whale sanctuary off Maui to
mate, sing and give birth.
» Late December to April

⑦ Hudson Bay, Manitoba
Beluga congregate in
their thousands along the
Churchill River estuary.
» July to August

⑧ St Lawrence River & Gulf
The spring thaw sparks a
food-chain reaction that
lures a variety of whales,
including beluga, fin, minke,
humpback and blue.
» June to November;
Mingan Islands for blues,
August to November

⑨ Bay of Fundy
Humpback, fin and minke
whales are commonly seen,
with sei and sperm whales
encountered further
offshore. The Bay of Fundy is
an important feeding and
nursery area for the rare
northern right whale.
» August to November for
northern right whales; June
to October for other species

⑩ New England
Stellwagen Bank, off Cape
Cod, is a summer feeding
ground for several species,
including humpback, fin,
minke, pilot and right whale.
» April to October

⑪ Caribbean
The seas around Dominica
are home to sperm whales,
while humpbacks gather to
sing, mate and calve in the
marine sanctuary north of
the Dominican Republic.
» Year round for sperm
whales; January to April
for humpbacks

South America

⑫ Ecuador
Humpback whales at Puerto
López and further north at
Gorgona, a Pacific island
around 50 km off the
Colombian coast.
» June to mid September

⑬ Chile
Blue whales, Chiloé Island.
» December to March

⑭ Península Valdés
See southern right whales at
play, raising their tails out of
the water and using them to
'sail' across sheltered bays.
Orca have prey on their
minds, surfing onto beaches
in pursuit of sea lion pups.
» Mid-July to November for
southern right whales; orca
year round, but hunting sea
lions from mid-February
until mid-April

Europe

⑮ Iceland
Spot whales in the glow of
the midnight sun. Húsavik
has an excellent whale
museum and offers cruises in
search of minke and
humpback whales. Try
Stykkishólmur on the west
coast of Iceland for blue and
sperm whales.
» May to September

16 Norway
Orca hunt herring in Tysfjord, while sperm whales seek squid in the submarine canyons of the Andenes.
›› Late May to September for sperm whales; October to mid-November for orca

17 Scotland
Set sail for the Hebrides, Orkney or Shetland Islands for sightings of minke whales, plus humpback, fin and sperm whales if you're lucky. Large pods of orca are also possible, particularly in the seas around the Shetland Islands and off the northwest coast of Ireland.
›› May to October.

18 Azores
Sperm whales can be found in the deep waters off the south coast of Pico.
›› May to October.

19 Canary Islands
Boat trips from the west coast of Tenerife frequently encounter large pods of short-finned pilot whales.
›› Year round

20 Italy
Fin whales, Ligurian Sea.
›› June to September

21 Greece
Sperm whales can be found south of Crete.
›› June to September

Africa

22 South Africa
Whale watching for landlubbers. Drive the Whale Route from Cape Town to Durban for sightings of southern right whales close inshore and easily visible from cliff tops, or take a boat trip from Gansbaii.
›› July to November.

23 Madagascar
Humpbacks off Nosy Boraha.
›› July to September

Asia

24 Sri Lanka
The south coast, particularly off Dondra Head, has emerged as prime territory for blue and sperm whales.
›› January to April

25 Japan
Humpbacks over-winter in the Kerama and Ogasawara islands, while Bryde's whales visit Ogata.
›› February to April for humpbacks, March to October for Bryde's whales

Australasia & Antarctica

26 South Australia
Southern right whales are easily viewed from clifftops along the Nullarbor and around Adelaide.
›› May to October

27 Hervey Bay, Australia
A favourite stopover for migrating humpbacks.
›› August to October

28 Tonga
Humpbacks arrive to give birth and mate.
›› July to November

29 Kaikoura, New Zealand
Bachelor sperm whales hang out on the edge of the continental shelf, a short boat ride from shore.
›› Year round

30 Antarctica
Krill-rich seas create the ultimate feeding ground for baleen whales, while orca nose around pack ice on the lookout for unwary penguins and seals.
›› November to March

Whale watching | fieldcraft

They're out there, somewhere. There's no exact science to whale watching. All you need is patience, binoculars, a little bit of luck and a few tips on observation techniques.

Try to develop a roving eye. In other words, don't let your gaze become fixed on any one point for too long. Scan 360 degrees around the boat, from the horizon to near distance, looking for clues that might reveal the presence of whales.

One of four things is likely to catch your eye: blows, backs, splashes and seabirds. When whales surface they blow (see right). In calm conditions this forceful exhalation can hang above the surface, like a puff of telltale smoke – sometimes distinctive enough for you to identify the species. Splashes should also make you look twice. They could be made by distant whales breaching, flipper slapping or lobtailing. Seabirds feeding can also create white water (especially plunge-diving gannets). Look carefully – there might be whales feeding from below. Finally, keep your eyes open for whales surfacing, their backs rolling above the surface, gleaming wet and smooth.

One of four things is likely to catch you eye: blows, backs, splashes and seabirds

Blow by blow
Even from a distance you can identify a whale by the shape, size and direction of its spout. From top to bottom, the fin whale has a powerful, straight blow rising as a narrow column up to 6 m high; the grey whale has a V-shaped blow that forms a heart shape, while the sperm whale has a blow projected forwards and to the left due to the fact that its blowhole is on one side of its forehead.

it's a wild life

Brian Jackman | Writer | brian-jackman.co.uk

↘ My big five
❶ Masai Mara National Reserve, Kenya
❷ Serengeti National Park, Tanzania
❸ Ruaha National Park, Tanzania
❹ South Luangwa National Park, Zambia
❺ Okavango Delta, Botswana

❝❞ La Paz, Mexico. I'm in the Sea of Cortez on board a whale watching catamaran. Already I have seen 60 humpbacks and nine blue whales, but it's the dolphins I will remember most. Joyfully they race towards us and within minutes we are engulfed by a Mexican wave of leaping bodies. They are chasing fish as they charge along. It's a feeding frenzy and we are at the heart of it, with thousands of dolphins strung out on either side of us.

Fate sealed – an orca surfs ashore to snatch a sea lion

Orcinus orca
Punta Norte, Península Valdés, Patagonia, Argentina

Southern sea lion pups (*Otaria flavescens*) are born in January and begin learning to swim a few weeks later – something this unique population of orca knows only too well. The cetaceans prefer calm conditions when it is thought they can more accurately pinpoint the cries of sea lions. Surging ashore along the so-called 'Attack Channel', they intentionally strand themselves in order to grab a pup – a risky strategy that is being studied by Punta Norte Orca Research (pnor.org). The public viewing area is above the sea lion colony, while a closer viewpoint of the Attack Channel is for professional photographers and film-makers only.

Beluga
Delphinapterus leucas
Born grey or brown, belugas fade to white by the age of five. They also stand out from other cetaceans by having a flexible neck and an impressive vocal repertoire. Large pods migrate through sub-Arctic and Arctic waters.
3-5.5 m; up to 1.4 tons
150,000+

Blue whale
Balaenoptera musculus
Compared to the fin whale, the second largest cetacean, the blue whale has a taller, thicker spout and less pointed snout. Its mottled flanks reflect the sea and sky, giving rise to its common name.
21-34 m; up to 200 tons
10-25,000

Fin whale
Balaenoptera physalus
Supercharged cetaceans, fin whales can cruise at 40 km per hour. With luck you'll glimpse their distinctive asymmetrical colour pattern – white on the right side of the lower jaw, dark on the left.
19-27 m; up to 75 tons
Around 55,000

Grey whale
Eschrichtius robustus
Bulky, mottled grey and sporting copious barnacles and scars, grey whales are great travellers, the eastern Pacific population migrating between Alaska and Mexico in a round trip of 20,000 km See pages 106-109.
11-16 m; up to 36 tons
Around 20,000

Humpback whale
Megaptera novaeangliae
Humpbacks engage in all kinds of cetacean aerobics, from spy-hopping, rolling and breaching to splashing the surface with its huge 5m-long flippers. Individuals can be identified by their fluke markings.
11-19 m; up to 30 tons
Over 60,000

Minke whale
Balaenoptera acutorostrata
The smallest and most abundant of the rorqual whales, minkes are found in all oceans. Fast moving, they surface only briefly, but you may catch a glimpse of the dorsal fin and distinctive white-banded flippers.
7-10 m; up to 10 tons
750,000+

Orca
Orcinus orca
Easily identified by its tall dorsal fin and black and white markings, the orca is the largest dolphin species. Ranging from the equator to the poles, its diet includes fish, seals, penguins and other whales.
5-9 m; up to 9 tons
180,000+

Pilot whale
Globicephala macrorhynchus
Black body, rounded head and wide, curved dorsal fin – tick off all these features and chances are you're looking at a pilot whale. This social cetacean lives in large family groups, sometimes a 100 or more strong.
5-7 m; 2-3 tons
600,000+

Southern right whale
Eubalaena australis
Most easily seen when they migrate north to the inshore waters of Argentina, South Africa and Australia, southern right whales have distinctive callosities on their heads which can be used to identify individuals.
11-17 m; 40-80 tons
Around 12,000

Sperm whale
Physeter macrocephalus
The largest toothed whale, the sperm whale has a massive head (and the biggest brain of any animal). Look for the spout, which is directed forwards and to the left. Sperm whales can dive to depths of 3,000 m.
10-20 m; 35-45 tons
300,000+

greatest ticks

Whale watching | game plan

There are dozens of boats at the marina. How do I choose the right one?

Look for an operator that's signed up to a strict code for responsible whale watching. If in doubt, ask questions about how they minimize disturbance to whales. A good operator will talk about the correct way to approach cetaceans (sideways, never from the front or rear), minimum distances, no-wake speeds etc. Whale watching should be an educational experience with experts on hand to interpret behaviour, describe conservation measures and so on. Whale sightings should be logged for research purposes, while additional activities, like using hydrophones to listen in on whale and dolphin calls, provide a more rounded experience.

Where should I sit on the boat?

That often depends on weather and sea conditions! The bow and raised areas like fly decks provide the widest field of view for sighting spouts, but are more exposed to wind, spray and waves. It's not essential to be next to the guide as most use a clock system to direct your gaze (ie humpback at three o'clock) with the bow representing 12 o'clock.

What special gear do I need for whale watching?

You may spend long periods waiting and watching, the boat idle, rolling broadside on a swell, so if you're prone to seasickness take precautions before setting off. Windproof and waterproof clothing, sunscreen and hat are essential, even if the forecast is sunny and warm. Polarizing sunglasses are useful for reducing glare and cutting through reflections on the water surface to see whales and dolphins that approach the boat. Take a pair of x8 or x10 binoculars or, if you're watching from land, a spotting telescope. Other useful extras include camera (see below), a notebook for recording sightings and a field guide.

☺ How do you get those perfect tail-fluke shots?

It's not easy photographing whales. They're moving, the boat's moving and salt spray is a camera's worst enemy. Protect your gear in a splash-proof vinyl housing (aquapac.net) or use a lens hood to cut glare on the lens. Choose a telephoto zoom, select as fast a shutter speed as possible and switch to continuous

Whales watching you

Humpback whale
Megaptera novaeangliae
Australia

Inquisitive whales may swim right up to your boat and 'spy-hop' for a better look at its occupants. These encounters are entirely on the whales' terms, however, and they should never be pursued for such close-up views.

Whale-watching etiquette frowns on elbowing photographers and stampedes from port to starboard

Way to go

Boat trips Most whale-watching trips last around three hours, with vessels ranging from small, zippy RIBs (rigid inflatable boats) to large motor launches.

Liveaboards For enthusiasts, dedicated cruises roam the seas for a week or more in search of cetaceans. Top spots include the Maldives and Sea of Cortez.

Cruises Voyages to regions like Southeast Alaska, Antarctica and the Norwegian Fjords often reward keen-eyed watchers with sightings.

Sea kayaking Paddling quietly at sea level in the company of whales is an unforgettable experience. Guided trips are available in several locations, including British Columbia, Baja California and Australia.

Swimming with whales Whale swims in locations like Norway, Tonga and the Dominican Republic are undeniably exhilarating, but they can also be potentially dangerous to swimmers and stressful to cetaceans. Pending research into their potential impact, the Whale & Dolphin Conservation Society recommends that whale watchers stay out of the water (see box).

Conservation holidays Whale-based expeditions are offered by Earthwatch (earthwatch.org).

shooting mode. Whales that raise their flukes are often preparing for long, deep dives, so you may only get one or two chances at a decent fluke shot. Keep your camera focused on the whale while it rests on the surface, then take a sequence of photos as the back and tail start arching through the water. The closer you are to the water surface, the more impressive the fluke shot.

Are there specialist whale-watching companies?

Endorsed by the Whale & Dolphin Conservation Society (wdcs.org), Oceans Worldwide (oceansworldwide.co.uk) offers a programme of 'Out of the Blue' whale-watching holidays to destinations ranging from Scotland and the Bay of Biscay to Alaska and Patagonia. Also try Naturetrek (naturetrek.co.uk) and Wildwings (wildwings.co.uk).

Should I shout "Thar she blows!"?

Encounters with whales are supercharged with emotion, but don't drown the moment with shouting

Where can I see whales for free?

There are several locations around the world where you can watch whales from the shore – good news for landlubbers who get sea sick, as well as those travelling on a budget.

❶ Inside Passage Ferry journeys north from Vancouver are often accompanied by sightings of orca and humpbacks The Frederick Sound area in Southeast Alaska is particularly renowned for bubble-net feeding humpbacks.

❷ California Cruise Highway 1 following the grey whale migration, stopping at headlands like Point Reyes to check for spouts.

❸ Quebec Stake out whale-watching viewpoints at Cap-de-Bon-Désir, Pointe Noire and Pointe des Monts on the St Lawrence River.

❹ Azores Once used by whalers, watchtowers on islands like Pico and Faial are now used by researchers and tourists.

❺ Bay of Biscay Catch a ferry between Portsmouth and Bilbao or Plymouth and Santander for a chance to spot up to 20 species of cetacean. See also p116.

❻ Scotland Island-hop around the Hebrides and Shetlands on CalMac ferries (calmac.co.uk) for a glimpse of orca and minke whales.

❼ South Africa A 12-km stretch of low cliffs at Hermanus provides one of the world's best vantage points for land-based whale watching.

❽ Japan Bryde's whales come close inshore at Ogata, March–October.

❾ South Australia Bunda Cliffs on the Nullarbor coast offer superb views of southern right whales in the sea 70 m below.

❿ New South Wales Humpbacks pass below the cliffs of Cape Byron, June–July.

and whooping. At worst you'll disturb the whales, but you will also shatter the expectant silence as they draw breath ready to slip below the surface again. Whale-watching etiquette also frowns on elbowing photographers, stampedes from port to starboard and anyone who utters the phrase, "that's a seriously big fish."

Any advice on swatting up on spouts?

There are several excellent field guides to cetaceans, including *Whales, Dolphins and Seals: A Field Guide to the Marine Mammals of the World* (A & C Black, 2006) and Mark Carwardine's *Whales, Dolphins and Porpoises* (Dorling Kindersley, 2002).

Where can I swim with whales?

Very few countries permit whale swims. The risks to humans are obvious. Whales are not only massive animals with potentially lethal flukes and flippers, but they also tend to be found in deep waters with strong currents and surface chop – conditions that rapidly cause fatigue in swimmers. Sharks have also been known to attack swimmers, presumably mistaking them for whale calves. As with dolphins, potential adverse effects on whales stem from vessels approaching too close or inappropriate behaviour from swimmers. Swimming with humpback whales is permitted in Tonga, but opponents claim it can disturb mothers and calves when they are most vulnerable.

Whale watching code

✅ Slowly approach whales sideways, never from head-on or behind.

❌ Do not cross the paths of cetaceans to intercept them or anticipate their next move in order to increase the chances of a close encounter. This will only make them feel chased and avoid you.

✅ Slow down to 'no-wake' speed and maintain a constant direction, making the whales feel more secure.

❌ Never split a pod or group of cetaceans.

✅ Be aware of other boats. If it's already busy, consider leaving the area and looking elsewehere. Always avoid a situation where whales are encircled by tour boats.

✅ Be especially aware of the presence of mothers and calves.

❌ Never spend more than 20 minutes with cetaceans, unless they have approached you and choose to prolong the encounter.

❌ Never feed cetaceans or influence their natural nehaviour in any way.

✅ Try to make as little noise as possible and leave the area slowly if you notice any possible signs of distress.

Tales from the wild | the pacific lagoons of baja

Pacific lagoons, Baja California, Mexico

White water erupted from the lagoon ahead of our small flotilla of sea kayaks. I glimpsed dark shapes surging through the foam, straight and lethal as torpedoes. A fluked tail rose and fell, cracking the surface with the sound of gunshot. Then terns arrived at the scene, folding their wings like paper darts as they dived into the churning mêlée.

"Dolphins often herd fish against the mangroves," Morgan Davies, our kayaking guide, told me. "And seabirds are never far behind."

Such a plethora of life had been hard to imagine when, a few days earlier, I flew south from Los Angeles to Baja California. A gnarled peninsula of desert mountains and cactus-stubbled plains, Baja probes the Pacific like a skeletal finger. But where barren land meets cobalt sea, the 1,250-km-long Mexican frontier teems with life.

Each winter and spring, grey whales visit the sheltered Pacific lagoons of Magdalena Bay to give birth and mate before resuming their epic 8,000-km migration to the Bering Sea. Travelling through a mosaic of waterways and camping on uninhabited islands, I had joined a five-day kayaking expedition to explore the whales' wilderness nursery grounds and, if I was lucky, to paddle alongside them.

Our 'put-in' was deep in a mangrove swamp at the northern end of Magdalena Bay. Gradually, we cajoled a mountain of expedition paraphernalia (tents, cooking equipment, firewood, water containers) into the kayaks' storage compartments.

"Don't forget about intertidaling," Morgan told us. "You get two toilet flushes a day here," he explained. "One for each time the tide comes in." It was crucial to find somewhere below high-tide mark before scooping a pit, using biodegradable toilet paper and then burying everything. "There are plenty of crabs, worms and other critters in the mangroves that will gratefully receive your donation."

And so with a strange sense of satisfaction that our passing would actually benefit the local wildlife, we set off with nothing but Morgan's emergency radio between us and the wilderness. After an initial period of knuckle scraping mis-strokes, the paddling was straightforward and I soon relaxed into an easy rhythm, lulled by the chuckle of water running beneath the kayak's hull.

Bahía Magdalena hasn't always been so tranquil. In the mid-1800s, Captain Charles Scammon was sailing off the coast when he spotted whale spouts rising from behind the low barrier islands which protect the bay. The cheers from his shipmates sounded the death knell for Baja's grey whales. Scammon was an American whaler and, in the ten years that followed his fortuitous sighting, the whale population was decimated.

Scammon's initial efforts to reap this valuable marine harvest met little resistance. On one occasion, two of his small whaleboats were crushed by whales, but the 15-m-long cetaceans were no match for Scammon's bomb lances. In 1857, he sailed into San Francisco harbour laden with 740 barrels of oil – the product of a single year's whaling.

Today, the main draw for visitors to Magdalena Bay is still the grey whale. Following protection in 1946 its numbers have risen from just a few hundred to over 25,000 and Mag Bay, for all its remoteness, has become a leading whale-watching destination.

Daylight was fading as we paddled towards our first campsite. The lagoon, mirror-calm, had revealed no sign of whales. Flights of cormorants made for their roost as we beached the kayaks on a barrier island – one of a chain of sandy islets, each several kilometres long but only a few hundred metres wide, sandwiched between lagoon and ocean. Although hidden by a line of dunes, I could hear the distant surf, a gentle whisper, like wind in long grass.

A knotted shoulder muscle, stiff from paddling and a night on compacted sand, eased me awake sometime before dawn. Or, at least, that's what I

> **I found a set of neat paw prints in the cold ashes of our campfire and, while we dismantled the tents and packed the kayaks, I felt an acute sense of being watched. But, like the whales, the coyotes were elusive**

ⓘ No kayaks or private boats are currently allowed in the nursery lagoons of Baja's Pacific Coast including Magdalena Bay. However, licenced Mexican whale-watching boats can take you to see the grey whales, and safari-style island camps (see p108) provide an opportunity to explore the coast's stunning barrier islands.

thought had woken me. Suddenly I was aware of something licking the outside of the tent. I held my breath and shifted slightly into a better position, but whatever it was must have heard me. There was a muffled whimper, a soft scratching of retreating footsteps, then silence.

Over breakfast, I mentioned my mysterious visitor to Morgan. "Oh yeah – that'll be a coyote," he said. "They lick the kayaks too. Out here, the morning dew is a good source of fresh water."

I found a set of neat paw prints in the cold ashes of our campfire and, while we dismantled the tents and packed the kayaks, I felt an acute sense of being watched. But, like the whales, the coyotes were elusive.

We paddled all morning in the lee of the barrier island, pausing to glide silently towards herons, taut with concentration as they stalked fish. Every hour

seemed to herald a different species. From the brazen snowy egret to the skulking green-backed heron, Magdalena Bay was festooned with birds. Pacific loons, eared grebes and surf scoters bobbed in our wake, while turkey vultures, frigate birds and ospreys pirouetted overhead.

The manœuvrable kayaks allowed us to nose about in narrow backwaters, skim across shallow sand banks and haul out on pristine, untrodden shores. At midday, we walked across the interior of a barrier island, crossing dunes carpeted in pungent wild sage and scattered with vicious devil's claw seeds. On the ocean side of the island, wind scuffed row upon row of Pacific breakers, misting the air with spray and driving sea spume across a beach littered with sand dollars and shells. This wild coast was a desolate contrast to the island's lagoon shore. Half-digested

The rough with the smooth – a barrier island on Baja California's Pacific coast separates sheltered lagoon from rowdy ocean

Baja California is one of the world's top whale-watching locations, the desert peninsula separating two distinct areas rich in cetaceans – the Sea of Cortez and the Pacific lagoons.

by sand lay the twisted wreck of a small fishing boat, bearded with seaweed. Along the strandline, polystyrene floats, light bulbs and plastic bottles were piled against the carcass of a large green turtle, an incongruous still-life of flotsam.

After two days of kayaking we reached the first *boca*, a natural deep water channel breaching the chain of barrier islands and connecting Magdalena Bay to the Pacific. Bocas are a favoured haunt of grey whales, but looking ahead all I could see was a boiling pot of leaping waves as vicious currents and rip tides seethed through the cutting.

"Looks a bit choppy up here." Morgan's voice was whipped away on the wind. The six kayaks coalesced into a tight pod and we dug our paddles hard against the current. But Morgan had no intention of taking us across. The tide was wrong and there was a real risk of capsizing. It was 'right on the edge' as he put it.

Instead we turned towards shore to look for a suitable campsite. We pitched the tents a few hundred metres from a sea lion colony. There was little shelter from the ocean wind and fine sand hissed against the flysheets. It crunched between my teeth and stuck fast to my face, now smeared with two days of sunblock and salt grime.

The following dawn, I walked stiffly out of camp, probing sand from my ears, and made for a piece of driftwood. A pair of curlews scattered at my approach, piping with indignation as they flew low across the lagoon. I stopped to watch them go, unaware that I, too, was being observed. When I looked round, the coyote couldn't have stood more than a dozen yards away. His grizzled fur was speckled with sand and his eyes were pale yellow and flecked, like a wolf's. In seconds the encounter was over, the coyote slipping into the early morning mist like a fleeting shadow.

We set off to cross the *boca* at low tide when waves would be less threatening. Paddling furiously for thirty minutes we emerged in calmer waters beyond the boca, wet and exhausted, but otherwise unscathed. Morgan decided it was time to sit back, stow the paddles and enjoy a spot of relaxed sailing. Stashed away in each kayak was a small sail and a collapsible mast and it wasn't long before we were cruising at four knots before a brisk wind. As always, our eyes roved the lagoon for tell-tale signs of grey

whales surfacing: a spurt of haze or a barrel-shaped back cleaving the sea. But for the third consecutive day, the leviathans eluded us.

News of the whales' whereabouts reached us the following day. We were setting up camp by another *boca* when local fishermen informed us that whales were being sighted daily in the nearby channel. But our hopes of kayaking with them were still to be thwarted. The weather was deteriorating. By the following morning the wind had whipped the boca into a filigree of foam. To kayak in such seas would be madness. Clearly, the only chance we would have of seeing whales was to brave the boca in the fishermen's more substantial motor-boats, or *pangas*.

The defiant scream of outboard engines as the *pangas* fought the heavy swell was shocking after the tranquillity of kayaking. Over the past few days we had travelled in tune with the natural pulse of Magdalena Bay, respecting its tides, currents and winds; never challenging them. But like any wildlife safari, the anticipation of our first whale sighting was intense.

A cry went up as the first blow was sighted. For a fraction of a second I saw a miniature rainbow perfectly framed in the column of spray before the wind tore it to shreds. Then, in defiance of the agitated sea, the broad back of a grey whale parted the waves. Gripping the gunwale of our wildly pitching panga, I watched its barnacle-scarred body ride the swell with ease, a great tail fluke suddenly curling above the surface, streaming water from its serrated edge, as the ceteacean slipped from view.

For several hours we searched for grey whales, other pangas ferrying tourists from a nearby fishing village on the mainland. There's no doubt that whale watching has helped to secure the future of Baja's grey whales by raising income and awareness. But sometimes it's the wider view, not the close encounter, that can leave the most lasting impression.

On our last evening, I climbed wind-rippled sand dunes high above camp to gaze across the lagoon we had kayaked through over the past few days. To the west, the Pacific beat its steady thunder, bursting white along endless beaches. And there, beyond the rows of breakers, spouts of haze, tinted gold by the sunset, plumed repeatedly from a grey whale and its calf as they rested off Baja's wilderness coast.

California greys (from top, left to right) – wilderness kayaking camp on a Baja barrier island; flukes up as a grey whale dives; scallop shells piled on a Pacific beach; grey whale calf; marbled godwit; California sea lions; kayaks under sail

Magdalena Bay, Baja California. The whale sanctuary and biosphere reserve of El Vizcáino comprises two lagoons to the north – San Ignacio and Ojo de Liebre. For whale watching in the Sea of Cortez, see p162.

Baja California

Ojo de Liebre
San Ignacio   Sea of Cortez
Magdalena Bay   La Paz

Making tracks

Kayaking specialists **Ecosummer Expeditions** (ecosummer.com) offers Baja trips combining five days of paddling in the Sea of Cortez with two days of grey whale watching at a Magdalena Bay base camp. Also try **Sea Kayak Adventures** (seakayakadventures.com).
Several airlines serve La Paz and Los Cabos, while ferries link the Mexican mainland to Santa Rosalia and La Paz. **Sea Kayak Adventures** (seakayakadventures. com) has a Grey Whale Base Camp overlooking Magdalena Bay.
GMT-8
January to April.
visitmexico.com

Tales from the wild | the smile on the face of a dolphin

North Bimini, Bahamas

Since the mid-1990s, Bahamian dive operators Nowdla and Bill Keefe have developed a remarkable relationship with a pod of wild spotted dolphins. They don't feed, tag or try to entice them in any way. "These are wild encounters – totally on the dolphins' terms," Bill explains. "It's up to them if they want to come and play." They've developed a so-called 'ice cream van' theory: "We always trace the same triangular route. We think they recognise the sound of our boat's propellers and, just like kids when they hear the jingle of an ice cream van, they come and meet us."

But on this, the first of our six four-hour quests across the shallow waters of the Great Bahama Bank, the sea plays tricks with our eyes. Even if the dolphins are nearby, the turbulent wake of a thunderstorm makes it impossible to spot them.

We retreat to Alice Town, a one-street community that fills the entire width of skinny North Bimini. This low-lying sand island, just 80 km from South Florida, is dubbed the 'game fishing capital of the world'. The Keefe's 10-m-long *Delphine* shares its berth with dazzling white launches bristling with fishing rods. Restaurant walls are plastered with photographs of record-breaking blue marlin.

The following afternoon we are back onboard, scouring the sea, straining for a glimpse of a dark dorsal fin. Bimini crouches low on the horizon, dipping in and out of view as we ride the gentle swell. Gradually, the heat and humidity blunt our vigil. Bill slips the *Delphine* into neutral and encourages us to go for a swim. "It'll revive your enthusiasm," he says. "The dolphins know when it's a boat-load of sceptics."

The water is well over 26ºC and gin-clear. Through my mask, I can easily make out the sandy seabed 10 m below – a lone orange starfish lying on its rippled surface like a discarded button.

Bill is the first to hear them. Like a long-wave radio struggling to tune, there are clicks, whirrs, squeaks and all manner of dolphin-talk. Below me, a pale streamlined shape cruises past and I have a brief glimpse of a spotty, smiling face. On an instinct I gulp a breath of air, fold at the waist and dive.

At first all I can see are shades of turquoise. I pinch my nose and blow gently to ease the pressure in my ears, then spin upright and begin ascending. Almost immediately, the dolphin is there beside me – so close, I could embrace it. Its eyes are bright and focused – level with mine – and with a surge of elation, I realise that we are staring at each other!

Bill told us that the dolphins seem intrigued when people free-dive towards the bottom. They often gather around to investigate, almost as if they are admiring, perhaps encouraging, our efforts to share their world.

Moments later, my head breaks the surface. I clear my snorkel and dive again, but the dolphins have gone. Bill calls us back to the *Delphine*. "They've finished playing for now," he says.

Encounters can last for anything from a few minutes to over an hour. Sometimes the dolphins are too engrossed with feeding, mating or sleeping to take much notice of the boat.

But the next morning, we are only an hour out of Alice Town before a mother and calf join us. The youngster seems beside itself with excitement, racing around the boat like a faulty torpedo, while its mother swims nearby keeping a watchful eye.

Once we are in the water, the youngster teases us with surging 'swim pasts', never appearing from the same direction twice. Eventually, the mother comes smoothly to the infant's side and they swim off in perfect synchrony.

Two hours later, when we come across the main pod. Unravelling a long rope off the stern, Bill instructs three of us to hold on to a series of loops tied in its length. As the *Delphine* accelerates to a mere three knots, I feel my arms stretch under the strain of being towed along. But the dolphins seem fascinated by this sudden transformation in our speed. Soon, seven or eight are alongside me. Another swims inches beneath my stomach, occasionally rolling on its back to peer up at me. I grin, my mask half-full of water. No wonder the dolphins are smiling.

> ### Like a long-wave radio struggling to tune, there are clicks, whirrs, squeaks and all manner of dolphin-talk

---

Atlantic spotted dolphins

Stenella frontalis
Great Bahama Bank, Bimini, Bahamas

Spotted dolpins only begin to get their spots once they have been weaned. Adults can reach about 2.3 m in length and weigh up to 140 kg. A fast swimmer and keen bow-rider, spotted dolphins often accompany boats.

Bahamas
Miami · Bimini · Nassau

Making tracks

- Bill & Knowdla Keefe's Bimini Undersea (biminiundersea.com) offers six-day Wild Dolphin Adventures, including five dolphin excursions and three snorkelling trips.
- Bahamas Express (flybahamasexpress.com) flies between Fort Lauderdale and Bimini. A ferry service between Miami and Bimini was planned for 2011.
- Development of the **Bimini Bay Resort** was widely criticised for damaging fragile mangrove habitat. Alice Town has several local guest houses.
- GMT-5
- May to September.
- bahamas.com

Wildlife cruises

Few types of wildlife travel tingle with a greater sense of discovery or anticipation than an expedition cruise to some remote corner of the world's oceans. A fleeting glimpse of an albatross riding the rollercoaster of a Southern Ocean swell; crouching quietly at the edge of a 100,000-strong penguin colony; meeting the gaze of a marine iguana that shows no fear of humans; hearing the sigh of breath as a whale surfaces, shattering reflections in some pristine bay... these are the kinds of moments that make wildlife cruises so special. And so addictive.

Charles Darwin started it. His voyages onboard the *Beagle* still fire our imagination, and his most famous landfall – the Galápagos Islands – are now one of the world's most popular wildlife cruise destinations.

Like a modern-day version of *HMS Beagle*, Jacques Cousteau's *Calypso* also became famous for its globetrotting, fact-finding voyages. Unlike Darwin's ship, however, Cousteau's trusty, wooden (and recently restored) vessel was equipped to explore the mysteries of the ocean floor. As well as scuba gear (which Cousteau himself helped develop in 1943), *Calypso* had a submersible and underwater observation chamber. The ship's expeditions have become the stuff of legends.

Then there are the great polar explorers – Shackleton, Amundsen and Scott to name a few – who might not have ventured to the Arctic or Antarctica with the aim of finding wildlife but, nonetheless, embody the free-spirited adventure of expedition cruising.

There is something of Darwin, Cousteau and Shackleton in all modern-day expedition voyagers – even if we're used to rather more comfortable accommodation and rely on the expert leadership of naturalist guides. From polar icebreakers to Amazon riverboats, wildlife cruise vessels follow in the wake of some of the most historically important voyages ever undertaken. Crossing the equator, reaching 80°N or stepping ashore on Antarctica will always be milestones on these trips, but ultimately it's the wildlife and wild places that lure us there.

Antarctica and sub-Antarctic islands like South Georgia promise a heady cocktail of ice, mountains and penguins galore, while High Arctic regions like Svalbard and Baffin Island offer a polar extreme of ice bears, walruses and equally astonishing scenery.

In the tropics, the Amazon and Galápagos provide two very different wildlife cruise experiences – one a river journey, gleaning precious glimpses of secretive jungle wildlife; the other an oceanic island odyssey, tiptoeing around brazen colonies of seabirds, sea lions and marine iguanas.

Less well known, but just as rewarding to wannabe-Darwins, are wildlife cruises in Indonesia (sailing to the land of Komodo dragons), Baja California's Sea of Cortez (a whale-watcher's paradise) and the Coral Sea (visiting the reefs and rainforests of Queensland and Papua New Guinea).

Mark Twain's impassioned plea (right) will strike a chord with any wildlife cruise-goer. Just remember to add 'treasure' and 'preserve' to the end. The places you will be visiting are some of the most wildlife-rich and ecologically vulnerable on earth.

Into the heart of Honduras

Probing the largest remaining tract of tropical rainforest in Central America, the Río Plátano is a fine excuse for a challenging river expedition (lamoskitiaecoaventuras.com). Heading upstream from the fabled Mosquito Coast, you'll need expert guiding, copious insect repellent and buttocks capable of withstanding several days' travel by dugout canoe. You'll experience virgin jungle, visit remote communities of Miskito and Pech Indians and see mysterious petroglyphs that stir rumours of ancient lost cities. Needless to say, the wildlife in this biosphere reserve is mind-boggling, with everything from jaguar, sloth and howler monkey to harpy eagle, crested guan and scarlet macaw.

Twenty years from now you will be more disappointed by the things that you didn't do than by the ones you did do. So throw off the bowlines. Sail away from the safe harbour. Catch the trade winds in your sails. Explore. Dream. Discover.

Mark Twain

Here be dragons – marine iguanas crowd old lava flows in the Galápagos Islands

Amblyrhynchus cristatus
Fernandina, Galápagos Islands

Early mapmakers used to place the phrase 'Here be dragons' at the edges of their known world. Had they known about Galápagos iguanas or Indonesia's Komodo dragons, the annotations might have had more cartographic credit.

Cruise embarkation ports

North America

1 Alaska & British Columbia
Cracks in crazy paving. That's what they look like on a nautical chart. Except the paving slabs are hundreds of forested islands, wedged against the mainland of British Columbia and Southeast Alaska – and the cracks form a coastal highway stretching 1,600 km north from Seattle to the old gold rush town of Skagway. The Inside Passage is firmly etched on cruise-liner itineraries, but travel by small ship or local ferry and you'll see more and often spend less. Highlights in BC include Vancouver Island, the Great Bear Rainforest and Queen Charlotte Islands – realm of bear and orca, and the heartland for cultures like the Haida and Tlingit.

In Southeast Alaska, ships visit Ketchikan, Juneau and the fabled Glacier Bay. Frederick Sound is a good place to keep watch for humpback whales.
» May to August
Seattle, Vancouver, Prince Rupert, Juneau, Ketchikan

2 Arctic Canada
Small ship expeditions in the Canadian territories of Nunavut and Nunavik promise encounters with walrus, polar bear, narwhal and other Arctic wildlife, as well as a fascinating insight into Inuit culture. Cruises can often be combined with Labrador and the west coast of Greenland (see below).
» August to September
Iqaluit

3 Greenland
Iceberg-strewn bays, Arctic wildlife and insights into

Inuit and Viking cultures all feature on Greenland cruises. The east coast can be combined with both Iceland and Svalbard.
» August to September
Kangerlussuaq, Reykjavik, Longyearbyen

Latin America & Antarctica

4 Baja California
Cruises in the Sea of Cortez ripple with the anticipation of whale sightings. Blue, humpback, fin and sperm whale are just some of the species likely to be seen, while cruise itineraries also include kayaking, snorkelling with sea lions and excursions into Baja's desert interior.
» Year round
La Paz

5 Caribbean
There's a huge choice of cruise options available

in the Caribbean. When it comes to watching wildlife and getting off the beaten track, however, the choice between a 3,000-passenger mega-ship and a skippered yacht is a no-brainer.
» December to June
Various islands

6 Galápagos Islands
Land-based trips are possible on the island of Santa Cruz, but only by cruising around the Galápagos can you fully appreciate the archipelago's wonderful wildlife. Each island has a special lure, from the petrel-hunting owls of Genovesa to the waved albatross of Española. Although the wildlife is totally unfazed by human presence, small- to medium-sized vessels help to minimize human impact.

» Year round
Baltra

7 Amazon River
The best boats for cruises on the Amazon are small with shallow draughts, enabling you to probe wildlife-rich backwaters, lagoons and flooded forest.
» March to October
Manaus

8 Tierra del Fuego
Cruceros Australis (australis. com) operates small ship cruises through the Straits of Magellan and Beagle Channel, visiting Cape Horn, penguin rookeries and Patagonian glaciers.
» September to April
Punta Arenas, Ushuaia

9 Falkland Islands
Sometimes combined with a cruise to the Antarctic

Africa

15 Indian Ocean
Liveaboard diving cruises operate in the Red Sea, Seychelles, Maldives and Mozambique Channel.
» Year round
⚓ Various

Asia

16 Kamchatka Peninsula
Spot bears, seabirds and cetaceans against a mesmerising backdrop of volcanoes, and explore the little-visited Kuril and Commander Islands.
» June to July
⚓ Petropavlovsk-Kamchatskiy

17 Southeast Asia
Adventure dive cruises are available in the Philippines (hcadivecruise.com), while sailing cruises venture to Indonesia's Komodo Island (komodocruise.com).
» Year round
⚓ Various

Australasia & Antarctica

18 North Australia
Cruises operate around the Kimberley and Queensland coast, with some venturing across the Coral Sea to Papua New Guinea and the Solomon Islands. Vessels range from luxury launches to sailing yachts and expedition ships.
» Kimberley: May to September; Queensland: April to November
⚓ Cairns, Darwin

19 Fiji & South Pacific
Tui Tai cruises (tuitai.com) island-hop around Vanua Levu, Rabi, Taveuni and the Ringgold Atolls, with plenty of time for hiking, snorkelling and kayaking.
» Year round
⚓ Natewa Bay

20 New Zealand's Sub-Antarctic Islands
A staggering number of breeding seabirds converge on these remote, blustery outposts each southern summer, transforming them into one of the world's greatest wildlife spectacles. Macquarie Island has 850,000 pairs of royal penguin, 218,000 pairs of king penguin and 150,000 southern elephant seals; Campbell Island has a colony of 7,500 pairs of southern royal albatross, while 340-ha Snares Island has two million sooty shearwaters, plus albatrosses, petrels, prions and crested penguins.
» November to December
⚓ Invercargill

21 East Antarctica
Sail beyond the Sub-Antarctic Islands (above) to reach the East Antarctic Coast where abundant wildlife includes snow petrels and emperor penguins at Dumont d'Urville. Venturing further south, Ross Sea is the historic gateway of many Antarctic explorers, as well as the breeding ground for millions of Adélie and emperor penguins. Highlights of this ultimate Antarctic voyage include Cape Adare, the Ross Ice Shelf and Mt Erebus and Shackleton's hut.
» January to early March
⚓ Invercargill

Peninsula (and South Georgia), the Falklands also make an excellent land-based destination. Cruise ship passengers often visit the penguin colonies at Bluff Cove or Volunteer Point.
» October to March
⚓ Ushuaia, Port Stanley

10 South Georgia
Worth pushing the boat out for, a visit to this wild, mountainous island adds considerably to the duration and expense of an Antarctic cruise, but the wildlife is legendary. You'll see colonies of 200,000 king penguins, as well as wandering albatross, giant petrel and fur seal.
» November to March
⚓ Ushuaia

11 Antarctic Peninsula
The classic voyage to the Great White Continent crosses Drake Passage to the South Shetland Islands and ice-choked bays of the Antarctic Peninsula and Weddell Sea. Typically a 10-day cruise, highlights include orca, humpback and minke whales, leopard, crabeater and fur seals, large rookeries of chinstrap, gentoo and Adélie penguins and the opportunity to go kayaking, diving or camping out on the ice.
» November to March
⚓ Ushuaia

Europe

12 Scottish islands
Set sail for the Orkneys, Shetlands, Hebrides and far-flung St Kilda, exploring one of Europe's richest areas for cetaceans and seabirds.
» April to September
⚓ Oban

13 Norwegian Fjords
Wildlife hotspots in this popular cruise destination include the Vesterålen Islands (for sperm whales) and the Lofoten Islands (for sea eagles).
» May to September
⚓ Bergen, Kirkenes

14 Svalbard
Voyage around the Arctic wilderness of Spitsbergen, venturing ashore in zodiacs to view glaciers, seabird cliffs, and walrus haul-outs. Svalbard cruises are always supercharged with the possibility of a polar bear encounter. The coastal scenery is a spectacular procession of mountains, while Ny-Ålesund offers a fascinating insight into an Arctic research station.
» May to October
⚓ Longyearbyen

Wildlife cruises | fieldcraft

6 of the best ferry trips for wildlife

1 Inside Passage The Alaska Marine Highway (dot.state.ak.us) and BC Ferries (bcferries.com) connect island communities throughout coastal British Columbia and Southeast Alaska. Keep watch for orcas, humpback whales, bald eagles and Stellar's sea lions. Parks Canada naturalists join summer midday sailings between Vancouver and Victoria and Nanaimo.

2 Isles of Scilly Travelling between Penzance, Cornwall, and St Mary's on the Scilly Isles (a voyage of 2hrs 40 min), the *Scillonian III* (islesofscilly-travel.co.uk) often provides sightings of common dolphins, seabirds, grey seals and even basking sharks. An expert from the Royal Society for the Protection of Birds accompanies Friday sailings.

3 Bay of Biscay Brittany Ferries (brittany-ferries.co.uk) works with the Marine Conservation Society to help passengers spot whales, dolphins and seabirds on its Portsmouth-Santander route.

4 Scottish Hebrides Caledonian MacBrayne (calmac.co.uk) plies routes throughout the Hebrides where you can see harbour porpoise, grey seal, dolphins, minke whale, orca, white-tailed sea eagle, gannets and other seabirds.

5 Sunderbans Explore the mangrove maze of the Sunderbans in Bangladesh where a small fleet of podgy, bright orange paddleships, known as Rockets, ply the myriad channels between Dhaka and Khulna. With luck, you may catch a glimpse of a rare Ganges river dolphin.

6 Cook Strait Linking North and South Island, the three-hour voyage between Wellington and Picton (interislander.co.nz) combines stunning scenery with a chance to spot whales, dolphins and fur seals.

Coast with the most – for many travellers, Antarctica is the ultimate expedition cruise destination

Paradise Bay, Antarctic Peninsula

Getting misty-eyed over all that panoramic perfection is all well and good, but if you're serious about wildlife you need to start focusing on details. Brown stains on distant snow-clad mountain slopes, for example, usually indicate large penguin rookeries (some are conspicuous enough to be visible from space). Check ice floes and bergs for seals and penguins hauled out to rest, and double-take any splash – it could be a leopard seal on the prowl, a whale surfacing or seabirds feeding.

Wildlife cruise code of conduct

❌ Do not touch or feed wildlife. If it appears to be agitated, then you are too close. Take binoculars and use them for close views, particularly of animals that are breeding.

✅ Use filtered drinking water from the ship, rather than purchase disposable water bottles.

✅ Watch where you are walking. Even pebble beaches can be nesting sites for plovers, terns and oystercatchers, while burrows are used by puffins, penguins and shearwaters. Also try to avoid trampling delicate plant life in dune or tundra areas. Keep to established trails and follow your guide's directions.

✅ Try to reduce the amount of packaging you take onboard with you. All non-recyclable items should be taken home.

❌ Do not leave behind litter or food scraps or throw anything overboard.

✅ Consider picking up one piece of rubbish from any beach you land on.

❌ Do not paint names or graffiti on rocks.

✅ Leave everything as you found it. Do not take souvenirs of rocks, fossils, bones, eggs or feathers.

✅ During close encounters with wildlife, remain quiet and avoid using flash when taking photographs.

✅ When whale watching, follow the guidelines on page 105.

✅ Do everything possible to avoid introducing alien species to island ecosystems. This can include anything from discarded fruit seeds to insects inadvertently carried in luggage.

guiding star

Cathy Iturralde Dillon

Isabela II, Galápagos
Metropolitan Touring,
Ecuador, (metropolitan-
touring.com)

**Most memorable wildlife
encounter** Watching
orcas playing with a huge
sunfish for an hour.

**Top tip for travellers on a
wildlife cruise** Be prepared
for unusual things to
happen, like changing
weather, rough seas and
unpredictable wildlife.

Favourite animal
Galápagos penguins are
faithful and elegant, and
amazingly fast swimmers.

**What does responsible
travel mean to you?**
Our commiment to the
Galápagos is to ensure that
its natural resources are
never damaged for future
generations. We organize
projects such as coastal
clean-ups, recycling and
diver training.

How to identify seabirds

A new species of storm petrel was identified off the coast of Chile as recently as 2011. Closely related to the white-vented
storm petrel (*Oceanites gracilis*) shown above, it was the first new seabird discovery in 55 years. It's perhaps not surprising
that these ocean wanderers can elude birdwatchers for so long. Not only do they cover vast areas of sea, but reliable
identification is made notoriously difficult by brief sightings, bad weather, rough seas and the often similar markings of
various pelagic species. Use the following checklist to sort out your prions from your petrels:

Size Compare the size of the bird you're trying to identify with other seabirds in the area.

Bill shape Is it tube-nosed (as in albatrosses, petrels and shearwaters), slender and hooked (as in frigatebirds and
cormorants) or long and dagger-like (as in gannets and boobies)?

Plumage This is where identification gets tricky. Most seabirds are black (or grey) and white. However, look closely at the
cap, eye band, collar, rump and tail – variations in markings on these areas will help you narrow down the species.

Flight Is the bird soaring like an albatross on long, stiff wings, banking above the waves like a shearwater, dancing on the
surface like a storm petrel, plunge-diving like a gannet, skipping along with short sharp wingbeats like a tern, fussing
behind your ship like a gull or chasing other seabirds like a frigatebird?

Wildlife cruises | game plan

There are cruises and then there are *expedition* cruises, voyaging to far-flung places in small ships, exploring wildlife-rich islands in the company of expert guides and experiencing the thrill of an oceanic quest. Cruising is no longer the preserve of the 'newly wed or nearly dead'.

Apart from choosing where to go, there are several factors to consider when arranging a wildlife cruise. Cost is likely to be an important issue. A typical 10-day cruise to the Antarctic Peninsula will easily sink US$3,500 of your hard-earned savings (excluding flights to the embarkation port). However, don't forget that expedition cruises are pretty much all-inclusive and enable you to reach remote places often impossible to visit in any other way.

You can sometimes save money by travelling during an off-peak season and choosing a bigger boat. The downside to this, of course, is that you may miss the prime period for wildlife (or hit bad weather) and big ships inevitably mean more protracted logistics (and potential environmental impact) shuttling passengers back and forth to shore.

Aim for an expedition vessel that carries up to around 150 passengers. Apart from sleeping, you probably won't spend much time in your cabin, so look for other features, like natural history libraries, the ratio of guides to passengers and whether the ship carries sea kayaks or snorkelling gear.

Finally, look carefully at the itinerary and weigh up the balance between landfalls and days at sea.

ⓘ The following companies offer wildlife cruises. The International Association of Antarctic Tour Operators (iaato.org) has a list of environmentally responsible Antarctic cruise operators.

- adventurecanada.com
- allrussiacruises.com
- amazonclipper.com.br
- australis.com
- discover-the-world.co.uk
- exodus.co.uk
- greenlandcruise.com
- heritage-expeditions.com
- hurtigruten.no
- metropolitan-touring.com
- innerseadiscoveries.com
- naturetrek.co.uk
- noble-caledonia.co.uk
- northernlight-uk.com
- northstarcruises.com.au
- oceansworldwide.com
- pacificcatalyst.com
- quarkexpeditions.com
- steppesdiscovery.co.uk
- tuitai.com

A typical day onboard

» **0630** Wake-up call. Often, the ship will have spent the night relocating to a new island or point of interest.
» **0700** Breakfast.
» **0800** Disembark in zodiacs for morning landing.
» **0815** Naturalist guides lead you on a short walk, stopping often to identify and photograph wildlife.
» **1100** Opportunity for additional activities, such as snorkelling from the beach, sea kayaking or a zodiac ride along the coast looking for seabirds and whales, or admiring icebergs.
» **1200** Return to ship. Rinse off your snorkelling gear and visit the natural history library to read up on wildlife you've seen.
» **1230** Lunch.
» **1330** The ship may navigate to a different site for the afternoon landing. There's time to search for wildlife from the deck, watch a presentation from one of the guides or simply to relax. This would also be the format for days at sea.
» **1530** Afternoon landing, guided walk and activities.
» **1800** Return to ship. Evening drinks and briefing on following day's schedule.
» **1930** Dinner.
» **2100** Natural history talk.
» **2200** Time for a spot of star-gazing before bed or, if you are enjoying the long days of a polar summer, there will be enough daylight for spotting whales and seabirds. On some polar cruises, 24-hr daylight means that some landings can be scheduled late at night.

Eyes wide open
An observation deck is perfect for spotting whales, sea birds (like this waved albatross) or even star-gazing on clear nights.

Rinsing off
Divers and snorkellers can rinse off their gear under the outdoor showers at the ship's stern, before hanging wetsuits on drying racks.

Power to the paddle
Ideal for paddling close inshore and gliding quietly and unobtrusively past wildlife, sea kayaks are stable, easy to use and provide a unique sea-level perspective.

Ship stats | *Isabela II*
Length: 53.7 m • Beam: 11.58 m
Capacity: 40 passengers, 24 crew

Plain sailing | anatomy of an expedition ship

Safety at sea
As well as sophisticated navigation equipment, the ship carries life boats and life rafts and has an onboard medical officer.

Through the looking glass
A window on marine life, this Boston Whaler can be launched for glass-bottom boat trips.

Reading matters
A well-stocked natural history library contains wildlife identification guides, maps and internet resources.

Room for less
Just 21 double cabins keep passenger numbers to a level where shore landings have less environmental impact than larger ships.

Ship to shore
Zodiacs are used for shore landings – either dry (onto rocks or a jetty) or wet (wading onto a beach as shown here).

Natural know-it-alls
Onboard naturalist guides co-ordinate the expedition itinerary, provide lectures and accompany shore landings.

Spitsbergen, Svalbard Archipelago

It only takes a brief tutorial and a few blistered palms to get us underway. As the tawny sails bloom overhead, the *Noorderlicht* cants dramatically and begins to sing with the wind – rigging chiming against twin steel masts; canvas thrumming and the Arctic Ocean bursting white beneath her bowsprit. Slowly, Longyearbyen, Svalbard's capital, falls astern – a cluster of brightly-coloured wooden houses shrinking to Lego blocks against a dramatic meringue-whip of mountains.

"We want to go north," explains Jan Belger, the guide onboard the 50-m schooner (with its crew of five). "But how far we get will depend on the pack ice." Throughout winter and much of spring, the seas around Svalbard freeze over. It's only around mid-June, with 24-hour daylight and temperatures creeping to 5°C, that such a voyage can even be contemplated.

It is midnight on our second day when the *Noorderlicht* drops anchor off the spindly island of Prins Karls Forland. Jan scans the beach for signs of life and soon we are being shuttled ashore in the ship's zodiac. Arctic terns patrol the shallows, dropping into the sea like fluted arrows, while puffed-up purple sandpipers scour seaweed on the strandline. But Jan has bigger game in his sights.

He leads us slowly to what appears to be a heap of smooth brown boulders. It's only when one twitches and lifts a wrinkled, moustached face above the aggregation that we freeze. There must be over 100 walruses – all males according to Jan – lounging about the pebbles snoring, belching and breaking wind under the midnight sun.

Early the next morning, hugging the jagged shoreline of Spitsbergen, we continue north. The soft light of night flares into another vivid arctic day – a gas-flame sky; the sea dancing with diamonds. Drifting into Magdalena Fjord we tease and tug the pristine reflections of mountains before mooring near the site of an old whaling station.

The following day there is a tense silence onboard. Somewhere, close ahead, lies the permanent pack ice. Already, we've nudged a large free-floating chunk – the *Noorderlicht* shivering from the impact, staining the ice red from paint scraped from her hull.

Slowly, the northern tip of Spitsbergen sinks behind us, the mountains snuffed out by stinging sleet that plunges the temperature to −20°C. But our spirits begin to soar. All eyes turn to the GPS in the map room as it plots our progress north. At 4.47pm everyone cheers, the ship's bell is rung and we raise glasses of steaming punch. We have reached 80°N – a nautical milestone in these waters every bit as momentous as crossing the equator. A few hundred metres ahead lies the ragged edge of the pack ice, a white skin gnawed by waves, but solid and impregnable as far as the eye can see. Less than 600 miles away is the North Pole.

Retreating to the mainland, we anchor near Ny-Ålesund at the foot of a huge glacier; blocks of blue ice skewed along its front, like teeth in disarray. Jan leads us on a hike through its crystal maze landscape.

There must be over 100 walruses – lounging about the pebbles snoring, belching and breaking wind under the midnight sun

The polar bear was probably watching us all the time. But it's only once we've looped back to our landing point that we spot the creature ambling casually across pack ice below the glacier.

In the days that follow, we have other privileged encounters with Arctic wildlife. At Alkhornet the cliffs are festooned with tens of thousands of nesting seabirds, the skies above us peppered with a blizzard of guillemots and little auks. An arctic fox tiptoes amongst the boulder-scree beneath the colony, a large turquoise egg clamped in its jaws.

But the most enigmatic encounter is also the most ephemeral. Anchored in a pristine bay, we hear the haunting siren calls of belugas pulsing mysteriously through the *Noorderlicht's* hull. We never see the white whales – apparently their song can carry underwater for many miles.

It was a sign of true wilderness that such a subtle sound could prove so captivating. Along with the cooing of eider ducks and the creaking of ancient glaciers, it came to symbolise our voyage through this extraordinary arctic realm.

Northern highlights (from top, left to right) – the *Noorderlicht* anchored in Magdalena Fjord; walruses hauled out on Prins Karls Forland; Svalbard reindeer browsing on the tundra; rock ptarmigan in winter plumage; bearded seal on pack ice; purple saxifrage; mountain reflections

From the end of February, the *Noorderlicht* is frozen in the ice at Tempelfjorden, Spitsbergen, where it acts as a unique winter base camp for exploring by dog sled and snowmobile.

Making tracks

🌊 **Oceans Worldwide** (oceansworldwide.co.uk) offers 10-day voyages around Spitsbergen onboard the *Noorderlicht*, while **Discover the World** (discover-the-world.co.uk) offers cruises on the *Polar Star* and *Expedition* – both capable of carrying around 100 passengers.
✈ **SAS** (flysas.com) operates flights to Longyearbyen via Oslo.
🛏 **Spitsbergen Hotel** (rica-hotels.com).
🕐 GMT+1 (GMT+2 Mar-Oct)
📅 June to October
ℹ svalbard.com

Tales from the wild | exploring the enchanted isles

Galápagos Islands, Ecuador

On the island of Española, surf blooms white on the cliffs at Punta Suárez – a relentless procession of sinewy waves hurling themselves onto the rocks and filling the air with the salty sweat of their exertions. Anywhere else in the world and you would be spellbound by such a vibrant seascape. But this is the Galápagos and the boulder beach below us is twitching with sea lions and marine iguanas. Sally lightfoot crabs daub the rocks with splashes of red and gold; waved albatross cartwheel overhead and Nazca boobies stand sentinel on rocky pedestals, their fluffy white chicks crouched in crevices like snagged cotton wool. The sea can flex its muscles all it likes, but it will never upstage the wildlife on Darwin's 'Enchanted Isles'.

Many places in the world have amazing wildlife. Some of them boast extraordinary biodiversity or a superabundance of animals. Others are renowned for endemic species, or allow intimate close-up encounters. It's a rare place, though, that combines all these attributes, and the Galápagos archipelago is one of them.

Punta Suárez on Española is only the third shore excursion on our week-long Galápagos cruise, but already we have seen several of the island's trademark wildlife highlights: blue-footed boobies dancing on North Seymour, hundreds of sea lions dozing on the beach at Gardner Bay, a Galápagos hawk feeding on one of Darwin's finches – evidence for the theory of natural selection ripped apart before our very eyes.

Over the next few days, our small expedition ship (with just 24 passengers onboard) loops through the archipelago. Each morning, we wake to find a new island. Zodiacs (or *pangas*) shuttle us ashore and we spend the next few hours walking slowly along trails that grapple with old lava flows or thread through forests of palo santo trees.

There is no need to walk far. At Punta Cormorant on Floreana Island (our fourth landing), we have barely strolled a dozen metres before our guide delivers a double whammy of Galápagos penguin and Caribbean flamingo. It's probably the only place in the world where the two can be seen together in the wild.

On Genovesa, there's another incongruous spectacle as we watch short-eared owls hunting storm petrels in broad daylight – the raptors waiting in ambush, perfectly camouflaged in clifftop lava fields, as swarms of the dainty seabirds return to their nesting burrows.

Then there are the Galápagos icons: flightless cormorants preening stubby wings; male frigatebirds shaking bright red, party-balloon throat pouches in courtship frenzies; marine iguanas snorting salt from their nostrils, and, of course, the high-stepping, head-bowing courtship dances of blue-footed boobies.

Then, just when you think the Galápagos has exhausted its cache of surprises, someone suggests you go snorkelling.

During an hour's drift along the rocky coast of Targus Bay on Isabela Island, we count 26 green turtles, sometimes in twos and threes, grazing on algae or drifting in watery space. Anywhere else in the world, this would be exceptional, but turtles are so common here they almost become part of the background. Sea lions steal the show in surging swim-pasts; penguins zip along at the surface like overwound bath toys, and flightless cormorants dive alongside you, their plumage wrapped in silver cocoons of trapped air.

And as if all this wasn't enough, the sea is squirming with fish – stately king angelfish parading from cover, vast shoals of yellowtail surgeonfish, wrasse, damselfish, parrotfish and even a brief encounter with an octopus.

Climbing into the zodiac and heading back to ship, I feel a warm glow of satisfaction. It's been another exceptional day of wildlife. I can't help but wonder whether the cruise will end in anticlimax, but early the next morning, the ship anchored in another pristine bay, I glance down and there, cruising off the stern, is an enormous manta ray...

> **Sea lions steal the show in surging swim-pasts; penguins zip along at the surface like overwound bath toys, and flightless cormorants dive alongside you**

Spiny wonder – detail of a marine iguana

Amblyrhynchus cristatus
Fernandina, Galápagos Islands

Marine iguanas are found throughout the Galápagos archipelago, hundreds often seen basking together along the shoreline. The only true marine lizard, it feeds on algae, diving to depths of up to 10 m in order to graze.

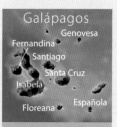

Galápagos

Genovesa
Fernandina
Santiago
Santa Cruz
Isabela
Floreana
Española

Making tracks

Metropolitan Touring (metropolitan-touring.com) operates four- and seven-night cruises on its expedition ships: *Isabela II*, *La Pinta* and *Santa Cruz*. Packages combining Galápagos cruises with the Ecuadorian Andes and Amazon are available from **Wildlife Worldwide** (wildlifeworldwide.com).
Lan Ecuador (lan.com) and **Tame** (tame.com.ec) connect Quito and Guayaquil with Baltra in the Galápagos – a 90-minute flight.
Finch Bay Eco Hotel (finchbayhotel.com), Puerto Ayora, Santa Cruz Island, offers a land-based option for the Galápagos.
GMT-6
Year round.
galapagospark.org
darwinfoundation.org

Wilderness trips

Escapists' utopia, adventurers' dream, explorers' great unknown. Wilderness is a subjective thing. Look it up in a dictionary and it's blandly written off as a 'wild uncultivated area' – more 'unkempt allotment' than Mongolian steppe. To a traveller, the word carries far more depth and meaning. Wilderness is one of travel's 'tingly' words, guaranteed to titillate the weariest of globetrotters. It is the promise of remoteness, the challenge of a new frontier, the privilege of glimpsing wildlife that knows no boundaries and of scanning a wide, unblemished horizon.

People will always crave the pristine beauty, spiritual renewal and sense of escape that accompanies a journey somewhere totally removed from the noise, pollution and clutter of everyday life. And, ironic as it may seem, the best way to preserve wilderness is to give people direct experience of it. Only then can they develop the empathy and enthusiasm that's so vital for ensuring its future.

Wilderness? I didn't think there was any left.
It's true that humans have laid claim to the most far-flung places on earth, mapped each one from space and wrought a great deal of environmental havoc, but large swathes of wilderness do still exist. Every continent has wild places full of opportunities for the adventurous traveller (see pages 126-127).

Call me a wimp, but I'm no Ranulph Fiennes. Rope burns and frostbite are not my idea of a holiday.
No one is suggesting you set off solo across the Arctic wastes. There are plenty of operators that specialise in taking small groups into wilderness areas and bringing them out again, fingers and toes intact. Safety is their paramount concern. Just make sure you choose a reputable company that employs expert local guides, uses the best possible equipment and practices environmentally responsible tourism.

Will I have to carry my own backpack, eat dry meals and sleep in a coffin-sized tent?
No. On some trips you can play the pampered explorer, staying in luxury wilderness ecolodges and comfortable camps. It's a matter of taste and budget. Having said that, however, I would urge you, at least once in your life, to set off into the wilds with everything you need carried on your back (or strapped to a horse, stowed in a kayak etc). There is something wonderfully liberating about travelling lightly through a wilderness. Your daily rhythm synchronises with natural cues, such as the passage of the sun, the rise and fall of tides and the movement of wildlife.

That's all very well if you're Ray Mears. My bushcraft skills are limited to blackberry picking.
You could always learn more about bushcraft by joining one of Ray's Woodlore courses (raymears.com). Naturally, it's vital that you know your limitations. Never embark on a wilderness journey unless you are fully prepared for what lies ahead.

Just you and the great outdoors

It's a jungle out there (or a desert, ice cap, mountain range…). You've packed the essentials: sleeping bag, insect repellent, water filter, first aid kit, map, compass, knife, torch and spare batteries, food, clothing and sun protection. Here's a list of some easily overlooked, but nifty little extras that you should also find room for:
Gaffa tape Sticky stuff for weather-resistant repairs.
Biodegradable soap Use this if you're going to wash (but let's face it, there won't be many people around to complain if you don't).
Fire starter Making fire is an essential skill for wilderness travel, so take waterproof matches or one of those nifty flint-sparking gizmos.
Journal Non-essential, but the wilderness is certain to inspire you and, in any case, you'll enjoy reading it years later and marvelling at how you survived all those bug bites, blisters and irregular bowel movements.

Wilderness is one of travel's 'tingly' words, guaranteed to titillate the weariest of globetrotters. It is the promise of remoteness, the challenge of a new frontier, the privilege of glimpsing wildlife that knows no boundaries

Chapman's baobab

Adansonia digitata
Makgadikgadi Pans, Botswana

Livingstone, Selous, Baines and other European explorers used this colossal, 3,000-year-old tree as a landmark and campsite during their expeditions into the African wilderness. Today, it is still an icon of a wild and remote corner of the continent.

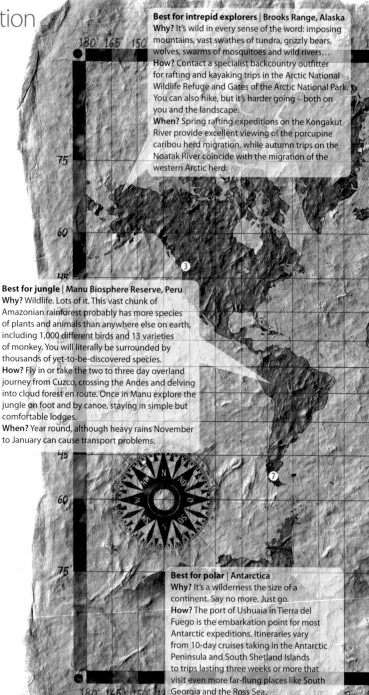

Best for intrepid explorers | Brooks Range, Alaska
Why? It's wild in every sense of the word: imposing mountains, vast swathes of tundra, grizzly bears, wolves, swarms of mosquitoes and wild rivers…
How? Contact a specialist backcountry outfitter for rafting and kayaking trips in the Arctic National Wildlife Refuge and Gates of the Arctic National Park. You can also hike, but it's harder going – both on you and the landscape.
When? Spring rafting expeditions on the Kongakut River provide excellent viewing of the porcupine caribou herd migration, while autumn trips on the Noatak River coincide with the migration of the western Arctic herd.

Best for jungle | Manu Biosphere Reserve, Peru
Why? Wildlife. Lots of it. This vast chunk of Amazonian rainforest probably has more species of plants and animals than anywhere else on earth, including 1,000 different birds and 13 varieties of monkey. You will literally be surrounded by thousands of yet-to-be-discovered species.
How? Fly in or take the two to three day overland journey from Cuzco, crossing the Andes and delving into cloud forest en route. Once in Manu explore the jungle on foot and by canoe, staying in simple but comfortable lodges.
When? Year round, although heavy rains November to January can cause transport problems.

Best for polar | Antarctica
Why? It's a wilderness the size of a continent. Say no more. Just go.
How? The port of Ushuaia in Tierra del Fuego is the embarkation point for most Antarctic expeditions. Itineraries vary from 10-day cruises taking in the Antarctic Peninsula and South Shetland Islands to trips lasting three weeks or more that visit even more far-flung places like South Georgia and the Ross Sea.
When? November to February.

What if I break my leg in the middle of nowhere?

On an organised trip your group leader should have enough first aid experience (and appropriate kit) to deal with most injuries – at least until some kind of emergency evacuation procedure kicks in. Make sure your travel insurance is comprehensive enough to cover the activities you'll be doing.

Wilderness would be fine if it wasn't so wild. Tell me I'm not going to be molested by mosquitoes, ransacked by racoons or beaten up by bears.

To be frank, most wilderness travellers who run into trouble with the local wildlife ask for it! If, for example, you are hiking in North American bear country it's sensible to take precautions like wearing bear bells or clapping your hands (to warn animals of your approach) and suspending your food (and other high odour items) out of reach of a bear on tiptoes. Similarly, venturing into a swampy region without mosquito repellent, long-sleeved clothing and a head net is asking to be bitten. It all comes down to researching your destination, understanding the wildlife and taking appropriate safety measures. Of course, there are several wilderness areas where you'll find yourself dislodged from the top of the food chain by predators such as big cats and polar bears. While this undoubtedly adds a certain thrill factor to the experience you must treat these creatures with the utmost respect.

ⓘ Should wilderness be sacred? It's one of travel's big dilemmas. See page 17.

Minimal impact

✅ Always choose an operator that sets a stringent code of conduct to minimize environmental impact.

✅ Travel in a small group with a local guide.

✅ Put something back into the local economy by choosing operators that employ local people.

❌ Don't harass wildlife in pursuit of that 'perfect' photo. Instead, savour the encounter from a respectful distance.

✅ Leave no trace when camping and, where they are permitted, restrict fires to safe areas.

✅ Rubbish takes longer to decompose at high altitude, so be especially vigilant in packing out all your refuse.

Best for mountains | Pamirs, Tajikistan
Why? A tangled knot of peaks, glaciers and wind-scoured plateaux, the Pamirs are one of the world's least visited mountain ranges – an austere land sparsely inhabited by Tajik tribespeople and home to snow leopard and other rare Asian wildlife.
How? Don't expect teashops or lodges. Apart from scant trails and a few shepherd huts that's it. Make sure you're well equipped for some challenging trekking.
When? July to September.

Best for coast | Skeleton Coast, Namibia
Why? Few places have more forbidding or evocative names than the coastal frontier of the Namib. Littered with the remains of ships and whales this vibrant fusion of desert and ocean lures visitors into a spectacular realm of vast dune fields, crowded seal and seabird colonies and the poignant legacy of the San Bushmen.
How? Venture out on short forays from the coastal towns of Swakopmund and Ludertiz or join an organized safari, camping along the coast's stark, yet beautiful hinterland.
When? Year round.

10 more ways to find your perfect wilderness

① **Most spiritual | West MacDonnell Ranges, Australia**
Follow in the footsteps of the Aboriginal Dreamtime by hiking the long-distance Larapinta Trail through the gorges and valleys of the arid Outback.

② **Most surreal | Makgadikgadi Pans, Botswana**
Tread lightly on vast Kalahari saltpans, the remains of an ancient 'superlake'; pluck Stone Age tools from its surface and trace the uncluttered curve of the earth.

③ **Most spooky | Olympic Peninsula, USA**
Trek beneath moss-strewn stands of giant hemlock and spruce in one of the last corners of wilderness in the lower United States (see p96).

④ **Most pampered | Serengeti, Tanzania**
Choose from luxury lodges or tented camps for safaris in search of big cats and the ground-swallowing wildebeest migration (see p64).

⑤ **Most cosy | New Zealand**
South Island has several luxury wilderness lodges where you can enjoy quality accommodation and cuisine right in the thick of things.

⑥ **Most northerly | Svalbard**
Although on a smaller scale to Antarctica, Svalbard also has ice-clad mountains, tidewater glaciers and plenty of wildlife, from polar bears to walruses.

⑦ **Most awe-inspiring | Patagonia, Chile**
Wilderness doesn't get any more breathtaking than the imposing pinnacles of Torres del Paine in Chile's Patagonian Andes. Other spectacular mountain wildernesses include the Wrangell-St Elias mountains of Alaska and Asia's Tien Shan.

⑧ **Most spine-tingling | Ndoki, Congo**
Venture into mysterious 'heart of darkness' jungle peppered with clearings or bais frequented by forest elephant and lowland gorilla.

⑨ **Most forbidding | Chang Tang Reserve, Tibet**
The world's second largest conservation area covers some 330,000 sq km of windswept plateau.

⑩ **Most accessible | Cairngorms, Scotland**
Hiking is superb in the mountains and ancient Caledonian pine forest of this national park where you may catch a glimpse of rarities like the capercaillie and pine marten.

Conservation trips

Throughout the world there are thousands of scientists, conservation organizations, government departments and local communities faced with the huge task of protecting wildlife and other natural resources. They have expertise and vision – but time is against them. Not only are environments declining faster than ever, but we have barely identified an estimated 10% of the world's species. Effective conservation stems from scientific understanding, but it can take months, sometimes years, of data-collecting, monitoring and analysis to develop a case that's sound enough to convince decision-makers to take action. That's where conservation holidays can help. By placing paying volunteers with existing projects around the world, targets can be achieved in a fraction of the time. Conservation holidays are also a superb way of boosting environmental awareness, sharing and learning skills and experiencing some of the wildest places on earth.

Conservation holidays get under the skin of a place and provide a depth of insight, awareness and satisfaction that is rarely experienced on a 'normal' holiday. At one end of the scale are trips which combine more traditional wildlife viewing with opportunities to visit and participate in research and conservation projects. Organizations like Earthwatch (earthwatch.org) go a step further by offering full-participation holidays lasting around two weeks. During this period you play an active role in a conservation project – either assisting scientists with their research or carrying out practical management work. This category offers the most choice and is a good option if you have limited time or want to try out a conservation holiday for the first time.

Full-blown conservation expeditions from organizations like Coral Cay Conservation (coralcay. org) are a different matter altogether. Lasting several weeks or months, they are popular with university and gap-year students, as well as retired professionals and those taking a career break. They rely on teamwork to carry out surveys in remote areas or to accomplish major physical projects, such as the construction of nature trails or research centres. Training is comprehensive and includes first aid and other essential aspects of basic expedition life, as well as skills relevant to conservation work. Although these trips are not for the faint-hearted, they often prove to be life-changing experiences.

Whichever conservation holiday you opt for, it's worth thinking carefully about your limitations. It's one thing to have passionate beliefs about conserving rainforests, but quite another to spend time working in such a hot, humid and demanding environment. Similarly, you may think coral reefs are the most beautiful natural treasures on earth, but if the prospect of donning an aqualung fills you with dread, think twice about joining a diving expedition. Have realistic expectations. Conservation holidays based on projects to protect wolves and other charismatic rarities may sound irresistible, but most of your work will probably involve looking for tracks – rather than contact with the creatures themselves.

ⓘ See pages 130-131 for a directory of conservation holiday operators.

Conservation holidays are a superb way of boosting environmental awareness, sharing and learning skills and experiencing some of the wildest places on earth

No PhD? No problem

You don't need to be a scientist to join a conservation holiday. All you require is enthusiasm, dedication and a strong commitment to the environment. Training is provided on site by fully qualified staff and will include wildlife identification, survey techniques and any other skills you need in order to make a positive contribution to the project. In addition, courses in specialist activities like scuba diving may form part of the holiday. Some organizations also offer a pre-departure briefing to enable you to find out more about the environmental issues involved and to meet past volunteers.

Taking the plunge

Conservation volunteers prepare for a diving trip in the Philippines as part of a survey programme by Coral Cay Conservation (CCC). Launched in 1985, CCC volunteers have not only collected data that has been used in the creation of marine and forest protected areas in Central America, the Caribbean and Southeast Asia, but have also worked on numerous community projects.

Conservation trips | directory

African Conservation Experience
conservationafrica.net
Non-profit organization, established 1999.
◉ Range of projects in southern Africa, including hands-on animal care, wildlife veterinary work, field research, marine conservation and ranger courses.
➲ South Africa, Botswana, Mauritius.
★ Monitor elephant populations in the Limpopo-Shashe trans-frontier conservation area, study whales and dolphins off South Africa's coast, learn how to track and identify wildlife and other ranger skills.

Coral Cay Conservation
coralcay.org
Non-profit organization with associated charitable trust, established 1986.
◉ Expeditions and shorter projects designed to help sustain livelihoods and alleviate poverty through the protection and management of coral reefs and tropical forests.
➲ Cambodia, Philippines, Tobago, Kenya.
★ Surveys forests in Kenya and reefs in Southeast Asia and the Caribbean, collecting data for new reserves. Full diving training available if needed.

Biosphere Expeditions
biosphere-expeditions.org
Non-profit organization, established 1999.
◉ Hands-on wildlife conservation expeditions lasting either one or two weeks, plus a range of taster days.
➲ Altai, Oman, Namibia, Brazil, Honduras, Peru, Azores, Slovakia, Maldives, Western Australia.
★ Survey snow leopards in Central Asia, cheetah in Namibia and jaguar in Brazil; study whales and dolphins in the Azores, monitor wolves in Slovakia and flatback turtles in Western Australia.

Earthwatch
earthwatch.org
Established Boston, 1971, and as a UK charity in 1985.
◉ Wide range of projects supporting the work of scientists in the field, and lasting 7-15 days. Topics range from climate change to endangered species.
➲ Worldwide.
★ Monitor the ecology of wildlife on the Mongolian Steppes, study manta rays off the Queensland coast, investigate climate change in Ecuador, study meerkat behaviour in the Kalahari.

British Trust for Conservation Volunteers
btcv.org.uk
UK's largest practical conservation charity, established 1959.
◉ Over 200 projects in the UK and worldwide, ranging from practical projects, such as trail maintenance, to wildlife surveys of endangered species.
➲ UK, Albania, Bulgaria, Cameroon, Estonia, France, Germany, Iceland, Italy, Japan, Lesotho, Portugal, Romania, Sovakia, South Africa, Taiwan, USA.
★ Maintain trails in Iceland's Vatnajökull National Park, manage woodland in Scotland, create artificial nesting sites for terns and avocets in Bulgaria.

Frontier
frontier.ac.uk
Non-profit organization, established 1989.
◉ Variety of 10- or 20-week expeditions carrying out practical conservation tasks and surveys, as well as community work, teaching placements and medical volunteering.
➲ Worldwide, including over 200 projects in Africa and Asia.
★ Survey wildlife in Tanzania's Kilombero Valley, study the behaviour of gibbons in Thailand, monitor dolphin populations in the Mediterranean, work at an animal rescue and rehabilitation centre in Guatemala.

Operation Wallacea

opwall.com

Non-profit organization with associated charitable trust, established 1995.

◉ Conservation research projects assisting scientists with marine and forest surveys and working with local people on a range of educational, community and cultural projects.

➋ Indonesia, Honduras, Egypt, South Africa, Mozambique, Cuba, Peru, Madagascar, Guyana, Mexico.

★ Survey pristine rainforest in Guyana, help produce a biodiversity atlas in Egypt, study sifakas in Madagascar and coral reefs in Cuba.

Raleigh International

raleighinternational.org

Charity, first established in 1978 as Operation Drake.

◉ Ten- or five-week expeditions focus on community, the environment and adventure/conservation.

➋ Costa Rica, Borneo, Nicaragua, India.

★ Help develop a conservation centre for sun bears in Borneo, construct solar-powered electric fences and dig elephant-proof trenches around villages and cultivated land in India to help reduce human/elephant conflict, construct a wildlife viewing platform in Costa Rica's La Cangreja National Park.

136 North America
140 Alaska
144 Western US
148 Eastern US
150 Florida
152 Western Canada
154 Eastern Canada
155 Newfoundland

**158 South &
Central America**
162 Mexico
164 Caribbean
164 Belize
165 Honduras
166 Costa Rica
168 Venezuela
169 Guyana
170 Brazil
172 Ecuador
173 Galápagos
178 Peru
180 Bolivia,
     Argentina &
     Chile

186 Europe
190 Britain
192 France
194 Spain
197 Azores & Canary
     Islands
198 Italy
200 Eastern Europe
202 Scandinavia
203 Iceland

206 Africa
210 Gabon & West
     Africa
212 Kenya
216 Tanzania
221 Uganda,
     Rwanda &
     Ethiopia
222 Zambia
226 Zimbabwe,
     Malawi &
     Mozambique
228 Botswana
230 Namibia
232 South Africa
236 Madagascar
243 Seychelles

244 Asia
248 India
251 Sri Lanka, Nepal
     & China
252 Malaysian Borneo
256 Indonesia

260 Australasia
264 Australia
270 New Zealand
272 Papua New
     Guinea

278 Polar regions
284 Svalbard
286 Antarctica
288 Falklands
290 South Georgia

Destinations

**Surf's up – gentoo penguins in
the South Atlantic Ocean**

Pygoscelis papua
Sea Lion Island, Falkland Islands

For penguins, the transition from
elegant swimmer to clumsy land-
waddler is an awkward one.

Destinations | At a glance

Antarctica
Wildlife highlights 286

Arctic
Wildlife highlights 284

Argentina
Patagonia 182
Tierra del Fuego NP 181
Valdés Peninsula 180

Australia
Daintree NP 265
Fraser Island 265
Great Barrier Reef MNP 268
Kakadu NP 264
Kangaroo Island 268
Kimberley 265
Lamington NP 268
Ningaloo MP 265
Phillip Island 265
Tasmania 265
West MacDonnell Ranges 265

Belize
Wildlife highlights 164

Bolivia
Madidi NP 180
Sajama NP 180

Botswana
Central Kalahari GR 228
Chobe NP 228
Linyanti Marshes 228
Makgadikgadi Pans 228
Okavango Delta 229

Brazil
Brazilian Amazon 170
Pantanal 170

Britain
Cairngorms 191
Pembrokeshire 190
Scottish Hebrides 191

Canada
Algonquin PP 154
Aulavik NP 153
Banff NP 153
Bay of Fundy 154
Churchill 153
Elk Island NP 153
Grasslands NP 153
Great Bear Rainforest 153
Gwaii Haanas NP 153
Haliburton Forest 154
Jasper NP 152
Johnstone Strait 152
Kluane NP 153
Mingan Archipelago NP 154
Pacific Rim NP 152
Saguenay-St Lawrence MP 154
Torngat Mountains NP 154
Wapusk NP 153

Chile
Chiloé Island 180
Lauca NP 180
Patagonia 182

China
Wildlife highlights 251

Costa Rica
Barra del Colorado WR 167
Braulio Carrillo NP 167
Cahuita NP 167
Cocos Island NP 167
Corcovado NP 166
Guanacaste NP 167
Las Baulas NMP 167
Los Quetzales NP 167
Manuel Antonio NP 167
Monteverde Cloud Forest 166
Tortuguero National Park 166

Cuba
Ciénaga de Zapata NP 164

Ecuador
Galápagos Islands 172
Wildlife highlights 172

Ethiopia
Wildlife highlights 221

Finland
Martinselkonen NR 202

France
Camargue 192
Cévennes NP 192
Corsica 193
La Brenne 193
Mer d'Iroise 193

Gabon
Loango NP 210

Gambia
Wildlife highlights 211

Guyana
Iwokrama Forest 169
Kaieteur NP 169
Rupununi Savannah 169

Iceland
Wildlife highlights 203

India
Bandhavgarh NP 249
Kanha NP 249
Kaziranga NP 248
Manas NP 249
Pench NP 249
Periyar NP 249
Ranthambhore NP 248
Satpura NP 248
Sundarbans NP 249
Tadoba-Andhari TR 249

Indonesia
Komodo NP 256

Italy
Abruzzo NP 198
Gran Paradiso NP 199

Kenya
Amboseli NP 212
Arabuko Sokoke FR 213
Kakamega FR 213
Lake Turkana 213
Marine national parks 213
Masai Mara NR 212
Mt Kenya NP 213
Rift Valley Lakes 213
Samburu NR 213
Tsavo NP 212

Madagascar
Andasibe-Mantadia NP 236
Berenty PR 236
Masoala NP 236
Ranomafana NP 236

Malawi
Wildlife highlights 226

Malaysia
Danum Valley CA 254
Gunung Mulu NP 252
Kabili-Sepilok FR 254
Kinabalu NP 254

Mauritania
Banc D'Arguin NP 210

Mexico
Copper Canyon 163
Monarch butterflies 163
San Ignacio Lagoon 162
Sea of Cortez 162
Sian Ka'an ER 163

Mozambique
Wildlife highlights 226

Namibia
Caprivi Strip 230
Damaraland 230
Etosha NP 230
Mundulea NR 230
Namib-Naukluft NP 230
Skeleton Coast 230

Nepal
Wildlife highlights 251

New Zealand
Wildlife highlights 272

Panama
Darién NP p164

Papua New Guinea
Wildlife highlights 226

Peru
Manú BR 178
Pacaya Samira NR 178
Tambopata NR 178

Poland
Bialowieza NP 201

Portugal
Azores 197

Romania
Carpathian Mountains 200
Danube Delta 200

Rwanda
Wildlife highlights 221

South Africa
Greater St Lucia WP 233
Karoo NP 233
Kgalagadi TP 233
Kruger NP 232
Madikwe GR 234
Namaqualand 232

Spain
Andalucía 195
Balearic Islands 195
Canary islands 197
Coto Doñana 194
Extremadura 194
Picos de Europa 195
Sierra de Guara 195
Spanish Pyrenees 195
Straits of Gibraltar 194

Sri Lanka
Wildlife highlights 251

Tanzania
Gombe Stream NP 217
Katavi NP 217
Lake Manyara NP 217
Mafia Island MP 217
Mahale Mountains NP 216
Mt Kilimanjaro NP 217
Ngorongoro CA 216
Ruaha NP 217
Selous GR 216
Serengeti NP 216
Tarangire NP 217

Uganda
Wildlife highlights 221

United States
Acadia NP 148
Admiralty Island NM 141
Arctic NWR 141
Big Bend NP 144
Big Cypress NP 151
Biscayne NP 151
Cape Canaveral NS 151
Channel Islands NP 145
Corkscrew Swamp 150

Crystal River NWR 151
Denali NP 140
Everglades NP 150
Florida Keys 151
Gates of the Arctic NP 141
Glacier Bay NP 140
Grand Canyon NP 140
Great Smoky Mountains NP 148
Isle Royale NP 149
Katmai NP 142
Kenai Fjords NP 142
Kodiak NWR 141
Lake Clark NP 141
Monterey Bay 145
Redwood NP 144
Rocky Mountain NP 144
Shenandoah NP 149
Tallgrass Prairie NP 149
Voyageurs NP 148
Wrangell-St Elias NP 141
Yellowstone NP 146
Yosemite NP 146

Venezuela
Amazonas 168
Canaima NP 168
Cueva del Guacharo 168
Henri Pittier NP 168
Los Llanos wetlands 168
Orinoco Delta 168
Sierra Nevada de Mérida NP 168

Zambia
Bangweulu Wetlands 223
Kafue NP 222
Kasanka NP 222
Liuwa Plain NP 222
Lochinvar NP 223
Lower Zambezi NP 224
Mosi-oa-Tunya NP 223
North Luangwa NP 223
South Luangwa NP 224
Sumbu NP 223
Zambezi River 225

Zimbabwe
Wildlife highlights 226

Note: This book does not attempt to provide an exhaustive directory of every wildlife destination in the world. Instead, this section describes the wildlife highlights of each continent, along with a selection of the very best places to visit. You will also find numerous other ideas in the Encounters section.

Half-Tail and her daughter Zawadi (also known as Shadow)

it's a wild life

Jonathan & Angie Scott | Photographers, authors & presenters | jonathanangelascott.com

↘ Our big five
1. Masai Mara, Kenya
2. South Georgia, Antarctica
3. Okavango Delta, Botswana
4. Ranthambhore National Park, India
5. Katmai National Park, Alaska

66 99 One morning while filming *Big Cat Diary* I left Angie to keep an eye on Half-Tail the leopard. When I returned many hours later Angie was still sitting in her Land Cruiser, but there was no sign of Half-Tail. "What happened?" I asked. Angie smiled and pointed under her car. There was our favourite leopard curled up fast asleep. No other animal has brought us quite so much pleasure – not even Kike the cheetah sitting on the roof of our vehicle (and peeing on us!) could match having a wild leopard accept our company so completely. At one point Half-Tail looked up and made eye contact with Angie – no sense of fear or aggression, just a look of mild curiosity. Bliss!

❶ Masai Mara, Kenya

If I only had one day in Africa I would spend it in the Masai Mara. We have a permanent base at Governor's Camp which borders the Musiara Marsh, home to the lions of the Marsh Pride which we have been following for nearly 35 years. The Mara in a nutshell: There's no better place to see all three big cats, a stunning variety of wildlife and superb birding. Add to this the spectacle of hundreds of thousands of wildebeest and zebra criss-crossing the Mara's rolling plains in the dry season from June to the end of October and you simply could not ask for more.

❷ South Georgia, Antarctica

The Serengeti of the Southern Ocean. What better place to provide a contrast to the magic of Africa, with equally spectacular scenery and mind-boggling numbers of animals and birds. The whites, greens and blues of Antarctica paint a picture of a land beyond reality. A visit to Antarctica is a journey of the soul as much as the body!

❸ Okavango Delta, Botswana

I had my first taste of living among Africa's wild animals in the Jewel of the Kalahari (I lived on a houseboat called the *Sitatunga* at Shakawe for a few weeks in 1975). The Delta is one of the best places to view wild dogs – another of our favourite animals. It is worth finding out where wild dog packs are likely to be denning and then plan accordingly, based on advice from lodge managers. The Delta is also good for big cats, especially during September and October – the height of the dry season. Mombo and Chiefs Camp are top spots for all round game viewing.

❹ Ranthambhore National Park, India

The combination of beautiful scenery, abundant lakes and water birds, combined with the chance of seeing a tiger, make this one of our favourite destinations for viewing Indian wildlife. We also love Kanha National Park and Bandhavgarh, which is undoubtedly the easiest place to see tigers in India – but we prefer the scenery and wildlife experience that Kanha and Ranthambhore offer.

❺ Katmai National Park, Alaska

We filmed *Big Bear Diary* in Katmai. Here is what our friends at Hallo Bay Bear Camp (hallobay.com) had to say about timing: 'The best time to visit for photography depends on what you would like to observe the bears doing. The salmon run is always a pretty exciting time frame, but our other favourite period is mid-June to mid-July when you can see the bears in the lovely green sedge grass meadows. The photos are much more colourful and you have a better chance to see cubs when they are very small. You also get to watch the bears clamming on the tidal flats during this time. For the salmon runs, visit between mid-August and the start of September. The bears will be busy fishing up and down the creek and hopefully the foxes and wolves will make an appearance at the creek as well.'

North America

When Scottish-born naturalist John Muir set out in 1867 to walk 1,600 km from Louisville, Kentucky to the Gulf of Mexico, he later wrote in his book: 'My plan was simply to push on in a general southward direction by the wildest, leafiest and least trodden way I could find'. Muir's boundless enthusiasm for nature later saw him venturing into the high Sierra of California. Of all his worldwide travels, nowhere stoked his burning passion for wilderness more than Yosemite Valley and he fought hard to protect it from commercial exploitation.

The tenacious Scot founded The Sierra Club (now one of the largest environmental organizations in the United States) and long after his death in 1914, he is still acclaimed as 'Father of the National Parks'.

Some of North America's finest wildlife areas are found within the national parks, wildlife refuges, national forests and marine reserves of Canada and the United States – a liberal scattering of protected areas that extends from the Alaskan panhandle to the Florida Everglades. They include Yellowstone, the world's oldest national park, established in 1872, and numerous nature reserves and sanctuaries pioneered by organizations like The Nature Conservancy and National Audubon Society.

John Muir's spirit lives on in the wonderfully diverse and uplifting travel experiences to be had in these wild places – from paddling a canoe on the pristine lakes of Ontario's Algonquin Provincial Park to hiking the forests and alpine meadows of Colorado's Rocky Mountain National Park.

Outside of Africa, there is nowhere better than North America for close encounters with large mammals, whether it's tracking wolves in Yellowstone, watching grizzlies forage along the kelp-strewn shores of British Columbia or glimpsing bighorn sheep clattering along a cliff in the Grand Canyon.

North America still has wilderness areas big enough to support the ground-swallowing Arctic migrations of the great caribou herds, while salmon runs and herring spawnings in the Northwest Pacific sustain healthy populations of whales, bears and seabirds.

But not everything is as John Muir would have liked it. North America's flower-rich prairie lands have all but vanished; wildernesses are threatened by mining and oil drilling, and even national parks must contend with urban encroachment, climate change, pollution and visitor pressure. Responsible wildlife travellers can do their bit to ensure the future of Muir's legacy by treating North America's wild places with the respect and sense of wonder they deserve.

ⓘ Find out more about conservation and protected areas in North America by visiting the following websites: US National Park Service (nps.gov), Parks Canada (pc.gc.ca), National Audubon Society (audubon.org), The Nature Conservancy (nature.org) and The Sierra Club (sierraclub.org).

Hawaii | North America's hottest wildlife destination

Two of the world's most active volcanoes, Kilauea and Mauna Loa, regularly put on pyrotechnic shows for visitors to Hawaii's Volcanoes National Park (nps.gov/havo). Of equal interest to wildlife enthusiasts, however, is the range of plants and animals that manage to colonize lava flows. Exploiting new opportunities is a trademark of Hawaiian wildlife. The archipelago is home to 23 endemic songbirds, including the apapane and i'iwi honeycreepers, as well as the endangered nene (or Hawaiian goose), Hawaiian petrel and 'io (or Hawaiian hawk). Offshore, the Hawaiian Islands Humpback Whale National Marine Sanctuary (hawaiihumpbackwhale.noaa.gov) protects an important breeding, calving and nursing area for North Pacific humpbacks. Whale-watching trips operate from Maui, November to May, or you can watch the cetaceans from coastal lookouts like Makapu'u Lighthouse on O'ahu.

Great outdoors – North America's national parks promise some of the world's ultimate wildlife adventures

Yosemite National Park, California

Naturalist John Muir once wrote, "No temple made with hands can compare with Yosemite." He might well have have been contemplating the sheer cliffs of El Capitan at the time, shown here rising above autumn-flecked forest on the banks of the River Merced.

Urban sprawl and agriculture may have seeped across much of North America, but the continent still has large swathes of forest, particularly in Canada. Tundra, desert, mountain, swamp and some spectacular coastal areas add to its rich and varied tapestry of habitats.

Natural zones

Permanent ice caps smother all but the fringes of Greenland, while Baffin, Ellesmere and other islands in the Canadian Arctic shed the frigid grip of pack ice for only a few months each summer. The exposed tundra is a blanket of bogs and mosses, freckled here and there with hardy alpine flowers. Tundra extends across the northernmost reaches of Alaska and the Canadian provinces of Labrador, Nunavut and Northwest Territories. As you head south, however, the barren plains become scattered with stunted conifers – resilient outliers of the huge boreal forest that shrouds much of Canada and the Alaskan interior.

The mighty conifer forests extend southward along the western mountains of the Coast and Cascade Ranges, greening British Columbia and

Tundra tumble – polar bears at home in North America

Ursus maritimus
Churchill, Manitoba

The great white bear is found right across Arctic and sub-Arctic regions of Canada and the United States, from Alaska to Labrador – even venturing on winter pack-ice as far south as Newfoundland.

reaching their crowning glory in the redwood forests of California. Boreal forest also marches along the Rockies, the continental divide bulging around the stark plains and sagebrush of the Great Basin before finally crumpling near the Arizona canyonlands and deserts of New Mexico.

East of the Rocky Mountains, the Great Plains lap at the foothills. This vast expanse of native grassland once flowed through central North America, from Alberta to northern Texas, but only a few protected islands of prairie remain in a sea of agriculture.

Broadleaved forests cloak the Appalachian Mountains, an ancient range that mirrors the eastern seaboard from Alabama to Newfoundland.

Sandy beaches, estuaries and rocky shores rim the Atlantic coast, culminating in the subtropical wetlands of Florida and the salt marshes of the Gulf of Mexico. To the north, the gaping maw of the St Lawrence seems to gulp at the North Atlantic, its curling 1,200-km-long gullet perfectly framed in the wolf-head profile of Québec.

North America's high-plains drifters

Barrenland caribou are constantly on the move, huge herds migrating up to 5,000 km a year between summer calving grounds on the tundra and winter refuges in the boreal forest. It's a natural spectacle every bit as epic as the Serengeti wildebeest migration. The caribou must run the gauntlet of wolves, cross lakes and rivers and contend with swarms of mosquitoes and blackflies. Another subspecies, the woodland caribou is more restricted to the boreal forest and tends to migrate over much shorter distances.

Wild city | Victoria, British Columbia

Three resident orca pods (comprising nearly 100 whales) cruise the Juan de Fuca and Haro Straits off the southern tip of Vancouver Island, making Victoria perfectly placed for whale-watching cruises. In fact, during the prime months of April to October, some operators boast a 100% success rate. Tours last around three hours and you can step straight from Victoria's waterfront onto either a high-speed zodiac, jet-powered catamaran or a more sedate motor cruiser – just make sure it's a member of the Pacific Whale Watch Association (pacificwhalewatch.org) which abides by guidelines for minimizing disturbance to cetaceans. If you're lucky you'll see orca breaching and spy-hopping. Keep your eyes peeled for Dall's porpoise torpedoing through the waves or the more leisurely passage of a grey or humpback whale. Sea lions are almost guaranteed and it's also worth casting an occasional glance skyward – you never know when a bald eagle might make an appearance. For a view of what lies beneath, the marine sanctuary at Ogden Point Breakwater, a few minutes from downtown Victoria, promises some of the world's best cold-water diving (divevictoria.com). Dive sites range from 8 to 35 m in depth and you're likely to see octopus, wolf eel, harbour seal and king crab.

The mighty conifer forests extend southward along the western mountains of the Coast and Cascade Ranges, greening British Columbia and reaching their crowning glory in the redwood forests of California

Day 1 Arrive Calgary, drive to Banff National Park in the heart of the Rocky Mountains **Day 2** Full day exploring Banff **Day 3** Golden, visit the Northern Lights Wildlife Wolf Centre **Day 4** Drive along the Icefields Parkway to Jasper **Day 5** Hike one of the many trails in Jasper National Park **Day 6** Overnight in Clearwater beside the Thompson River **Days 7 and 8** Sample the activities on offer in Whistler **Day 9** Drive to Vancouver **Day 10** Ferry to Vancouver Island; whale watching in Johnstone Strait **Day 11** Explore Pacific Rim National Park; overnight in Tofino **Day 12** Return to Vancouver **Day 13** Depart Vancouver

↻ Based on a tailor-made itinerary from **Wildlife Worldwide** (wildlifeworldwide.com), this trip would cost from around £2,500 per person, including flights from the UK, car hire, ferries, 12 nights B&B accommodation and guided activities. The **Great Canadian Travel Co** (greatcanadiantravel.com) offers a seven-night itinerary from Vancouver to Calgary from around C$1,650 per person, including three nights in Vancouver, one in Jasper and two in Banff, a whale-watching trip, rail travel between Vancouver and Jasper and three days car rental.

Wildlife travel

With its extensive system of parks, wildlife refuges and wilderness areas, a sophisticated tourist infrastructure and almost limitless travel options, North America is a superb natural history destination. You can make your forays into the wild as simple or as challenging as you like. Take bears, for example. At one extreme you can watch them on a guided tour from the comfort of a wilderness lodge; at the other, you could plan a week-long camping trip, hiking through grizzly country.

Independent travel is straightforward in North America, but be sure to obtain any necessary permits and wilderness experience before venturing off the beaten track. Also bear in mind the heavy tourist pressure that some national parks face during busy holiday seasons – travelling in quieter months may offer more rewarding wildlife watching opportunities.

By visiting national parks, you play a part in their protection. Most offer ranger-led activities – an excellent way to learn about wildlife and conservation (the US Parks Service even has a Junior Ranger Program for children). Several First Nations communities also operate tours and ecolodges, providing a unique insight into the deep-rooted links between culture and wildlife in North America.

Wild places

Alaska's premier national parks like Denali, Katmai and Kenai Fjords ❶ mix wildlife, wilderness and wow factor. Those with a yearning for truely remote places should plan a backcountry expedition to the Gates of the Arctic National Park ❷. Alternatively, travel through Southeast Alaska ❸ on the state ferry system, a marine highway that extends south from Glacier Bay through the forested islands and Pacific coast of British Columbia's Great Bear Rainforest ❹. Searching for orcas in Johnstone Strait ❺ is one of the main draws of Vancouver island, but don't miss Pacific Rim National Park ❻ where temperate rainforest meets the ocean. More woodland wonders can be explored in the Pacific Northwest states of Washington and Oregon where Olympic National Park ❼ can be combined wth visits to Mount Rainier and the North Cascades. In California, tree-lovers should head for Redwood National Park ❽. In the Sierra Nevada, meanwhile, Yosemite National Park ❾ epitomises the great outdoors of the western United States. National parks in the Canadian Rocky Mountains ❿ include Banff, Jasper, Kootenay and Yoho – all boasting spectacular scenery and wildlife ranging from moose and beaver to wolf and brown bear. In Colorado, Rocky Mountain National Park ⓫ and Grand Teton National Park ⓬ showcase the United States' high places with magnificent snow-capped peaks, alpine meadows, sapphire lakes and forests. Offering a lifeline to large mammals like wolf and grizzly bear, Yellowstone National Park ⓭ is North America's ultimate 'big game' destination, while the fragile remnants of the great prairie grasslands (protected in places like Tallgrass Prairie Reserve, Oklahoma ⓮) provide a safe haven for plains bison. Wildlife also makes a stand in the watery wilderness of Midwest nature reserves like Voyageurs National Park ⓯ where you can paddle a canoe in search of moose, black bear and bald eagle. Further north, Churchill ⓰ has become established as one of the world's top wildlife destinations, with tours to see polar bear in autumn and beluga whales in summer. Eastern Canada's natural highlights include whale watching in the Gulf of St Lawrence ⓱ and Bay of Fundy ⓲, while the Eastern United States has wild woods in the Appalachian Mountains ⓳ and the teeming wetlands of the Everglades ⓴.

Making tracks | Alaska

Alaskan wildlife tour operators include **AAT** (alaskatours.com), **Alaska Wildland Adventures** (alaskawildland.com) and **Explore Tours** (exploretours.com).

Alaska Airlines (alaskaair.com) flies from Seattle to Anchorage (3.5 hours) and connects major towns and cities throughout the state. One of the world's great drives, the 2,400-km **Alaska Highway** starts in Dawson Creek, British Columbia and ends at Delta Junction. Cruise ships and ferries ply the **Alaska Marine Highway** (dot. state.ak.us/amhs) from the Inside Passage, across the Gulf of Alaska and west to the Aleutian Islands. Destinations on the **Alaska Railroad** (alaskarailroad. com) include Anchorage, Denali, Fairbanks, Portage, Seward and Talkeetna. Bush planes reach remote areas.

Range of wilderness lodges, cabins (fs.fed.us/ recreation) and hostels (alaskahostelassociation.org).

GMT-9

High season is June to August when daytime temperatures range from 15-27°C. May and September have lower prices. Expect unpredictable weather at any time of the year. Layered clothing is best.

Backcountry hikers should be aware of bear safety measures (p93).

US dollar ($).

travelalaska.com

alaskaconservation.org

Denali National Park & Preserve

★ Dall sheep, moose, caribou, grizzly bear, wolf

Established in 1917 as Mount McKinley National Park, Denali takes its name from the Athabascan word for 'High One'. North America's highest peak (6,194 m) lords over this 24,300-sq-km wilderness – the glaciers and valleys of the Alaska Range sweeping down to vast tracts of lake-studded tundra and a tentative stubble of boreal forest.

Winter hits hard in Denali and its wildlife either stays put and copes, or heads south to warmer climes. Year-round residents like caribou, Dall sheep, moose, wolf, ptarmigan and gyrfalcon simply tough it out, while others, like the grizzly bear, hibernate. When spring arrives, there's a flurry of activity as groggy bears emerge from their dens and millions of migratory birds (including golden eagles from as far afield as Mexico) arrive to breed. Wild flowers bloom from early June to late July. It can be light for 20 hours a day and wildlife is at its most active – including mosquitoes. By early August, the winged menace has disappeared from all but the wettest areas. Autumn colours begin to flush the tundra, bears start to gorge on berries and birds have migration on their minds once more. As bull moose gather harems for the mating season, the first glimmers of the Northern Lights may start to be seen. If snow falls in September, it usually stays until spring.

Denali's 'big five' (moose, caribou, Dall sheep, wolf and grizzly bear) can often be seen on a bus ride along the 137-km park road – the sole vehicle access into the heart of the park. This provides a better chance of seeing wildlife than hiking, as you have a higher vantage point and the benefit of many eyes. If you plan to explore Denali on foot, be sure to take bear safety precautions (see page 93).

There are approximately 1,800 moose in the park, with bulls weighing up to 630 kg. The Denali caribou herd has similar numbers; calves are born mid-May to early June. Keeping to ridges and steep slopes to avoid predators, Dall sheep are found in mountain regions in the east and west of the park, the valleys reverberating with the clash of headbutting rams during the late-November rut. Denali's wolf numbers fluctuate at around 100. Roaming large areas, the packs feed primarily on caribou, moose and Dall

sheep. Grizzly bears, meanwhile, have a very mixed diet in Denali, eating everything from caribou calves and carrion to roots, blueberries and salmon.

Directions 390 km north of Anchorage on Alaska Route 3; Alaska Railroad between Anchorage and Fairbanks passes park entrance.
Getting around Private car access as far as Savage River Bridge; shuttle bus and bicycles for destinations further into park.
Seasons Park open year round; bus service operates along park road mid-May to mid-September; winter activities also available.
Visitor centres Summer visitor centre May to September; Murie Science & Learning Centre year round.
Things to do Guided tours, ranger activities, backpacking, hiking, cycling, fishing, skiing, dogsledding, mountaineering, photography.
Places to stay Campsites, backcountry camping, wilderness lodges.
Further information nps.gov/dena

Glacier Bay National Park & Preserve

★ Humpback whale, Steller's sea lion, harbour seal, sea otter

Star of many an Alaskan cruise, Glacier Bay's tidewater glaciers calve icebergs into deep fjords where abundant fish attract marine mammals, such as humpback and minke whale, orca, harbour and Dall porpoise, harbour seal and Steller's sea lion. In the 200 or so years that the ice has retreated, exposing the 100-km-long bay, a forest of spruce and hemlock has taken root, providing a habitat for black bear, wolf and moose. Occasionally, you can spot bears working the shoreline, turning over rocks in search of tideline morsels. With luck, you may even see a 'glacier bear', a rare, silver-coloured form. Offshore, sea otters (which number around 1,500 in the park) dive for crabs, molluscs and sea urchins, while sea cliffs throng with nesting colonies of guillemots and puffins.

Two of the best adventure activities in Glacier Bay are rafting the Tatshenshini and Alsek rivers and sea kayaking in Muir Inlet. Local outfitters can kit you out or arrange guided tours.

Directions West of Juneau; accessible only by sea (tour boat, cruise ship etc) or air. Alaska Airlines has a daily summer service between Juneau and Gustavus, 16 km by road from the park headquarters at Bartlett Cove. Alaska Marine Highway Ferry *LeConte* calls twice weekly at Gustavus during summer months.
Getting around Buses run between Gustavus and Bartlett Cove, where boat tours are available to tidewater glaciers.
Seasons Late May to mid-September.
Visitor centres Bartlett Cove, May to September.
Things to do Boat tours, ranger activities, hiking, camping, mountaineering, kayaking, rafting, fishing, flightseeing.
Places to stay Backcountry camping, wilderness lodge, cruise ships.
Further information nps.gov/glba

Beaufort Sea

Gates of the Arctic National Park & Preserve
Access to this spectacular wilderness – home to bears and herds of muskoxen and caribou – is usually by float plane. Best time to visit is late June to early September, but be prepared for unpredictable weather. Once the floatplane leaves, you're on your own, so be sure to plan carefully. Experience in low-impact wilderness camping is also essential.
nps.gov/gaar

• **Prudhoe Bay**

Brooks Range

Arctic National Wildlife Refuge
Stretching from the Arctic coast deep into the Brooks Range, this breathtaking place supports a greater diversity of wildlife than any other protected area in the Arctic. Polar bears give birth in snow dens along its northern fringe, grizzly bears roam the coastal plains and foothills, while black bears can be found in boreal forest further south. Add to this huge herds of caribou, muskoxen, Dall sheep, wolves and 300,000 snow geese (late August to September) and you have one of the world's finest wildernesses.
alaska.fws.gov/nwr/arctic

Kobuk Valley National Park ○
Migrating caribou

Lake Clark National Park & Preserve
Quintessential Alaska, with active volcanoes, glaciers, wild rivers and prolific wildlife. There's no highway access, you'll need to charter an air taxi. Wilderness camping, kayaking and fishing are all possible for those who plan carefully.
nps.gov/lacl

Wrangell-St Elias National Park & Preserve
This vast national park (almost six times bigger than Yellowstone) demands at least a week if you want to explore its backcountry of mountains, glaciers and rivers. Activities include hiking, rafting and kayaking. Look for Dall sheep on rocky ridges, moose near lakes and bears at salmon spawning streams. With less time, take Richardson Highway to the park visitor centre which has trails and views.
nps.gov/wrst

Bering Sea

• **Fairbanks**

Denali National Park
see page140

△ **Mt McKinley**

Alaska Chilkat Bald Eagle Preserve
Bald eagle numbers on the Chilkat river flats can swell from a resident 300 to over 3,000 between October and February.
dnr.alaska.gov/parks/units/eagleprv

○ **Yukon Delta National Wildlife Refuge**
Shorebirds, muskoxen, marine mammals

Anchorage •

• **Valdez**

Prince William Sound

• **Haines**

• **Seward**

Homer •

Kenai Fjords National Park see page142

Glacier Bay National Park see page140

Juneau •

Katmai National Park see page142

Gulf of Alaska

Tongass National Forest

Bristol Bay

Kodiak National Wildlife Refuge
A haven for some 3,500 Kodiak brown bears, 600 breeding pairs of bald eagle, plus thriving populations of sea otters and sea lions, this fjord-riven island is a port of call for the Alaska Marine Highway Ferry *Tustumena* (dot.state.ak.us/amhs) which departs Homer monthly, April to October, for the four-day run to Dutch Harbour on the Aleutian Island of Unalaska. The voyage is a great opportunity to observe the whales, seals, sea lions, otters and migratory birds of the Alaska Peninsula.
alaska.fws.gov/nwr/kodiak

Alaska Peninsula National Wildlife Refuge
Brown bear, caribou, moose, marine mammals

Admiralty Island National Monument
A 30-minute floatplane ride from Juneau, Pack Creek Brown Bear Viewing Area is the best place to view some of Admiralty Island's 1,500 bears. Known to native Tlingit as 'Kootznoowoo' or 'Fortress of the Bears', the island is a riot of old growth rainforest, mountain lakes and wild salmon creeks.
fs.fed.us/r10/tongass/districts/admiralty

Katmai National Park & Preserve

★ Brown bear, moose, lynx, river otter, sea otter, sea lion

Each summer, when the sockeye salmon migrate from Bristol Bay into the creeks, rivers and lakes of the Naknek drainage, Katmai's Alaskan brown bears rub their paws in anticipation. Around 100 stake out the Brooks Falls area, snatching leaping fish in their jaws and pounding through shallows in pursuit of a slippery feast. Various wooden platforms provide superb (and safe) views of the spectacle.

Bears hog the limelight in Katmai, but take a hike in the Valley of Ten Thousand Smokes and you stand a good chance of seeing other wildlife, such as red fox, wolf, lynx, wolverine, porcupine, moose and caribou. Named after the 1912 eruption of Novarupta, which dumped ash over 64 sq km and caused fumaroles to steam from buried rivers and glaciers, the starkly beautiful valley can be accessed along a rough road between Brooks Camp and Three Forks Overlook.

Katmai's coastline is also worth exploring. You can stay in wilderness lodges or join a wildlife cruise in search of sea lion colonies. Grey whales and orcas are also regular visitors to the Shelikof Strait between Katmai National Park and Kodiak island.

Directions 470 km southwest of Anchorage by plane.
Getting around Alaska Airlines flies Anchorage to King Salmon, the park headquarters; air taxi charters and boats serve Brooks Camp and various lodges in the park's interior and along the coast.
Seasons Park open year round; national park services at Brooks Camp available June to mid-September; prime bear-viewing months July and September.
Visitor centres Brooks Camp and King Salmon.
Things to do Bear watching, hiking, backpacking, fishing, boating, ranger activities, bus tour to Valley of Ten Thousand Smokes.
Places to stay Brooks Camp campground, backcountry camping, wilderness lodges, coastal cruises.
Further information nps.gov/katm

Kenai Fjords National Park & Preserve

★ Sea otter, sea lion, Dall's porpoise, humpback whale, bear

The Ice Age lingers in Kenai Fjords, its coastal peaks smothered in the Harding Icefield – source of some 38 glaciers. You can drive to Exit Glacier and explore a network of trails through cottonwood forest and across a gravel moraine to the frozen snout of the glacier itself. The more demanding, full-day Harding Icefield Trail climbs high above the tree line for stunning views across a panorama of ice and snow.

You're likely to see black bears on this trail (particularly in salmonberry thickets), so make some noise to avoid surprising them. Boat trips depart Seward throughout the summer. The park's tidewater glaciers are only within range of a full-day tour, while a half-day cruise in Resurrection Bay will still give you opportunities to spot Kenai's outstanding marine life.

Directions Near Seward, 200 km south of Anchorage, via Seward Highway or Alaska Railroad (May to September only).
Getting around Shuttle bus service to Exit Glacier, boat tours, water taxis to coastal backcountry areas.
Seasons Park open year round, but Exit Glacier road closed winter.
Visitor centres Seward and Exit Glacier, May to September.
Things to do Boat tours, ranger program, hiking, camping, mountaineering, kayaking, fishing, flightseeing, dogsledding.
Places to stay Backcountry camping, lodges, cabins.
Further information nps.gov/kefj

Southeast Alaska | Highlights of the Inside Passage

Ketchikan is a gateway to the Misty Fjords National Monument – over two million acres of rugged, brooding wilderness, perfect for hiking, kayaking or fishing. The Southeast Alaska Discovery Centre provides an excellent introduction to the region (including a fascinating glimpse into the culture of the First Nations people), while nearby Saxman Village boasts the world's largest collection of standing totem poles and a chance to watch modern-day carvers at work. At **Wrangell** you can search for ancient petroglyph rock carvings on the beach or venture by kayak into the mouth of the Stikine River. **Petersburg** offers the chance to appreciate the workings of a busy Alaskan fishing port. Facing the open Pacific and built in the shadow of Mt Edgecumbe, an extinct volcano, **Sitka's** many historical treasures include the Russian Orthodox St Michael's Cathedral, Sitka National Historic Park and the Sheldon Jackson Museum (containing one of Alaska's best collections of indigenous culture). The Alaska Raptor Centre (a hospital for bald eagles) is also worth a visit. For outdoor enthusiasts **Juneau** provides access to some of Southeast Alaska's most spectacular scenery. You can hike to the Mendenhall Glacier, fly over the 3,900-sq-km Juneau Ice Field, take a boat trip to Tracy Arm Fjord (with its tidewater glaciers) or visit Admiralty Island to view brown bears. Juneau is also the starting point for trips into Glacier Bay National Park. More wild sights await visitors to the Alaska Chilkat Bald Eagle Preserve, near **Haines**, while **Skagway** offers a nostalgic and captivating glimpse into the gold rush days. The more adventurous can hike the five-day Chilkoot Trail in the prospectors' footsteps or ride the White Pass & Yukon scenic railway.

Autumn gold – the Alaska Range during Fall.
Left: Willow ptarmigan in winter plumage, the
nimble-hooved dall sheep and the ever-watchful
grey wolf.

For wildlife tours in Yellowstone, try **Yellowstone Safari Co** (yellowstonesafari.com). Guided hiking in Grand Canyon, Yellowstone and Rocky Mountain National Parks is available from **Wildland Trekking** (wildlandtrekking.com). **Green Tours** (greentours. co.uk) features Redwood NP on its Northern California small-group trip, while **WWF Tours** (worldwildlife.org) has a wildlife trek in Big Bend NP.

Major airline hubs include Los Angeles, San Francisco, Seattle and Denver, served by numerous airlines, such as **American** (aa. com), **British Airways** (britishairways.com) and **United** (united.com). **Greyhound** (greyhound. com) and **Amtrak** (amtrak. com) provide bus and rail services in the region.

Wide range of lodges, hostels and campsites.

GMT-8 (Los Angeles), GMT-7 (Denver)

Climate varies from cool summer fog along the Redwood coast to blistering heat in Big Bend NP and snow in the Rockies.

Backcountry hikers should be aware of bear safety measures (p93).

US dollar ($)

Tourist information websites include arizonaguide.com, colorado.com, experiencewa.com, travelnevada.com, visitcalifornia.com, wyomingtourism.org

Big Bend National Park

★ Cacti, mountain lion, bull snake, great horned owl, tarantula

Clinched in a loop of the Rio Grande, this 3,100-sq-km chunk of the Chihuahuan Desert supports a surprising diversity of plants and animals, including 60 cacti, 32 snakes, 12 owls and 75 mammals. This is mountain lion country, although you're more likely to see black-tailed jackrabbit and the pig-like javelina, or collared peccary. Top bird ticks include Lucifer hummingbird, Mexican jay and and black-capped vireo.

Directions West Texas, 110 km south of Marathon. Nearest major airports are Midland/Odessa and El Paso.
Getting around No public transport into park.
Seasons Park open year round.
Visitor centres Panther Junction Visitor Centre open daily.
Things to do Ranger activities, backpacking, hiking, cycling, Rio Grande float trips, birding, climbing.
Places to stay Campsites, Chisos Lodge (foreverresorts.com).
Further information nps.gov/bibe

Grand Canyon

Grand Canyon National Park

★ California condor, mountain lion, bighorn sheep

Scan the cliffs and fir trees along the Grand Canyon's South Rim late in the afternoon (Bright Angel Lodge is a good spot) and you may glimpse North America's largest bird. There are just 370 California condors left in the world and around 70 are found in northern Arizona and southern Utah – a mixture of captive-bred individuals and broods raised in wild nest caves in the Grand Canyon. With a wingspan of 2.9 m, these carrion feeders can soar effortlessly on thermals high above the 29-km wide, 1.6-km deep canyon. The South Rim is predominantly Sonoran desert scrub, inhabited by mule deer, bighorn sheep, rock squirrels and grey fox, while the North Rim lies in the Boreal zone – home to the secretive mountain lion and endemic Kaibab squirrel.

Directions South Rim is 95 km north of Williams, 128 km northwest of Flagstaff. Flights serve Phoenix, Flagstaff, Las Vegas and Grand Canyon Airport. Greyhound bus and Amtrak rail stop at Flagstaff, with shuttles to Grand Canyon Village. North Rim village is 48 km south of Jacob Lake, Utah and is only accessible by road.
Getting around Free shuttle bus around South Rim village and to various trailheads, including South Kaibab.
Seasons South Rim all year, North Rim mid-May to mid-October.
Visitor centres South and North Rim.
Things to do Ranger activities, hiking, mule treks, river trips.
Places to stay Campsites and lodges (xanterra.com).
Further information nps.gov/grca

Redwood National & State Parks

★ Coast redwood, Roosevelt elk, Pacific tree frog, sea lion

Rising high and mighty in old-growth forest, the coast redwood (*Sequoia sempervirens*) is the undisputed crowd-puller of this park. However, the world's tallest tree – exceeding 100 m in height – is just one species in an extraordinarily diverse mosaic of ecosystems, ranging from forest and prairie to rockpool and beach. In a single visit, you could see everything from giant salamanders and black bears in shady forest to giant sea anemones and Steller's sea lions along the Pacific-raked shore. Grey whales also migrate along the coast (December/January and March/April), while herds of Roosevelt elk can be seen grazing areas of prairie.

Directions 520 km north of San Francisco on Highway 101. Park headquarters is at Crescent City.
Getting around Redwood Coast Transit offers public transport.
Seasons Park open year round.
Visitor centres Five centres, including Crescent City and Thomas H Kuchel Visitor Centres, open daily.
Things to do Ranger activities, backpacking, hiking, cycling, scenic drives, kayaking, horseback riding and horsepacking.
Places to stay Currently only campsites only in the park (hostel closed in 2010).
Further information nps.gov/redw

Rocky Mountain National Park

★ Elk, bighorn sheep, moose, marmot, golden eagle

Boasting more than 60 peaks over 12,000 ft (3,657 m), Rocky Mountain National Park protects vast swathes of alpine tundra, as well as the headwaters of the Colorado River. Glacial moraines give way to meadows and lakes, while stands of ponderosa and aspen thicken to forests of spruce and fir. Although grizzly bear, grey wolf and bison are locally extinct, the park provides perfect habitat for several species of large mammal, including a summer population of over 3,000 elk (dwindling to 1,000 in winter). Standing up to 1.5 m at the shoulder, bull elk rut during the

North Cascades NP

Glacier NP

Olympic National Park see pages 96-97

Seattle

Mt Rainier

Skagit River
Thousands of bald eagles descend on the Skagit River each December and January to feast on chum salmon.
nature.org

Great Falls

Badlands National Park
A surreal landscape of eroded pinnacles and gullies in the mixed-grass prairie, the Badlands are home to bison, pronghorn antelope, mule deer and bighorn sheep. The bison are best viewed from the Sage Creek Rim Road, while the pronghorns can sometimes be seen from the Badlands Loop Road. Look for golden eagles around Badlands Wall and western meadow larks and burrowing owls out on the prairie.
nps.gov/badl

Portland

Pacific Ocean

Cascade Range

Redwood National Park see page 144

Crater Lake NP

Yellowstone National Park see page 146

Grand Teton NP

Jackson

Platte River, Nebraska
Sandhill cranes gather in their thousands in March.
rowesanctuary.org

Lassen Volcanic NP

Great Salt Lake

Sierra Nevada

Salt Lake City

Rocky Mountain National Park see page 144

Rocky Mountains

Sacramento

Yosemite National Park see page 146

Denver

Pikes Peak

San Francisco

Canyonlands NP

Arapaho National Wildlife Refuge
A sanctuary for thousands of waterfowl, as well as waders such as eared grebe and Wilson's phalarope. Pronghorn antelope, beaver and coyote are also regularly seen.
fws.gov/arapaho

Sequoia & Kings Canyon NP

Zion NP

Bryce Canyon NP

Grand Canyon National Park see page 144

Monterey Bay
Boat trips to watch grey whales (Jan-Mar) and blues and humpbacks (Apr-Dec).

Las Vegas

Death Valley National Park
Desert bighorn sheep, bobcats and other hardy species survive in this land of extremes. Wildflowers in April.
nps.gov/deva

Albuquerque

Los Angeles

Carlsbad Caverns National Park
Witness the exodus of Mexican free-tailed bats at dusk during summer.
nps.gov/cave

San Diego

Phoenix

Tuscon

El Paso

Guadalupe Mountains NP
Fossil reef, desert reptiles

Channel Islands National Park
Swept by the nutrient-rich waters of the Santa Barbara Channel, this cluster of five islands supports a wealth of marine life, from superpods of common dolphin and large haul-outs of California sea lion and northern fur seal to migrating grey whales (December to March) and breeding colonies of tufted puffin, brown pelican, guillemots, storm petrels, murrelets and auklets. The islands are home to distinct subspecies of fox and deer mouse. Activities include boat trips, snorkelling and kayaking.
nps.gov/wrst

Big Bend National Park see page144

autumn when they are best observed in Kawuneeche Valley, Horseshoe Park, Moraine Park and Upper Beaver Meadows. Listen for their call, or bugle – deep, resonant tones, rising to a high-pitched squeal, then dropping to a series of grunts.

Numbering around 800, bighorn sheep are most easily viewed at Sheep Lakes from May to mid-August; mule deer are common throughout the park, while moose favour willow thickets along the Colorado River in Kawuneeche Valley. Above the treeline, you'll probably hear the whistles and squeaks of marmots and pikas before you spot the rodents busily foraging in alpine meadows. They'll be alert for predators like mountain lion, coyote and golden eagle. Other birds in the park include Steller's jay, prairie falcon, white-tailed ptarmigan, American dipper and broad-tailed hummingbird. Butterfly spotters won't be disappointed either – no less than 139 species have been identified here.

Directions Two-hour drive from Denver International Airport.
Getting around Free bus shuttles operate within the park and connect Estes Park with visitor centres and trailheads.
Seasons Park open year round.
Visitor centres Five visitor centres: Beaver Meadows, Fall River and Kawuneeche (open year round), Alpine and Moraine (May-October).
Things to do Ranger activities, backpacking, hiking, cycling, fishing, climbing, Trail Ridge road tours, horse riding, skiing, snow shoeing.
Places to stay Campsites, backcountry camping, lodges.
Further information nps.gov/romo

Yellowstone National Park

★ Grizzly bear, wolf, bison, elk, bighorn sheep

Established in 1872 as America's first national park, Yellowstone has 3,122-m Mt Washburn, a 32-km-long canyon, waterfalls over 90 m high and more than 300 geysers (60% of the world total). It is also big game country, supporting the largest concentration of large mammals in the lower 48 states, including bears and bison. Hayden Valley is one of the park's prime wildlife-viewing sites. You can often see herds of bison here. Grizzly bears prey on calves during spring and early summer, while the bison rut occurs in late July and August. Coyotes are frequently spotted in the valley, while birdlife includes nesting sandhill cranes, bald eagles and white pelicans.

Yellowstone's bison population fluctuates from 2,300 to 4,500 animals. Grizzly bears, meanwhile,

number around 500, with a similar size population of black bears (preferring forested areas in the Lamar and Hayden Valleys). In contrast to the common coyote, Yellowstone's bobcats, lynx, mountain lions, wolverines and wolves (see page 88) are much harder to see. Top of the menu for wolves, elk are the most abundant large mammals in the park, with some 30,000 split between seven or eight summer herds. Other native ungulates include mule deer, moose, bighorn sheep, pronghorn and white-tailed deer.

Directions Sprawling through parts of Wyoming, Montana and Idaho, Yellowstone has several entrances. Nearest airports include Cody, Jackson, Bozeman, Billings and Idaho Falls. Buses link Bozeman and West Yellowstone.
Getting around Bus tours (including snowcoach tours in winter).
Seasons Park open year round; most entrances close in November while roads are prepared for the winter season.
Visitor centres Albright (Mammoth Hot Springs), open year round; other visitor centres seasonal (Canyon, Fishing Bridge, Grant, Old faithful, West Yellowstone).
Things to do Guided tours, ranger activities, hiking, cycling, fishing, horse riding, llama packing, skiing, snow-shoeing, snowmobiling.
Places to stay Campsites and lodges (xanterra.com).
Further information nps.gov/yell

Yosemite National Park

★ Mule deer, black bear, bighorn sheep, mountain lion, red fox

Yosemite's waterfalls, giant granite cliffs and groves of giant sequoia are an irresistible lure to wilderness lovers. Scenic highlights include the 739-m-tall Yosemite Falls and 2,695-m Half Dome. While hiking the park's trails, keep an eye out for Yosemite's abundant wildlife, whether it's mule deer in Yosemite Valley or Sierra Nevada bighorn sheep above the treeline. Be sure to visit the Mariposa Grove of giant sequoias and the subalpine Tuolumne Meadows (accessible around late May along Tioga Road).

Directions Allow five hours to drive from San Francisco to Yosemite Valley. Amtrak runs a train/bus service to the valley; Greyhound serves Merced, from where transfers are available to Yosemite.
Getting around Free shuttle bus to some areas of the park.
Seasons Park open year round, although some roads are closed during winter due to snow. Most waterfalls reach peak flow in May or June, running dry by August. Most wildflowers bloom in June.
Visitor centres Yosemite Valley and Tuolumne Meadows (open daily), Wawona Information Station (summer only).
Things to do Guided tours, ranger activities, hiking, cycling, fishing, horse riding, rock climbing, cross-country skiing, snow shoeing.
Places to stay Campsites and lodges (xanterra.com).
Further information nps.gov/yose

Steaming ahead – a herd of bison treks beside Firehole River towards the Midway Geyser Basin. Left: Bull elk in his prime; grizzlies play-fighting.

Making tracks | Eastern US

One of North America's leading wildlife tour operators, the **Environmental Adventure Company** (eactours. com) offers nature trips worldwide, including several on home turf to destinations ranging from Alaska to the Everglades. Tours in the Eastern United States feature the Great Smoky Mountains, Lake Superior and Isle Royale. Whale-watching trips depart Boston's Long Wharf, April to November; operators include **Boston Harbor Cruises** (bostonharborcruises.com).

✈ Major airline hubs include New York, Washington DC, Boston and Chicago, served by numerous airlines. **Greyhound** (greyhound. com) and **Amtrak** (amtrak. com) provide bus and rail services in the region.

🛏 Wide range of lodges, hostels and campsites.

🕐 GMT-5 (New York), GMT-6 (Dallas).

☼ Climate varies from hot and humid year round in New Orleans and along the Gulf Coast to a typical Atlantic climate of warm summers and cold, snowy winters in Maine. All of the areas featured here offer activities year round.

☺ Backcountry hikers should be aware of bear safety measures (p93).

💲 US dollar ($)

ⓘ Tourist information websites in the region include visitmaine.com, exploreminnesota.com, virginia.org and visitnc.com

Acadia National Park

★ Peregrine falcon, loon, eider duck, beaver, harbour seal

The Maine coast at its most diverse, Acadia National Park is a rugged patchwork of forested islands, lakes, marshes, sheltered inlets and rocky shores. The fact that it also straddles the transition zone between eastern deciduous and northern coniferous forests only adds to its biodiversity. An impressve 338 bird species have been recorded in the park, including no less than 23 varieties of warbler. Seabirds, eiders, peregrines and bald eagles also breed here, while the estuaries are an important wintering site for shorebirds such as purple sandpiper and harlequin duck. From mid-August to mid-October, rangers and volunteers carry out a HawkWatch survey from Cadillac Mountain (the park's highest point), counting migratory raptors like American kestrel and sharp-shinned hawk as they head south for the winter.

Directions Approximately six hours north of Boston, most of the park is located on Mount Desert Island, accessible by vehicle. In summer, buses operate between Boston and Bangor (80 km from park), and on to Bar Harbor on the east coast of Mt Desert Island.
Getting around Free Explorer Bus on Mount Desert Island mid-June to early October; Island Explorer bus links park to nearby villages and campgrounds, as well as Hancock County aiport.
Seasons Park open year round; most facilities close during winter.
Visitor centres Hulls Cove (mid-April to late-October).
Things to do Cycling, birdwatching, boating, climbing, fishing, hiking, horse riding, scenic drives, rock-pooling, sea kayaking.
Places to stay Two campsites on Mt Desert Island.
Further information nps.gov/acad

Great Smoky Mountains National Park

★ Black bear, elk, spring flowers, salamanders, woodpeckers

The Appalachian Mountains rucked up in all their glory, Great Smoky Mountains National Park lays a leafy cloak across the border of North Carolina and Tennessee. America's most visited national park, most people arrive with the hope of glimpsing one of its 1,500 or so black bears. Open areas like Cataloochee and Cades Cove are probably your best bet for bear-spotting (you may also see white-tailed deer, raccoon, and woodchuck). However, there's a lot more to Great Smoky than bears. The park supports over 1,660 species of flowering plants. At the peak of spring blooming (usually mid-April), trilliums, orchids, irises, columbines and violets carpet the ground, the display continuing into summer with lilies and cardinals.

Great Smoky Mountains

The park also supports 30 species of salamander and a wonderful variety of birds. Explore spruce forest on the highest ridges for red-breasted nuthatch, or try your luck in the lower-elevation hardwood forests for downy woodpecker, belted kingfisher and summer-visiting scarlet tanager and Acadian flycatcher.

Directions Cherokee, Gatlinburg and Townsend provide access to the park's three main entrances. Trolley service from Gatlinburg; bus service from Cherokee.
Getting around Extensive road and trail network.
Seasons Park open year round; some roads and campgrounds closed winter; fall colours best from October to early November. Avoid crowds by visiting outside weeknds during summer and fall.
Visitor centres Cades Cove, Oconaluftee, Sugarlands (open daily).
Things to do Ranger activities, hiking, cycling, fishing, horse riding.
Places to stay Le Conte Lodge (lecontelodge.com), plus various campsites for group, horse riders and backcountry hikers.
Further information nps.gov/grsm

Voyageurs National Park

★ Black bear, wolf, moose, beaver, otter, bald eagle

Some 200 years ago, fur traders paddled this watery maze in birch bark canoes piled high with animal pelts, and it's still very much somewhere to explore afloat. Canoeing on lakes and drifting silently past forested islands, you'll slow down to the natural rhythm of Voyageurs National Park, pausing to listen to the haunting call of a common loon, or snapping alert as you hear a bear or deer moving through the woods. If you're lucky, you might even witness the paddle-arresting howl of wolves.

Directions Falls International, Minnesota, is the nearest airport, five hours' drive from the park. There's no public transport to Voyageurs.
Getting around Canoes and boats available to rent; boat tours.
Seasons Park open year round; lakes frozen in winter.
Visitor centres Rainy Lake (open year round), Kabetogama and Ash River (open mid-May to late September).
Things to do Boat tours, canoeing, kayaking, boating, guided tours, ranger activities, hiking, fishing, snowshoeing, cross-country skiing.
Places to stay Campsites, backcountry camping.
Further information nps.gov/voya

Voyageurs National Park see page 148

Hawk Mountain Sanctuary
From mid-August to mid-December, around 20,000 hawks, eagles and falcons are observed from Hawk Mountain's lookout during the annual raptor migration.
hawkmountain.org

Delaware Bay
Horseshoe crabs spawn on beaches during May and June, the eggs attracting up to a million shorebirds.
horseshoecrab.org

Acadia National Park see page 148

Isle Royale National Park
Accessible only by boat or floatplane, this remote archipelago is the perfect setting for a wilderness journey by foot, canoe or kayak. No bears are found here, but you could well see red squirrel, moose, otter and beaver, and perhaps hear the howl of one of Isle Royale's famous wolves (part of a long running predator-prey study). Birdlife includes ospreys, loons and various waterfowl.
nps.gov/isro

Shenandoah National Park
Just 120 km from the nation's capital, Shenandoah's scenic Skyline Drive gives access to miles of woodland trails.
nps.gov/shen

Mason Neck National Wildlife Refuge

Tallgrass Prairie National Preserve
A tiny remnant of the wild grasslands that once covered vast swathes of the United States, this preserve is home to a rich flora and small herd of bison.
nps.gov/tapr

Great Smoky Mountains National Park see page 148

Alligator River National Wildlife Refuge

Cape Hatteras National Seashore
Sea turtles, shore birds

Wichita Mountains Wildlife Refuge
Bison, elk, white-tailed deer

Holla Bend National Wildlife Refuge
Wintering ducks and geese

Lake Superior

Lake Huron

Lake Michigan

Lake Ontario

Lake Erie

• Boston

• Buffalo

• Detroit

• Cleveland

• Chicago

• Pittsburgh

• New York

• Philadelphia

• Washington DC

Chesapeake Bay

• Norfolk

Appalachian Mountains

• Kansas

St Louis •

• Louisville

• Knoxville

• Nashville

• Oklahoma City

• Memphis

• Atlanta

• Birmingham

• Dallas

• Jackson

Mississippi

Florida p150

Atlantic Ocean

• New Orleans

• Houston

Gulf of Mexico

Bahamas

Making tracks | Florida

⌇ **Everglades Day Safari** (ecosafari.com) offers a full-day, guided ecotour; **Crystal Seas Kayaking** (crystalseas.com) runs single- and multi-day paddling trips in the Everglades (Dec-Mar); **Central Florida Nature Adventures** (kayakcentralflorida.com) offers more offbeat kayaking adventures.

✈ Several airlines fly to Florida gateways, Miami and Orlando. There is no public transport to Everglades National Park or Corkscrew Swamp Sanctuary. A rental car will get you to all visitor centres and points of interest from where you can walk, canoe or cycle deeper into the Everglades.

🛏 There is plenty of accommodation outside the protected areas. In Everglades NP, there are drive-in campsites at Flamingo and Pine Island. Numerous backcountry campsites in the national park and neighbouring Big Cypress National Preserve.

🕐 GMT-6

☀ The best time to visit is from late November to late April when it is drier and cooler with daytime temperatures reaching 29°C. Thunderstorms occur during the hot and humid summer season (May to October), which is also the worst time for mosquitoes.

🦟 Take insect repellent.

💲 US dollar ($)

ⓘ visitflorida.com

🦅 **Audubon Society** (audubon.org)

Wood stork

Osprey

Little blue heron

Black skimmer

Corkscrew Swamp Sanctuary

★ Wood stork, little blue heron, red-shouldered hawk

Purchased by the Audubon Society in the 1950s to protect its cypress forest from loggers, Corkscrew Swamp is a little gem. Its 3.6-km boardwalk threads through pinewoods, open prairie and the largest forest of ancient bald cypress in North America, some of which tower 40 m tall. The 4,450-ha sanctuary is also renowned for supporting the United States' largest nesting colony of endangered wood storks. Following the boardwalk, you'll glimpse the wood storks' nests through a wild tangle of branches, festooned with bromeliads, ferns and orchids. Walking deeper into the sanctuary, you enter a lost world of giant trees and swamp ferns that riot through ponds the colour of well-brewed tea. Alligators and turtles languish in lakes smothered with floating water lettuce, a little blue heron tiptoeing across the leafy raft in search of crayfish. Other wetland species to look out for include red-bellied turtle, purple gallinule, American bittern, anhinga and river otter. Black bears occasionally enter the sanctuary in search of food.

Directions Northeast of Naples, 24 km east from Exit 111 on I-75, following Immokalee Road.
Getting around Self-guided boardwalk trail.
Seasons Sanctuary open year round.
Visitor centres Blair Audubon Centre (open daily).
Things to do Walking, birdwatching.
Places to stay Campsites, hotels nearby.
Further information corkscrew.audubon.org

Everglades National Park

★ Osprey, black skimmer, great egret, anhinga, alligator

North America's great subtropical wetland, the Everglades is actually a shallow, 80-km-wide river flowing south from Lake Okeechobee to the coast. Occupying the southernmost fifth of this dynamic ecosystem, Everglades National Park has habitats ranging from pineland and hardwood hammock to freshwater prairie and mangrove forest. Its biodiversity is astonishing. You can find everything from tiny grass frogs to 4-m-long alligators; 40 species of mammal slosh through the wetland, including river otter, white-tailed deer, bobcat, racoon and the highly endangered Florida panther. But first and foremost, the Everglades is about birds. Over 366 species have been reported here, including common waders like white ibis and great white heron. Flocks of black skimmers fly offshore; ospreys nest in mangroves; turkey vultures and swallow-tailed kites spiral overhead, while dozens of various warblers and flycatchers can be found in grasslands and woodlands.

Four visitor centres provide excellent background to the 607,500-ha park. Near the Ernest F Coe Visitor Centre, the 800-m Anhinga Trail promises close-up views of birds and alligators. Continuing south towards Flamingo, there are several short, well-interpreted trails leading from parking areas along the 61-km park road. At Flamingo Visitor Centre, boat tours explore Florida Bay and the backcountry. There are also several canoe and walking trails nearby. At Shark Valley Visitor Centre, off the Tamiami Trail, a tram tour leads to an observation tower providing views across sawgrass prairie or the 'sea of grass'. The Gulf Coast Visitor Centre at Everglades City is the gateway to the Ten Thousand Islands, a mecca for canoeists, anglers and birdwatchers.

Directions Access is from Tamiani Trail (I-41) or main park road, near Homestead, south of Miami. Self-drive or guided tours.
Getting around Shark Valley tram tours, boat tours, canoeing.
Seasons Park open year round.
Visitor centres Four (see above) open year round.
Things to do Guided tours, ranger activities, hiking, camping, fishing, boating, canoeing, kayaking.
Places to stay Campsites in park, lodging in nearby communities.
Further information nps.gov/ever

Atlantic Ocean

Tallahassee ⊙

Gulf of Mexico

● Jacksonville

Cape Canaveral National Seashore
Each summer, Loggerhead, green and leatherback turtles nest on 39 km of pristine barrier island beach at Cape Canaveral. Add the adjacent Merritt Island National Wildlife Refuge into the equation and you also have great birding. As well as herons, egrets, ibises, and pelicans, special ticks include wood stork and roseate spoonbill.
nps.gov/cana

● Daytona Beach

Crystal River National Wildlife Refuge
Unable to tolerate water temperatures below 20ºC, endangered West Indian manatees congregate in the warm, spring-fed waters of Kings Bay each winter (November to March) to rest and feed. Sharing this 'sirenian spa' are ospreys, cormorants, herons, ibises and anhingas, along with fish, such as alligator gar, mangrove snapper, mullet, bass and crevalle. The nearby town of Crystal River offers manatee snorkel tours, allowing you to swim with these gentle marine mammals. It's a strictly 'hands-off' experience, with federal and state laws prohibiting any kind of harrassment towards the manatees – and that includes touching a resting manatee, approaching a manatee before it approaches you, feeding a manatee or separating a cow from its calf.
fws.gov/crystalriver

⊙ Orlando

Biscayne National Park
Coral reefs, mangrove forests and subtropical islands all within sight of downtown Miami. Snorkel, dive, kayak, camp and watch wildlife, ranging from West Indian manatees, sea turtles and angelfish to terns, plovers and pelicans.
nps.gov/bisc

● Tampa

St Petersburg ⊙

Big Cypress National Preserve
Rent a canoe and spend a day paddling in this water wonderland (mosquitoes are more tolerable November to March) and you'll spot several typical Florida species, including alligators, egrets and anhingas. Protecting nearly 300,000 ha of freshwater swamp adjacent to the Everglades, Big Cypress National Preserve is also home to less commonly seen critters, such as river otter, bobcat, black bear and the highly elusive Florida panther. Stretching from the Gulf Islands National Seashore, the Florida National Scenic Trail winds through prairie and stands of dwarf cypress in the south of the preserve – it's well-marked and easy to walk in winter, but you'll be wading knee-deep during the rainy season.
nps.gov/bicy

Lake Okeechobee

West Palm Beach ⊙

Cape Coral ● ● Fort Myers

Bonita Springs ⊙
Corkscrew Swamp Sanctuary see page 150

Fort Lauderdale

Naples ●

Florida Panther National Wildlife Refuge

Miami ⊙

Florida Keys
Three national wildlife refuges punctuate the pilgrimage to Key West at the tail-end of the Florida Keys. Cross Seven Mile Bridge between Knight's Key and Little Duck Key and you enter National Key Deer Refuge where numbers of Key deer have bounced back from a low of just 27 in 1957 to around 800 today. A subspecies of Virginia white-tailed deer, they can be seen throughout Big Pine and No Name Keys. Only accessible by boat, Great White Heron and Key West National Wildlife Reserves (both administered by the Key Deer Reserve) are protected nesting areas for 250 species of birds, along with green and loggerhead turtles.
fws.gov/nationalkeydeer

Ten Thousand Islands National Wildlife Refuge

Everglades National Park see page 150

Florida Bay

Key West ●

Making tracks | W Canada

Banff Adventures (banffadventures.com) offers a range of guided tours in the Canadian Rockies, while **Overlander Trekking & Tours** (overlandertrekking.com) runs both day treks and backcountry adventures in Jasper National Park. **Ecosummer Expeditions** (ecosummer.com) offers sea kayaking, backpacking trips and coastal cruises in Johnstone Strait, Great Bear Rainforest and Haida Gwaii (Queen Charlotte Islands). Sea kayaking, including mothership voyages, is also available from **Northern Lights Expeditions** (seakayaking.com), while **Orca Kayak Trips** (orca-kayak-trips.com) operates a sea kayak camp.

Vancouver and Calgary are the major gateways for flights to the region. **BC Ferries** (bcferries.com), **Via Rail** (viarail.com) and **Greyhound Canada** (greyhound.ca) combine efficient public transport with sightseeing.

National parks offer plenty of opportunities for camping – some, like Banff, have hotels and lodges. For wilderness lodges see pages 156-157.

GMT-8 (Vancouver)

Whale watching is generally best from May to October, bear watching in spring and September.

Backcountry hikers should be aware of bear safety measures (p93).

Canadian dollar (C$)

canada.travel, hellobc.com

raincoast.org

Jasper National Park

★ Bighorn sheep, pine marten, lynx, wolverine, elk, bear

The largest and one of the wildest national parks in the Canadian Rockies, Jasper covers 10,878 sq km of mountain wilderness. The possibilities for backcountry hiking are almost endless. Hit the trails during the quieter spring and fall seasons and you stand a better chance of seeing wildlife. Jasper is home to 69 mammal species, ranging from the common Columbian ground squirrel and alpine-dwelling hoary marmot to bigger critters like moose, elk, woodland caribou, bighorn sheep, coyote and both black and grizzly bear. Wolf and mountain lion are also present, but rarely seen. Wildlife aside, another highlight of Japser is the 90-minute Snocoach adventure to the 389-sq-km Columbia Icefield that will take you out on to the crevasse-riddled Athabasca Glacier.

Directions 370 km west of Edmonton on Trans-Canada Highway 16 which connects with the Icefields Parkway. Via Rail operates trains to Jasper via Edmonton and Vancouver; Greyhound runs buses.
Getting around Snocoach tours (summer, daily, brewster.ca).
Seasons Park open year round; peak months July and August.
Visitor centres Jasper Information Centre (open daily).
Things to do Hiking, camping, cycling, fishing, horse riding, boating, canoeing, rafting, guided tours.
Places to stay Campsites in national park; nearby lodges, hostels.
Further information pc.gc.ca/eng/pn-np/ab/jasper, jasper.travel

Johnstone Strait

★ Orca, humpback, Dall's porpoise, black bear, bald eagle

This glacier-carved channel between Vancouver Island and the mainland of British Columbia delves into a realm of giants – where towering red cedars grow to 1,000 years old and where bald eagles, black bears and orcas gain mythological stature in the minds and carvings of the local Kwagiulth people. Boat tours in fast zodiacs are available from various ports, but the best way to explore Johnstone Strait is by sea kayak. Paddling from island to island, carrying your food and fresh water and camping on pebbly beaches or in forest clearings, a kayak tour will enable you to nose about in flat-calm inlets and gain sea-level views of porpoises, seals, sea lions and, with luck, orcas.

There are around 200 resident orca in Johnstone Strait, each one identified by the shape of its dorsal fin or the black and white markings along its flanks. Over several decades, life histories and family trees

Johnstone Strait

have been logged, births and deaths catalogued and behaviour recorded. Transient orcas are found further offshore, travelling in smaller pods and feeding predominantly on seals, sea lions and other cetaceans – unlike resident orcas which eat salmon. Out of bounds to all vessels, Robson Bight Ecological Reserve is one of the most mysterious whale sanctuaries in the world. Orcas visit here not to feed on salmon, but to rub their bodies on the steeply shelving beaches that occur along this section of Vancouver Island.

Directions Port McNeil on the northern tip of Vancouver Island is the main centre for sea kayaking operations.
Getting around Sea kayaking tours range from multi-day wilderness camping expeditions to centre-based trips, staying at a kayak camp. Mother ship cruises (in which kayaks are carried onboard) are also available. More traditional whale-watching tours using fast motorboats are available from Vancouver or Victoria with Eagle Wing Tours (eaglewingtours.com), Orca Spirit (orcaspirit.com) and Prince of Whales (princeofwhales.com). Fisheries and Oceans Canada (pac.dfo-mpo.gc.ca) publish guidelines for responsible whale watching.
Seasons Year round; best time for whale watching is mid-July to mid-September when orca feed on the salmon run.
Visitor centres Port McNeil Visitor Centre (open daily).
Things to do Sea kayaking, boat tours.
Places to stay Campsites, lodges, hostels, hotels, cruises.
Further information vancouverisland.travel

Pacific Rim National Park | Life on the edge

Where British Columbia's temperate rainforest meets the Pacific Ocean, two of Canada's richest ecosystems form a vibrant cocktail of habitats where, in the space of a few hundred metres, you might find sitka spruce rearing from thick, springy carpets of moss, giant green anemones studding a tidal pool and grey whales feeding in kelp beds offshore. West Vancouver Island's Pacific Rim National Park includes the 76-km, five- to seven-day West Coast Trail, a backpacking route that links a succession of sandy, log-strewn beaches, sandstone cliffs and old-growth forest. Make sure you're clued up on tides before you set off, and keep an eye out for bears, wolves, whales and sea lions.
pc.gc.ca/eng/pn-np/bc/pacificrim

Kluane National Park

At 5,959 m, Mt Logan reigns supreme over this wilderness of peaks, glaciers and forests. The Alsek River valley is a good place to look for wildlife, such as Dall sheep, mountain goat, grizzly bear, moose and golden eagle.

pc.gc.ca

Aulavik National Park

Over 12,000-sq-km in area, Aulavik is home to 70,000 muskox, as well as polar bear and Arctic wolf.

pc.gc.ca

Churchill

Best known for its polar bear gathering in October and November (see p94), Churchill's summer wildlife spectacles are equally impressive. From late June to mid-August, thousands of beluga whales gather in the Churchill River estuary to calf and feed on capelin. May, June and September witness the mass migration of birds such as snow and Canada geese, descending on Churchill's tundra, alongside grebes, loons, terns, gulls, cranes, swans and ducks. These are also good months to observe tundra plants, with late-June-flowering Lapland rhododendron giving way to crimson-leaved bearberry in August.

churchill.ca

Gwaii Haanas National Park

Complemented by the Haida Heritage Site and a National Marine Conservation Area, Gwaii Haanas protects nearly 5,000 sq km of island and ocean – home to thousands of seabirds, as well as black bear, orca and humpback whale.

pc.gc.ca

Great Bear Rainforest

Wedged between the Pacific Ocean and the Coast Mountains, this vast tract of lush, moss-shrouded temperate rainforest, sheltered creeks and salmon-spawning rivers is home to black, brown and white ('spirit') bears. The Bella Coola Valley offers some of the best chances for an encounter, either on foot or by drifting downstream in a boat. Hiking, sea kayaking and whale watching are all on offer too.

raincoast.org

Wapusk NP

Meaning 'white bear' in Cree, Wapusk has one of the world's largest polar bear denning areas.

pc.gc.ca

Elk Island National Park

Elk Island supports plains and wood bison, moose, elk, white-tail and mule deer, beaver, porcupine and lynx. The trumpeter swan has been reintroduced here, joining pelicans, great blue herons and a range of other waterbirds.

pc.gc.ca

Johnstone Strait
see page 152

Jasper National Park see page 152

Pacific Rim National Park see page 152

Banff National Park

Picture-perfect Banff is Canada's oldest and most famous national park – a jewel in the Canadian Rockies, with turquoise lakes and emerald forests topped off with glittering snow-capped peaks. Nearly half of the park is above treeline, a mixture of alpine meadows, rocky moraines, snow, ice and scree. This merges with the predominant subalpine zone of fir, spruce and pine and a lower montane zone of open forest and grassland. This trio of ecosystems suits a wide variety of mammals, including bighorn sheep, elk, mountain goat, woodand caribou, lynx, wolverine and grizzly bear. Attracting some four million visitors a year, Banff has numerous activities on offer year round, from hiking, canoeing, climbing and horse riding to snowshoeing and soaking in hot springs.

pc.gc.ca

Grasslands National Park

One of North America's most endangered habitats, prairie grasslands is a refuge for species like the black-tailed prairie dog, pronghorn antelope, sage grouse and burrowing owl.

pc.gc.ca

Ivvavik National Park

Beaufort Sea

Banks Island

Victoria Island

Dawson City

Great Bear Lake

Mt Logan

Pacific Ocean

Whitehorse

Yellowknife

Great Slave Lake

Gwaii Haanas

Wood Buffalo National Park
Bison

Lake Athabasca

Hudson Bay

Churchill

Prince Rupert

Lake Winnipeg

Bella Coola

Rocky Mountains

Johnstone Strait

Port McNeil

Vancouver Island

Coast Mountains

Edmonton

Yoho National Park

Banff

Calgary

Vancouver

Victoria

Waterton Lakes National Park

Winnipeg

Hudson Bay

Torngat Mountains National Park
Nearly 10,000 sq km of glacial valleys, brooding peaks and Labrador coast, this is a realm of polar bears and migratory caribou.
pc.gc.ca

Mingan Archipelago NP
Over 1,000 granite islands and reefs, dense seabird colonies and seas rich in seals, dolphins and whales.
pc.gc.ca

Gros Morne
National Park

St John's

Newfoundland

Saguenay-St Lawrence Marine Park
Where the waters of Saguenay Fjord mix with those of the world's largest estuary, rich upwellings sustain a marine foodchain that supports beluga, blue, fin and minke whales. Boat tours are available, while the best land-based viewpoint is Cap-de-Bon Désir.
pc.gc.ca, parcmarin.qc.ca

Gulf of St Lawrence

Forillon
National Park

Bay of Fundy
see below

Cape Breton
Highlands
National Park

Atlantic Ocean

Fathom Five National Marine Park
A pristine example of the Great Lakes' freshwater ecosystem, plus islands rich in orchids.
pc.gc.ca

Quebec

Halifax

Montreal

Ottawa

Lake Superior

Lake Huron

Lake Ontario

Cap Tourmente National Wildlife Area
A staging post for thousands of migrating snow geese each spring and autumn.
captourmente.com

Algonquin Provincial Park
Launch a canoe and paddle silently through a pristine patchwork of forests and lakes, home to beaver, moose, river otter and white-tailed deer. The park has 1,500 km of canoe trails, from short loops lasting a few hours to backcountry epics lasting a week or more. Local outfitters can kit you out with all your paddling and camping gear.
algonquinpark.on.ca

Toronto

Niagara Falls

Lake Erie

Haliburton Forest
Trek along the Pelaw River, canoe across a lake, then climb into the forest for one of the world's longest treetop boardwalks.
haliburtonforest.com

Making tracks | E Canada

⊙ **Great Canadian Travel** (greatcanadiantravel. com) has an 11-day trip tracing the St Lawrence seaway and a more offbeat expedition cruise along the remote Labrador coast. **Wildland Tours** (wildlands. com) operates wildlife holidays in Newfoundland.
◴ GMT-5 (Toronto)
ⓘ canada.travel, ontariotravel.net, bonjourquebec.com, novascotia.com, tourismnewbrunswick.ca, newfoundlandlabrador.com

Bay of Fundy

★ Northern right whale, humpback whale, fin whale
Every day, a staggering 100 billion tonnes of seawater flows in and out of the Bay of Fundy, creating the world's biggest tides of up to 16 m between high and low water extremes. The resultant currents spawn nutrient-rich waters that attract several species of cetaceans, including humpback, fin and minke whale, as well as the endangered northern right whale. Boat trips in the mouth of the bay (around Grand Manan Island) offer excellent whale-watching opportunities, while sea kayaking tours and low-tide beachcombing walks enable you to explore Fundy's tide-scoured coast. Good spots include Hopewell Rocks, a series of tottering sea stacks, arches and caves. Fundy's tides also cause tidal bores – best viewed from shore in the Hantsport and Maitland areas of Nova Scotia or during a zodiac ride on the nearby Shubenacadie River.

Directions For whale watching, head for Digby in Nova Scotia or the St Andrews area in New Brunswick.
Getting around All whale-watching companies endorsed by Bay of Fundy Tourism adhere to a strict code of ethics. Islands in the mouth of the bay are linked by ferry to the mainland.
Seasons August to November for northern right whales; June to October for other species of cetacean.
Things to do Whale watching, sea kayaking, hiking, boat trips.
Places to stay Heritage inns, B&Bs and hotels.
Further information bayoffundytourism.com, bayoffundy.com

The Cabot Trail | A drive beside the Atlantic

A 300-km loop around the tip of Cape Breton Island, the Cabot Trail scenic highway passes fishing villages and links trailheads for hikes in Cape Breton Highlands National Park.
cabottrail.com

Wild side | newfoundland

1 Spot icebergs from Quirpon Lighthouse
Around 800 bergs pass Quirpon Island each spring, numbers peaking in June.
linkumtours.com

2 Kayak along the dramatic north coast
Paddle close to seabirds, whales and icebergs in Iceberg Alley.
wildnfld.ca

3 Trek the Tablelands of Gros Morne National Park
Explore a rugged wilderness forged from the crust of an ancient ocean floor.
pc.gc.ca

4 Spot humpback whales and dolphins
Daily cruises run from St Anthony; late June to early September is best.
discovernorthland.com

5 Hike to Western Brook Pond, Gros Morne NP
This inland fjord is reached via a boardwalk across wildlife-rich wetlands.
pc.gc.ca

1

2

3

4

5

Knight Inlet Lodge
Glendale Cove, Knight Inlet, British Columbia

A floating lodge tucked into a sheltered anchorage on the forest-draped coast of British Columbia, Knight Inlet oozes remoteness and adventure. Reached by floatplane, 80 km from Campbell River, the former logging camp dates from the early 1940s and accommodates up to 30 guests in cedar-panelled splendour. Crab, salmon, prawns and other delicious seafood comes fresh from Knight Inlet, while nights are spent cosying up to wood burners in the lodge's lounge areas. It's bears, not pampering, however, that guests come here for. Glendale Cove supports one of British Columbia's highest concentrations of grizzly bears – up to 50 can be located within 10 km of the lodge during the autumn salmon-feeding frenzy. The bears are present from late April, emerging with cubs from winter dens to feed along the estuary. Numbers drop off during mid-summer when the heavy berry crop encourages them to disperse through the forest. A combination of boat trips and viewing platforms at Knight Inlet promises some wonderful encounters. As well as bear viewing, the lodge offers boat trips to observe seals, sea lions, porpoises, dolphins, minke whales and other marine life. From July, there's the added attraction of orcas in Johnstone Strait; humpback whales arrive in September. Jetboat tours, sea kayaking and hiking are also available.
grizzlytours.com

Sadie Cove Wilderness Lodge
Kachemak Bay State Park, near Homer, Alaska

Operating solely on an alternative energy system of wind and hydro power, this driftwood ecolodge tiptoes on stilts over a remote beach, 16 km by boat from Homer. The rustic handcrafted cabins sleep a maximum of 10 guests. You can take a sauna overlooking a rushing creek, stroll trails through old-growth forest or paddle kayaks in search of sea otters, whales and eagles. A place to relax and soak up the wilderness.
sadiecove.com

Quirpon Lighthouse Inn
Great Northern Peninsula, Newfoundland

A spectacular clifftop bolt-hole on Quirpon Island at the very tip of Newfoundland, this restored 1922 lighthouse keeper's cottage overlooks the Straits of Belle Isle where the confluence of the Gulf of St Lawrence and the North Atlantic creates a feeding ground for 22 species of cetacean. Icebergs also pass by on the Labrador Current. Reached by a 45-minute boat trip from the mainland, the 10-room inn offers delicious home cooking, as well as hiking and kayaking.
linkumtours.com

Tweedsmuir Park Lodge
Bella Coola Valley, British Columbia

Originally built as a hunting lodge in the late 1920s, this 10-chalet ecolodge now has bears and other wildlife frequently wandering across its lawns. Bordering the Atanarko River in the heart of the Great Bear Rainforest, Tweedsmuir is perfectly placed for observing grizzly bears feeding on salmon during the autumn. Other activities include guided forest walks, river drifts, birdwatching, fishing, heli-hiking and storytelling by First Nations Nuxalk.
tweedsmuirparklodge.com

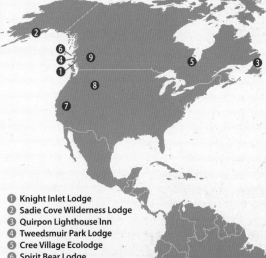

1. Knight Inlet Lodge
2. Sadie Cove Wilderness Lodge
3. Quirpon Lighthouse Inn
4. Tweedsmuir Park Lodge
5. Cree Village Ecolodge
6. Spirit Bear Lodge
7. Yosemite Lodge at the Falls
8. Amangani
9. Cathedral Mountain Lodge

Cree Village Ecolodge
Moose Factory Island, near James Bay, Ontario

One of Canada's flagship eco-friendly properties, the 20-room Cree Village combines traditional architecture of the MoCreebec people with modern environmental features, such as no-water, zero-odour composting toilets (using red wiggler worms to create organic fertiliser), natural wool carpets and efficient natural ventilation. Located between Moose River and James Bay, the community-run lodge offers nature walks, boat trips and cultural tours.
creevillage.com

Spirit Bear Lodge
Klemtu, Princess Royal Island, British Columbia

Opened in 2011, this 12-room waterfront lodge is built in the spirit of BC's West Coast First Nations. Inside, you'll find Tsimshian art and solid cedar dining tables alongside modern touches like 6-m-high picture windows – perfect for viewing passing orca, white-sided dolphins and sea lions. Each day, local guides lead boat trips into the Great Bear Rainforest searching for spirit bears, grizzlies and other wildlife and exploring the estuary shores on foot.
spiritbear.com

Yosemite Lodge at the Falls
Yosemite National Park, California

Accommodation in Yosemite ranges from the upmarket Ahwahnee Hotel to the more basic High Sierra Camps (accessible only by foot or on horseback). Yosemite Lodge at the Falls is a good mid-range option, with 249 rooms, including new, prototype green rooms with eco-friendly features like recycled newspaper insulation and reduced water consumption. Numerous activities are available, from cycling, rafting and horse riding to cross-country skiing.
yosemitepark.com

Amangani
Jackson Hole, Wyoming

A stunning luxury lodge with magnificent views of the Grand Tetons, Amangani offers an exclusive, year-round wilderness escape. Wildlife safaris are available to Yellowstone National Park, and you can also go mountain biking in the Tetons, hot-air ballooning over Jackson Hole and fly-fishing on the Snake River. Amangani has 29 sensational suites, a 35-m outdoor heated pool and local art and craft gallery. During winter, it's one of North America's top ski hotels.
amanresorts.com

Cathedral Mountain Lodge
Yoho National Park, British Columbia

Yoho might not be the best known national park in the Canadian Rockies, but its scenery and wildlife is just as spectacular. Opened in 2010, these stylish cabins have fireplaces and hot tubs, while the main lodge building offers fine cuisine with views of the glacier-fed Kicking Horse River. An onsite adventure specialist can recommend the best places to view wildlife, or organise activities ranging from hiking and canoeing to paragliding and climbing.
cathedralmountain.com

South & Central America

It was the ultimate wildlife cruise: a five-year voyage charting the coast of South America, with Tahiti, New Zealand, Australia and the Cape of Good Hope lined up as homeward-bound stopovers. When Robert FitzRoy, captain of the *HMS Beagle*, put the word out that 'some well educated and scientific person should be sought who would profit by the opportunity of visiting distant countries yet little known', a young medical graduate called Charles Darwin jumped at the chance. He was subsequently enrolled as the ship's unpaid naturalist.

When the *Beagle*, a cramped 27-m-long brig-sloop with 74 crew, set sail from Plymouth in December 1831, Darwin was almost immediately seasick. He left the ship at every opportunity to explore inland, collecting specimens and making observations of geology, natural history and culture. Some of his journeys ventured far into the interior of South America, including the Brazilian rainforest, Chilean Andes and Patagonia. It was his landfall on the Galápagos Islands in September 1835, however, that would eventually form the bedrock of his evolutionary theories and establish Darwin as one of the greatest biologists that has ever lived.

Darwin's ground-breaking book, *On the Origin of Species*, was published in 1859, but from a traveller's point of view, his account of the *Beagle's* voyage (published 20 years earlier) is just as fascinating. *The Voyage of the Beagle* (originally entitled *Journal and Remarks*) describes Darwin's encounters with capybaras, armadillos, guanacos, condors, hummingbirds, giant tortoises and a wealth of other species that have become firm favourites of modern-day wildlife adventurers in South America.

Admittedly, there were some animals that Darwin didn't seem to care for. The Galápagos marine iguana, for example, he described as 'a hideous-looking creature, of a dirty black colour, stupid, and sluggish in its movements'.

Darwin's voyage was nothing if not an eye-opener – and that same sense of wonder and discovery still awaits travellers who seek out the wild places of South and Central America. Whether you're planning a horse-riding expedition in Patagonia, a river trip in the Amazon, a trek in the Andes or a voyage to the Galápagos, you can't help but feel a tingle of 'Darwinian curiosity'.

If he was alive today, the great naturalist would no doubt have been relieved to see the continent's network of national parks and biosphere reserves – precious repositories of natural selection – and even more gratified to learn that many of them were managed by local communities. This is a continent where ecotourism is evolving and flourishing.

Manú | Journey to the heart of the Amazon

At 1.5 million hectares, Manú Biosphere Reserve in Peru is quite possibly the most species-rich protected area on Earth, with an ever-increasing inventory that features 1,200 species of plants, 850 varieties of birds and 200 different mammals, including 13 monkeys and over 100 bats. Part of the reason for this extraordinary biodiversity is Manú's range of habitats, rising in tiers from lowland tropical rainforest, through cloud forest on the eastern slopes of the Andes to *puna* grassland at 4,200 m above sea level. You can reach the jungle heart of Manú by taking a light aircraft flight from Cuzco, followed by a riverboat trip, but the overland journey is far more rewarding. After crossing the high-altitude *puna* and cresting a pass in the Andes, the first night is spent in a cloud forest lodge, close to courtship leks of the Andean cock-of-the-rock. From there, it's a long drive on a gravel track that spirals into the Amazon basin, passing remote communities like Pilcopata before reaching the Manú and Madre de Dios Rivers. Transferring to motorised longboats you can navigate shallow rapids and flood-stranded driftwood to reach rainforest lodges, like Manú Wildlife Centre, six hours travel downstream. See also pages 178 and 185.

That condor moment – few sights are more majestic than a wild Andean condor in flight

Vultur gryphus
Ecuador

This wild condor was photographed in a canyon near Hacienda Zuleta (haciendazuleta.com), the site of a rehabilitation project for condors that have been found injured or kept as pets. Known as Condor Huasi (House of Condor in the native Quechua language), the project seeks to reintroduce captive-bred birds to the wild and also raise awareness of the importance of wildlife conservation in the Andean *páramo* grassland – of which the condor is a crucial 'anchor' species.

From rampant Amazonia to rarified altiplano, South America is a land of extraordinary contrasts. Coral reefs flourish off the coast of Belize, while winter sea ice clogs the channels of Tierra del Fuego. Vast wetlands and savannahs pour their own special mix of species into the continent's rich stew of biodiversity, while the Andes add a flourish of snow-capped peaks, cloud forest and high-altitude desert.

Natural zones

Few countries symbolize the natural wealth and variety of South America better than Ecuador. In a two- or three-week journey, travelling west from the Amazon basin, you pass through an unrivalled variety of habitats brimming with biodiversity: tropical rainforest, cloud forest, high-altitude *páramo* grassland, Andean volcano, Pacific shore and the evolutionary treasure chest of the Galápagos Islands.

Other biodiverse hotspots include Central America where, in a country as small as Costa Rica, you can experience mist-shrouded cloud forest, lowland rainforest and dry coastal forest – each with their own extravagant cast of creatures. Add wetlands, mangroves, mountains, turtle-nesting beaches and coral reefs and it's small wonder that Central America boasts the world's greatest concentration of animal and plant life.

However, it is the Amazon – the oldest and largest tropical forest on earth – that most people associate with wildlife in South America. Covering over 6.5 million sq km of land, this magnificent green mantle is looking increasingly ragged in places as logging, mining and ranching take their toll, but it is still home to an incredible variety and abundance of species, from pink river dolphins swirling through flooded forests to spider monkeys swinging high in the canopy.

Less well known, but a haven for South American species like jaguar, capybara and caiman, the Pantanal of southwest Brazil is a seasonal wetland half the size of France. It merges with the wooded grasslands and swamps of the Gran Chaco which extend south across the Río de la Plata basin and is home to the maned wolf, Chacoan peccary and some 18 armadillo species.

South of this lie the pampas grasslands of Argentina (prime habitat for birds like the rhea) and the rugged frontier of Patagonia. Wild and dramatic, this southern extreme of South America has a coastline rich in penguin and seal colonies; twisted forests of sub-Antarctic beech trees cower at its fringes, while puma, grey fox and guanaco roam its plains and mountains.

Forming the western boundary of Patagonia, Gran Chaco and the Amazon basin, the Andes rise in an 8,000-km-long wall of ice-clad volcanoes, desert plateaus and cloud forests along the length of South America. A refuge for mountain dwellers such as the Andean condor and spectacled bear, this towering wilderness also supports a varied assemblage of endemic plants. The same is true of the Guiana Highlands of Venezuela and Guyana where flat-topped mountains, or *tepuis*, like Mt Roraima nurture lost worlds of unique orchids and pitcher plants. For South America's ultimate experience of 'evolution in isolation', however, you need to travel 1,000 km off the coast of Ecuador where the Galápagos Islands are renowned for birds and reptiles that are found nowhere else on earth and show no fear of humans.

Booted racket-tail hummingbird

Ocreatus underwoodii
Bellavista Cloud Forest Reserve, Ecuador

Hummingbird watching is addictive. The variety of these zippy little beauties is mind-blowing, and you'll often get close-up views if you spend some time around the nectar feeders at your lodge.

> **Wild and dramatic, the southern extreme of South America has a coastline rich in penguin and seal colonies; twisted forests of sub-Antarctic beech trees cower at its fringes, while puma, grey fox and guanaco roam its plains and mountains**

Wild city | Iquitos, Peru

Only accessible by plane and boat, Iquitos is an urban oasis on the west bank of the Amazon, 3,646 km from the river's mouth. It has a lively, pioneer feel, best experienced in the waterfront district of Belén where you can hire canoes to nose about the stilted huts. Grander houses dating from the rubber boom of the 1890s and early 1900s can be seen on Plaza de Armas. A 23-km drive or three-hour boat trip south of the city, Allpahuayo-Mishana Reserve protects a large swathe of white-sand jungle that not only boasts one of the highest levels of biodiversity in the Amazon, but is also home to several endangered species, including two primates – the equatorial saki and collared titi. Half a dozen varieties of bird new to science have also been discovered here in recent years. Just 4 km from Iquitos, Lake Quistococha has canoes for hire, plus a two-hour walking trail through surrounding rainforest. A 20-minute boat ride from the Iquitos suburb of Bellavista, the Amazon Animal Orphanage and Pilpintuwasi Butterfly Farm (amazonanimalorphanage. org) at Padre Cocha rears several species of butterfly and moth, including giant blue morphos and swallowtails, and also rescues orphaned wild animals. Current lodgers include a jaguar, anteater, squirrel monkey and uakari.

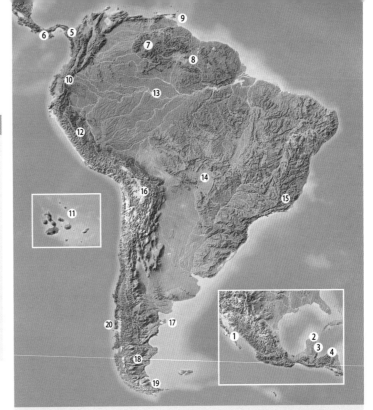

Day 1 Arrive San José, overnight in the city **Day 2** Excursion to Poás volcano; optional whitewater rafting **Day 3** Drive through cloud forest to Braulio Carrillo National Park, then by riverboat for three to four hours to Tortuguero National Park **Day 4** Explore Tortuguero by boat **Day 5** Return by 30-minute flight to San José; drive to Monteverde Cloud Forest Reserve and overnight in a nearby lodge **Day 6** Explore the cloud forest on foot **Days 7 and 8** Drive to Arenal and spend two days exploring the area around the active volcano **Days 9-11** Drive four hours to the Pacific coast at Manuel Antonio National Park for a few days relaxing n the sandy beach and exploring the rainforest **Day 12** Return to San José by light aircraft **Day 13** Depart San José

↻ Based on a tailor-made itinerary from **Journey Latin America** (journeylatinamerica.co.uk), this trip would cost from around £1,800 per person, excluding international flights, but including domestic flights, road and boat travel, accommodation, some meals and excursions.

Wildlife travel

You need time to do justice to large countries like Brazil or Argentina, but several Latin American nations embody the wild appeal of the continent in a relatively small area. In Honduras, for example, the Río Platano rainforest is like a 'little Amazon' where you can explore virgin jungle by dugout canoe, stay in remote lodges and visit indigenous communities. Belize blends reef and rainforest into a comfortable two-week wildlife holiday, while Costa Rica's extensive network of national parks and reserves is easily visited, even by independent travellers.

On the whole, however, wildlife travel in Central and South America requires a good deal of planning and, for this reason, many people choose to join an organised trip. Local operators smooth out the logistics of travelling to remote areas, while guides can take you to the most wildlife-rich places and help overcome potential language barriers.

There are numerous opportunites fo supporting community-run ecotourism initiatives in the region. Several Amazonian lodges, for example, are run by indigenous groups; fishermen in Baja California supplement their income through small-scale whale watching tours, while locally owned ranches, or *estancias*, immerse you in gaucho culture with the added bonus of exploring wild places on horseback.

Wild places

Mexico's desert peninsula, Baja California ❶ is a magnet to whale watchers, while Sian Ka'an Ecological Reserve on the Yucatan Peninsula ❷ combines well with the coral reefs, tropical forests and Mayan ruins of Belize or the Guatemalan jungle at Tikal or the Río Dulce ❸. For intrepid eco-travellers, a journey by dugout canoe deep into the Río Platano rainforest of Honduras ❹ comes a close second to adventure treks in Panama's Darien Gap wilderness ❺. Also worth exploring in Panama are the wildlife-rich islands of Bocas del Tora. Peaceful, calm, politically stable and lavishing over 25% of its land area to national parks and reserves, Costa Rica ❻ is a natural choice for wildlife travellers, while those in search of emerging ecotourism destinations should consider Venezuela ❼ for its Los Llanos wetlands, forest-draped *tepuis* and Caribbean coastline, or Guyana ❽ for pristine rainforest, the mighty Kaieteur Falls and wildlife-rich Rupununi savannah. The Caribbean, meanwhile, has no shortage of natural riches, especially in the biodiverse duo of Trinidad & Tobago ❾. Ecuador combines Amazon and Andes ❿ with the mesmerising Galapágos islands ⓫, while Peru ⓬ offers all kinds of jungle jollies, Inca treks and adventure activities. The incredible fauna and flora of the Brazilian Amazon ⓭ can be glimpsed on river cruises or from lodges near Manaus, although the Pantanal ⓮ offers a more visible display of the country's wildlife. The remaining fragments of Brazil's Atlantic coast rainforest ⓯ are home to endangered primates, while the salt lakes of Bolivia's altiplano ⓰ are blushed pink by flamingos. Argentina's Valdés Peninsula ⓱ has no shortage of wildlife spectacles, from breeding southern right whales and colonies of elephant seals to encounters with rheas and hairy armadillos. Darwin would have kicked himself had he realized that the *Beagle* sailed straight past this wildlife wonderland. There are plenty of Darwinian connections in Patagonia ⓲ where wildlife travel hotspots include the hiker's paradise of Torres del Paine National Park. Far more than a stepping-off point for Antarctic cruises, Tierra del Fuego ⓳ has fascinating, weather-beaten forests, penguin colonies and glaciers. Also off the beaten track, Chiloé Island ⓴ has an intriguing mixture of hummingbirds and blue whales.

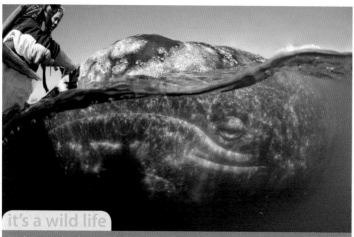

it's a wild life

Mark Carwardine | Zoologist, writer, photographer, TV presenter | markcarwardine.com

↘ **My big five**
1. Baja California, Mexico
2. South Georgia Island
3. Sipadan Is, Borneo
4. Great Bear Rainforest, British Columbia
5. The Pantanal, Brazil

" I've been whale watching for more than 25 years, in over 50 countries, and San Ignacio Lagoon is by far the best place for the closest encounters. I'm addicted to the place and go several times every year to see the friendly grey whales that congregate there every winter to breed. My most recent visit was as good as ever: at one point, we had three mothers and their calves rolling around our tiny boat for well over an hour. Normally, I would encourage people not to touch wild animals, but these gentle giants are exceptional – if you don't scratch and tickle them they will go and find someone who will. It's often hard to tell who is getting the most from the encounter.

San Ignacio Lagoon
Pioneered by local fisherman Francisco 'Pachico' Mayoral in the 1970s, whale watching in Ignacio Lagoon is best between January and mid-April, allowing the grey whales time to recover from their long migration and nurse newborn calves. Exploring the lagoon in small, open pangas, you'll often experience close encounters with the whales (see left) and observe other wildlife such as sea lions, dolphins and turtles.
pachicosecotours.com

Sea of Cortez

Loreto Bay National Marine Park

Los Mochis

Bahía Magdalena
see page 106

La Paz

Baja California

Wildlife cruises in the Sea of Cortez
Join an expedition cruise to the Sea of Cortez (also known as the Gulf of California) and you will be entering seas that support one of the world's greatest concentrations of cetaceans. They're attracted here by plankton blooms sustained by nutrient-rich upwellings from a submarine maze of canyons and sea mounts. It's all eyes on deck as you scan the deep azure waters for the 12-m-tall spout of surfacing blue whales and the blows, breaches and flukes of fin, humpback, minke, sperm and Bryde's whales. Common dolphins can often be seen in superpods 1,000 or more strong, while more elusive cetaceans include dwarf sperm whale, pygmy killer whale and orca. As well as whale watching, you will stop at remote islands to visit fur seal and sea lion colonies. There will be opportunities for sea kayaking, snorkelling and birdwatching (desert specials include the gila woodpecker, crested caracara and Xantu's hummingbird). For divers, meanwhile, there's the chance of unforgettable encounters with manta rays, turtles, hammerhead and whale sharks.

Copper Canyon

Rattling 656 km between Los Mochis and Chihuahua, the Ferrocarril Chihuahua al Pacífico railway traverses a vast network of deep ravines which includes the mighty Barrancas del Cobre, or Copper Canyon. It's a 14-hour ride straight through, but spread the journey over several days to track down some of the endemic birds of the Sierra Madre's pine-oak forests. There are woodpeckers, trogons, warblers and eagles here, but top of most birdwatchers' list is the thick-billed parrot.

Monarch butterfly sanctuaries

The 3,000-m mountains of Michoacán province in central Mexico provide a winter refuge for hundreds of millions of monarch butterflies between October and February. Coating the branches of oyamel fir trees in shimmering cloaks of orange, black and white wings, the insects cluster together in a state of torpor. Come early spring, however, and the monarchs start to twitch and flutter as lengthening days and warmer temperatures cue their 3,000-km migration north to the United States and Eastern Canada where females lay their eggs on milkweed plants. In late summer/early autumn, the insects return to Mexico again, completing the only annual, two-way migration in the butterfly world. Accessible from the town of Angangueo, El Rosario and Sierra Chincua monarch butterfly sanctuaries are two of the best places to witness the overwintering masses.

Sian Ka'an Ecological Reserve

A short distance from the Mayan ruins of Tulum, this biosphere reserve protects rainforest, mangrove and marsh as well as a large marine section containing a barrier reef. Its rich fauna includes over 300 species of birds. A small ecotourism and education centre, Centro Ecologico Sian Ka'an offers kayaking and boat tours.
cesiak.org

Making tracks | Mexico

Several operators offer wildlife voyages in the Sea of Cortez, including **Naturetrek** (naturetrek. co.uk) and **WildOceans** (wildwings.co.uk). Diving live-aboards include the **Solmar V** (solmarv.com). Sea kayaking holidays in Loreto Bay and Isla del Carmen are run by **Sea Kayak Adventures** (seakayakadventures. com) and **Ecosummer** (ecosummer.com).
GMT-6
See boxes, left, for prime seasons for whale watching and monarch butterfly viewing. Watch out for hurricane season on the Caribbean coast from June to November.
visitmexico.com

Chihuahua

Río Grande

Sierra Madre Occidental

Sierra Madre Oriental

Monterrey

Tampico

Gulf of Mexico

Mérida

Cancún

Yucatán

León

Guadalajara

Mexico City

Veracruz

Puebla

Pico de Orizaba

Pacific Ocean

Oaxaca

Acapulco

Ciénaga de Zapata National Park, Cuba
Beyond the classic cars and cigar culture, Cuba shows its wilder side at this wetland reserve – home to 18 of Cuba's 22 endemic bird species, including the Zapata rail and 5.5-cm-long bee hummingbird. A large colony of greater flamingos forms a pink slick across the reserve which is also a refuge for the Cuban crocodile and manatee.
lata.org/cuba

Dominican Republic
Watch humpback whales at Samaná Bay and explore the coastal wetlands of Los Haitises National Park.
godominicanrepublic.com

Cayman Islands
Encrusted with corals and sponges, the drop-offs of the Cayman Islands are dive meccas.
caymanislands.co.uk

Darién National Park, Panama
A bridge between continents, this jungle wilderness is for intrepid travellers only. Join an organised trip to experience untouched rainforest inhabited by jaguar and harpy eagle.
visitpanama.com

Trinidad & Tobago
A birdwatcher's paradise, this pair of Latin American beauties is well known for its scarlet ibis – best seen at Trinidad's Caroni Swamp where thousands arrive to roost each dusk. Macaws and bitterns are also found here, while highland reserves like Asa Wright Nature Centre (Trinidad) and Main Ridge Forest (Tobago) are home to little gems like the blue-backed manakin and tufted coquette hummingbird.
gotrinidadandtobago.com

Leeward Is
Lesser Antilles
Bahamas
San Juan
Puerto Rico
Dominican Republic
Santa Domingo
Grand Etang National Park, Grenada
Havana
Cuba
Haiti
Trinidad & Tobago
Cayman Islands
Jamaica
Caribbean Sea
Kingston
Gulf of Mexico
Belize
see below
Caracas
Venezuela p168
Mexico
Guatemala
Honduras see opposite
Cartagena
Colombia
Nicaragua
Costa Rica p166
San Salvador
Panama City
Panama
Pacific Ocean

Wildlife highlights of Belize

Over 40% of Belize is protected in tropical forest reserves, including the Cockscombe Basin Wildlife Sanctuary, established in 1984 to protect a large jaguar population. A short distance from Belize City, the Community Baboon Sanctuary (see page 74) has witnessed equal success with the conservation of black howler monkeys. To the north, Crooked Tree Wildlife Sanctuary is a haven for waterbirds, such as Jabiru storks, snail kites and several species of kingfisher, heron and duck, while the tropical forests of Tapir Mountain Reserve, near Belmopan, provide a refuge for Belize's national animal, the Baird's tapir.

Rainforests are just one half of the picture when it comes to natural treasures in Belize. The country also boasts the world's second longest barrier reef system (see page 48) – a 295-km chain of reefs, coral cays and mangroves, plus three offshore atolls (Turneffe Islands, Lighthouse reef and Glover's Reef). A world heritage site, the reef supports over 500 varieties of fish and several endangered species, including the West Indian manatee, hawksbill turtle and American crocodile. Breeding colonies of magnificent frigatebirds, brown and red-footed boobies and brown noddies can be found on islands like Man O' War Caye and Half Moon Caye. The diving opportunities are outstanding. Ambergris Caye and Caye Caulker are the most popular, but many divers venture to the smaller marine reserves and to the world-famous Blue Hole.

Seasons The wet season is June and August; hurricane season September and October. Wildlife watching can be particularly rewarding during June and July when fresh rains bring relief after the stifling heat of May.
Further information travelbelize.org, belizeaudubon.org

Paradise found – Hunting Cay

Over 450 sand and mangrove cays are found along the Belize Barrier Reef.

① Travel by dugout into the Río Plátano rainforest
Explore the fabled *Moskitia* (Mosquito Coast), venturing upriver through a vast rainforest biosphere reserve.
honduras.com/moskitia

② Explore the mangrove estuary of Cuero y Salado
Paddle a canoe through this sanctuary in search of manatees, monkeys and boat-billed herons (pictured).
letsgohonduras.com

③ Take a boat trip to Punta Sal National Park
Rainforest, mangroves, sandy beaches and coral reefs can all be found in this Caribbean jewel.
letsgohonduras.com

④ Dive the Bay Islands
Located 29 km off the coast, Utila has superb diving on coral reefs, plus encounters with whale sharks, March to May and August to October.
aboututila.com

⑤ Spot birds in Pico Bonito National Park
It's home to 420 species, from hummingbirds to eagles. Pico Bonito Lodge is birding heaven.
picobonito.com

Making tracks | Costa Rica

Several wildlife travel companies feature Costa Rica (see p26-29). Local operators include **Costa Rica Tour** (costaricatour.com) and **Pizotes Eco Adventure Tours** (costaricawildlifetours.com).

Major airlines serving San José include **American** (aa.com), **Continental** (continental.com) and **Delta** (delta.com). The world's first carbon-neutral airline, **Nature Air** (natureair.com) flies to 17 destinations across Costa Rica. Buses are cheap and far-reaching if you have more time. Independent self-drive is also possible.

A variety of places to stay is available, including several ecolodges.

GMT-6

Expect some rain at any time of the year, although it's generally drier from December to April. At sea level, temperatures average 30-35°C, tempered by sea breezes, while the highlands and cloud forest can be a cool 10-15°C. From May to November (Costa Rica's 'green' season), expect clear mornings and heavy rain storms in the afternoons.

Seek local advice before swimming. Although surfing is excellent in some areas, rip currents pose a real danger. Estuaries can be home to crocodiles, bull sharks and stingrays.

Colón (CRC)

visitcostarica.com

Costa Rican Conservation Foundation (fccmonteverde.org)

Red-eyed tree frog

White-faced capuchin

Resplendent quetzal

Keel-billed toucan

Corcovado National Park

★ Baird's tapir, jaguar, ocelot, scarlet macaw, squirrel monkey

For a country rich in wildlife (a quarter of Costa Rica is protected as national parks and reserves), Corcovado boasts extraordinary biodiversity. Its rain-drenched tropical lowland forest is a glorious tangle of some 500 tree species, while the animal inventory stands at 104 mammals, 370 birds and 117 amphibians and reptiles. All four species of Costa Rica's monkeys are found here – spider monkey, squirrel monkey, mantled howler and white-faced capuchin – while the notoriously shy Baird's tapir is often spotted near the Sirena Biological Station (see below). Follow trails along the rainforest-fringed beaches for great views of capuchins, coaties and peccaries or delve into the jungle for fabulous birdwatching (Corcovado has Central America's largest population of scarlet macaws).

Directions Flights from San José serve Puerto Jiménez, the largest town on the Osa Peninsula; buses got to La Palma and Drake from where Drake Bay Wilderness Resort offers boat trips to Corcovado. Alternatively hike into the park to stay at Sirena Biological Station.
Getting around Hiking, boat trips.
Seasons See 'Making tracks', left.
Things to do Hiking, birdwatching, sea kayaking, whale watching.
Places to stay Written permission is required to stay at the only accommodation in the park, Sirena Biological Station (corcovado.org); ecolodges outside the park include Drake Bay Wilderness Resort (drakebay.com); Lapa Ríos ecolodge (laparios.com).
Further information sinac.go.cr (Spanish only)

Monteverde Cloud Forest Reserve

★ Resplendent quetzal, hummingbirds, orchids

No less than 30 species of hummingbirds flit through the moss-drizzled cloud forest of Monteverde, but it's the resplendent quetzal (best seen between January and July) that most dedicated birders want to see. Non-feathered highlights in the reserve include an astonishing 420-plus varieties of orchid and, if you are extremely lucky, you may also glimpse a Baird's

tapir or one of Monetverde's five species of cats. The network of trails in the park is well maintained, but come prepared for fog or rain.

Directions Buses travel daily between San José and Santa Elena (4 hrs), from where buses and taxis operate to Monteverde.
Getting around Walks, tours, Trainforest Railroad (trainforest.com).
Seasons See 'Making tracks', left.
Things to do Hiking, birdwatching, guided walks, horse riding, canopy tours (including zip-lining and suspended walkways).
Places to stay Lodges in the area include Cloud Forest Lodge (cloudforestlodge.com) and El Establo (elestablo.com).
Further information monteverdeinfo.com

Tortuguero National Park

★ Sea turtles, three-toed sloth, howler monkey, otter

Canals and coastal lagoons provide the main access to this exotic mix of flooded forest and Caribbean coast. Slipping quietly along water channels and nosing about in mangroves, a kayaking or boat trip offers the best chance for spotting wildlife such as howler and spider monkey, white-faced capuchin and three-toed sloth. Don't forget to occasionally glance down from the trees – Tortuguero is a good place to see southern river otter, spectacled caiman and basilisk lizards, along with wading birds, such as herons and jacanas. It's the beach, however, that's the real wildlife crowd-puller. A major nesting site for hawksbill, leatherback, loggerhead and green turtles, the park's beaches are one of the best places in the world to see the marine reptiles hauling themselves ashore to lay eggs.

Directions 80 km north of Limón; boat and air access only to Tortuguero Village, just north of the park.
Getting around Boat trips and walking tours.
Seasons Green and hawksbill turtles nest from July to September; leatherbacks February to April. Hatchlings emerge from November.
Things to do Boat trips, sea kayaking, canoeing, beach walks (to observe nesting turtles), canopy tour, hiking.
Places to stay Various lodges and B&Bs in Tortuguero Village.
Further information tortuguerovillage.com

Guanacaste National Park
Linked to Santa Rosa National Park, Guanacaste provides a wildlife corridor for wide-ranging species like the jaguar, as well as birds and insects that migrate seasonally between the coastal dry forest and inland cloud forest.

Braulio Carrillo National Park
This huge swathe of virgin rainforest and cloud forest is easy to reach from San José, but take time to explore its hiking trails and you'll see toucans, toucanets, trogons, tanagers, hummingbirds and some of the other 500-plus species of birds recorded here. Mammals include tapirs, monkeys and jaguar. Don't miss the aerial tram – an open gondola ride through the treetops.

Nicaragua

Barra del Colorado Wildlife Refuge
A watery paradise for birds like wood stork, snail kite, anhinga, glossy ibis and green-backed heron.

Santa Rosa Park

Liberia

Barra Honda National Park

Las Cañas

Volcán Arenal

Sarapiqui

Tortuguero National Park
see page 166

Tamarindo

Nicoya Peninsula

Quesada

Monteverde National Park
see page 166

Voicán Poás

Caribbean Sea

Puntarenas

Alajuela

Volcán Irazú

San José

Limón

Ostional Wildlife Refuge

La Amistad International Park

Las Baulas National Marine Park
A nesting site for leatherback turtles (October to April), Las Baulas offers night time, ranger-led tours to witness the spectacle of these marine heavyweights (weighing up to 900 kg) dragging themselves up the beach to dig pits in which to lay their eggs. When visiting, take care not to use flashlights which can disorientate the turtles, and avoid walking above the high-tide mark where concealed clutches of eggs are easily damaged. Adjacent to the marine park, Tamarindo National Wildlife Refuge protects mangroves, home to frigatebirds, monkeys and crocodiles.

Cerro Chirripó

Cahuita National Park
Elkhorn and staghorn corals festoon the reefs of Cahuita, while a rare swamp forest along the coast is a good spot to look out for boat-billed herons, kingfishers, coatis, racoons and sloths.

Manuel Antonio National Park
An easily accessible strip of rainforest and unspoilt golden-sand beaches, Manuel Antonio is a popular park with a good network of beaches. The chic ecolodge Arenas del Mar makes a good base.
arenasdelmar.com

Ballena Marine National Park

Palma Sur

Los Quetzales National Park
One of Costa Rica's newest national parks, Los Quetzales was inaugurated in 2008 and protects a healthy population of quetzals on the Pacific slopes of the Talamanca Range.
sinac.go.cr/principal

Osa Peninsula

Panama

Corcovado National Park
see page 166

Pacific Ocean

Cocos Island National Park
Located 550 km off the Pacific coast of Costa Rica, uninhabited Cocos not only supports a unique island rainforest, but its surrounding seas are revered by adventurous divers for vast migratory shoals of hammerhead sharks, plus abundant manta rays, dolphins, whale sharks and humpback whales. Join a live-aboard from Puntarenas, 36 hours' cruise away.

South America | Venezuela

Netherlands Antilles

Coro

Islas Los Roques

Caribbean Sea

Morrocoy National Park

Caracas

Mochima National Park

Trinidad & Tobago

Maracaibo

Cabimas

Maracay

Cumana

Barcelona

Caripe

Trujillo

Cueva del Guacharo
Oilbirds – 15,000 of them – nest in this cave, filling the darkness with bat-like clicks.

Lago de Maracaibo

Barinas

Henri Pittier National Park
Established in 1937, this reserve protects a range of bird-rich habitats, from cloud forest in the Cordillera de la Costa to mangrove forest at sea level.

Delta de Orinoco

Mérida

Cálabozo

Ciudad Guayana

Pico Bolívar

Sierra Nevada de Mérida National Park
Where the Andes divide in two, the southern ridge of the Sierra Nevada de Mérida contains snow-capped peaks and high-altitude grassland, or *páramo*.

Ciudad Bolívar

San Cristóbal

Orinoco

Orinoco Delta
River dolphin and manatee are highlights of a boat trip in this mangrove maze, but you could also see howler monkey, hoatzin and macaws.

Los Llanos

Guiana Highlands

Making tracks | Venezuela

↻ Local operators include **Orinoco Tours** (orinocotours.com). **Naturetrek** (naturetrek. co.uk) offers various wildlife holidays in Venezuela, including birding tours, while **Geodyssey** (geodyssey. co.uk) operates tailor-made and group trips.

✈ Numerous airlines serve the capital, Caracas. The country is well served by internal flights, while the road network is generally good in the north.

🛏 Places to stay range from plush hotels in Caracas to cattle ranches in Los Llanos and remote, basic jungle lodges.

🕐 GMT-4.5

☀ Visit year round, although the drier months are October to April.

💲 Bolívar fuerte (Bs).

ⓘ think-venezuela.net

Angel Falls

Auyan Tebuy

Guyana

La Gran Sabana

Mt Roraima

Los Llanos wetlands
Though not quite on the scale of Brazil's Pantanal, this large tropical grassland floods between July and November to create a seasonal wetland where scarlet ibis, capybara, anaconda, giant anteater and Orinoco crocodile can be found alongside herds of cattle tended by *llanero* cowboys. Saddle up and explore the region on horseback, or paddle a canoe through flooded areas. Tours are available from operators in Mérida.

Canaima National Park
The highlands of La Gran Sabana are characterized by flat-topped mountains (*tepuis*) from which stunning waterfalls – including 979-m Angel Falls – cascade in misty plumes. Over 900 species of plants, including many carnivorous varieties, are endemic to the *tepuis*, while the surrounding rainforest supports giant anteater, giant armadillo, jaguar, river otter and ocelot.
angel-ecotours.com

Amazonas

Amazonas
The densely forested drainage basin of the Orinoco is a little-visited swathe of the Amazon, scattered with *tepuis*. Serranía de la Neblina National Park is located in the far south of the region and is named after the mist-shrouded mountain that rises on the Brazilian border.

Serranía de la Neblina

Angel Falls

Shell Beach
Leatherback turtle
nesting site

Charity

Matthews
Ridge

Venezuela

Atlantic Ocean

Georgetown Botanical Gardens
Dust off your binoculars at this rich floral oasis in the heart of Guyana's capital. Blood-coloured woodpecker and festive parrot are just two of the birding highlights here.

Georgetown

Kaieteur National Park
Plunging 228 m into a mist-shrouded gorge, mighty Kaieteur Falls is usually visited as a fly-in daytrip from Georgetown. If you have time, though, travel overland (allow four days) and spend longer delving into the pristine rainforest around the waterfall. The tank bromeliads are often home to frogs, and it's also possible to see courting leks of the Guianan cock-of-the-rock, as well as various primates and jungle cats. Watch the falls carefully at dusk and you'll spot swifts darting through the curtain of water to their roosts in the rocks behind.
kaieteurpark.gov.gy

Bartica

**Arrowpoint
Nature
Resort**

**New
Amsterdam**

Wineneru

Linden

Essequibo

Issano

Ayangganna

Mt Roraima

Mahdia

Kaieteur Falls

Ituni

Suriname

Guiana
Highlands

Making tracks | Guyana

Local operators include **Wilderness Explorers** (wilderness-explorers.com). **Wildlife Worldwide** (wildlifeworldwide.com) can arrange international packages to Guyana.
Flights operate via Miami, Toronto and Barbados. Buses link Georgetown and Lethem, but many visitors fly to remote sites like Iwokrama and Kaieteur. Regular river ferries operate to Bartica.
There is a scattering of ranches and ecolodges in the interior, including the Iwokrama River Lodge (see page 185).
GMT-4
The main wet season is May to July, with another rainy period from late-December to late January.
Guyana dollar (G$).
guyana-tourism.com
guyanabirding.com

Iwokrama Forest
The Iwokrama International Centre for Rainforest Conservation and Development manages this 3,710-sq-km swathe of rainforest for the benefit of wildlife and the 16 local communities that have a stake in the area's ecotourism, research and sustainable timber operations. Few places in the world offer better chances of seeing jaguar, while the Iwokrama River Lodge (p185) also makes an excellent base for exploring the Rupununi wetlands and savannah.
iwokrama.org/wp

**Iwokrama River Lodge
& Research Centre**

Annai

Karanambu

Letham

Kanuku Mountains

Rupununi

Rupununi Savannah
Ranches here provide excellent bases from which to roam grasslands, wetlands and forests by 4WD vehicle, boat, canoe, horseback or on foot. You may well spot giant river otter, giant anteater, woolly, spider and howler monkey, black caiman, anaconda, capybara, ocelot and numerous species of birds, including the endangered red siskin and sun parakeet.The Kanuku Mountains, meanwhile, have one of South America's densest populations of harpy eagle.

Dadanawa

Harpy eagle

Making tracks | Brazil

🌀 Wildlife tour operators in Brazil include **Brazil Ecotravel** (brazil-ecotravel.com) and **Metropolitan Touring** (metropolitan-touring.com), while international companies featuring the country's natural highlights include **Reef & Rainforest Tours** (reefandrainforest.co.uk), and **Tribes** (tribes.co.uk).

✈ Numerous airlines serve major cities like São Paulo and Rio de Janeiro. Internal flights are often the most practical means of getting around. **TAM** (tam.com.br) offers air passes linking up to nine destinations within Brazil, including Campo Grande, Cuiabá and Manaus.

🛏 **Hidden Pousadas Brazil** (hiddenpousadas brazil.com) lists inns, ecolodges and B&Bs.

🕐 GMT-2 (Brasília and coast), GMT-3 Mato Grosso), GMT-4 (West Amazonas)

☀ Weather patterns vary across such a vast country, but the climate is generally tropical with average temperatures around 27°C. See opposite for specific wildlife seasons. Mid-December to February is the national holiday season and can be very busy.

⚕ Take precautions against malaria if visiting the Amazon.

💲 Real (R$).

ℹ braziltour.com, lata.org/brazil

🌍 **The World Land Trust** (worldlandtrust.org) is funding the protection of Brazil's Atlantic rainforest.

The Brazilian Amazon

★ River dolphin, sloth, pygmy marmoset, hoatzin, macaws

Unlike the Pantanal, below, it's sometimes a case in the Amazon of not being able to see the animals for the trees. Immersing yourself in this immense tropical forest, however, still ranks as one of the world's most exciting and rewarding wildlife travel experiences. Simply being there, staying in a jungle lodge or cruising upstream in a small riverboat, will give you a strong sense of the forest's vibrant biodiversity. With patience, you'll glimpse tapirs, monkeys and otters by the water's edge, macaws flashing scarlet and blue over the forest canopy or caiman skulking in the backwaters, just their eyes and nostrils protruding above the surface. Boost your chances of wildlife sightings by staying at places like Uakari Lodge and Cristalino Jungle Lodge which have canopy towers, hides and trails. A 60-km river trip from Manaus, the Anavilhanas Archipelago is also a good base. The forest floods here in April and May, allowing canoe trips through the treetops in search of river dolphins, manatees and giant, air-gulping pirarucu fish.

Directions Manaus is the major gateway, reached by flights.
Getting around Join a riverboat trip or transfer to a jungle lodge.
Seasons Rainy season occurs from mid-October to March.
Things to do Boat trips, hiking, canoeing, fishing.
Places to stay Several lodges are within a day's river journey from Manaus, including the floating Uakari Lodge (uakarilodge.com.br) and the treetop Ariaú Amazon Towers (ariautowers.com).

The Pantanal

★ Jaguar, giant anteater, giant river otter, hyacinth macaw

Where there's a wetland, there's usually abundant wildlife. Make that a tropical wetland covering 210,000 sq km and you're guaranteed a natural spectacle. The Pantanal is just that – a water wonderland squirming with 30 million caiman, half a million capybara, copious birds (656 species and counting) and one of the continent's most visible populations of jaguar. In the northern Pantanal, the Transpantaneira Highway links a succession of lodges from where you can stroll boardwalks in search of wildlife, gaze across the patchwork floodplains from viewing towers or simply relax in gardens watching capybara graze the lawns and hummingbirds fuss around bird feeders. This is also ranch country, so you will be able to track down wildlife on horseback. Boat trips, meanwhile,

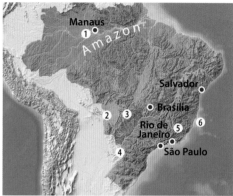

Wild places

❶ **Amazon** – Manaus is the starting point for jungle jollies.
❷ **Pantanal** – visits to the southern part of the wetland have the added bonus of snorkelling in the crystal clear and wildlife-rich river near Bonito.
❸ **Emas National Park** is pimpled with termite mounds and roamed by maned wolf, rhea and giant anteater.
❹ **Iguazú Falls** can be visited from Brazil or Argentina.
❺ Rare **Atlantic forest** has high numbers of endemic trees.
❻ **Abrolhos Marine National Park** and the Bahia coast have nesting green turtles and humpback whales (Jul-Nov).

offer some of the best opportunities for seeing jaguar, as well as caiman, capybara, howler monkey, marsh deer, tapir and giant river otter. Travelling along the Transpantaneira, look out for anacondas basking on the roadside and giant anteaters trundling across the grasslands. Night drives can turn up anything from ocelot and maned wolf to armadillos and nightjars.

Directions Access the Northern Pantanal from Cuiabá, travelling south along the Transpantaneira Highway between Poconé and the Cuibá River. The Southern Pantanal is reached via Aquidauana, Campo Grande and Miranda.
Getting around Hire a driver and guide for the Transpantaneira (there is no public transport). Lodges offer boat trips and safaris.
Seasons During the dry season (July to September), wildlife concentrates around dwindling pools. Floodwaters advance during the rains (October to December) crowding wildlife on higher ground during the full flood (December to March). The floodwaters recede between April and June when migrant birds arrive.
Things to do Safaris by vehicle, boat, horseback and on foot.
Places to stay Range of *pousadas* (lodges) along the Transpantaneira, including Araras Ecolodge (araraslodge.com.br) and Jaguar Ecological Reserve (jaguarreserve.com) and Pantanal Wildlife Centre (pantanalwildlifecenter.com).
Further information pantanal.org

Panther on the prowl – the Pantanal is thought to support the world's largest population of jaguar; they are often seen sunbathing on riverbanks, allowing close-up views on boat trips.
Left: Capybara, the world's largest rodent, is frequently spotted in the Pantanal and you're guaranteed seeing caiman (the wetland is home to no less than 30 million of them).

Ubiquitous sally lightfoot crabs

Wildlife tour operators in Ecuador include **Metropolitan Touring** (metropolitan-touring. com), which operates several Galápagos vessels as well as the Finch Bay Ecohotel on Santa Cruz. For a full list of operators, go to lata.org/ecuador.

Airlines include **Continental** (continental. com), **Iberia** (iberia.com) and **LAN** (lan.com).

Galápagos boats range from yachts to motor cruisers. You spend less time embarking and disembarking on a small boat, but they are less stable than larger ones and may not reach as many islands. Usually, the better quality (and more expensive) boats have the best guides. See also pages 176-177. Amazonian ecolodges include **Huaorani** (see page 185), **Napo Wildlife Centre** (napowildlifecentre.com), **Sacha Lodge** (sachalodge. com) and **Secoya Lodge** (secoyalodge.com).

GMT-5 (mainland), GMT-6 (Galápagos)

Visit year round. It's warmer in the Galápagos between December and March (and good for snorkelling), while June to September can be cooler and drier on the mainland.

Take anti-malarials if visiting the Amazon.

US dollar (US$).

ecuador.travel

Darwin Foundation (darwinfoundation.org), **Galápagos National Park** (galapagospark.org).

Wild places

① Galápagos Islands – wildlife-watcher's paradise, a 90-minute flight from the mainland.
② Cloud forest reserves like Bellavista buzz with hummingbirds and other star species like tanager finch and plate-billed mountain toucan.
③ Cotopaxi National Park's *páramo* grassland and high-altitude lake attracts Andean lapwings, Andean gulls and several species of waterfowl.
④ The Ecuadorian Amazon has several superb ecolodges.

Isla de la Plata
A budget alternative to the Galápagos, boat trips to this island will enable you to see blue-footed booby, albatross, frigatebird and sea lion, plus the bonus of humpback whale between June and September.

Wildlife highlights of Ecuador

For nature lovers, Ecuador's terrific trio (Galápagos, cloud forest and Amazon) can be easily combined on a two- or three-week itinerary. Spend a day or two in Quito visiting the old colonial centre before striking northwest to the cloudforest where valleys like the Tandayapa support over 340 species of birds. Hummingbirds and tanagers are the most conspicuous (you'll see plenty around bird feeders at various lodges), while a walk in the woods will immerse you in a misty, mesmerising world, where earthworms grow to a metre long and tiny frogs dwell in water-filled bromeliads. You can fly or travel overland to the Amazon. Most visitors spend around three nights at a lodge, exploring the rainforest by canoe and using walkways and canopy towers to spy on wildlife. Five- or seven-day cruises are the most popular option for experiencing the Galápagos, although land-based trips are also available, staying on Santa Cruz and taking day trips to nearby islands.

Galápagos Islands | Landing sites

① **North Seymour** A good introduction to Galápagos wildlife, this small, flat island has sea lions, marine and land iguanas, blue-footed boobies and frigatebirds. Dry landing on black basalt lava.
② **South Plaza** The jetty on South Plaza is often taken over by sea lions. Land iguanas are common. A trail leads across the island to seabird cliffs.
③ **Santa Fé** From a sea lion-strewn bay on the northeast of Santa Fé, a trail winds through cactus forest – home to land iguanas. Spot rays and turtles in the bay.
④ **Punta Pitt** Cliff trail provides encounters with all three species of booby: blue-footed, red-footed and Nazca.
⑤ **Gardner Bay** Wade ashore on a dazzling 2-km-long coral-sand beach smothered in sea lions. Snorkelling around the offshore islet is excellent.
⑥ **Punta Suárez** Spectacular rocky headland, often pounded by surf and the site of a blowhole on the southern coast. Wildlife is outstanding: marine iguana, lava lizard, Nazca and blue-footed booby, swallow-tailed gull, red-billed tropicbird, three species of Darwin's finch, Galápagos hawk and (from April to December) a colony of waved albatross.
⑦ **Punta Cormorant** Wet landing on olivine beach (you may see Galápagos penguin in the bay), followed by a trail that heads inland past a brackish lagoon (flamingos, stilts and other waders) to a sandy beach that's used as a nesting ground by green turtles. Look for stingrays in the shallows and lava lizards on the rocky headlands.
⑧ **Genovesa** Remote and spectacular, the flooded caldera of Genovesa has over a million nesting seabirds. Great frigatebirds, red-footed boobies, lava and swallow-tailed gulls and yellow-crowned night herons are best seen around the sandy beach at Darwin Bay. At Prince Philip Steps a short climb leads onto basalt cliffs where daytime-hunting short-eared owls can be observed snatching white-vented storm petrels as they return to their nesting burrows. The trail also leads through dry woodland with nesting Nazca and red-footed boobies. Mockingbirds are common. Snorkel along the base of the cliffs near Prince Philip Steps to see large numbers of king angelfish, Moorish idol, yellow-tail surgeonfish and, possibly, a few Galápagos sharks and fur seals.
⑨ **Bartolomé** A small island off the east coast of Santiago, Bartolomé has a boardwalk that climbs through a volcanic landscape of ash fields, lava tubes and cinder cones to a viewpoint overlooking Pinnacle Rock. You can snorkel at the Pinnacle, often with penguins and reef sharks.
⑩ **Puerto Egas (James Bay)** Snorkelling from the black-sand beach is good, while a walking trail follows the coast to a series of tide pools teeming with marine iguanas and sally lightfoot crabs. Don't miss the fur seal grottoes.

Pinta

Marchena

Genovesa
8

Isabela's volcanoes
Measuring 130 km in length, Isabela is the largest island in the Galápagos. Its six peaks include Volcán Wolf, the highest at 1,646 m, and Volcán Ecuador – eroded in half by wave action and a spectacular sight as you sail around the northwest tip of the island. Giant tortoises are found throughout the highlands of Isabela, but you are only allowed to climb Volcán Alcedo, a 20-km round trip.

What's happening when?
See page 176. Wildlife Worldwide (wildlifeworldwide.com) also has a comprehensive online Galápagos calendar with month-by-month natural history highlights.

Pacific Ocean

Equator

Volcán Wolf

Volcán Ecuador

Volcán Darwin

Volcán la Cumbre
11

12

13
Volcán Alcedo

Fernandina

Santiago
10

Rábida

Bartolomé
9

North Seymour

Baltra
1

Charles Darwin Research Station
A short walk from Puerto Ayora, this scientific research station has a giant tortoise breeding facility. Boardwalks connect a series of enclosures, some containing hatchlings, others serving as retirement homes for old-timers like Lonesome George – the sole survivor of the Pinta Island subspecies. The research station also works with the Galápagos National Park to restore the ecosystem of Isabela Island which is threatened by goats and other alien species.

Santa Cruz
2

Pinzón

Isabela
14

Volcán Santo Tomás

Volcán Cerro Azul

Puerto Villamil

Puerto Ayora

Santa Fé
3

4
San Cristóbal

Puerto Baquerizo Moreno

El Chato Tortoise Reserve
See wild giant tortoises (pictured below) on private farms in the highlands. Tours depart Puerto Ayora.

Post Office Bay
Wade ashore in the footsteps of pirates, whalers and fishermen who, since the late 1700s, have used a large wooden barrel here to leave mail for homebound voyagers. The tradition continues today with postcard-toting tourists.

7
Floreana

Española
6 5

11 **Punta Espinosa** The shield volcano of La Cumbre looms over black lava fields where the Galápagos' biggest concentration of marine iguanas can be found. Pioneer cactus, lava lizards and sally lightfoot crabs have also claimed the ropy coils of lava, while sea lions lounge on coves of crushed shell and pencil urchin spines. Look out for whales and dolphins in Bolivar Channel.

12 **Targus Cove** This sheltered, steep-sided bay is excellent for snorkelling – green turtles are abundant and you should also see flightless cormorants, penguins, sea lions, marine iguanas, large shoals of fish and even manta rays, sharks and

dolphins. A panga ride along the shore will get you close to penguins and flightless cormorants, while a short hike above the bay has wonderful views across a flooded crater known as Darwin's Lake. Look for finches, flycatchers and yellow warblers in the surrounding woodland.

13 **Urvina Bay** Wet landing on a steep beach. Giant tortoise, land and marine iguanas, plus flightless cormorants.

14 **Punta Moreno** After navigating a maze of mangrove channels, you make a dry landing on pahoehoe lava before following a scant trail to a series of brackish lagoons – home to flamingos, pintail ducks and brown pelicans.

Giant tortoise

Natural selection | galápagos

This page: Galápagos sea lion, marine iguana and waved albatross (Punta Suárez, Española). Opposite (from top left): plumage detail of great frigatebird (Genovesa), short-eared owl (Genovesa), Galápagos hawk (Española), Great frigatebird in flight (Genovesa), Galápagos penguin swimming (Isabela), Galápagos mockingbird washing (Genovesa), flightless cormorant preening (Isabela), Nazca boobies (Española), adult lava heron (Fernandina).

Wild nights out | Galápagos cruise vessels

Galápagos calendar | Monthly guide to wildlife highlights

January As the rainy season starts, marine iguanas become brightly coloured and land birds begin nesting. Green turtles start egg laying and warming sea temperatures are ideal for snorkelling.

February Galápagos dove courtship is in full swing; flamingos and pintail ducks are also breeding, along with marine iguanas on Santa Cruz. Sea temperatures reach 25°C.

March Expect frequent downpours this month. Marine iguanas are nesting on Fernandina, but the big event in late March is the mass arrival of waved albatross to Española.

April Waved albatross waste no time in practising their courtship dances. Frigatebirds are also engaged in frenzied mating rituals. Green turtle and Isabela land iguana eggs hatch. As the rains come to an end, the islands are at their greenest.

May As North Seymour's blue-footed boobies begin their courtship, waved albatross are laying eggs on Española and turtle hatchlings are emerging. Marine iguana eggs are also hatching on Santa Cruz.

June The first of the season's mists appear as giant tortoises descend from the Santa Cruz highlands in search of nesting sites. Seas can become choppy. This is a good month for spotting migratory birds and humpback whales.

July Sea temperatures will drop to around 21°C this month. Everywhere you go, seabird colonies are a riot of courtship, egg-brooding and chick-feeding. It's another good month for whale watching.

August Sea temperatures fall to around 18°C. Sea lions begin to pup, and it's a good time to look for courting Galápagos hawks and nesting Nazca boobies and swallow-tailed gulls. Migrant shore birds arrive, while giant tortoises head back to the highlands.

September It's a good month to brave the waters around Bartolomé where Galápagos penguins are usually active. Most seabirds are also still busy nesting and rearing chicks. Male beachmaster sea lions start fighting over females.

October The misty (Garúa) period is coming to an end. Galápagos fur seals start mating, lava herons begin nesting and blue-footed boobies have chicks on Española and Isabela.

November Seas are calmer and water temperatures start rising. Snorkellers can enjoy encounters with sea lion pups. Storm petrels are busy nesting on Genovesa and dodging the island's short-eared owls.

December Giant tortoise eggs hatch between now and April; green turtles are mating in offshore waters, while the first waved albatross chicks fledge.

One for landlubbers | Finch Bay Eco Hotel

A small hotel on the edge of Puerto Ayora, Santa Cruz island, the 27-room Finch Bay Eco Hotel (finchbayhotel. com) is well located for visits to the Charles Darwin Research Station, El Chato Tortoise Reserve and the beach at Tortuga Bay. An excellent snorkelling spot (Las Grietas) is also nearby and, if your sea legs are up to it, boat trips can whisk you to nearby islands for the day. Other activities include mountain biking, sea kayaking, scuba diving or simply lazing by the hotel pool.

Cachalote

Type Steel-hulled, ketch-rigged, motor sailor, refurbished in 2002.
Length 21 m
Berths 16 passengers in eight double/twin cabins, each with private shower and toilet.
Facilities Bar, saloon, dining area, three wooden decks, including sundeck, air conditioning throughout, sea kayaks onboard.
Crew Four crew and one naturalist guide.
Price category Mid-range.
Islands usually visited Baltra, Santa Cruz, Española, Isabela, Santiago and Bartolomé.
galapagosislands.com

Isabela II

Type Motor-yacht.
Length 53 m
Berths 40 passengers in ensuite double/twin cabins.
Facilities Lounge, bar, restaurant, library, gift shop, sundeck, jacuzzi, sea kayaks, glass-bottom boat, snorkelling gear, lecture areas, air conditioning throughout.
Crew 24 crew, one doctor and three naturalist guides.
Price category Luxury.
Islands usually visited Baltra, North Seymour, Española, Floreana, Santa Cruz, Genovesa, Isabela, Fernandina, Santiago and Bartolomé.
metropolitan-touring.com

La Pinta

Type Motor-yacht.
Length 63 m
Berths 48 passengers in ensuite cabins, some interconnecting for families.
Facilities Lounge, bar, restaurant, library, gift shop, sundeck, jacuzzi, outside bar, sea kayaks, glass-bottom boat, snorkelling gear, lecture area with cinema screen, air conditioning.
Crew 24 crew, one doctor and four naturalist guides.
Price category Deluxe.
Islands usually visited San Cristobal, North Seymour, Santa Cruz, Floreana, Fernandina, Isabela, Bartolomé and Española.
lapintagalapagoscruise.com

Sagitta

Type Swedish built triple-masted sailing yacht.
Length 36 m
Berths 16 passengers in 10 double cabins, each with a double lower and single upper berth and ensuite shower and toilet.
Facilities Bar, salon, library, sundeck, shaded alfresco dining area, air conditioning, snorkelling gear.
Crew Eight crew and one naturalist guide.
Price category Luxury.
Islands usually visited North Seymour, Santa Cruz, Española, Floreana, Isabela, Fernandina, Santiago and Bartolomé.
naturegalapagos.com

Samba

Type Steel-hulled motor-sailor with stabilising sail.
Length 24 m
Berths 14 passengers in seven ensuite cabins, six of which are air-conditioned.
Facilities Salon, large forward deck, aft dining deck area, sundeck, air conditioning, mini library and large-screen TV lecture area, two pangas.
Crew Six crew and one naturalist guide.
Price category Mid-range.
Islands usually visited Baltra, North Seymour, Santa Cruz, Floreana, Fernandina, Isabela, Santiago, Bartolomé and Española.
galapagos-ecuador.com

Santa Cruz

Type Motor-cruiser.
Length 72 m
Berths 90 passengers in 43 ensuite cabins, including spacious suites.
Facilities Lounge, bar, restaurant, library, gift shop, sundeck, stargazing program, jacuzzi, glass-bottom boat, snorkelling gear, aromatherapy centre, air conditioning.
Crew 52 crew, one doctor and six naturalist guides.
Price category Luxury.
Islands usually visited Baltra, Bartolomé, North Seymour, Santa Cruz, San Cristobal, Española, Fernandina and Isabela.
galapagosvoyage.com

Making tracks | Peru

Owned by non-profit conservation group, Peru Verde, **InkaNatura Travel** (inkanatura.com) runs jungle lodges in Manú and Tambopata and can organise specialist birding and archaeology tours as well as biology workshops and treks. For international operators covering Peru, visit lata.org/peru.

Flights to Lima are available with **American Airlines** (aa.com), **KLM** (klm.com) and **Iberia** (iberia.com).

Accommodation ranges from Amazon riverboats and jungle ecolodges to city hotels and camping on the Inca Trail.

GMT-5

Temperatures in the jungle remain at a fairly steady level in the high 20s and you can expect short, intense bursts of rain at any time of year. It tends to be hotter and drier, however, from April to October. The reverse is true for the coast which is driest from December to April.

Take precautions against malaria if visiting the Amazon.

Nuevo sol (S/.).

peru.info

Blue-and-yellow macaw

Pacaya Samira National Reserve

★ Pink river dolphin, three-toed sloth, caiman, hoatzin

Covering 20,000 sq km, Pacaya Samiria extends east from the official source of the Amazon (where the Ucayali and Marañon rivers meet). The world's largest flooded forest, it is only accessible by boat from December to April when 85% of the reserve is inundated. Wildlife is prolific with nearly 1,000 species of plants recorded, along with 450 species of birds, 102 mammal species and 130 varieties of reptiles and amphibians. Pink river dolphins use sonar to navigate through the flooded forest, while hoatzin can often be seen perched in trees over lagoons and oxbow lakes. Four species of caiman – black, white-bellied, smooth-fronted and dwarf – can be found lurking among rafts of floating lettuce or basking on fallen tree trunks.

Directions 180 km southwest of Iquitos along the Amazon River.
Getting around Riverboats operate from Iquitos. One of the longest established is Delfin (delfinamazoncruises.com) which operates two vessels – one with six cabins, the other with 14. Hiking is possible in the reserve during low-water season.
Seasons The flooded season (December to April) has temperatures of around 30°C and rivers running 7 m higher than normal.
Things to do River cruises, canoeing, boat trips, fishing.
Places to stay In addition to riverboat cruises (see 'Getting around') accommodation includes the Pacaya Samiria Amazon Lodge (pacayasamiria.com.pe) located in the reserve's buffer zone.

Manú Biosphere Reserve

★ Scarlet macaw, giant river otter, emperor tamarin, tapir

The overland journey through Manú (see page 159) traverses high Andean passes and cloud forest before following rivers deep into the jungle. The Manú Wildlife Centre (page 180) has canopy towers for spotting some of Manú's 1,000 bird species and 13 different primates, a tapir-viewing platform (for observing this largely nocturnal creature at close quarters) and excursions to a riverbank clay lick that attracts flocks of macaws and parrots. Boat trips to a nearby oxbow lake often reveal giant river otter, howler monkey, three-toed sloth and black caiman.

Directions Fly from Cusco or travel overland.
Getting around Jungle trails, boat trips, canoeing.
Seasons Late March through December.
Things to do Birdwatching, boat trips, jungle trails.
Places to stay Cloud forest lodges include Cock-of-the-Rock Lodge (inkanatura.com) and Manú Paradise Lodge (manuparadiselodge.com); rainforest lodges include Manú Wildlife Centre (manuwildlifecenter.com).

Iquitos

Amazon

1

Trujillo

2

Inca Trail
Hiking the Inca Trail will give you an opportunity to experience cloud forest rich in hummingbirds and orchids.

Lima

Machu Picchu

6

5

3

Cusco

4

Wild places

❶ From the jungle city of Iquitos (see page 160) delve into the Amazon at Pacaya Samiria National Reserve.
❷ Huascarán National Park offers spectacular hiking in the Cordillera Blanca, with the chance of spotting Andean condors, viscachas and, if you're particularly lucky, puma.
❸ Scoured by the Humboldt Current, the rocky peninsula of the Paracas National Reserve has sea lions, inca terns, brown pelicans, Peruvian boobies and Guanay cormorants. Whales can be seen offshore around the Ballestas Islands.
❹ The Colca Canyon is one of the best places in South America to see Andean condors.
❺ Tambopata National Reserve is part of the great Tambopata Madidi Wilderness on the Peru-Bolivia border, protecting some of the most species-rich forest on Earth.
❻ Manú Biosphere Reserve (see also page 159) rivals even Tambopata for biodiversity – its habitats range from high-altitude grassland to lowland tropical rainforest.

Tambopata National Reserve

★ Macaws, parrots, capybara, harpy eagle, otter, primates

Renowned for its clay licks (attracting up to 260 macaws and a dozen species of parrots), Tambopata's Heath River and Sandoval Lake are also rich in wildlife.

Directions A 25-minute flight from Cusco, Puerto Maldonado is the departure point for boats to various lodges in the reserve.
Getting around Jungle trails, boat trips, canoeing.
Seasons August through April; clay lick best August to October.
Things to do Birdwatching, boat trips, jungle trails.
Places to stay Heath River Wildlife Centre (inkanatura.com) is close to a floating hide overlooking a clay lick and also runs night-time caiman-spotting trips; Sandoval Lake Lodge (inkanatura.com).

❝ ❞ It was almost as if a door had closed behind us. One moment we were driving in brilliant sunshine across the high-altitude *puna*, the next we were descending through cloud that parted occasionally to reveal a gravel road, unravelling through forested valleys like a wayward strand of dental floss. From a 3,500-m pass, high in the Andes, we traced the road eastwards until it was snuffed out by the misty expanse of the Amazon rainforest, lapping at the mountains like a green tide.

William Gray

Big on biodiversity – it is not unusual for a single hectare of rainforest in Manu to support over 200 different varieties of trees. Left: Local people call hoatzins 'stink birds' because the aromatic oils in their diet of leaves gives them a distinctive odour; the male Andean cock-of-the-rock performs complex courtship lek displays in the cloud forests of Manu; this leaf-shaped katydid is part of the ever-increasing inventory insects found in Manu – one of the world's most biodiverse hotspots.

South America | Bolivia, Argentina & Chile

Making tracks | BO/AR/CL

Wildlife tour operators in Bolivia include **Ruta Verde** (rutaverdebolivia.com). For Patagonia, try **Aventura Argentina** (aventuraargentina.com) and **Blue Green Adventures** (bluegreenadventures.com). **The Latin American Travel Association** (lata.org) has a directory of operators.

Buenos Aries and Santiago are major international gateways to the region with **LAN** (lan.com) and **TACA** (taca.com) providing a comprehensive internal network. Long-distance bus services are also excellent throughout the region.

GMT-3 (Argentina), GMT-4 (Bolivia and Chile).

Weather varies enormously across the region. Bolivia's wet season is October to March; southern Patagonia is gripped by winter June to September; central parts of Chile and Argentina are best in spring and autumn.

Take precautions against malaria if visiting the Amazon.

Argentine peso (ARS$), Boliviano (Bs), Chilean peso (CLP).

Argentina: tourismo. gov.ar/eng/menu; Bolivia: lata.org/bolivia; Chile: chile.travel

Guanaco, Torres del Paine

Madidi National Park, Bolivia

★ Primates, pink river dolphin, macaws, toucans, otters

Part of a group of Amazon reserves that includes Tambopata in Peru (see page 176), Madidi rivals even Manú in terms of species richness. Covering an area of some 26,000 sq km, Madidi ranges from glacier-clad Andes and rapid-strewn canyons to dense tropical rainforest and open pampas. At least 11% of the world's 9,000 bird species are thought to live here. A new species of monkey – the brown and orange titi (*Callicebus aureipalatii*) – was discovered in Madidi's jungle as recently as 2005, while other wildlife highlights in this huge national park include jaguar, giant river otter, river dolphin, tapir, spider monkey, ocelot, anaconda and a profusion of orchids, amphibians and invertebrates.

Directions A 50-minute flight from La Paz, Rurrenabaque is one of the main access points to Madidi's rainforest. From here, a 6hr boat trip on the River Beni takes you to Chalalán Ecolodge (see below).
Getting around Jungle trails, boat trips, canoeing.
Seasons October to July.
Things to do Birdwatching, boat trips, jungle trails, night safaris.
Places to stay Chalalán Ecolodge (chalalan.com), see page 185.

Valdés Peninsula, Argentina

★ Orca, sea lion, Magellanic penguin, southern right whale

Protruding from the Atlantic coast of northern Patagonia like a hammerhead pounding the ocean, the Valdéz Peninsula surged into the limelight when orca were filmed surfing onto its beaches to snatch hapless sea lion pups (see pages 102 and 103). However, this is just one of the region's many wildlife highlights. Each austral winter, southern right whales migrate into the huge bays of the Peninsula. You can often see mothers with calves, courtship displays and a curious 'sailing' behaviour where the whales raise their tail flukes above the surface and cruise across the bay. Commerson's dolphin is also regularly sighted, while other marine mammals include elephant seal and sea lion. Punta Tombo has a colony of several hundred thousand Magellanic penguin.

Directions Puerto Madryn is the main base for exploring Valdés. You can fly there from Buenos Aires or travel overland by bus.
Getting around Guided tours are available.
Seasons Orca February to April; southern right whale mid-July to November; Magellanic penguins September to mid-March.
Things to do Whale watching trips, birdwatching.
Places to stay Various hotels in Puerto Madryn and nearby.

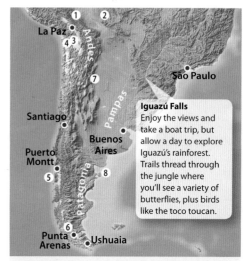

Iguazú Falls
Enjoy the views and take a boat trip, but allow a day to explore Iguazú's rainforest. Trails thread through the jungle where you'll see a variety of butterflies, plus birds like the toco toucan.

Wild places

❶ Like Peru's Manú and Tambopata reserves, Madidi National Park, Bolivia, is considered one of the most biodiverse protected areas on the planet.
❷ A little gem if you can reach it, the remote Noel Kempff Mercado National Park in Bolivia has rainforest, scrub and Pantanal, so you can expect to see superb birdlife.
❸ Sajama National Park protects a rugged swathe of Bolivian Andes that includes snow-capped volcanoes, the world's highest forest (gnarled kenua trees at 5,200 m) and high-altitude specialists like vicuña and Andean flamingo.
❹ Bordering Sajama (above), Lauca National Park, Chile, has a spectacular landscape of volcanoes, lava fields and lakes. Easily reached by bus from Arica, the high altitude reserve (Lago Chungara is at 4,500 m) is home to vicuña, flamingos, Andean fox and puma.
❺ The unique Valdivian temperate rainforest on Chiloé Island has many endemic bird species, including parakeets and hummingbirds, while the surrounding coast is home to Magellanic and Humboldt penguin, kelp goose, flightless steamer duck, migrant waders and numerous other shore and seabirds. Sea lions, dolphins and blue whales (December to March) can also be seen.
❻ Iconic mountain scenery, wilderness hiking and the chance to spot guanaco, flamingo, condor, Andean deer and puma make Chile's Torres del Paine National Park a highlight of many Patagonian wildlife itineraries.
❼ El Ray National Park has habitats ranging from cloud forest to semi-desert – with diverse wildlife to match.
❽ Argentina's Valdés Peninsula is a hotspot for marine mammals, seabirds and Patagonian wildlife.

" Sailing into the Strait of Magellan, our ship began to be jostled by an agitated sea. Clouds snuffed out the mountains, rain and sea grime smeared the windows, but the petrels and albatrosses were up and about, wheeling over the whitecaps, making a mockery of the squalls.

William Gray

①

① Cruise along the Strait of Magellan
Brave the elements to see mountains, glaciers, whales, seabirds and the penguin colony at Magellan Island.
australis.com

② Discover the wildlife of Beagle Channel
A short boat ride from Ushuaia, the Beagle Channel supports large colonies of king cormorant.
canalfun.com

③ Hike in Tierra del Fuego National Park
This sub-Antarctic beech forest is home to the showy Magellanic woodpecker and austral parakeet.
canalfun.com

④ Explore Cape Horn
A boardwalk protects the island's fragile vegetation. Visit the lighthouse, chapel and albatross memorial and gaze south across the Southern Ocean.

⑤ Set sail for Antarctica
Ushuaia is the main embarkation port for cruises to Antarctica. The South Shetland Islands are usually sighted after two days crossing the Drake Passage.

Above: Catching the rays – Magellanic penguins preen in the golden hours of dusk.
Far left: Dawn view of Laguna Torre and Grande Glacier below the 3,102-m peak of Cerro Torre, Los Glaciares National Park, Argentina.
Left: Hairy armadillo; southern right whale breaching off Argentina's Valdés Peninsula; male and female elephant seal.

Lapa Ríos Ecolodge
Osa Peninsula, Costa Rica

Set in a 376-hectare private nature reserve with dreamy views across pristine rainforest to the Pacific coast, Lapa Ríos has 16 bungalows built and furnished using sustainably harvested materials, including palm-thatched roofs. The lodge only employs local people, providing them with educational and training opportunities. Combine this with the lodge's passive design, renewable energy schemes, sustainable waste and water management and its deep-rooted respect for wildlife and the environment and it's small wonder that Lapa Ríos has been awarded Costa Rica's highest sustainable tourism certification.

The reserve acts as a buffer and wildlife corridor for the Osa Peninsula's Corcovado National Park where naturalist-led day hikes are a highlight. Other activities include birdwatching walks, boat trips in the mangrove forest, whale watching and kayaking. You can also spend a night even closer to nature by sleeping on a special outdoor platform. Visits to local conservation and education projects are available, while those in search of some pampering can enjoy massages and yoga.

laparios.com

Kuyimá Ecolodge
San Ignacio Lagoon, Baja California, Mexico

A community-run ecolodge, with 11 rustic cabins and solar-heated showers, Kuyimá has been granted environmental certification by Green Globe 21. Local guides run boat trips in open *pangas* to see the grey whales that migrate annually to Ignacio Lagoon. Rock art tours in El Vizcaíno Biosphere Reserve are also available, as well as mule-supported treks into Santa Teresa Canyon, observing desert wildlife and sleeping under the stars.
kuyima.com

Bellavista Cloud Forest
Ecuador

This peaceful lodge almost feels like an organic part of the forest, its thatched roofs smothered in epiphytes. Imaginative rooms include the dome with spiral staircase and ladders climbing to a den overlooking the canopy. Smart Voyager certified, Bellavista is grounded in sustainable practices and offers internships to students in ecotourism. The lodge is a paradise for hummingbirds, while numerous trails probe the surrounding cloud forest.
bellavistacloudforest.com

Iwokrama River Lodge
Iwokrama Forest, Guyana

Located on the west bank of the Essequibo River, Iwokrama River Lodge has eight cabins, each with wrap-around verandahs. Highlights of a stay at this role model for commercially sustainable community-based ecotourism include a 154-m canopy walkway, excellent chances of spotting jaguar and visits to the Makushi settlement of Fair View Village. A trip to the Turtle Mountain satellite camp, deep in the jungle, is also not to be missed.
iwokrama.org

1. Lapa Ríos Ecolodge
2. Kuyimá Ecolodge
3. Bellavista Cloud Forest
4. Iwokrama River Lodge
5. Araras Ecolodge
6. Huaorani Ecolodge
7. Manú Wildlife Centre
8. Chalalán Ecolodge
9. Ecocamp Patagonia

Araras Ecolodge
Pantanal, Brazil

Located right in the heart of the Pantanal, 19-room Araras Ecolodge frequently has capybara wandering through its grounds. Two tree-top lookouts provide a wonderful view across the wetlands and a chance to spot hyacinth macaws (over 40 nest in the lodge area). Canoeing, horse riding, trekking and jeep safaris are also available. The lodge runs a giant river otter conservation programme and supports local communities through employment.
araraslodge.com.br

Huaorani Ecolodge
Yasuní Biosphere Reserve, Ecuador

This intimate 10-person, palm-thatched ecolodge was developed by the Huaorani (uncontacted by the outside world 55 years ago) to help maintain the integrity of their culture while conserving the rainforest and generating an income through ecotourism. As well as superb wildlife viewing, you will gain a privileged glimpse into the Huaorani's traditional lifestyle, getting to know individual households and exploring the jungle by dugout canoe.
huaorani.com

Manú Wildlife Centre
Manú National Park, Peru

This 44-bed riverside lodge is part-owned by Peru Verde, a non-profit NGO involved in rainforest conservation projects. Constructed in local Machiguenga style, its bungalows are made from wood collected from the river each rainy season when trees are naturally washed away from riverbanks. The lodge sponsors onsite researchers and is just a short boat ride from clay licks and oxbow lakes. Two canopy platforms and a nocturnal blind provide excellent opportunities for observing rainforest wildlife.
manuwildlifecenter.com

Chalalán Ecolodge
Madidi NP, Bolivia

A local community-run project, this outstanding ecolodge offers comfortable accommodation for up to 30 people. Cabins built with traditional materials, such as copa plam, have balconies overlooking Chalalán Lagoon, while solar energy and effective waste treatment ensure minimal impact to the environment. Local Quechua and Tacana guides can arrange boat trips on the Beni and Tuíchi Rivers, night-time canoeing on Chalalán Lagoon and nature walks in the rainforest.
chalalan.com

Ecocamp Patagonia
Torres del Paine NP, Chile

Inspired by the traditional huts of the nomadic Kawesqar of Patagonia, this seasonal, minimal impact camp consists of spacious dome-shaped tents built on raised platforms and linked by walkways to avoid damaging the ground. As well as solar and wind energy, Ecocamp Patagonia uses composting toilets and was the first operator in Chile to receive ISO 14001 Environmental Management System certification. Expert local guides arrange treks and horse riding.
ecocamp.travel

Europe

Some of the natural world's most evocative sights can be found in Europe – bluebells carpeting a beech wood in spring; vast, shimmering flocks of waders pulsing across tidal mudflats; red deer roaring during the autumn rut; Atlantic cliffs ringing with the cries of seabirds... It's only through a conscious effort to nurture and conserve, however, that many of these wildlife wonders survive in the continent's increasingly crowded spaces. Hail the conservation movements of Europe! Without them, the world would not only be a poorer place, but biodiversity would have been dealt a devastating blow.

Home to 80% of the UK's rarest or most threatened bird species, the 200 nature reserves of the Royal Society for the Protection of Birds (RSPB) cover an area of 130,000 ha. Add to that 2,200 nature reserves managed by the Wildlife Trusts, over 1,100 km of coastline protected by the National Trust, 15 national parks and around 150 marine protected areas, and you can begin to appreciate the scale of conservation activity in just one European nation.

Even the nature-loving Brits, however, would be the first to admit that much more needs to be done to safeguard wildlife both in the UK and across Europe.

Driving new initiatives, the RSPB – now one of Europe's largest wildlife conservation charities – was founded in 1889 in protest against the trade in exotic bird feathers used to accessorize women's hats. But if there was one person who can be singled out as a pioneer of conservation in the UK, Europe and beyond, it has to be the late Sir Peter Scott.

Son of the famous Antarctic explorer, Scott not only founded the UK's Wildfowl & Wetlands Trust in 1946, but he was also a founder of the World Wildlife Fund and architect of the IUCN Red Data Books on endangered species. Naturalist, artist, broadcaster and author, Scott – who died in 1989 – was described by Sir David Attenborough as conservation's 'patron saint'.

Scott's legacy pervades the wild places of Europe. You can sense it in the far north, where geese, ducks and waders – popular subjects for many of Scott's paintings – migrate each summer to nest. And you can see it, too, at his beloved Slimbridge reserve in Gloucestershire, where many of those same species spend the winter months. Scott's conviction that wildlife conservation relied on safeguarding habitats and inspiring people is as relevant now as it was several decades ago. In Europe, it underpins projects as diverse as protecting Scotland's ancient Caledonian forest to pulling the Iberian lynx back from the brink of extinction.

It also lies at the heart of responsible wildlife travel. You only have to visit the Carpathians of Romania, for example, to find local people taking great pride in showing visitors the bears and wolves that still roam the area's mountain forests.

There's certainly no shortage of enthusiasm for nature conservation in Europe – and, with a wealth of fabulous wildlife sites to visit, ecotravellers can become some of its best ambassadors.

Flights of fancy | Best of Britain's birding spectacles

Snettisham RSPB Nature Reserve in Norfolk hosts two of Britain's great avian events – vast flocks of wading birds swirling over The Wash as high tide forces them to leave the mudflats, plus the winter roosting (at dawn and dusk) of thousands of pink-footed geese. Hides are ideally placed to witness the 'touchdown' of both events. During summer, avocets and ringed plovers nest on the beach in front of the hides. At Bempton Cliffs on the North Yorkshire coast, meanwhile, the sound (and *eau de poisson*) of Britain's largest mainland gannetry wafts your way long before you peer down from the RSPB viewpoint at the swirling, squawking spectacle of up to 200,000 seabirds nesting on the cliffs below. It's just one of several seabird cities in Britain. Others include Hermaness (pictured left) and Pembrokeshire's islands (page 190).

Seabird cities – one of the wildlife spectacles of Europe

Hermaness National Nature Reserve in the far north of Scotland's Shetland Islands has been left to the seabirds – over 100,000 of them. The cliffs and nearby islets are painted white by their guano, as if a winter storm has dusted the coastline with fresh snow. Crouching on soft turf at the cliff's edge, you can watch fulmars, gannets and puffins gyrate on the fickle ocean breeze, filling the air like shreds of tickertape flung from a New York skyscraper.

Densely populated, widely cultivated and cast in a dense web of roads and railways, Europe is still a wonderful destination for wildlife. Look to the continent's mountains and remote borders; to its wetlands and islands; to fragments of the great wildwood and, most of all, to its superb network of national parks and nature reserves.

Natural zones

Europe was once a land of trees. Broadleaf forests of oak, beech and birch cloaked much of western and central Europe, but now only remnants survive – the most famous being Poland's Bialowieza Forest. Conifer forest still claims much of the continent's high ground, along with large swathes of Scandinavia, where it merges with Russia's mighty taiga forest.

Europe's major mountain ranges – the Alps, Pyrenees and Carpathians – are strongholds for large mammals such as brown bear, wolf and ibex. Transboundary conservation efforts are helping many of these species expand their ranges and reclaim old haunts. Beavers have been reintroduced to the Scottish Highlands, while the dry, scrubby slopes of Spain's Sierra Morena provide a lifeline to Iberian lynx. Cleaner rivers now support healthy populations of otters; numerous wetlands and offshore islands have been declared sanctuaries for breeding and migratory birds, and perhaps most importantly, Europe's man-made landscapes – its farmland, parks and canals – are being managed in a more wildlife-friendly way.

Wildlife travel

Europe's extensive and efficient transport network – even to far-flung islands and distant Arctic outposts – smooths the way for wildlife travellers. Wherever you choose to go, chances are there will be places to stay, expert naturalist guides and probably a national park or nature reserve with trails, hides and a visitor centre.

Europe also has numerous wildlife tour operators, ranging from specialists such as Transylvanian Wolf (a Romanian company offering wolf-tracking holidays – see box, right) to generalists covering large parts of the continent. Naturetrek (naturetrek.co.uk) offers one of Europe's most comprehensive selection of wildlife tours, including butterfly watching holidays in support of the charity Butterfly Conservation.

it's a wild life

Simon King | Wildlife film-maker | simonkingwildlife.com, wildlifewhisperer.tv

❝❞ I am hot and panting despite the bracing wind that blows into my face from the north-east. I have been running along the Shetland coastline trying to keep up with one of the most charismatic of the islands' natural inhabitants: an otter. Now she surfaces from a hunting dive and I freeze, my silhouette shielded from the sky, and her gaze, by the peat bank that runs along the foreshore. She heads towards me, a large fish in her jaws, and I sink to my knees to further reduce my profile. No more than 4 m away, she comes ashore and begins to chew on the lumpsucker. For a moment I am as much a part of her world as the gulls and lapping water that offer a rhythm to her day.

↘ My big five

❶ **Shetland Islands, Scotland**
Sea birds, otters and orcas
❷ **Masai Mara, Kenya**
Big cats, wildlife spectacle
❸ **South Georgia**
Penguins and albatrosses
❹ **Peninsula Valdés, Argentina**
Orcas
❺ **False Bay, near Cape Town, South Africa**
Great white sharks hunting fur seals

guiding star

Dan Marin

Transylvanian Wolf, Romania (transylvanianwolf.ro)
Most memorable wildlife encounter A pack of six wolves chasing off a bear at a kill. We had a great sight of the wolves feeding and socializing, a full moon rising behind them above the Carpathian Mountains of Transylvania.
Top tip for travellers Apart from opportunities to spot animals like wolves and bears, you have a great chance to discover traditional culture.
Favourite animal The wolf – both for the animal itself as a symbol of wilderness and for its role as a central character in our traditional culture.

What does responsible travel mean to you? Romania has one of the last true wilderness areas in the whole of Europe and we must do our best to preserve that for the future. We have managed to place Zarnesti and its surrounding part of the Carpathian Mountains on the world map of ecotourism, with all its benefits for the environment and local communities.

Day 1 Fly to Kajaani via Helsinki and transfer to Hotel Kalevala (approx 90 minutes) **Day 2** Explore the taiga forest of the Finnish wilderness by bike, canoe or on foot **Day 3** Visit the Petola Nature Centre and walk to a special wildlife-viewing hide deep in the forest for a night of bear watching **Day 4** Return to your hotel, catch up on some sleep, then make the most of the long summer evenings for some final birdwatching **Day 5** Transfer to Kajaani for flight to Helsinki

⟳ Based on an itinerary from **Discover the World** (discover-the-world.co.uk), this trip would cost around £850 per person, based on twin-share and including international flights between the UK and Kajaani, airport transfers, half-board accommodation and bear watching at Petola Nature Centre. Available April to October.

Wild city | Stockholm, Sweden

Scattered liberally along the edge of the Gulf of Bothnia in the Baltic Sea, the 25,000 or so islands of Sweden's Stockholm Archipelago are a popular playground for the city's inhabitants. Many have holiday homes there, while tour boats and ferries regularly ply between the capital and day-trip islands such as Vaxholm, Sandhamn and Utö. To get a more intimate feel for the wildness of the archipelago, however, nothing beats a sea-kayaking or canoeing trip, slipping quietly and unobtrusively between forested islands inhabited by white-tailed eagle, osprey, elk, roe deer and pine martin. Large colonies of seals, terns and guillemots can also be found here. Guided tours are run by Stockholm Adventures (stockholmadventures. se) which also operates a kayak camp on Runmarö Island – one of the best spots for accessing the wild scenery of the outer archipelago. On the mainland, Stockholm Adventures operates safaris from the capital to nearby undisturbed meadows and forests where elk and wild boar can often be seen foraging during summer evenings.

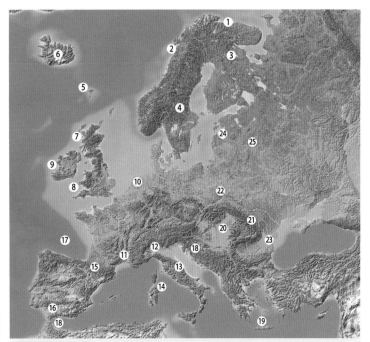

Wild places

The extreme north of mainland Europe is a little-visited land of rugged beauty where you can search for seabirds, snowy owls and Arctic foxes at Norway's Varanger Fjord ❶. White-tailed eagles and sperm whales can be seen around the lofty Lofoton Islands ❷, while the taiga forest of northeast Finland ❸ is one of the best places in the world to observe brown bears in the wild. The forests and lakes of Sweden ❹ are also rich in mammals, including beaver, elk and wolf. In the Faroe Islands ❺ seabirds rule the roost, with some two million pairs staking out the cliffs of this North Atlantic archipelago. Iceland ❻ has seabird cities on its western fjords, thousands of breeding waterfowl at lake Myvatn and excellent whale watching in Skjalfandi Bay. Whales, seabirds, eagles and otters feature on island safaris in the Scottish Hebrides ❼, while the Pembrokeshire islands of Skomer, Skokholm, Grassholm and Ramsey ❽ are bustling with puffins, shearwaters and gannets each spring. The natural treasures of Ireland ❾ include the unique flora of the Burren and the migratory birds of the Ballycroy blanket bogs. In the Netherlands ❿ coastal areas are crucial for waders, as are the lagoons and reedbeds of the Camargue in southern France ⓫. An extensive network of national parks covers the Alps ⓬, including the long-established Swiss National Park and Italy's Gran Paradiso. Mountain species, from butterflies to lammergeiers, also find protection in the Italian Apeninnes ⓭, the rugged interior of Corsica ⓮ and the Pyrenees ⓯. One of Europe's finest wildlife destinations, the Coto Doñana of Andalucía ⓰ is a stronghold for the highly endangered Iberian lynx and a magnet to waterbirds. Northern Spain isn't short of wildlife appeal either – its Picos de Europa mountains still support bears and wolves, while the Bay of Biscay ⓱ rewards whale watchers with sightings of everything from common dolphins to blue whales. Cetaceans are also widespread in the Mediterranean, particularly in the Straits of Gibraltar ⓲ and off the south coast of Crete ⓳. Largest of the Greek Islands, Crete also puts on a spectacular display of wildflowers. Highlights of Eastern Europe include the steppes of Hungary ⓴, the bear forests of the Carpathian Mountains ㉑ and the ancient wildwood of Poland's Bialowieza Forest ㉒. The pearl of the region for birdwatchers, however, is the Danube Delta ㉓: des-res for thousands of pelicans, herons, cormorants and other waterbirds. Estonia ㉔ is also a birding hotspot, while offbeat Belarus ㉕ is gaining popularity as a wildlife destination, thanks to reserves like Berezinsky and Pripiatsky – home to European bison, wolf, bear and lynx.

↗ Many of Britain's national parks and wildlife sites have excellent visitor facilities, making them easy to incorporate in an independent holiday. Specialist wildlife watching tours are also available. In Scotland, try **Great Glen Wildlife** (greatglenwildlife.co.uk), **Heatherlea** (heatherlea. co.uk), **Shetland Wildlife Holidays** (shetlandwildlife. co.uk) and **Speyside Wildlife** (speysidewildlife. co.uk). In Wales, contact **Welsh Wildlife Breaks** (welshwildlifebreaks.co.uk). UK-based **Naturetrek** (naturetrek.co.uk) has a selection of British and Irish breaks in its extensive worldwide portfolio.

✈ Overseas travellers can reach Britain through any of its major airports, or by ferry or Channel Tunnel from mainland Europe.

🛏 Some of the best options for places to stay in or near Britain's wild places include farm stays (farmstays.co.uk), youth hostels (yha.org. uk and syha.org.uk), campsites and lodges with **Forest Holidays** (forestholidays.co.uk) and **National Trust Cottages** (nationaltrustcottages.co.uk).

🕐 GMT

☀ Year round, although summer holidays (late July and August) can be busy.

💷 GB pound (£).

ℹ visitbritain.com

💻 naturalengland.org.uk, rspb.org.uk, wwt.org.uk, wildlifetrusts.org, woodland-trust.org.uk

Puffin emerging from burrow

Gannet with seaweed

Pembrokeshire's seabird islands

★ Puffin, Manx shearwater, gannet, guillemot, razorbill

Each year, in early April, around 6,000 pairs of puffins arrive to breed on Skomer Island off the coast of Pembrokeshire. They take up residence in nesting burrows on grassy slopes above sea cliffs thronging with guillemots, razorbills, kittiwakes and fulmars. By May, the whole island is ablaze with red campion, bluebells and thrift. Grey seals loll offshore, while great black-backed gulls prowl the coast, waiting to snatch unwary puffins. With luck, you might also spot one of the island's short-eared owls. Overnight visitors can witness one of Britain's greatest wildlife spectacles as 120,000 pairs of Manx shearwaters return to their nesting burrows under cover of darkness – the night suddenly reverberating with their eerie, wailing cries.

Shearwaters, along with puffins and storm petrels, also nest on nearby Skokholm, while further offshore, Grassholm appears dusted with summer snow as 32,000 pairs of gannets settle down to nest. Boat trips to Grassholm often have the added bonus of dolphin, basking shark and minke whale sightings.

On the northern edge of St Brides Bay, boat trips around Ramsey Island often turn up sightings of porpoises and gannets feeding in Ramsey Sound. Kittiwakes, razorbills and guillemots stream from the island's cliff-face rookeries, while grey seals rest in shingle coves or bob to the surface to watch you pass.

Directions Skomer is a 15-minute boat trip from Martin's Haven on the mainland, landings April to October only. Boats to Ramsey Island operate from St Justinians, near St David's.
Getting around Dale Sailing (sale-sailing.co.uk) runs boat trips to Skomer, Skokholm and Grassholm. For Ramsey Island, try Thousand Islands Expeditions (thousandislands.co.uk).
Seasons Puffins begin to leave the islands at the end of July.
Things to do Boat trips, walking trails on Skomer.
Places to stay Basic self-catering on Skomer.
Further information rspb.org.uk, welshwildlife.org

Wild places

❶ Fallow, red, roe and sika deer can be seen in the New Forest, plus unusual insects like the stag beetle.

❷ The chalk downlands of Kent and Sussex support a wealth of orchids and butterflies.

❸ The Pembrokeshire islands of Grassholm, Skokholm, Skomer and Ramsey are important seabird nesting sites.

❹ Rare alpine plants survive in the mountains of Snowdonia National Park, along with birds like the chough.

❺ A popular haul-out for common and grey seals, the north Norfolk coast also hosts half of the world's overwintering pink-footed geese, while the reedbeds of East Anglia are an important nesting site for bitterns.

❻ Bass Rock in the Firth of Forth has 75,000 pairs of nesting gannets. Other well-known gannetries in Britain are found at Bempton Cliffs, Yorkshire, and the remote sea stack of St Kilda, off the west coast of the Outer Hebrides.

❼ The ancient Caledonian forest of the Cairngorms is home to wildcat, pine marten, capercaillie and crested tit.

❽ One of the wildlife-rich Inner Hebrides, Islay is an overwintering site for thousands of barnacle and white-fronted geese. Otters and grey seals can be found around the coast, while corncrakes nest in undisturbed farmland.

❾ The wildflower-rich machair grassland of North Uist in the Outer Hebrides comes into bloom during May.

❿ Belfast Lough is a magnet to waders and wildfowl.

> ❝❞ A rising tide nuzzles rocks drizzled with honey-coloured seaweed. Each rhythmic swell chuckles through the heaped piles of kelp, massaging them to life until they are twitching, swirling and cavorting with the sea – playing otter-tricks with my mind.
>
> William Gray

①

① Spot an otter
For your best chance of seeing one, join a wildlife safari on Mull. Golden eagles and short-eared owls will also be in your sights. **torrbuan.com**

② Hike or bike in Cairngorms National Park
Red squirrel, pine marten, capercaillie and wild cat are just some of the highlights of this upland reserve. **cairngorms.co.uk**

③ Go whale watching
Sea Life Surveys has been running wildlife cruises around Mull since 1982, notching up 24 species of whale and dolphin. **sealifesurveys.com**

④ Track red deer
There are around 300,000 red deer in Scotland, but two of the best places to witness the rut are the Isle of Arran and the Knoydart peninsula. **visitscotland.com**

⑤ Watch sea eagles
Making a comeback in the Hebrides, sea eagles can be viewed from the hide at Loch Frisa, Mull. For ospreys, visit Loch Garten on the mainland. **rspb.org.uk**

②

3

4

5

Making tracks | France

🌀 Several operators offer regional wildlife tours in France. **Brittany Wildlife Tours** (brittanywildlife.com) covers northwest France; **Faunus Wildlife Tours** (faunus.co.uk) delves into the Ariege region of the French Pyrenees; **Northern France Wildlife Tours** (nfwt.online.fr) focuses on Brittany, Normandy and Pays de la Loire, and **Wildlife Provencale** (wildlifeprovencale.com) offers wildlife holidays in the South of France.

✈ **Air France** (airfrance.com) connects Paris to 200 destinations in 85 countries. As well as an extensive autoroute network, France has an efficient rail system, with high-speed TGV trains (tgv.com) linking major centres.

ℹ WWF's **Gîtes Panda** status (gites-panda.fr) is awarded to rental properties in natural areas that preserve traditional styles of architecture and offer sustainable tourism in a rural environment. Also consider **Camping France** (campingfrance.com) or cottage rental companies like **Allez France** (allezfrance.com).

🕐 GMT+1

☼ Visit during the spring and autumn for bird migrations; early to mid-summer for wildflowers and butterflies. August can be very busy and hot, particularly in the south.

💶 Euro (€).

ⓘ france.guide.com

ⓘ parcnationaux-fr.com

Greater flamingo, Camargue

Camargue

★ Greater flamingo, whiskered tern, bee-eaters, dragonflies

Just south of Arles, clutched between two arms of the Rhône, lies one of Europe's great wetlands – a 100,000-ha mosaic of lagoons, dunes and marshland. It's tempting to think of the Camargue as a watery wilderness, but people have not only played a major role in its creation (through drains, dykes and salt pans), but they continue to use the land for rearing the region's famous white horses and black bulls. That still leaves plenty of room for birds though. Around 400 species have been recorded, including ducks, geese, avocets, herons, warblers and kingfishers. It's the greater flamingo, however, that draws the crowds. Pretty in pink, these leggy birds tiptoe through the briny pools feeding on tiny shrimps. Around 10,000 pairs nest at Ilot du Fangassier.

Other good birdwatching spots include the dunes at La Pointe de Beauduc (migrants and waders), the pastures of Le Grenouillet (herons, bee-eaters, waders and terns) and the roadside observation deck at Mas Neuf (stilts, godwits, pratincoles, herons and warblers). Located 4 km from Saintes-Maries-de-la-Mer, Parc Ornithologique de Pont de Gau (parcornithologique.com) is a 60-ha bird sanctuary in the heart of the Camargue with nature trails and hides. Elsewhere in the region, make a beeline for Les Apilles (a range of limestone hills where eagle owls and Egyptian vultures can be found) and La Crau, a strange pebbly landscape that's home to hoopoe, larks and shrikes.

Directions From Arles, take the D570 through the western side of the Camargue to Saintes-Maries-de-la-Mer. At Albaron, the D37 heads to Étang de Vaccarès, the largest of the Camargue's lagoons.
Getting around You can tour the Camargue by car in a day. Saintes-Maries-de-la-Mer is a good base for cycling or walking to La Gacholle lighthouse along the sea dyke.
Seasons Park open year round; even winter is good for birds.
Visitor centres Located in the core Camargue National Reserve,

Capelière has an information centre on the region's wildlife. There are also visitor centres at La Gacholle lighthouse and Saintes-Maries-de-la-Mer.
Things to do Guided tours, nature trails, birdwatching, walking, cycling, horse riding
Places to stay Campsites, B&Bs and hotels in surrounding area
Further information reserve-camargue.org

Cévennes National Park

★ Orchids, butterflies, eagles, little bustard, green lizard

A varied region on the southeast edge of the Massif Central, the Cévennes has granite peaks, limestone plateaux and gorges, meadows, forests and rivers. Gorges du Tarn and Corniche des Cévennes are excellent for raptors, including booted, golden and short-toed eagles. The stunning blue rock thrush can also be found, along with fragrant, green-winged and lesser butterfly orchids. Griffon vultures have been reintroduced to Gorges de la Jonte, while the 1,699-m massif of Mont Lozere is the haunt of Montagu's harriers. The remarkable diversity of the Cévennes unfolds further as you drive towards the summit of Mt Aigoual through beech and chestnut woodland inhabited by hoopoe and red deer, or west towards the short-grass prairies of the Causses – a breeding site for little bustard and stone curlew.

Directions Easily accessed from Montpellier and Nîmes.
Getting around In addition to roads, there are over 3,500 km of hiking paths, 400 km of horse riding trails and mountain biking routes on the Causse Méjean and the Aigoual massif.
Seasons Park open year round; visit in spring for orchids.
Visitor centres Around 30 throughout the region, plus Eco-Museums (networks of museums and heritage trails for each massif).
Things to do Guided tours, nature trails, birdwatching, walking, cycling, horse riding
Places to stay Gîtes d'étape allow hikers to stay overnight at various points along trails in the park.
Further information eng.cevennes-parcnational.fr

French Alps | A trio of mountain national parks

Three of the nine national parks in France (parcsnationaux.fr) are found in the Alps. Better known for its skiing, **La Vanoise National Park** has a large population of ibex, as well as nesting golden eagles and lammergeiers. More than 100 peaks in **Les Ecrins National Park** are over 3,000 m high – perfect territory for some 15,000 chamois and 600 ibex. Curving towards Provence, **Mercantour National Park** is the most species-rich of the three parks, with no less than 2,000 plant species, 153 bird species and 58 mammal species, including a small population of wolves.

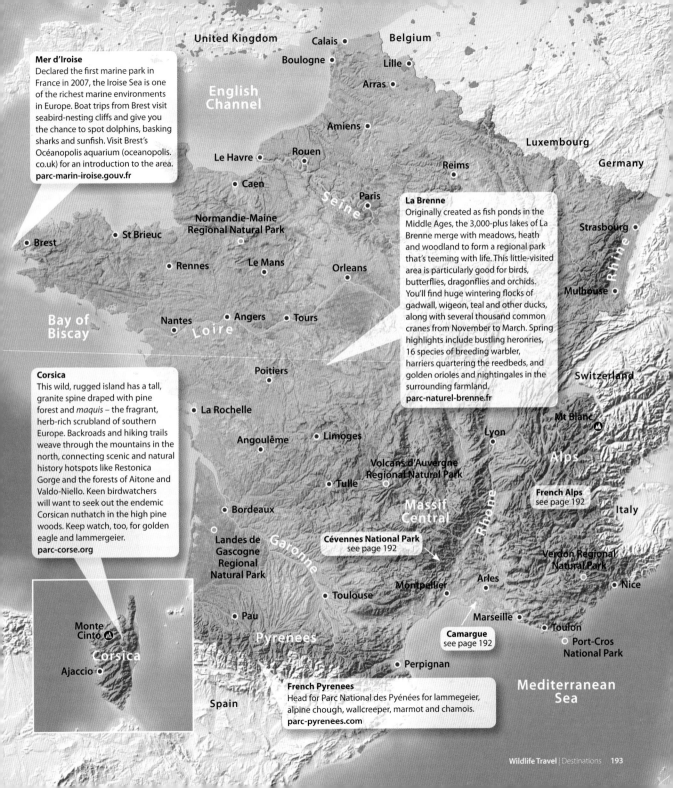

Mer d'Iroise
Declared the first marine park in France in 2007, the Iroise Sea is one of the richest marine environments in Europe. Boat trips from Brest visit seabird-nesting cliffs and give you the chance to spot dolphins, basking sharks and sunfish. Visit Brest's Océanopolis aquarium (oceanopolis.co.uk) for an introduction to the area.
parc-marin-iroise.gouv.fr

La Brenne
Originally created as fish ponds in the Middle Ages, the 3,000-plus lakes of La Brenne merge with meadows, heath and woodland to form a regional park that's teeming with life. This little-visited area is particularly good for birds, butterflies, dragonflies and orchids. You'll find huge wintering flocks of gadwall, wigeon, teal and other ducks, along with several thousand common cranes from November to March. Spring highlights include bustling heronries, 16 species of breeding warbler, harriers quartering the reedbeds, and golden orioles and nightingales in the surrounding farmland.
parc-naturel-brenne.fr

Corsica
This wild, rugged island has a tall, granite spine draped with pine forest and *maquis* – the fragrant, herb-rich scrubland of southern Europe. Backroads and hiking trails weave through the mountains in the north, connecting scenic and natural history hotspots like Restonica Gorge and the forests of Aitone and Valdo-Niello. Keen birdwatchers will want to seek out the endemic Corsican nuthatch in the high pine woods. Keep watch, too, for golden eagle and lammergeier.
parc-corse.org

French Pyrenees
Head for Parc National des Pyénées for lammegeier, alpine chough, wallcreeper, marmot and chamois.
parc-pyrenees.com

Cévennes National Park
see page 192

French Alps
see page 192

Camargue
see page 192

United Kingdom
Belgium
Calais
Boulogne
Lille
Arras
Luxembourg
Amiens
Germany
English Channel
Le Havre
Rouen
Reims
Strasbourg
Caen
Paris
Seine
Rhine
Brest
St Brieuc
Mulhouse
Normandie-Maine Regional Natural Park
Rennes
Le Mans
Orleans
Switzerland
Bay of Biscay
Nantes
Angers
Tours
Loire
Poitiers
La Rochelle
Mt Blanc
Lyon
Alps
Angoulême
Limoges
French Alps
Tulle
Volcans d'Auvergne Regional Natural Park
Italy
Bordeaux
Massif Central
Rhone
Verdon Regional Natural Park
Landes de Gascogne Regional Natural Park
Garonne
Nice
Arles
Montpellier
Toulouse
Pau
Marseille
Pyrenees
Toulon
Port-Cros National Park
Perpignan
Mediterranean Sea
Spain

Monte Cinto
Corsica
Ajaccio

Europe | Spain

Making tracks | Spain

🔎 **Iberian Wildlife Tours** (iberianwildlife.com) organises trips in Andalucía, Extremadura, the Picos de Europa and Pyrenees. Also try **Wildside Holidays Iberia** (wildsideholidays.com).

✈ **Iberia** (iberia.com) has an extensive flight network covering Spain and its islands, while **SATA** (sata.pt) operates to the Azores. Various low-cost and charter flights are also available. **Brittany Ferries** (brittany-ferries.co.uk) runs services between the UK and northern Spain; **Company of Whales** (companyofwhales.co.uk) offers whale-watching trips across the Bay of Biscay.

🏠 Consider renting a *casa rural* (rural house) through Andalucía's **RAAR** (raar.es), northern Spain's **Casas Cantabricas** (casa.co.uk) or Catalonia's **Ruralverd** (ruralverd.com).

🕐 GMT+1 (Spain), GMT (Canary Islands).

🌙 Try to avoid the heat and tourist crush of mid-summer. Spring and autumn are also the best periods to witness bird migrations, wildflowers etc.

💶 Euro (€).

ⓘ spain.info

Iberian lynx

Coto Doñana

★ Spanish lynx, greater flamingo

Struggling against ongoing threats such as drainage, urban development and pollution, the Coto Doñana is a resilient wetland wilderness on the Guadalquivir river estuary in Andalucía. Long exploited by humans, it now receives protection not only as a national park, but also as a Ramsar site, biosphere reserve and world heritage site. Why all the fuss? Put simply, birds love the place. Doñana is home to five threatened bird species, including the Spanish imperial (or Adalbert's) eagle and marbled teal. One of the Mediterranean's largest heronies is found here, while 500,000 waterfowl touch down in the reserve's lagoons and marshes each year to overwinter. Palaearctic migrants also use the wetland as a vital refuelling stop as they fly between Europe and Africa. Top ticks for birders include the purple gallinule, crested coot, whiskered and black terns, little egret, spoonbill, bittern, greater flamingo and slender-billed gull. In the park's drier areas of dune, woodland and *maquis*, you can expect to see azure-winged magpie, great spotted cuckoo, larks, pipits and nightjars.

But there's more to Doñana than birds. Anyone who visits this internationally significant wildlife reserve is constantly on the alert for a possible sighting of an Iberian lynx. Following a census in 2010, only 265 of these critically endangered cats were recorded – 30% in the scrublands of Doñana and the rest in the cork oak forests of Sierra Morena to the northeast. To increase your chances of spotting one of these elusive predators, you will need to be out and about at dawn and dusk when they are more likely to be active, hunting rabbits, ducks and deer fawns.

Directions Take the A483 south of Almonte to the main visitor centre at El Acebuche or head towards the village of El Rocío.
Getting around Access to the national park is strictly controlled, with official guided tours leaving from El Acebuche (0830 and 1500). You can explore nature trails at the visitor centre near El Rocío and go birdwatching along the edge of the park from Centro de Visitantes Antonio Valverde (30 km south of Villamanrique de la Condesa) and along Playa de Castilla, east of Matalascañas. A boat operates along the Guadalquivir from Sanlúcar de Barrameda.
Seasons Park open year round.
Visitor centres See 'Getting around'.
Things to do Guided tours, walks, boat trips, birdwatching.
Places to stay Nearest accommodation is in Matalascañas.
Further information reddeparquesnacionales.mma.es/parques/donana

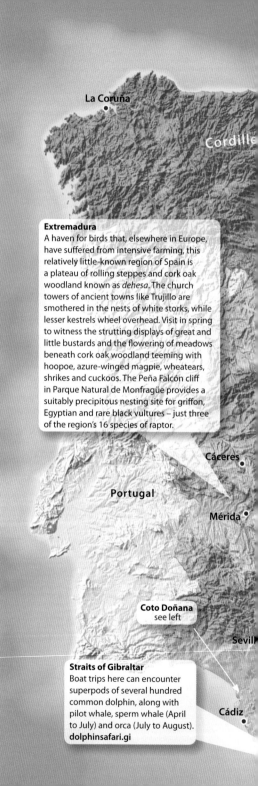

La Coruña

Cordille...

Extremadura
A haven for birds that, elsewhere in Europe, have suffered from intensive farming, this relatively little-known region of Spain is a plateau of rolling steppes and cork oak woodland known as *dehesa*. The church towers of ancient towns like Trujillo are smothered in the nests of white storks, while lesser kestrels wheel overhead. Visit in spring to witness the strutting displays of great and little bustards and the flowering of meadows beneath cork oak woodland teeming with hoopoe, azure-winged magpie, wheatears, shrikes and cuckoos. The Peña Falcón cliff in Parque Natural de Monfragüe provides a suitably precipitous nesting site for griffon, Egyptian and rare black vultures – just three of the region's 16 species of raptor.

Cáceres

Portugal

Mérida

Coto Doñana
see left

Sevil...

Straits of Gibraltar
Boat trips here can encounter superpods of several hundred common dolphin, along with pilot whale, sperm whale (April to July) and orca (July to August).
dolphinsafari.gi

Cádiz

Spanish Pyrenees
In Catalonia, Parc Nacional d'Aigüestortes is a beautiful tapestry of peaks, meadows, lakes and forests. The pine woods are a good place to spot capercaillie and black woodpecker, while golden eagle and lammergeier can sometimes be seen soaring overhead. Chamois inhabit rocky scree areas, while the park's lakes are home to otter and beaver. Parque Nacional de Ordesa is another wonderful haven for mountain wildlife. Both parks offer superb opportunites for hiking. Elsewehere in the Spanish Pyrenees, the Aragon, Hecho and Veral Valleys promise excellent birdwatching.

Picos de Europa National Park
Only 15 km inland from the coast of northern Spain, these craggy limestone peaks are rich in wild flowers during spring and summer. On a botanising ramble in undisturbed meadows you may come across bee, lizard, man and marsh orchids, while a cable-car ride to the limestone scree and pavement on Fuente Dé will be rewarded with displays of gentians and saxifrages. Brown bears and wolves still roam these mountains, but you are more likely to see chamois. Bird lovers won't be disappointed – the Picos de Europa have everything from griffon vultures to rock thrushes and wallcreepers.

Sierra de Guara
The dry southern slopes of this sierra in the foothills of the Pyrenees are favoured by birds of prey. The variety is astonishing, with Bonelli's eagle, booted eagle, Egyptian vulture, golden eagle, griffon vulture, hobby falcon, honey buzzard, lammergeier, peregrine falcon, red kite and short-toed eagle all present during summer months. The northern slopes have thicker forests where you might find pine marten and wild boar.

Andalucía
Covering a huge chunk of southern Spain, Andalucía is renowned for its wildlife. The two key locations for Iberian lynx are found here – Doñana National Park and Sierra de Andújar. Naturetrek (naturetrek.co.uk) runs dedicated lynx-watching trips in the spring and autumn. Almería, meanwhile, is the stepping-off point for visits to the Sierra Nevada (raptors, wild flowers and butterflies) and Cabo de Gata wetlands (flamingoes, ducks and waders).

Balearic Islands
Away from the busy tourist resorts, the Balearics have plenty to offer the wildlife traveller. The archipelago lies on a major bird mirgation route betwen Europe and Africa, with the freshwater marsh of Mallorca's Parc Naturel de S'Albufera providing a welcome rest and feeding ground for bee-eaters, terns and warblers. Mallorca's Tramuntana Mountains are the haunt of black vulture, while the Formentor Peninsula supports summer-visiting Eleonora's falcon. Menorca, meanwhile, has a vibrant coastal floral, a healthy bird of prey population (including breeding Egyptian vultures) and several wetland areas that attract a range of herons and warblers.

Santander
Bilbao
Torre de Cerredo
Pamplona
France
Pyrenees
Aneto
Ordesa National Park
Aiguestortes National Park
Andorra
Catalonia
Zaragoza
Barcelona
Mediterranean Sea
Madrid
Almanzor
Menorca
Palma
Mallorca
Valencia
Ibiza
Cabrera National Park
Migratory birds & seabirds
Formentera
Alicante
Sierra Morena
Córdoba
Sierra de Andújar Natural Park
Andalucía
Cartagena
Mulhacén
Cabo de Gata-Níjar Natural Park
Almería
Málaga
Sierra Nevada National Park
onfragüe Natural Park
ntábrica
ón

Flower power – *dehesa* grassland in full bloom in the Extremadura region of central Spain.
Left: A colony of white storks nesting on the roof of an old farmhouse; hoopoe with raised crest.
Top: Male great bustard in full-feathered courtship display – the puffed-up military-style strutting of these 22-kg birds is one of Europe's most mesmerizing wildlife spectacles. Witness it on the steppes of Extremadura in mid- to late April.

The Azores

Straddling the Mid-Atlantic Ridge, 1,500 km from Lisbon, each of the nine volcanic islands in the Azores has its own character and special appeal. The twin lakes of Sete Cidades – one blue, one green – are the main attractions on **São Miguel**, the largest of the islands. However, be sure to also visit the spa town of Furnas and nearby Terra Nostra Gardens – a tranquil haven of exotic and native flora. The northeast of the island is a good place to search for the Azores bullfinch (the only endemic land bird in the archipelago), while the northwest coast has breeding roseate terns. On **Terceira**, highlights range from the world heritage site of Angra do Heroísmo (once a hub of Atlantic maritime trade) to the quarry of Cabo do Praia where birdwatchers can track down American shorebirds. **Graciosa** is renowned for the Furnas do Enxofre, a sulphur lake located in a cave beneath the island's Caldeira, while **São Jorge** is a magnet to walkers with its dramatic sea cliffs and deep valleys covered in lush vegetation. Far to the west, **Flores** is claimed by many to be the most beautiful island in the Azores with a particularly stunning display of hedgerow hydrangeas in July. It's the islands of **Faial** and **Pico**, however, that are likely to be of most interest to wildlife travellers. Whale watching trips operate from the historic port of Horta on Faial and the old whaling centre of Lajes on Pico. Of the 27 species of cetacean recorded in the Azores, blue, fin and sei whales are present during March and April, while resident species include sperm whale, short-finned pilot whale, orca and bottlenose, common and Risso's dolphins. One of the best and most reponsible operators is Espaco Talassa (espacotalassa.com).

Canary Islands

Many of the Canary Islands have spectacular volcanic interiors, perfect for hiking, while offshore there's excellent diving and whalewatching. On **Tenerife**, make tracks for the Canarian pine forest surrounding Mount Teide National Park – home to the endemic blue chaffinch. Los Gigantes Diving Centre (divingtenerife.co.uk) offers scuba trips to see stingrays, eagle rays and bull rays at the base of sea cliffs on the island's northwest coast. Most whale watching tours operate out of Las Américas, but be sure to choose one that adheres to strict guidelines for minimising disturbance to the resident pods of short-finned pilot whales. Travelling by ferry around the islands offers another opportunity for spotting cetaceans, as well as shearwaters, storm petrels and other seabirds. On **Gomera**, the ancient laurel forest of Garajonay National Park is inhabited by the endemic Bolle's pigeon and laurel pigeon, while **Fuerteventura** has arid species more typical of North Africa. A day or two birding here should be rewarded with sightings of black-bellied sandgrouse, Egyptian vulture and the rare Houbara bustard.

Falling water and shearwater

Above: Salto do Prego, near Faial da Terra, São Miguel, The Azores.
Left: Cory's shearwater (*Calonectris diomedea*) is commonly seen in the Atlantic; 15,000 breed on the remote Selvagens, 130 km north of the Canary Islands.

Making tracks | Italy

⟳ **Naturetrek** (naturetrek.co.uk) has one of the best collections of Italian wildlife tours, covering destinations from the Dolomites and Abruzzo to Sardinia and Sicily.

✈ **Alitalia** (alitalia.com) flies from Europe and the United States to all major cities in Italy. There is also a wide choice of budget airlines. For train travel, **Trenitalia** (trenitalia.com) has an online reservation system, while ferry services from the mainland to Sardinia and Sicily are operated by **SNAV** (snav.it).

🏠 **Associazone per l'Agriturismo** (agriturist.it) offers a selection of farms, villas and mountain chalets across Italy. For campsites, try camping.it.

🕐 GMT+1

☀ Much of Italy has a typically Mediterranean climate with long, hot summers (temperatures consistently above 25°C) and mild winters. Expect cooler weather and more severe winters in the mountain regions of the Alps and Apennines.

€ Euro (€).

ⓘ enit.it

🖥 parks.it

Abruzzo

Alpine chough

Abruzzo National Park

★ Apennine wolf, Marsican brown bear, chamois

A royal hunting reserve until 1877, Parco Nazionale d'Abruzzo, Lazio e Molise was inaugurated in 1922 to provide a refuge for the wildlife of the Appennine range – Italy's 1,400-km-long backbone. The park's 66 species of mammal include the Marsican brown bear and Appenine wolf – long persecuted in the region, but now making a steady comeback. Spend some time walking in Abruzzo's ancient beech forests and you may catch a glimpse of one of these elusive predators – or get a worthy consolation prize of red deer or black woodpecker.

Wolves and bears also venture out onto the national park's high alpine pastures, but you're more likely to see chamois clattering about on surrounding rocky slopes – particularly in the dramatic amphitheatre of Camosciara. It's also worth scanning ridges for golden eagle and alpine chough. Don't overlook the detail at your feet. Abruzzo's meadows are festooned with stonecrop, gentians, saxifrages, orchids and other alpine wildflowers – many of them foodplants for the park's 100-plus species of butterfly. Visit during early summer and you should see blue-spot hairstreak, clouded yellow, grizzled skipper, purple emperor and scarce swallowtail varieties.

Directions From Rome, it is about a two-hour drive to Pescasseroli, a good base in the park from which to plan walks and excursions.
Getting around The S83 traverses the park. Abruzzo also has an extensive network of hiking trails.
Seasons Park open daily; snow likely November to April.
Visitor centres Pescasseroli.
Things to do Hiking, horse riding, climbing.
Places to stay Hotels, guesthouses and camping.
Further information parcoabruzzo.it

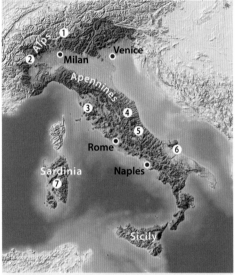

Wild places

❶ Green swathes beneath towering limestone pinnacles, the meadows of the Dolomites in northeast Italy support a fabulous array of orchids and alpine plants – irresistible habitat for dozens of varieties of butterfly, from pearl-bordered fritillaries to alpine blues.

❷ Adjoining the Vanoise National Park in France (see page 192), Italy's Gran Paradiso National Park covers a stunning tract of glacier-draped peaks, conifer forests and meadows.

❸ Ancient forest, home to goshawk, wild boar and elusive wolves, can be found in the Casentinesi Forest near Florence. The unspoilt Provence coastline of Marema Regional Park, meanwhile, has a diverse Mediterranean flora and fauna. Nearby Orbetello Lagoon supports various wader (including greater flamingo), while offshore Giglio Island has a colony of rare Audouin's gull.

❹ Sibillini National Park in Le Marche protects a chunk of the Apennines rich in alpine wildlife.

❺ Located in the heart of the Apennines, Abruzzo National Park has a mixture of alpine and Mediterranean species, including numerous wild flowers, butterflies and birds, and endemic races of bear and wolf.

❻ An orchid hotspot, the Gargano Peninsula has no less than 69 different varieties of these fascinating flowers.

❼ The 'Jewel of the Mediterranean', Sardinia has a rugged interior smothered in forests and herb-scented scrub, best seen at the WWF nature reserve of Monte Arcosu. Coastal wetlands in the Gulf of Cagliari have breeding avocet, bittern, flamingo and purple gallinule.

Mountain refuge – Italy's oldest national park, Gran Paradiso was established in 1922 to protect the alpine habitat of the threatened ibex.
Left: The chamois is also found in Gran Paradiso, along with mountain birds like the golden eagle and alpine chough; the park's stunning scenery attracts hikers and climbers.

Leading specialist **Ecotours** (ecotourswildlife.co.uk) runs trips to Albania, Belarus, Bulgaria, Croatia, Hungary, Poland, Romania, Slovakia, Slovenia and Ukraine. Local Romanian operators include **Absolute Carpathians** (absolute-nature.ro), **Aves Tours** (avestours.ro) and **Ibis Tours** (ibis-tours.ro).

Low-cost airlines cover many destinations in Eastern Europe. National carriers include **LOT Polish Airlines** (lot.com) and Romania's **Tarom** (tarom.ro). Bus and train travel is inexpensive and straightforward.

A wide range of accommodation options is available, from B&B guesthouses to Danube Delta riverboats.

GMT+1 (Croatia, Hungary, Poland, Slovakia), GMT+2 (Estonia, Romania).

Expect climate conditions ranging from Mediterranean to alpine.

Croatian kuna (HRK), Estonia euro (€), Hungarian forint (Ft), Polish zloty (PLN), Romanian new leu (RON).

croatia.hr, hungary.com, poland-tourism.com, romaniatourism.com, visitestonia.com.

White pelicans

Carpathian Mountains

★ Brown bear, wolf, lynx, golden eagle, woodpeckers

The Carpathians of Romania are a stronghold for the European brown bear. As many as 6,000 of these impressive mammals inhabit the mountain's forested slopes, along with perhaps half as many wolves and a much smaller population of lynx. Mountain villages like Zarnesti and Magura make ideal bases for exploring Piatra Craiului National Park where local guides can help you track all three species by identifying their prints, spoor and other signs such as territorial scratch marks. At dusk, special hides provide your best chances of seeing bears. Other wildlife in the Carpathian forests includes wild boar and red deer. Zarnesti Gorge is a good spot for chamois, wallcreeper, orchids and butterflies.

Directions Zarnesti is 30 km from the town of Brasoz and can be reached by bus, train or private vehicle.
Getting around Access to Piatra Craiului is often by traditional horse-drawn cart; hiking trails probe the national park itself.
Seasons The main wolf-tracking season begins in February; bear watching starts in May when the animals emerge from hibernation.
Visitor centre Located just outside Zarnesti.
Things to do Hiking, wolf tracking, bear watching from hides, horse riding, meet local shepherds.
Places to stay Elena Guesthouse, Zarnesti (pensiuneaelena.ro) is a 16-room, family-run pension that works closely with the Carpathian Large Carnivore Project (clcp.ro).
Further information pcrai.ro/lang-en/home

Danube Delta

★ White pelican, cormorant, marsh tern, white-tailed eagle

A wetland paradise for over 300 species of birds, the Danube Delta oozes across 2,200 sq km of rivers, lakes, reedbeds, flooded islets and riverine forest. It's a key nesting site for cormorant, pygmy cormorant, white pelican and Dalmatian pelican. Herons also breed in huge, mixed colonies, while other notable species include marsh tern, glossy ibis, white-tailed eagle and almost the entire world population of overwintering red-breasted geese.

Directions Tulcea is the main gateway to the Danube Delta.
Getting around Travel through the delta on a river cruise or base yourself in local guesthouses, taking day trips by boat; some of the larger islands can be explored on foot.
Seasons The best birdwatching is from April to late October.
Things to do River cruises, boat trips, birdwatching.
Places to stay Ibis Tours (ibis-tours.ro) operates a floating hotel sleeping 20 people for delta cruises lasting up to 10 days.
Further information romaniatourism.com

Wild places

① Smallest of the Baltic States, Estonia's wetlands, forests, coastal inlets and islands are some of Europe's top birdwatching locations – particularly during the spring migration when Matsalu Bay becomes a stopover for thousands of ducks, geese, swans, waders and cranes en route to their Arctic breeding grounds.

② A refuge for European bison, wolf and lynx, Poland's Bialowieza Forest protects the largest remaining fragment of the continent's original 'wildwood'. A mixed forest of oak, spruce, lime, hornbeam and alder, this World Heritage Site is also home to red deer, wild boar and no less than eight species of woodpecker – black, great-spotted, green, grey-headed, lesser-spotted, middle-spotted, three-toed and white-backed.

③ The steppes of Hortobágy National Park, Hungary, host 50,000 common cranes each October as they make their way south to wintering grounds in North Africa. The grasslands also support great bustard and imperial eagle.

④ Arguably Europe's finest wildlife destination, Romania's natural highlights include the Black Sea coast (a migratory flyway between Eurasia and Africa), the Danube Delta and Carpathian Mountains.

⑤ Bulgaria's Rhodope Mountains are a favourite for birdwatchers in search of eagles and vultures.

⑥ Croatia's national parks include Plitvice Lakes, Paklenica and Krka.

Wildwood – Straddling the border of Poland and Belarus, the Bialowieza Forest is a remnant of the ancient oak woodland that once covered much of lowland Europe.
Left: European bison is one of the large mammals that still survives here (others include wolf and wild boar); the forest is also home to eight species of woodpecker, including the middle-spotted.

Finnature (finnature.fi) arranges wildlife tours across Finland. **Wild Sweden** (wildsweden.com) runs moose and beaver safaris, wolf-tracking tours, as well as wildlife adventures at the Kolarbyn Ecolodge. International operators featuring Scandinavia include **Discover the World** (discover-the-world.co.uk).

Scandinavian Airlines (flysas.com) has an extensive flight network across the region. Other major airlines include **Finnair** (finnair.com) and **Icelandair** (icelandair.net). **Smyril Line** (smyril-line.com) connects Bergen with the Shetland Islands and Iceland, while **Hurtigruten** (hurtigruten.com) cruises the Norwegian coast.

Tourist office websites (below) have online booking facilities.

GMT (Iceland), GMT+1 (Norway, Sweden), GMT+2 (Finland).

Wildlife-watching activities are available all year, but be prepared for severe winter conditions and mosquitoes in summer.

Finland euro (€), Icelandic kroner (ISK), Norwegian kroner (NOK), Swedish krona (SEK).

visitfinland.com, visiticeland.com, visitnorway.com, visitsweden.com.

Great grey owl

Brown bear, Finland

Martinselkonen Nature Reserve, Finland

★ Brown bear, wolf, wolverine, moose, lynx, great grey owl

Where Russia's vast taiga forest spills across the border into northeastern Finland, it sets the scene for one of Europe's most exciting wildlife encounters. Keeping an all-night vigil from a hide in the Martinselkonen Nature Reserve, you have an excellent chance (with near-24-hour daylight during summer) of seeing brown bears up-close. Sometimes more than 30 individuals gather to feed here, including mothers with cubs and solitary males. The bears usually emerge from hibernation in late April, with July and early August often being the best months to see cubs. Wolverine and pine marten are also glimpsed occasionally, along with taiga birds such as three-toed woodpecker, Siberian jay, rustic bunting and Siberian tit. The forest also offers a great opportunity to search for owls. Up to 10 species are found here, including the great grey owl.

Directions Flights from Helsinki serve Kajaani, Kuusamo and Oulu – each offering access to the taiga wilderness of northeast Finland.
Getting around Walking trails in the forest.
Seasons May to August.
Things to do Bear watching hides, hikes, birdwatching
Places to stay A refurbished former frontier guard station, the Martinselkonen Wilderness Centre sleeps up to 26 people and is approximately 270 km from Oulu, 170 km from Kajaani and 150 km from Kuusamo. A 2-km forest trail leads to various hides around a bear-viewing area. The larger hides have room for 10 people (including sleeping areas), while the smaller ones are designed to accommodate two or three people with a particular interest in photography. Feeders around the lodge attract woodpeckers and red squirrels, while nesting boxes have been put up for pygmy, Tengmalm's and Ural owls.
Further information Finnature (finnature.fi) runs bear photography tours to Martinselkonen.

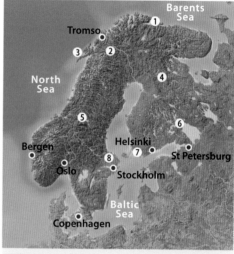

Wild places

❶ Cleft into the northern tip of Europe, Norway's Varanger Fjord, provides a sheltered refuge for large rafts of Steller's eider and other sea ducks. During summer, the island of Hornøya is alive with nesting seabirds, such as Brünnich's guillemot, puffin and kittiwake. Inland, the Arctic tundra and taiga forest is the haunt of the snowy owl.
❷ World renowned for its winter displays of the Aurora Borealis, Abisko National Park in Swedish Lapland is a brooding mountain wilderness with excellent hiking trails. Moose and reindeer are commonly seen.
❸ Sperm whales gather in summer to feed off the continental shelf near the Lofoten Islands, Norway, while the islands themselves have spectacular mountain scenery and thriving seal and seabird colonies.
❹ Taiga forest shimmering with countless lakes, the wilderness of northeast Finland is prime territory for brown bears and wolves.
❺ Breeding cranes are the star attraction at Ånns Jön Wetlands, Sweden, where an observatory (annsjon.org) provides views across lakes and bogs teeming with ducks, divers and waders.
❻ A popular hiking area, the Petkeljärvi National Park of Finland has glacial ridges (or eskers) cloaked in pine forest that is home to beaver, moose and wolf.
❼ Consisting of more than 2,000 islands, Archipelago National Park, Finland, is ideal for a canoeing expedition in search of Baltic seal, moose and white-tailed eagle.
❽ Covering a diverse range of habitats, from meadows and wetlands to evergreen forests and oak woods, Sweden's Färnebofjärden National Park is rich in birdlife.

❶ Spot ducks and divers around Lake Myvatn
A nesting site for red-throated diver (pictured) and 25,000 ducks, including Barrow's goldeneye and harlequin duck.

❷ Search for minke whales in Skjalfandi Bay
Operating from Husavik, North Sailing's oak-hulled herring trawlers are now used as whale watching boats. **whalewatchinghusavik.is**

❸ Go to hell (and back)
Travel by 4WD to Askja where the explosion crater of Viti (Icelandic for hell) is surrounded by a surreal volcanic landscape. **icetourist.is**

❹ Hike in Asbyrgi Gorge
A wooded oasis in northern Iceland, horseshoe-shaped Asbyrgi has carpets of wood cranesbill and is part of Vatnajökull National Park. **visitnortheasticeland.is**

❺ See birds in West Fjords
Rising to 440 m, Latrabjarg is the largest seabird cliff in Iceland with nesting colonies of razorbill, fulmars, guillemots and puffins. **westfjords.is**

Wild nights out | camping in the wilderness

Pitch perfect – wild camping
in Abisko National Park,
Swedish Lapland

Pitching a tent in one Europe's national parks or along a wild stretch of coast gets you to the heart of some of the continent's most wildlife-rich places. With the right kit and some basic bush skills, setting up camp in the wilderness can be liberating and hugely rewarding – but it also comes with a responsibility to leave little or no trace of your presence.

Responsible camping

✔ If possible, use an existing campsite.

✔ Before setting up camp, contact landowners for area restrictions and permit requirements. Seek advice on sensitive wildlife areas, particularly seasonal ones where, for example, ground-nesting birds may be rearing young. Always register with the appropriate authorities and advise friends or relatives of your itinerary and expected return date.

✔ Try to pitch your tent on non-vegetated areas, or at the very least, avoid particularly sensitive habitats, such as wildflower meadows and wetlands.

✔ When choosing a campsite, avoid disturbing wildlife or livestock, and avoid areas where access would cause unnecessary erosion.

✘ Do not set up camp near obvious wildlife trails, drinking or feeding areas.

✔ Avoid damaging historical, archaeological and palaeontological sites.

✘ Do not dig trenches around your tent unless flash flooding is a real threat.

✔ For cooking use a camp stove. If you need to build a fire, use only fallen timber. Allow the fire to burn down to a fine ash which can be raked out and disposed of. Aim to leave no trace of your fire. Be sure to observe any fire-use restrictions in place – particularly in dry areas such as the Mediterranean.

✔ If toilets, portable latrines or composting toilets are not available, dig latrines at least 50 m from water sources, trails and campsites. Cover the hole with natural materials and either burn or pack out your toilet paper.

✔ Wash clothing and cooking items well away from water sources and scatter grey water so that it filters through soil. If you must wash in streams, rivers or lakes, use biodegradable, phosphate-free soap.

✔ Pack out all rubbish and unused food, plus litter left by others. If camping in areas inhabited by bears, use robust sealed food containers and follow the bear-safety guidelines on page 93.

✔ Keep noise to a minimum, especially during the early morning and evening.

✔ Consider taking a bushcraft or wilderness camping course before venturing into the wilderness.

✘ Do not forage for wild food unless you are certain it is safe.

Africa

Following the mass extinction of the dinosaurs 65 million years ago, mammals were poised to steal the limelight. A remarkable process of diversification was about to take place that would ultimately lay the foundation for today's safari tick list. Curiously, however, most of Africa's familiar species – from zebras, giraffes and antelopes to lions, rhinos and wild dogs – began evolving not in Africa, but in Eurasia and North America.

Picture the scene 50 million years ago. Tropical forests smothered every scrap of land, from pole to pole. In this humid stew, African mammals were sprouting branches of evolution that would lead to elephants, primates, hyraxes and elephant shrews. Fast forward a few million years and the earth began to cool. North American and Eurasian forests thinned, giving rise to patchy plains – a new land of opportunity that began to be exploited by the ancestors of horses, camels, rhinos, buffalo, deer, cats and dogs.

Although Africa remained largely cloaked in jungle, its mammals also continued to diversify. In 2003, palaeontologists in Ethiopia discovered fossils of archaic elephants, as well as a veritable ark of other African mammals. Some were huge and, it has to be said, spectacularly ugly. Arsinoitherium, for example, stood 2 m at the shoulder, and sported a pair of massive horns protruding from either side of its snout – a kind of botched attempt at the modern-day rhino.

So why, you may ask, does Africa's treasured Big Five contain the descendant of a European import rather than Africa's homespun version? Well, scientists are still pondering the demise of Arsinoitherium, but it undoubtedly had something to do with the fact that 24 million years ago 'island Africa' collided with Eurasia (which had long been connected by a land bridge to North America). Mammals from all continents began to mix and compete for the first time and the evolutionary shakeout inevitably had winners and losers. While more primitive species became extinct, the Eurasian influx modernized Africa's fauna. Mammals cradled in Africa, such as hyraxes, elephants, aardvarks, monkeys, spring hares and golden moles held their own (and some, like the elephants, invaded new territory), while Eurasian herds began to roam Africa.

Around 13 million years ago, Africa's newly formed grasslands were witnessing an influx of antelope and buffalo. Short-necked giraffes, ancestral hippos and sabre-tooth cats spread from Eurasia, dogs arrived from North America, while Africa's primates began venturing from their ancestral forests to forage across the spreading savannahs.

This momentous 'meeting of mammals' reached its climax in the Pleistocene, about two million years ago, when Africa was home to an unrivalled range of mammal families. While the Ice Age reaped its toll of great mammals elsewhere in the world, Africa's megafauna got off lightly. Ironically, it was only with the arrival of humans – the continent's most recent mammalian progeny – that Africa's empire of mammals began to crumble.

Biodiversity hotspot | Eastern Arc Mountains

For spectacular big game, places like the Masai Mara, Serengeti and South Luangwa are hard to beat. And for abundant birdlife the Rift Valley lakes are a natural choice. But if you're after sheer biodiversity then head to the Eastern Arc Mountains and coastal forests of East Africa. Stretching from Tanzania's Udzungwa mountains to the Taita Hills in Kenya, this region supports a greater variety of species than anywhere in East Africa, including no less than 50 endemic species of reptile. Other wildlife unique to Kenya includes the Shimba Hills banana frog, the golden-rumped elephant shrew (found only in coastal forests north of Mombasa), the Malindi pipit (endemic to Kenya's coastal grasslands) and the Tana River red colobus monkey – of which only around 1,200 individuals remain in patches of gallery forest along the lower Tana River.

Golden cat – early morning sun highlights the scruff of mane on a young male lion

Madikwe, South Africa

A thrill to see on safari, but not so great to live with, lions frequently come into conflict with people living in rural parts of Africa. Rather than resorting to poison or guns to protect their herds, farmers are encouraged to use guard donkeys (more fearless than dogs and capable of packing a good kick) to keep big cats at bay, while chilli pepper bricks burnt around fields can deter crop-raiding elephants.

Africa | Wildlife highlights

Most people imagine endless plains covered with big game when they think of wildlife in Africa. But the quintessential savannah of the Serengeti and Masai Mara is just one facet of the continent's rich kaleidoscope of habitats.

Natural zones

The Sahara is perhaps the most impoverished part of Africa when it comes to species diversity – but even here you will find desert-adapted creatures like the fennec fox and dorcas gazelle.

It's a different story in the Congo Basin where a patchwork of rivers, swamps and flooded forests support more than 10,000 plant species, 1,000 species of birds and over 400 different mammals, including lowland gorilla and forest elephant. The variety of life is also astonishing in the Great Rift Valley where isolated mountains and lakes have led to a high level of endemism, particularly in areas like the Ethiopian Highlands, Ruwenzoris, Eastern Arc Mountains and Lakes Tanganyika and Nyasa (Malawi).

Spreading south from Tanzania into Zambia and Zimbabwe, vast miombo woodlands are home to huge herds of elephant and a wide range of antelopes. Africa's second great desert, the Kalahari covers much of Botswana – the Okavango Delta forming a verdant oasis on its northern fringes. Great rivers like the Zambezi, Luangwa and Orange also support teeming wildlife in southern Africa. The tip of the continent is characterised by the unique Cape Floral Kingdom where two-thirds of an estimated 9,000 plant species are found nowhere else. On Madagascar, no less than 80% of species are endemic.

Wildlife travel

Timing and logistics are crucial when planning a wildlife trip in Africa. Wet and dry seasons affect animal movements, seasonal floods can make entire areas inaccessible for months at a time, while many wildlife hotspots are remote or require special permits, and expert guides. Fortunately, there are numerous safari specialists that know exactly how to overcome these obstacles. The key to a successful trip is to talk to the experts and start planning well in advance. The standard of accommodation and guiding in Africa's wild places is second to none.

it's a wild life

Chris McIntyre | Managing Director of Expert Africa & guidebook author | expertafrica.com

↘My big five
1 Okavango Delta, Botswana
2 Etosha National Park, Namibia
3 Ngorongoro Crater, Tanzania
4 Mana Pools National Park, Zimbabwe
5 Galápagos Islands, Ecuador

" Skeleton Coast, May 1996. On the long drive north, we stopped to stretch our legs in a dry river bed. The desert sun gave little warmth through the damp, salty air. Tracks and white droppings intrigued me to follow the trail upstream. Disturbed from a reedbed, a big brown hyena bounded onto a sandy mound, fixing me with penetrating eyes from within its magnificent mane. We stared at each other in disbelief, before the hyena vanished silently into the mist. I've yet to see another of this secretive species, but I cherish the memory of finding that first sighting for myself.

guiding star

Richard Knocker

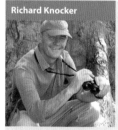

Guiding Principles Ltd (guiding-principles.com)
Country Tanzania, but guide in East and Southern Africa.
Most memorable wildlife encounter Hiding in a bush while around 1,500 buffalo walked past, metres away, completely unaware of us.

Top tip for travellers
Pack a sense of humour... this is Africa.
Favourite animal This would have to be elephant. Many animals are exquisitely beautiful – take the cheetah for instance. But you can't fail to be touched at a deeper level by elephants; they are symbolic of all that is best about humankind. Their future could be bleak; some of the worst of mankind.
What does responsible travel mean to you? Even the biggest parks depend on wild spaces beyond their boundaries for ecosystem health, and so symbiosis with the people living there is vital; we often visit community conservancies, where most of the revenue goes straight to the local people, thereby encouraging better management of the area. All our safaris have a carbon offset costed in, which supports a local reforestation project, geared to protecting biodiversity and water catchment.

Wild city | Nairobi, Kenya

If a cheetah sprinted north from Nairobi National Park, it would take barely four minutes – traffic permitting – to reach the city centre. Just 7 km from the matatu-mayhem of downtown Nairobi, this tenacious reserve is also home to lion, leopard, hyena, buffalo, giraffe, zebra, wildebeest, hippo and the world's highest concentration of black rhino. Only elephant is missing from the Big Five. You can visit the park on a guided tour or take the Kenya Wildlife Service bus from Nairobi city centre on Sundays. A taxi or matatu will get you to the main gates where the Nairobi Safari Walk weaves through wetland, forest and savannah. A rescue and rehabilitation centre for orphaned elephants and rhinos, the David Sheldrick Wildlife Trust (sheldrickwildlifetrust.org) is located in the southwest corner of the park and can be visited between 1100 and noon when nursery inmates are due their daily mudbath. At Langata Giraffe Centre (giraffecenter.org), 18 km from Nairobi city centre, you can hand-feed endangered Rothschild giraffe and get on the receiving end of a big sloppy, blue-tongued kiss. Out in the suburb of Karen, Butterfly Africa has hundreds of winged wonders fluttering inside a tropical hothouse, while Karura Forest (the largest of Nairobi's three suburban forests) is home to Syke's monkey and other secretive forest species such as bushbuck, dik dik, duiker, bush pig, genet and civet. Attractions in the 1,063-ha forest include waterfalls, bamboo forest and caves once used as Mau Mau hideouts during Kenya's struggle for Independence.

Wild places

Morocco's Atlas Mountains ❶ are ablaze with wild flowers in the spring and also provide a refuge for endangered birds, like the bald ibis. Birds are the main attraction at Banc D'Arguin in Mauritania ❷ – a wetland sanctuary for millions of migratory waders. In West Africa ❸, birdwatchers flock to Gambia and Senegal, while the pristine rainforests of Gabon ❹ offer exceptional wildlife-watching opportunities, from western lowland gorilla to humpback whale. Intrepid travellers can venture into the heart of the Congo Basin ❺ in search of lowland gorilla and forest elephant – a complete contrast to a relaxed diving holiday in the Red Sea ❻ where spectacular coral reefs are just one of many natural spectacles in Africa's Great Rift Valley. Further south in Ethiopia ❼, the escarpments and plateaux of the Simien and Bale Mountains are strongholds for the endemic Ethiopian wolf, gelada baboon and walia ibex. In Uganda and Rwanda ❽, mountain gorillas claim the high ground, while the Great Rift Valley is seen at its most majestic in the volcano-pimpled plains of the Serengeti-Mara ❾. Rift Valley lakes are renowned as hotspots of biodiversity, and none more so than Tanganyika and Nyasa (Malawi) ❿ with their endemic communities of colourful cichlid fish. Chimpanzees can be found in forests along the shores of Lake Tanganyika ⓫, while the vast wilderness reserves of Selous and Ruaha in southern Tanzania ⓬ promise some of Africa's best safari experiences, with high standards of guiding. The same is true for Zambia's Luangwa Valley ⓭ where you will be led through beautiful scenery on unforgettable walking safaris. Victoria Falls is a highlight of any visit to the Zambezi Valley ⓮, but there are national parks upstream and downstream of the falls with superb lodges and activities ranging from canoeing to night drives. Botswana's Okavango Delta ⓯ is one of Africa's most magical safari destinations – a verdant oasis on the edge of the Kalahari ⓰. Wildlife of the Namib Desert ⓱ is mainly confined to its coast, although a good guide will help you track down desert elephant, rhino and gemsbok in remote tracts of Damaraland and Kaokoland ⓲. South Africa's natural treasures cover everything from the proteas of the Cape Floral Kingdom ⓳ to Kruger's big five ⓴ and sharks along the Wild Coast ㉑. Further north, Africa's shoreline is peppered with wildlife-rich archipelagos, like the Quirimbas of Mozambique ㉒. Coral reefs fringe the East African coast ㉓, while the Seychelles (and Aldabra) ㉔ have reefs, seabirds, giant tortoises and the coco-de-mer palm. For pure island magic and lemurs galore, head to Madagascar ㉕.

Bar-tailed godwit

Limosa lapponica

Banc D'Arguin National Park, Mauritania

★ Shorebirds, orca, dolphins, monk seal, turtles, fennec fox

A mishmash of mudflats, mangroves, sand dunes and offshore islands, Banc D'Arguin hosts a staggering three million wintering shorebirds – a third of the entire population migrating back and forth along the Atlantic flyway. Over 100 species have been recorded, including vast numbers of bar-tailed godwit, black tern, broad-billed sandpiper, flamingo, knot, ringed and grey plover, redshank and spoonbill. Among the area's breeding birds are white pelican and several species of tern. Marine life is also abundant. Four species of turtle – green, hawksbill, leatherback and loggerhead – are found in the reserve's shallow seas, along with six species of dolphin (including orca, Atlantic humpbacked and Risso's) and a colony of around 150 endangered monk seals. Roaming the desert coast, meanwhile, are Dorcas gazelle, fennec fox, jackal and striped hyena.

Directions Take the coast highway 250 km north from Nouakchott.
Getting around Arrange permits from the national park service in Nouakchott, hire a 4WD vehicle with a guide, or join an organised expedition with Mauritanie Aventure (mauritanie-aventure.com).
Seasons Winter (November to February) for migrant shorebirds.
Things to do Birdwatching, desert safaris, swimming, dune walking, visits to the fishing villages of the local Imraguen people.
Places to stay Community tented camps.

Forest elephant

Loxodonta cyclotis

Loango National Park, Gabon

★ Western lowland gorilla, chimpanzee, turtles, whales

Surfing hippos, elephants strolling through the dunes, nesting sea turtles, humpback whales breaching offshore... Loango has become famous for its beach life, but the heart and soul of this stunning reserve lies in its virgin jungle, savannahs and swamps. Home to thriving populations of western lowland gorilla, forest elephant, nearly 200 other mammal species and 600 varieties of birds, Loango was described by American biologist Michael Fay as 'Africa's last Eden'.

Directions Operated by Africa's Eden (africas-eden.com), Loango Lodge can only be reached by light aircraft, but it was closed in September 2010 following a dispute with the national aviation authority. Check the website for latest information on reopening.
Seasons Leatherback turtles nest November to April, humpback whales migrate along the coast June to September, gorilla sightings at their best from April to July.
Things to do The lodge arranges boat tours, savannah safaris, forest and beach walks.
Places to stay Loango Lodge (see above) and satellite camps.

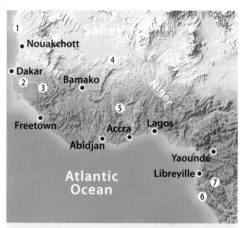

Wild places

❶ A coastal oasis teeming with wildlife on the fringes of the Sahara, Mauritania's Banc D'Arguin is one of the world's most important destinations for wintering shorebirds.
❷ Renowned for its birdwatching (see opposite), Gambia's wildlife hotspots include the Abuko Nature Reserve (a pocket of riverine forest near the coast), the Bao Bolon Wetland Reserve (floodplains and mangroves) and the River Gambia National Park – dense riverside forest and islands colonised by chimpanzees released by the Chimpanzee Rehabilitation Project (chimprehab.com).
❸ In Senegal, Langue de Barbarie promises excellent birding along the coast, while the World Heritage Site of Niokolo-Koba National Park protects gallery forest and savannah next to the River Gambia. Wildlife here includes chimpanzee, lion, leopard, eland, a large population of elephants and baboons and over 350 species of birds.
❹ A boat trip from Timbuktu along the River Niger not only provides a fascinating insight into the rural culture of Mali, but is also a good opportunity for spotting birds such as Egyptian plover, red-billed quelea and African fish eagle.
❺ Ghana's flagship reserve, Mole National Park is a good spot for walking and canoeing safaris where you will see abundant birdlife, a variety of antelope and perhaps buffalo and elephant. Lion are present, but rarely seen.
❻ Over 10% of Gabon was turned into national parks by the late President Bongo in 2002 – among them, the extraordinary Loango National Park with its mosaic of forests, savannahs, lagoons and sandy beaches.
❼ Lopé National Park is Gabon's oldest protected area and has a mixture of dense rainforest and savannah. Huge troops of mandrill, containing over 1,000 individuals, have been recorded here. You can reach the park on the trans-Gabon railway from Libreville.

Royal tern

African darter

Abyssinian roller

Northern red bishop

Egyptian plover

Red-throated bee-eater

Long-tailed nightjar

Malachite kingfisher

Feathered fancies – Gambia's bird checklist stands at around 570 species. For European travellers, the country offers an easily accessible introduction to the diverse and colourful birdlife of Africa, with short flights, little time difference, perfect climate and good value for money. Specialist operators like **The Gambia Experience** (gambia.co.uk) offer dedicated birdwatching tours visiting key areas like Abuko Nature Reserve, Tanji Bird Reserve, Brufut woods and the Makasutu river.

Making tracks | Kenya

Dozens of Nairobi-based operators offer safaris. One of the best is Gamewatchers Safaris (porini.com) which also runs camps in community-owned conservancies.

The hub of East African air transport, Nairobi is served by numerous airlines, including **Kenya Airways** (kenya-airways.com). Domestic airlines, like **Air Kenya** (airkenya.com) support connect Nairobi with the coast and popular safari destinations.

Wide range of excellent camps and lodges, as well as resorts and hotels on the coast.

GMT+3

Kenya has two rainy seasons (from March to May and November to December). Temperatures average around 20°C in the Central Highlands and Rift Valley – hotter and more humid at the coast.

Take precautions against malaria.

Kenya shilling (KSh)

magicalkenya.com

Kenya Wildlife Service (kws.org)

Up and away | Ballooning

In the Masai Mara National Reserve, hot-air balloon flights are available from Governors' Camp, Keekorok Lodge and the Sarova Mara Game Camp, as well as the Soysambu Conservancy near Nakuru National Park and the Loisaba Ranch in northern Kenya's Laikipia Plateau.

Elephants and egrets in Amboseli

Amboseli National Park

★ Elephant, spotted hyena, hippos, grey crowned crane

Amboseli's 1,500 elephants (studied by Cynthia Moss and her team since 1972) are the highlight of this iconic park. Matriarchal herds and lone 'big tusker' bulls roam its typically dry plains where dust-devils swirl against the hazy backdrop of Mt Kilimanjaro. Far outnumbering lions, spotted hyenas are the dominant hunters in Amboseli. You can observe a den on one of the safari circuits where, curiously, the hyenas share with warthogs. Climb Observation Hill for panoramic views across Amboseli Lake where closer inspection (by vehicle) reveals hippo, mud-wallowing buffalo and elephant, plus numerous waterbirds, including flamingo, spoonbill, goliath heron, black-winged stilt, ibis, blacksmith plover, jacana and yellow-billed stork.

Directions 265 km southeast of Nairobi; road access and airstrip.
Getting around Well defined circuits; no off-road driving allowed.
Seasons Dry seasons tend to concentrate game around the lake.
Things to do Game drives, birdwatching.
Places to stay Lodges in and around park, plus two campgrounds.
Further information Amboseli Trust for Elephants (elephanttrust.org)

Masai Mara National Reserve

★ Wildebeest, lion, cheetah, zebra, elephant, buffalo, topi

Time your trip right and your arrival in the Masai Mara may coincide with the Great Migration when legions of wildebeest and zebra arrive from the Serengeti in search of fresh pasture (see pages 64-65 and 218-219). Even without the migration, however, the Mara offers superb game viewing, excellent accommodation and a chance to learn about Maasai culture. Proud custodians of the Greater Mara area, which encompasses not only the national reserve but a patchwork of neighbouring conservancies, the Maasai are your best guides to this beautiful, big-sky country of rolling savannah, woodland-fringed river courses and rocky escarpments. See page 25 for profiles of two of the region's 'guiding stars'.

The Masai Mara is famous for its big cats – the BBC's *Big Cat Diary* was filmed here – and you would be unlucky not to see lion and cheetah. Leopard and spotted hyena are also common, while chance encounters with serval and caracal are not unheard of.

Out on the plains, topi stand sentinel on termite mounds, surrounded by mixed herds of Thomson's and Grant's gazelle, wildebeest, zebra, impala and eland. Warthog snuffle out roots and tubers; buffalo, elephant and giraffe browse areas of patchy woodland, and troops of baboon fan out across the savannah, picking at morsels of food and keeping a wary lookout for predators like the martial eagle.

The Mara has around 540 bird species, ranging from the plains-strutting ostrich, secretary bird and ground hornbill to smaller grassland specialists like cisticolas, francolins, larks and widowbirds. Among the 57 different raptors are six species of vulture.

Directions 270 km southwest of Nairobi; road access and airstrips.
Getting around 4WD vehicles are recommended. In the National Reserve you must keep to designated tracks; conservancies provide more freedom, but care must be taken to avoid habitat damage.
Seasons For migration timings, see page 219. Lion and cheetah cubs are often born during the April-June wet season.
Things to do Game drives, hot-air ballooning, walking safaris (in Mara conservancies), Maasai village visits.
Places to stay Wide range of operators, including Asilia (asiliaafrica.com), Basecamp Explorer (basecampexplorer.com), Fig Tree Camp (madahotels.com), Governor's Camp (governorscamp.com), Kicheche Camps (kicheche.com), Mara Bushtops (orion-hotels.net), Mara Plains Camp (greatplainsconservation.com), Ngerende Island Lodge (ngerende.com), Sanctuary Retreats (sanctuaryretreats.com), Serena (serenahotels.com) and Sopa Lodges (sopalodges.com).

Tsavo East & West National Parks

★ Elephant, gerenuk, black rhino, Kirk's dik-dik, sandgrouse

An arid wilderness the size of Wales, Tsavo supports at least 6,000 elephant. Stake out a waterhole and you will see an almost endless procession of red-dust-coated herds arriving to drink. Lion thrive in the reserve and there are also two black rhino sanctuaries. Drought-tolerant species include gerenuk and oryx.

Directions 300 km southeast of Nairobi, 200 km northwest of Mombasa. Year round access, even for 2WD vehicles.
Getting around Rough roads; off-road driving not permitted.
Seasons Stake out waterholes during dry seasons for best wildlife.
Things to do Game drives; walking at Mzima Springs.
Places to stay Several lodges and camps, including Tsavo East's Satao Camp (sataocamp.com) and Tsavo West's Severin Safari Camp (severin-kenya.com).

Ethiopia

Somalia

Uganda

Tanzania

Lake Victoria

Lake Turkana

Chalbi Desert

Great Rift Valley

Indian Ocean

Lake Turkana
Drive overland to Lake Turkana and you'll experience one of Africa's most compelling desert journeys, crossing mountain-studded plains roamed by nomadic herdsmen and braving the desolate Chalbi Desert. As well as an important hominid fossil site, Sibiloi National Park is a refuge for wildlife adapted to the region's arid conditions, such as reticulated giraffe, gerenuk and sandgrouse. Turkana's islands, meanwhile, are nesting grounds for one of Africa's largest populations of Nile crocodile.

Kakamega Forest Reserve
A remnant of equatorial jungle, Kakamega is thick with rainforest giants, some of its trees towering over 60 m high. Colobus, de Brazza, red-tailed and Sykes monkey live here, along with 350 birds species, including the stunning great blue turaco. Further north at Saiwa Swamps you can find the semi-aquatic sitatunga antelope, while Mt Elgon is famous for the salt-mining elephants of Kitum Cave.

Laikipia Plateau
One of Kenya's greatest conservation success stories, much of Laikipia is covered by community-run ranches and conservancies, combining traditional land use with the protection of wildlife (including 50% of Kenya's black and white rhino). There are over 40 tourism operations in the region, all promoted by the Laikipia Wildlife Forum. Places to stay include Ol Malo and Loisaba Lodges. **laikipia.org**

Samburu, Buffalo Springs & Shaba National Reserves
Acacia scrub studded with rust-coloured termite mounds, and rocky ridges sprouting spears of euphorbia and aloe characterise this trio of reserves. Grevy's zebra, reticulated giraffe, gerenuk, beisa oryx and Somali ostrich are indicators of their semi-arid environments, but more widespread species are also found here, such as lion, cheetah and elephant. The Ewaso Nyiro River is a favourite spot for drinking – and springing an ambush.

Marine national parks
Located off Wasini Island, Kisite Mpunguti Marine Park can be reached by dhow from Kenya's South Coast and offers some of the country's finest snorkelling and diving. In addition to coral reefs teeming with angelfish, snapper and grouper, it's not unusual to experience a breathtaking swim-past from the resident bottlenose dolphins – or a close encounter with a whale shark (December to February). On the North Coast, top snorkelling and diving spots in Malindi and Watamu Marine Parks include Stork Passage and Turtle Reef. Glass-bottom boat tours are also available.

Rift Valley Lakes
One of the world's great ornithological spectacles, saline Lake Bogoria is wreathed in pink by hundreds of thousands of lesser flamingo and smaller numbers of greater flamingo. Lake Nakuru is also pretty in pink, albeit with fewer flamingos, while the papyrus-fringed freshwater lakes of Baringo and Naivasha are all-of-a-flutter with African fish eagles, pied kingfishers, pelicans, storks, ducks, herons and cormorants. Kenya's Rift Valley Lake national parks also support abundant mammals – notably greater kudu at Bogoria, and Rothschild's giraffe and both black and white rhino at Nakuru.

Coastal forest reserves
Arabuko Sokoke is a haven for butterflies and rare species such as Fischer's turaco and golden-rumped elephant shrew. Shimba Hills has sable antelope and colobus monkey, while the neighbouring Mwalugange Elephant Sanctuary is a successful community project.

Sibiloi NP

Central Island NP

South Island NP

Maralal National Sanctuary

Mt Elgon

Kitale

Eldoret

Lake Baringo

Lake Bogoria

Nanyuki

Kisumu

Nakuru

Mt Kenya

Nyeri

Lake Nakuru

Lake Naivasha

Ruma NP

Aberdares National Park
Black rhino, bongo

Masai Mara National Reserve
see page 212

Mt Longonot

Nairobi

Nairobi National Park
see page 209

Amboseli National Park
see page 212

Lake Magadi

Mt Kilimanjaro

Tsavo East & West National Parks see page 212

Malindi

Malindi & Watamu Marine National Parks

Arabuko Sokoke Forest Reserve

Shimba Hills National Reserve

Mombasa

Kisite Marine National Park

Elephants of Tsavo

A tent at Satao Camp (sataocamp.com) in Tsavo East National Park offers a front-row seat on one of Kenya's – if not Africa's – best wildlife experiences. Each spacious tented suite, with its verandah, is barely 100 m from a waterhole that acts as a magnet to Tsavo's legendary elephants.

They come and go from all directions, following well-trodden game trails that radiate from the precious water source like spokes on a wheel. Sit in a canvas chair and you'll not have long to wait before a matriarch arrives, leading her herd at a brisk pace, youngsters jogging along to keep up with the adults. Smaller bachelor groups of bulls arrive stage left; zebra, waterbuck, hartebeest and impala enter stage right, baboons mingle in the foreground, while flocks of sandgrouse and doves cascade from above.

The scene is set for a fascinating performance of pachyderm behaviour: fifty or more elephants dipping and coiling their trunks as they satiate their thirst; bulls tossing black mud over their backs or blasting ochre-coloured dust between their legs; youngsters skittering about amongst the forest of elephantine legs; sub-adult males sparring with each other; females socialising with trunks entwined.

What makes the spectacle all the more captivating is how it constantly changes. Half a dozen bulls might stake out the waterhole for much of the day, but the family groups come and go – even by night you'll see their ghostly shapes illuminated by the waterhole's floodlights. Come morning and you may well find yourself forgoing a game drive in favour of a few hours sitting quietly in the presence of these magnificent animals.

" **"** Bachelor groups of bulls arrive
stage left; zebra, waterbuck,
hartebeest and impala enter stage right,
baboons mingle in the foreground, while flocks
of sandgrouse and doves cascade from above.
William Gray

TATO (tatotz.org) represents numerous leading tour operators. **Expert Africa** (expertafrica.com) has firsthand knowledge of camps and lodges across Tanzania.

British Airways (ba.com) flies direct to Dar es Salaam. **Kenya Airways** (kenya-airways.com) has flights to Kilimanjaro International Airport, via Nairobi. Internal flight operators include **Coastal Aviation** (coastal.cc) and the **Tanganyika Flying Co** (tanflyco.com).

Lodges and camps are run by **&Beyond** (andbeyondafrica.com) **Asilia** (asiliaafrica.com), **Serengeti Bushtops** (orion-hotels.net), **Mbalageti** (mbalageti.com), **Sanctuary Retreats** (sanctuaryretreats.com), **Serena** (serenahotels.com), **Serengeti Safari Camp** (serengeti-safari-camp.com) and **Singita** (singita.com) and **Sopa Lodges** (sopalodges.com).

GMT+3

The north is good all year, although the best time for climbing Kilimanjaro is March to September. The coast can be wet and stormy March to May, while southern parks can be inaccessible during April-June rains.

Yellow fever vaccination certificate required. Anti-malarials recommended.

Tanzania Shilling (TSh).

tanzaniatourist board.com

Tanzania National Parks (tanzaniaparks.com).

Mahale Mountains National Park

★ Chimpanzee, blue monkey, red colobus, red-tailed monkey

Tracking chimps in lush forest along the far-flung eastern shore of Lake Tanganyika is the highlight of a visit to this beautiful park. Members of the habituated Mimikire group are relaxed near human visitors, often enabling you to view them from close quarters.

Directions Light aircraft flights from Arusha or Dar-Selous-Ruaha.
Getting around Be prepared to walk for anything from 30 minutes to three hours to locate the chimps.
Seasons Forest paths are driest August to October.
Things to do Chimp tracking, kayaking, dhow trips, fishing, hiking.
Places to stay Greystoke Mahale (greystoke-mahale.com) is set on a sandy, lakeside beach and is renowned for its knowledgeable guides and expert trackers.

Eland, Ngorongoro Crater

Ngorongoro Conservation Area

★ Black rhino, lion, elephant, buffalo, leopard, spotted hyena

A spectacular natural arena for one of Africa's greatest concentrations of wildlife, Ngorongoro Crater is a vast caldera, up to 19 km wide and surrounded by 600-m-high walls. In addition to large herds of zebra, buffalo and antelope, the crater has over 30 black rhino and a thriving population of elephant – including some impressive tuskers. At least 500 hyena prowl the crater's grasslands, competing with the 60-odd lion for the position of top hunter. A few cheetah manage to hold out amongst these bolder predators, while leopard are sometimes seen in the forest of yellow-bark fever trees. Bat-eared fox and golden jackal are regularly spotted, while hippo are a regular feature of the swamp area. Flamingos and other waders can be found around Lake Magadi, but the plains are also teeming with birds, including kori bustard and crowned crane and rosy-throated longclaw. The only thing potentially spoiling this microcosm of Africa is the number of safari vehicles and the tendency for drivers to gravitate towards big cats and rhinos. However, for guaranteed sightings, magnificent scenery and a good chance of witnessing predator action, Ngorongoro is hard to beat.

Directions 165 km west of Arusha.
Getting around Game drives; 4WD vehicles are essential for negotiating the tracks in and out of the crater.
Seasons Year round; June to September can get very busy.
Things to do Game drives; access to crater restricted from 0630-1800.
Places to stay No accommodation in crater itself, but five lodges on the crater rim, including the luxurious Ngorongoro Crater Lodge (andbeyond.com) with its exotic suites, fine dining and butler service.

Selous Game Reserve

★ African wild dog, lion, elephant, buffalo, hippo, crocodile

Lying at the heart of Tanzania's less-trodden southern safari circuit, Selous covers 45,000 sq km of plains, forests and hills – plenty of space for you to immerse yourself in the solitude of a true African wilderness. The handful of camps in the Selous are found mainly along the Rufiji River – the reserve's wildlife artery, pulsing with birds, hippo and crocodiles. Boat trips are a highlight of any visit, as are walking safaris.

Directions Nearest entrance around 250 km from Dar es Salaam.
Getting around 4WD vehicles.
Seasons Some lodges close April to June.
Things to do Game drives, boat trips, walking safaris.
Places to stay Beho Beho (behobeho.com), Lake Manze Camp (lakemanze.com), Rufiji River Camp (rufijirivercamp.com), Sand Rivers (sand-rivers-selous.com), Selous Impala Camp (selousimpala.com) and Selous Safari Camp (selous.com). Some properties can arrange fly-camping, staying in simple, temporary bushcamps.

Serengeti National Park

★ Wildebeest, zebra, Thomson's gazelle, lion, cheetah

Grand stage for the wildebeest migration (see pages 64-65 and 218-219), the Serengeti is utterly transfixing – a 15,000-sq-km expanse of savannah and acacia woodland, populated with large herds of game and abundant predators. Although timing is crucial to witness the migration, some areas have good year-round wildlife – particularly Seronera and the Western Corridor. Neighbouring reserves, like Grumeti and Loliondo, offer exclusive accommodation and the bonus of walking safaris, horse riding and night drives – activities that are not permitted in the national park.

Directions Around 300 km northwest of Arusha.
Getting around 4WD vehicles.
Seasons Year round. See page 217 for migration timings.
Things to do Game drives, hot-air ballooning, walking safaris.
Places to stay Wide range (see box, left, and pages 64 and 219).

Mt Kilimanjaro National Park

Six well-maintained trails lead to Ulhuru Peak (5,896 m), passing through distinct vegetation zones. Look for colobus monkeys and turacos in the foothill forests, and scarlet-tufted malachite sunbirds feeding on the flowers of giant lobelia in the heather moorland.

Gombe Stream National Park

Jane Goodall's chimpanzee research site, Gombe Stream National Park can be reached by river from Kigoma. A tented camp and basic resthouse arrange hikes to see the habituated Kasekela chimps. A more affordable alternative to Mahale.

Serengeti National Park
see page 216

Ngorongoro Crater
see page 216

Lake Manyara National Park

Famous – but by no means unique – for its tree-climbing lions, this beautiful and diverse park protects a narrow strip of land between Lake Manyara and the western escarpment of the Great Rift Valley. From flamingo-flushed lakeshore to floodplains grazed by buffalo and elephant, it's the perfect introduction to Tanzania's northern safari circuit.

Mahale Mountains National Park
see page 216

Tarangire National Park

June to October is the most rewarding time to visit Tarangire – the dry season lures wildlife back to the national park's river channels and swamps. In good years, you can see large herds of elephant, buffalo, wildebeest and zebra. Lion are also relatively common. Explore the park's less-visited southern reaches, weaving through its photogenic acacia and baobab woodland.

Eastern Arc Mountains
see page 207

Saadani NP
see page 241

Katavi National Park

Very remote and little-visited, Katavi takes four or five hours to reach by light aircraft from Arusha. A few permanent camps dot its 4,500-sq-km expanse of savannah and acacia woodland. Wildlife viewing is at its best between June and November when the dry season forces large numbers of zebra, giraffe, buffalo, elephant and antelope to gather near the Katuma and Kapapa Rivers.

Selous Game Reserve
see page 216

Mafia Island Marine Park

Protecting the coral reefs at the southern end of Mafia Island, as well as the rich mangrove habitat in the Rufiji Delta, this marine park offers excellent diving and snorkelling. Some of the best sites include Chole Bay, Ukuta and Tutia Reefs. The best season to visit is from August to March before heavy rain starts.

Ruaha National Park

Easily combined with the Selous on a fly-in safari, Ruaha and its neighbouring game reserves form Tanzania's largest national park, covering over 50,000 sq km. A mixture of rolling savannah and woodland, it has a scattering of rustic camps along the Great Ruaha River – the lifeline of the park.
tanzaniasafaris.info

Lake Victoria · Musoma · Mwanza · Lake Natron · Lake Eyasi · Ol Doinyo Lengai · Mt Meru · Arusha · Mt Kilimanjaro · Moshi · Kenya · Usambara Mtns · Eastern Arc Mtns · Great Rift Valley · Tanga · Pemba Island · Pangani · Zanzibar Island · Zanzibar Town · Dodoma · Morogoro · Dar es Salaam · Indian Ocean · Mikumi NP · Rufiji · Udzungwa Mtns · Mafia Island · Lake Tanganyika · Lake Rukwa · Mbeya · Poroto Mtns · Zambia · Lake Nyasa · Ruvhma · Mozambique · Kigoma · DRC

Africa | Tracking the Great Migration

The ultimate game plan for witnessing the Great Migration

The stage is set: 40,000 sq km of tawny savannah, flushed green in places by recent rains and scattered here and there with acacia woodland and jumbled rocky outcrops. A few rivers claw their way across the plains, while distant hills and volcanoes pimple an otherwise unblemished horizon, stretched taut beneath towering African skies.

Enter the leading cast: 1.5 million wildebeest, 500,000 Thomson's gazelle, and 200,000 plains zebra. Waiting in the wings, lion, cheetah, hyena and crocodile prepare for their killer cameos. The supporting cast completes the scene: everything from the hippo to the dung beetle has a role to play in this wildlife extravaganza. Just don't expect a big curtain raiser.

The Great Migration is more fringe theatre than West End blockbuster. It has no fanfare opening or edge-of-seat finale. Instead, you can drop in, any time you choose, to witness a small but utterly transfixing part of this perpetual performance. The big question is where to go and when. To answer that, you need to know the script, the game plan for the Great Migration – but be warned, wildebeest are notoriously bad at learning their parts, while the vagaries of seasonal rains can also play havoc with your carefully planned safari.

Essentially, the Great Migration is an endless search for food. The grazers move to where the grass is freshest – and that depends on where the rains have fallen. It's the weather that controls the herds, spinning them in a giant clockwise rotation through the Serengeti-Mara ecosystem. Red tape is trampled under some eight million hooves as the ungulate legions cross back and forth between Tanzania and Kenya. Nor do they respect the boundaries of the two flagship reserves in the area (the Serengeti National Park and Masai Mara National Reserve), instead spilling out into neighbouring conservancies to mingle with Maasai cattle.

Don't run away with the idea that this is some kind of irrepressible stampede, a wave of wildebeest flooding the savannah in a single amorphous mass of clattering hooves and tossing heads. When the herds are on the move they break up, threading single-file for miles across the plains, and where grazing is good, they speckle the land for as far as the eye can see.

That's not to say, however, that the pilgrimage isn't punctuated by drama. Far from it. When the herds reach the legendary crossing points of the Grumeti and Mara rivers, they bottleneck in nervous, skittish hordes, well aware of lurking crocodiles and strong currents. The urge to migrate, however, is overpowering and it only takes a single bold zebra (or gung-ho gnu) to wade in before the rest follow, churning the river to a boiling stew of flailing legs, straining necks, leaping white water and reptilian lunges. A feast for predator and photographer alike.

Wherever (and whenever) you witness the Great Migration, however, it is the sheer wonder that such a wide-ranging natural spectacle still exists in our crowded world that ultimately leaves the most lasting impression. Spend a few hours in the midst of a 100,000-strong herd of wildebeest and zebra, striped flanks and bearded faces ebbing around you in ceaseless currents, and you'll almost feel part of the show.

Common wildebeest

Connochaetes taurinus
Masai Mara National Reserve, Kenya

A single wildebeest is thought to walk at least 30,000 km in its lifetime. Within three minutes of being born, a newborn wildebeest is able to stand and walk.

Migration map

January
🐃 The migration settles in the short-grass plains of the southern Serengeti, near Lake Ndutu. The short rains usually fall here in November and December, (sometimes as early as October), luring herds from the central Serengeti in search of fresh pasture. Nourished by phosphorous-rich volcanic soils, the grasslands offer nutritious grazing. Wildebeest, zebra and gazelle begin calving at the end of the month.
🏠 Seasonal camps, including Olakira Camp, Serengeti Safari Camp and Serengeti Under Canvas, pitch up near Lake Ndutu, while permanent accommodation includes Ndutu Safari Lodge.

February
🐃 Calving continues, with up to 500,000 wildebeest born on the southern plains during a two- to three-week window. Far from being static, the wildebeest move around the plains.
🏠 You should be in easy driving distance of the herds from Ndutu and Kusini. Due to its central position in the Serengeti, Seronera can be used as a base for viewing the migration from about November to June.

March
🐃 Several weeks of grazing have taken their toll on the southern plains. There are rumblings of thunderstorms to the north and west; soon the herds will be following their noses in search of rain and fresh grass.
🏠 The Ndutu region is still the best base.

April
🐃 The migration moves towards the Western Corridor of the Serengeti National Park as the long or heavy rains set in. It's a slow plod through patchy woodland and long-grass plains, the herds streaming past Moru Kopjes and the Mbalageti River.
🏠 Tucked into the Moru Kopjes, Dunia Camp has a lion's eye view of the plains, while the Serengeti Serena Safari Lodge has an equally panoramic outlook.

May
🐃 As the long rains dwindle, columns of wildebeest continue to enter the Western Corridor of the Serengeti. There is a sense of expectation as the migration piles into the narrow wedge of land between the forest-lined river courses of the Mbalageti and Grumeti.
🏠 Properties in the Seronera region are still a good bet, while Mbalageti Camp is well placed near the entrance to the Western Corridor. As the month progresses, everyone wants to be based near the Grumeti River.

June
🐃 By June the rains have stopped and the wildebeest rut is well underway. The grasslands reverberate to the bellows and grunts of testosterone-fuelled males as they chase rivals and round up females. The migration begins to coalesce into a 'mega herd', bunched up along the southern bank of the Grumeti River. Crossings can start early in the month, herds

splashing through what is usually a series of pools and channels rather than a continuous, flowing river. As the frequency of crossings intensifies during June, Grumeti's large crocodiles enjoy their annual glut of wildebeest and zebra flesh.
🏠 Prime spots for Grumeti River crossings, Grumeti Serengeti Tented Camp and Kirawira Camp are located in the Serengeti National Park, while Faru Faru River Lodge, Sabora Tented Camp and Sasakwe Lodge are three stylish Singita properties in a 138,000-ha private concession to the north of the river.

July
🐃 With the Grumeti River in their wake, the herds push northwards, the sweet scent of the Mara grasslands in their nostrils. They spread out on a broad front that extends from the Grumeti Game Reserve and Ikorongo Game Controlled Area to northern reaches of the Serengeti National Park. The migration can enter the Mara as early as mid June; in other years wildebeest can linger in the northern Serengeti well into August and September. You can stake out likely Mara River crossing points in both the Serengeti and Masai Mara throughout July and August.
🏠 The northern Serengeti, between the Mara River and Kenyan border, the Lamai Wedge is easily accessed by Sayari Camp and Lamai Serengeti. Serengeti Bushtops is also located near the Mara River, while seasonal camps include Lemala Mara, Olakira and Serengeti Under Canvas.

August
🐃 The northward thrust continues. In a typical year, you can expect the migration to reach the Masai Mara by early August. River crossings often reach their frenzied climax this month as large herds take a leap of faith into the Mara River, sometimes doubling back on themselves a few days later – much to the delight of waiting crocs and lions.
🏠 Kenya's finest wildlife sanctuary has plenty of superb camps and lodges, both in the national reserve itself and in neighbouring conservancies. If you're here specifically to witness the migration, Serena Lodge, Mara Intrepids, Rekero Camp and the Governor's Camps are located in the western half of the Masai Mara National Reserve, within easy reach of river crossing points. All camps and lodges in the wider Mara can organize day trips into the national reserve.

September
🐃 The focus of the migration is firmly in Kenya where the wildebeest edge slowly eastwards through the Masai Mara. They'll wander wherever there is fresh grass, so you can also expect to encounter large herds in the conservancies surrounding the reserve.
🏠 Choice picks for (top end) places to stay include Kichwa Tembo and Bateleur Camps, Basecamp Masai Mara, Fig Tree Camp, the Governor's Camps, Kicheche Mara and Bush Camps, Mara Plains Camp, Mara Bushtops, Mara Porini and Porini Lion Camps, Naibosho Camp, Ngerende

Island Lodge, Rekero Camp and Sanctuary Olonana. For budget options, you can camp near the Oloolaimutiek and Talek gates.

October
🐃 The herds begin to move with renewed purpose. Any week now, rains start falling on the short-grass plains of the southern Serengeti and the wildebeest need to be there when fresh green shoots have pushed to the surface. And so begins the long trek south.
🏠 Perched below the Kuka Hills in the Loliondo Game Controlled Area, &Beyond's Klein's Camp often has a grandstand view of the migration, while Nomad's Serengeti Safari Camp and Nduara Loliondo Camp are also well placed at this time of year. Further south, Lobo Wildlife Lodge and Migration Camp both make good bases.

November
🐃 The herds pick up the pace as the short rains lure them southwards. They form long columns stretching from Lobo to the Serengeti's central Seronera area.
🏠 Lobo Wildlife Lodge can still be a good option, but as the month progresses look more to the south. Serena's Mbuzi Mawe Tented Camp and Bilila Lodge Kempinski are near the migration corridor.

December
🐃 The herds reach the southern Serengeti, completing the cycle.
🏠 Lodges and camps in the Seronera and Ndutu areas once more become the focus of migration viewing.

Mother's pride – a lioness greets her eight-week-old cub that has been left hidden in a marshy area of dense reeds near the Ndutu Plains of the southern Serengeti.
Left: Crowned cranes take flight, while plains zebra make the daily pilgrimage to a waterhole in the Ngorongoro Crater.
Top: Unfurling its wings in a flash of electric blue, a lilac-breasted roller uses a prominent perch to hawk for insects.

Uganda

Africa in miniature, Uganda packs the best of the continent into a small, beautiful and easily accessible destination. In the far north (and bordering the potentially volatile Sudan) lies semi-arid **Kidepo Valley National Park** where stony scrub and savannah host 80 species of mammal, including elephant, lion, zebra and cheetah. In lush contrast, the forested **Ssese Islands** of Lake Victoria in Uganda's south are the haunt of black-and-white colobus monkeys and a wide range of birds. The Victoria Nile snakes northwest from the lake, erupting in a plume of white water at **Murchison Falls National Park** where boat trips sidle up to large numbers of hippo and crocodile, and perhaps an elusive shoebill standing motionless in the papyrus beds. You may also see elephant, buffalo, Rothschild's giraffe, Uganda kob, defassa waterbuck and lion. **Queen Elizabeth National Park** provides another opportunity for game-viewing afloat. Drifting slowly along Kazinga Channel, you will also spot some of the park's 612 species of birds – an impressive tally that reflects the area's rich mixture of swamp, savannah and rainforest. To the north, **Kibale Forest National Park** protects a swathe of rainforest that's home to 13 primate species, including a large population of chimpanzees. Guided chimp-tracking tours are available here, as well as the nearby **Semliki Forest** (see page 82). Most primate-watching trips in Uganda, however, focus on the mountain gorillas of **Bwindi Impenetrable National Park** where you can hike trails through exuberant rainforest for an unforgettable encounter with the great apes.

Rwanda

Like Uganda (above), most visitors to Rwanda have primates in their sights. **Volcanoes National Park** (see page 80) is the place to go for mountain gorilla tracking, while **Nyungwe National Park** is a veritable primate paradise with everything from chimpanzees and Angolan colobus to blue monkey, grey-cheeked mangabey, l'Hoest's monkey and greater galago. Exploring forest trails, you may also glimpse giant forest hog, various squirrels and some of the park's 275 bird species, such as the African crowned eagle, black-and-white-casqued hornbill and Rwenzori turaco. Rwanda also gets a slice of the more classic East African safari experience in its **Akagera National Park**, a mosaic of grassland, swamps and lakes along the Tanzanian border. Wetland-loving antelope such as waterbuck, reedbuck and sitatunga are found here, along with buffalo, topi, zebra and lion.

Ethiopia

With stomach-swooping escarpments, broad river valleys and mountain plateaux rising to over 4,000 m, the **Simien Mountains** have some of Africa's most dramatic scenery. Allow anything from three to 10 days for a trek taking in Geech Abyss and 4,543-m Ras Dashen, keeping an eye out for the area's indigenous wildlife. Large groups of 500 or more gelada baboon – formed by several harems joining together – graze grassy meadows, retreating at dusk to sheer cliff faces which offer better protection against predators. Walia ibex also inhabit precipices and knife-edge ridges beyond the reach of the highly endangered, coyote-sized Ethiopian wolf. Among the 180 species of birds in the Simien Mountains, two of the most conspicuous are the lammergeier and thick-billed raven. **Awash National Park** has acacia-dotted grasslands inhabited by more typical East African plains species, while **Lake Abiata** – one of a string of Rift Valley lakes in Ethiopia – has shores thick with cormorants, flamingos, herons and storks.

Holding on – mountain gorillas can be seen in Uganda's Bwindi Impenetrable National Park and Rwanda's Volcanoes National Park

See pages 72-85 for the ins and outs of primate watching.

Africa | Zambia

Making tracks | Zambia

🧭 **The Zambian Safari Company** (zambiansafari.com) organises trips throughout Zambia and southern Africa. Other leading operators include **Robin Pope Safaris** (robinpopesafaris.net), **Voyagers** (voyagerszambia.com) and the **Zambezi Safari & Travel Co** (zambezi.co.uk). **Expert Africa** (expertafrica.com) and **Wildlife Worldwide** (wildlifeworldwide.com) also have highly specialist knowledge of the country.

✈ **British Airways** (ba.com) flies direct between London and Lusaka; **South African Airways** (flysaa.com) connects Lusaka with Johannesburg, while **Kenya Airways** (kenya-airways.com) has flights from Nairobi. You can also reach Zambia by long-distance bus from South Africa (intercape.co.za) or by train from Tanzania (tazara.co.tz).

🛏 Wide choice of places to stay, from budget campsites to luxury safari lodges and tented camps.

🕐 GMT+2

☀ Cool and dry (May to August), hot and dry (September to November) and hot and wet (December to April). Access can be difficult during the latter 'green season', although lodges that remain open offer birdwatching and river safaris.

➕ Malaria is widespread.

💲 Zambian kwacha (Kw).

ℹ zambiatourism.com.

🛡 **Wildlife Authority** (zawa.org.zm), **WECSZ** (conservationzambia.org).

Kafue National Park

★ Antelopes, zebra, lion, cheetah, hippo, Pel's fishing owl

From the 'mini Serengeti' of Busanga Plains in the north to dense miombo woodland further south, Kafue National Park covers 22,400 sq km – an area similar in size to Wales or New Hampshire. The wide range of habitats in this huge reserve is reflected by its extraordinary diversity of antelopes. No less than 16 species are found here, including blue wildebeest, bushbuck, defassa waterbuck, grysbok, impala, kudu, Lichtenstein's hartebeest, oribi, puku, reedbuck, roan, sable, red lechwe and sitatunga. You can spot the largest member of the family – the eland – and one of its smallest – the common duiker. Predators, such as lion and cheetah, are also commonly seen, particularly near open areas like the Busanga and Nanzhila Plains. The Kafue River and Lake Itezhi Tezhi are good places to look for hippo and the rare Pel's fishing owl – one of around 450 bird species found in the national park.

Directions Travel overland from Lusaka or Livingstone, or fly to one of the park's lodges or camps using small, light aircraft.
Getting around A 4WD vehicle is essential.
Seasons Year round, except in the Busanga Plains region where seasonal flooding means camps are only open June to November.
Things to do Game drives, walking safaris, fishing.
Places to stay Wide range, including Busanga Bush Camp (wilderness-safaris.com), Kaingu Safari Lodge (kaingu-lodge.com), Lufupa River Camp (wilderness-safaris.com), Mikambi Safari Lodge (mukambi.com) and Puku Pan Safari Lodge (pukupan.com).

Kasanka National Park

★ Sitatunga, straw-coloured fruit bat, wetland birds

With its water-repellent fur, splayed hooves and ability to dive underwater when threatened, the sitatunga is a truly amphibious antelope – and there is no better place in Africa to see one than Kasanka, particularly if you spend time in the park's Fibwe Hide. Perched 18 m off the ground in a mahogany tree, the hide also offers spellbinding views of the mass exodus of a million straw-coloured fruit bats as they leave their roost in the swamp forest on nightly feeding forays.

Directions Kasanka NP has an airstrip for light aircraft charter flights, or you can drive from Lusaka via Kapiri Moshi and Serenje.
Getting around Drive yourself or join a guided safari.
Seasons Birdwatching best from November to March, game-viewing May to October, fruit bats November to December.
Things to do Game drives, walking safaris, fishing, canoeing.
Places to stay Lodges and campsites (see page 241).
Further information kasanka.com

Chimfunshi Wildlife Orphanage

A rescue centre for wild chimpanzees orphaned by hunting and deforestation, Chimfunshi rehabilitates these threatened primates to various social groups in large forested enclosures. Another area has been repopulated with once-indigenous antelope. African Impact coordinates a volunteer programme at Chimfunshi. africanimpact.com

Liuwa Plain National Park

The setting for one of Africa's last undisturbed wildebeest migrations (usually arriving late October), the 3,660-sq-km grasslands of Liuwa Plain National Park are also home to wild dog and lion. However, the area is remote and difficult to access. Safaris are occasionally organised by experienced operators like Robin Pope Safaris, or you can organise your own 4WD expedition, staying in the national park's community-run campsites. robinpopesafaris.net

Nchi
Wildl
Reser

Angola

Liuwa
Plain

Zambez

• Mongu

Ngonye
Falls

Sioma Ngwezi
National Park

Sumbu National Park
Located on the shores of Lake Tanganyika, Sumbu National Park is a popular angling spot. Lodges also arrange game drives and boat trips to view the park's wildlife which includes elephant, reedbuck and the shy sitatunga antelope. Birds are particularly abundant along the lake shore – look out for African fish eagle, African skimmer, grey-headed gull and whiskered tern.

Bangweulu Wetlands
Seasonal floodwaters ebb and flow across the plains east of Lake Bangweulu, creating one of the world's most important wetlands. Around 30,000 endemic black lechwe – sometimes in herds a thousand strong – can be found here, along with a kaleidoscope of waterbirds, ranging from the shoebill (a steely-blue, storklike bird with an enormous bill used for catching lungfish) to large flocks of waders, ducks, geese, wattled crane, white and pink-backed pelican and spoonbill. Drier areas are stalked by ground hornbill, Denham's bustard and crowned crane, while Montagu's harriers quarter overhead. The only practical place to stay is Shoebill Island Camp which arranges canoe trips (best May to August for seeing shoebills) and supports local community and anti-poaching initiatives in the area. **kasanka.com**

Lochinvar National Park
With splayed hooves and powerful hindlegs designed for leaping through waterlogged grasslands, over 30,000 Kafue lechwe inhabit the floodplains of Lochinvar's Kafue Flats. This internationally renowned wetland is also teeming with wading birds, ducks, geese and raptors. Top ticks include pygmy goose, wattled crane, pelican and flamingo.

Upper Zambezi
Elephant, giraffe and waterbuck often come down to the water's edge to drink. Bee-eaters excavate nesting colonies in the sandy riverbanks, while herons, kingfishers, hamerkops and African fish eagles are frequently sighted. Hippos and crocodiles are common too. See also page 225.

North Luangwa National Park
Almost pure wilderness, North Luangwa National Park covers an area of 4,636 sq km between the Luangwa River and Muchinga Escarpment. Poaching took its toll here during the early 1980s – something that was vividly portrayed in the book *Survivor's Song* written by American scientists Mark and Delia Owens. Today, the park is thriving. A black rhino reintroduction scheme was successfully initiated in 2003, while large herds of buffalo roam North Luangwa's plains and forests. Lion, elephant and leopard can also be seen, as well as Cookson's wildebeest, eland and reedbuck. There are no permanent lodges in the park. Only a few safari operators are granted concessions to operate bush camps for walking safaris and game drives. **remoteafrica.com, shiwasafaris.com**

Mosi-oa-Tunya National Park
Covering just 67 sq km, Mosi-oa-Tunya National Park takes in the eastern section of Victoria Falls, some spectacular gorge scenery further downstream and a riverside game area that is home to reintroduced white rhino and a variety of other species.

Kasanka National Park
see page 222

South Luangwa National Park
see page 224

Lower Zambezi National Park
see page 224

Kafue National Park
see page 222

Chimfunshi Wildlife Orphanage
see box, top left

Chaminuka Nature Reserve

Blue Lagoon National Park
Lechwe, wetland birds

Busanga Plains

DRC

Mbala

Tanzania

Nyika Plateau

Lake Bangweulu

Malawi

Lavushi Manda National Park

Kitwe

Ndola

Kafue

Luangwa

Chipata

Kabwe

Mozambique

Lusaka

Lake Nyasa

Lake Kariba

Zimbabwe

Livingstone

Namibia

Victoria Falls

Lower Zambezi National Park

★ Elephant, buffalo, African fish eagle, kingfishers

The Zambezi flows past floodplains and silty islands in the Lower Zambezi National Park. Fig, ebony and sausage tree jostle for space on the riverbanks, merging with stands of winterthorn acacia and miombo woodland as the valley floor rises to meet the northern escarpment. Elephant and buffalo are abundant. You can sometimes see large herds wading in the river, or even crossing over to Mana Pools National Park in Zimbabwe. The bird life is also stunning. The plaintive, almost gull-like, cry of the African fish eagle is quintessential Lower Zambezi. You can often see the majestic raptors perched on dead trees near the water's edge. Also look out for white-fronted bee-eater, giant, malachite and pied kingfishers, various egrets and storks, plus the exotic narina trogon and Meyer's parrot – preferably from the seat of a Canadian canoe being paddled gently along a backwater of the Zambezi River.

Directions Most visitors book all-inclusive safaris which include transfers to the park, accommodation and activities. Lower Zambezi is a 40-minute flight from Lusaka. It is also possible to drive, but you will need well-equipped 4WD vehicles.
Getting around Once you are in the park, 4WD vehicle and canoe are the two main forms of transport.
Seasons Most accommodation is open April to November, although temperatures soar in late October. The 'green season' (December to April) is particularly good for birdwatching.
Things to do Game drives, walking safaris, fishing, canoeing.
Places to stay Upmarket properties include Chiawa Camp (chiawa.com), Chongwe River Camp (chongwe.com), Kanyemba Lodge (kanyemba.com), Redcliff Zambezi Lodge (redcliff-lodge.com), Royal Zambezi Lodge (royalzambezilodge.com) and Sausage Tree Camp (sausagetreecamp.com), while mid-range options are limited to Mvuu Lodge (mvuulodge.com). Most lodges offer canoeing trips lasting a few hours, but Safari Par Excellence (victoriafalls.net) organises overnight canoe safaris lasting three or four days.

South Luangwa National Park

★ Thornicroft's giraffe, leopard, carmine bee-eater

Ranking alongside Africa's great wildlife wonders, like the Serengeti, Okavango and Etosha, South Luangwa National Park covers 9,050 sq km of woodland, grassland and wetland – a veritable Eden, teeming with over 60 species of mammals and well over 500 species of birds. The endemic Thornicroft's giraffe (distinguished from the more widespread southern giraffe by its darker body patches) and Cookson's   >>

it's a wild life

Chris Breen | Founder of Wildlife Worldwide | wildlifeworldwide.com

↘ **My big five**
1 **Luangwa Valley, Zambia**
2 **Great Bear Rainforest, British Columbia**
3 **Northern Territory, Australia**
4 **Pantanal, Brazil**
5 **Kanha National Park, India**

66 99 I was desperate to see black lechwe. In fact, I had flown to Zambia specifically to visit the Bangweulu Wetlands to see the endemic black lechwe at the very best time of year – the end of March. This is when the grassy floodplains are a foot-deep in water and conditions are perfect for these most beautiful of water-loving antelope. Morning broke and it was a sight to behold – as far we could see in every direction were black lechwe, tens of thousands of them. And, overhead, pallid harriers, Montagu's harriers, ducks, geese and no less than 83 wattled cranes.

> 66 99 **Canoeing on the Zambezi provides the perfect opportunity for paddling silently past riverside wildlife (from egrets to elephants). Just remember that surprised hippos can be dangerous – regularly tapping the side of your canoe usually makes them surface and allows you to steer clear.**

William Gray

❶ Canoe down the river
Paddle past hippos and elephants in Zimbabwe's Mana Pools NP or Zambia's Lower Zambezi NP, camping overnight on the riverbank.
zambezi.com

❷ Spot big game
You will often see elephants and other wildlife drinking at the river's edge during a boat trip on Lake Kariba or on the Upper Zambezi. The birdlife is also spectacular.

❸ Watch white rhino
Zambia's Mosi oa Tunya NP has a small breeding herd of reintroduced white rhino. Calves were born in early 2011, a positive sign in the face of increasing poaching.

❹ Walk in the mist
Sustained by spray from Victoria Falls, a rainforest of ebony, palm and fig is home to shy bushbuck. Look for swifts, black eagles and taita falcons in the gorge.

❺ Head upriver
Islands and riverbanks upstream of Victoria Falls have several superb camps and lodges – great bases for birdwatching and boat trips.
tongabezi.com

❶

❷

❸

❹

❺

wildebeest are found here. South Luangwa also supports around 15,000 elephant and one of the Africa's densest leopard popuations. Lion and hyena are also abundant, while antelopes (14 species in total) range from bushbuck and waterbuck to sable and roan. Pods of hippo clog lagoons and river channels, particularly during the hot, dry season in September and October when enormous flocks of red-billed quelea stream across the valley, gathering to drink around dwindling pools. Carmine bee-eaters arrive to nest around this time – technicoloured heralds of the imminent rains when many camps and lodges are forced to close. A few remain open, however, making the most of the verdant 'green season' to operate boat trips or even microlight safaris. It's the walking safari, though, that has become synonymous with a visit to South Luangwa National Park. Pioneered in South Luangwa by the visionary Norman Carr, who worked with local chiefs in the mid-1900s to extend reserve boundaries and ensure that nearby villagers received income from South Luangwa's first camps and lodges, walking safaris are now available at several locations. Some lodges offer short morning or afternoon strolls, while others operate multi-day trails, linking rustic bush camps. Always accompanied by a guide and armed scout, these footloose forays into the bush fine-tune your senses to every crackle of leaf, whiff of dung or slightest movement. There is no better way to wise up on bushlore or learn about the traditional uses of plants.

....

Directions Most safari packages include flights to Mfuwe, the park's main transport hub which also lies on three overland routes – from Chipata, Mpika and Petauke.
Getting around You will be driven around the park in 4WD vehicles
Seasons Many camps and lodges are seasonal, opening only after floodwaters have subsided in April/May. Walking safaris and game drives are available during the main season from June to October. Temperatures can reach 45°C by November when wildlife concentrates around shrinking lagoons. River safaris are available during the flood period of February to April.
Things to do Walking safaris, game drives, boat trips, canoeing, microlight safaris, cultural visits to villages and community projects.
Places to stay The following – generally top-end – operators run lodges with satellite bushcamps, linked by overnight walking trails: Bushcamp Company (bushcampcompany.com), Kafunta Safaris (luangwa.com), Norman Carr Safaris (normancarrsafaris. com), Remote Africa Safaris (remoteafrica.com), Robin Pope Safaris (robinpopesafaris.net) and Shenton Safaris (kaingo.com). Excellent budget options include Flatdogs Camp (flatdogscamp.com) and Wildlife Camp (wildlifecamp-zambia.com).

Walk on the wild side – tracking wildlife on foot in South Luangwa is guaranteed to get the adrenaline flowing

Norman Carr Safaris (see page 241) pioneered walking safaris in South Luangwa National Park. Getting this close on foot to large mammals – let alone a lion – is a rare privilege. Most bush walks focus on small wonders, like birds, insects, tracks and droppings.

Wild places | Zimbabwe, Malawi & Mozambique

❶ Zimbabwe's bastion of conservation, Hwange National Park covers over 14,600 sq km of wooded savannah and teak forest. A stronghold for African wild dog, the park also has thriving populations of elephant, brown hyena, sable antelope and gemsbok.
❷ Gonarezhou National Park in southeastern Zimbabwe will form part of the proposed 100,000-sq-km Great Limpopo Transfrontier Park with Mozambique's Limpopo National Park ❸ and South Africa's Kruger National Park.
❹ Zimbabwe's Mana Pools National Park lies along the south bank of the Zambezi and is a beautiful, wildlife-rich area for canoeing and walking safaris.
❺ On the southern shore of Lake Kariba in Zimbabwe, Matusadona National Park is a sanctuary for black rhino and also has good numbers of lion.
❻ Malawi's premier wildlife destination, Liwonde National Park has plenty of hippo and crocodile in the stately, palm-fringed Shire River, while surrounding bush is roamed by elephant, buffalo, black rhino and sable.
❼ Lake Nyasa (or Malawi) is renowned for its colourful and endemic cichlid fish, best seen on a snorkelling trip at Cape Maclear or Lake Malawi National Park.
❽ A rolling grassland plateau cleft by wooded gorges, Nyika National Park protects a spectacular chunk of the Rift Valley in northern Malawi. Explore on foot or horseback, mingling with zebra and eland.
❾ With work underway to restore Gorongosa National Park in Mozambique to its former glory, large numbers of zebra, buffalo and wildebeest have been reintroduced.
❿ Mozambique's Bazaruto Archipelago and the more remote Quirimbas ⓫ offer spectacular diving on coral reefs, as well as turtle-nesting beaches, mangroves and dugongs. Various lodges provide barefoot luxury.

Making a beeline for Luangwa – when the carmine bee-eaters return to the Luangwa Valley each September to begin nesting, they form colourful, noisy colonies along the riverbanks.
Left: Hippos are abundant in South Luangwa National Park, emerging at dusk to graze on land. A newly-born puku fawn does its best to remain hidden in a patch of grassland near the Luangwa River – prime hunting territory for leopards.

Okavango

Caprivi Strip

Namibia

Shakawe

Tsodilo Hills

Okavango Delta
see page 229

Selinda Spillway

Linyanti Marshes
see box, below left

Kasane

Savute

Savuti Channel

Moremi Game Reserve

Maun

Toteng

Nxai Pan National Park

Makgadikgadi Pans

Chobe National Park

Classic big-game country, Chobe supports between 30,000 and 50,000 elephant, along with enormous herds of buffalo. Popular with visitors, the Chobe River is often packed with pachyderms, particularly during the dry season (April to November). Lions have learnt to hunt elephant here, although buffalo still make up the bulk of their kills. Flooded in 2010 for the first time in over 25 years, Savute Marsh is another prime wildlife area in Chobe. During the green season (December to April) wildlife migrates south to the Kalahari's open plains before returning to Chobe's permanent water in the dry winter months. Easily accessible from Livingstone and Kasanae, Chobe has a variety of upmarket camps and several campsites, and offers game drives and boat trips.

Kwando River & Linyanti Marshes

A trio of reserves – Kwando, Linyanti and Selinda – cluster around the Kwando-Linyanti river system, supporting abundant wildlife, including several packs of African wild dog. Like the private reserves in the Okavango, walking safaris and night drives are allowed here, enabling you to get on intimate terms with the area's riparian forest, mopane woodland and patches of grassland. The Selinda Spillway – which flowed in 2009 for the first time in decades – is an ancient watercourse linking the Okavango and Linyanti Marshes, and can be explored on an exciting four-day canoe trip (May to October) with Wilderness Safaris. Also in Selinda Reserve, Motswiri Camp offers mokoro trips and horse riding in addition to the usual safari activities.
wilderness-safaris.com

Makgadikgadi & Nxai Pans

Vestiges of an ancient 'superlake', these vast saltpans are rejuvenated by seasonal rains. Shallow pools attract up to 30,000 breeding flamingo, while flushes of grass lure nomadic zebra and wildebeest. Complete with tea tent, the 1940s-style Jack's Camp makes a superb base for exploring the Makgadikgadi Pans. Bushmen guides track down desert-adapted wildlife and show you Stone Age tools littering the surface of the pans, while five-night quad-bike safaris to Kubu Island rank as one of the most exhilarating adventures in Africa. Nxai Pan also has a camp which makes a good base for visiting the famous Baines' Baobabs. unchartedafrica.com

Francistown

Zimbabwe

Khama Rhino Sanctuary

Serowe

Tuli Block

Mahalapye

Limpopo

Kalahari Desert

Central Kalahari Game Reserve

Created to protect the hunter-gatherer lifestyle of the indigenous Khwe Bushmen, the CKGR covers over 50,000 sq km and is remote and largely inaccessible. Summer rains (January to May) nourish grasslands in inter-dune valleys, attracting huge herds of springbok and gemsbok and a surprising number of other species, such as wildebeest, cheetah and the famous black-maned Kalahari lions. Accommodation in and around the northern fringes of the reserve include Tau Pan Camp, Kalahari Plains Camp and Deception Valley Lodge.

Molepolole

Gaborone

Kgalagadi Transfrontier Park

Tshabong

South Africa

Making tracks | Botswana

Operators include **&Beyond** (andbeyond.com), **Sanctuary Retreats** (sanctuaryretreats.com) and **Wilderness Safaris** (wilderness-safaris.com).

The easiest way to reach Botswana is to fly to Maun or Livingstone via Johannesburg.

Safari camps and lodges tend to be remote, exclusive and expensive.

GMT+2

Dry season (May to November) best for game viewing, except in the Central Kalahari (see left).

Botswana pula (BWP).

botswanatourism.co.bw

Exploring the Okavango by mokoro

Okavango Delta

★ Red lechwe, African wild dog, elephant, African fish eagle

Reaching like a green-fingered hand into the Kalahari, the Okavango is a water-wilderness of floodplains, reedbeds, papyrus swamps and wooded islands – a unique inland delta laced with a vein-like network of channels. Expanding and shrinking with the seasonal ebb and flow of floodwaters from Angola (see pages 68-71), the Okavango is one of Africa's most enigmatic wildlife destinations. From tiny frogs perched on reed stems to herds of lechwe splashing through the shallows, the delta supports a plethora of species. You'll find abundant birdlife, the big five (rhino were reintroduced in 2001) and one of the continent's largest surviving populations of African wild dog.

Moremi Game Reserve protects the core of the delta. A wonderfully diverse area, it has a little bit of everything that the delta can offer, from permanent lagoons to a dry peninsula covered in mopane trees. Over 400 species of birds have been recorded here, including the secretive Pel's fishing owl. Moremi is also excellent for sightings of wild dog, lion, elephant and buffalo. Two of the reserve's most rewarding areas are the floodplain of the Khwai River and the Xakanaxa Lagoon, where the dry Mopane Tongue meets a beautiful mosaic of pools and channels.

The Okavango also has a patchwork of private reserves – exclusive concessions that promise just as good wildlife as Moremi, but with the added bonus of walking safaris, night drives and – if you stay at Abu Camp – elephant safaris where you can either walk with the herd or ride on top in special saddles.

Although accommodation in the delta tends to be expensive, many private reserves are part-owned by local communities. By staying in Vumbura or Duba Plains Reserves, for example, a large part of your fee goes towards wages for local staff, supplies from the communities and the development of projects like medical clinics and schools.

Directions Moremi Game Reserve is around 95 km north of Maun. Many camps in the delta are reached by light aircraft flights.
Getting around 4WD vehicles essential.
Seasons Dry season (May to November) is best for game viewing.
Things to do Mokoro (dugout canoe) rides, game drives, walking safaris, elephant back safaris.
Places to stay Numerous camps and lodges. Key operators include Wilderness Safaris (wilderness-safaris.com), see also page 238.

Jumbo offering – in the Kalahari, dung means dinner for insects in search of moisture, nutrients and salts. Here, butterflies swarm over fresh elephant droppings, while a dung beetle prepares a tasty ball that it will roll away to eat at leisure.
Left: Keeping a cool head – gemsbok, or oryx, have special networks of blood vessels and nasal passages that cool the animal's blood before it reaches the brain.

Africa | Namibia

Kunene

Angola

Kaokoland

Etosha National Park
Namibia's flagship reserve protects a vast saltpan surrounded by plains and woodland. Wildlife watching here is fabulous. Simply park your car next to a waterhole (most people drive themselves around the park), sit quietly and you'll observe a procession of animals arriving to drink. Etosha has large numbers of wildebeest, zebra, springbok and gemsbok, along with elephant, giraffe, black and white rhino, lion, leopard and cheetah. There are four inexpensive restcamps in the park, each with basic rooms, a campsite, shop, swimming pool and floodlit waterhole. **nwr.com.na**

Caprivi Strip

Mudumu
National
Park

Damaraland
A spectacular arid wilderness of gravel plains and granite monoliths, Damaraland is the realm of black rhino and the elusive desert-adapted elephant. Camps like Etendeka have expert guides who will take you on wildlife-tracking walks and drives.

Etosha
Pan

Bwabwata
National
Park

Mamili
National
Park

Mundulea
Nature Reserve
see box, below right

Grootfontein

Caprivi Strip
Riverside lodges offer boat trips, fishing and game drives in Namibia's lush panhandle. Hippo, buffalo, elephant and lion are regularly seen, while the birdlife is outstanding.

Okonjima
Home of the AfriCat Foundation, Okonjima is dedicated to protecting Namibia's cheetah, leopard, lion and caracal, and has a lodge and bushcamp. **okonjima.com**

Twyfelfontein

Otjiwarongo

Brandberg

Waterberg
Plateau

Mundulea Nature Reserve
A private 120-sq-km reserve in the Otavi Mountains, Mundulea promises an intimate insight into wildlife and bushlore with owner Bruno Nebe – one of the most knowledgeable and enthusiastic guides in the business. Using the reserve's comfortable bushcamp as a base, you'll set out on foot to explore a ruggedly beautiful area of wooded gorges, caves and bushveldt. Eland, wildebeest, kudu and oryx are frequently seen, along with predators like leopard, cheetah, hyena, honey badgers, jackal, serval and caracal. **mundulea.com**

Cape
Cross
Fur seals

Swakopmund

Walvis Bay

Windhoek

**Atlantic
Ocean**

Namib
Desert

Sesriem

Mariental

Botswana

Kalahari
Desert

Sossusvlei

Namib-Rand
Nature Reserve

Skeleton Coast See also page opposite.
You can drive from Swakopmund north to the fur seal colony at Cape Cross (see page opposite), but for a unique perspective of the Skeleton Coast nothing compares with a fly-in safari, skimming along this surf-fringed desert shore in an eight-seater Cessna, dropping in on a succession of wilderness camps in Damaraland and Kaokoland. The Schoeman family have been running these trips for over 30 years and know the area intimately. Highlights include the flamingos of Walvis Bay, the silver-grass plains of Hartmann's Valley and the Kunene River – a vibrant ribbon of sparkling rapids, calm pools and dense stands of river acacias full of birdlife. **skeletoncoastsafaris.com**

Keetmanshoop

Namib-Naukluft National Park
The world's driest and most ancient desert, the Namib was spawned by the relentless waves of the Skeleton Coast some fifty million years ago. If enough rain falls on the mountains to the east, the Tsauchab River springs to life and rages towards the desert, a flash flood tearing through Sesriem Canyon before surging along the Corridor. But the rejuvenated river never reaches the coast. At Sossusvlei it is choked by a range of immense sand dunes. On the rare occasions (roughly once every 10 years) when the *vlei*, or clay pan, is full it forms a natural oasis teeming with flamingos, dragonflies, frogs and other wildlife.

Fish
River
Canyon

Making tracks | Namibia

Turnstone Tours (turnstone-tours.com) organises camping safaris to Sossusvlei and Damaraland. **Expert Africa** (expertafrica.com) also knows the country well.

Flights to Windhoek are available via Frankfurt and Johannesburg.

Namibia is an excellent self-drive destination, with a good range of B&Bs, guest farms, restcamps and campsites.

GMT+1

Visit year round.

Namibian dollar (N$).

namibiatourism.com.na

South Africa

> **Drift silently above the heat-shattered mountains and apricot-coloured sand dunes in the Sossusvlei area of the Namib Desert, lifting off from Sesriem or the Namib Rand Nature Reserve. Some of the world's tallest sand dunes, reaching heights of 380 m, can be found here, while keen-eyed balloonists may spot mountain zebra, oryx, springbok and ostrich.**
>
> **William Gray**

❶ Drift above the desert
Namib Sky offers hot-air balloon flights over the Sossusvlei area, including a celebratory champagne breakfast upon landing.
namibsky.com

❷ Read the sands
A good guide will bring Sossusvlei to life, revealing the antics of tok-tokkie beetles, shovel-nosed lizards and horned adders by deciphering their tracks.

❸ Skeleton Coast
Explore this forbidding shore on a fly-in safari, spying shipwrecks, whale bones and seal colonies from the air.
skeletoncoastsafaris.com

❹ NamibRand Reserve
This huge private nature reserve of dunes, sandy plains and mountains borders the Namib-Naukluft and has excellent camps.
namibrand.com

❺ Seals and birds galore
Join a 4WD tour from Swakopmund to see pelicans and waders at Walvis Bay or the seal colony at Cape Cross.
turnstone-tours.com

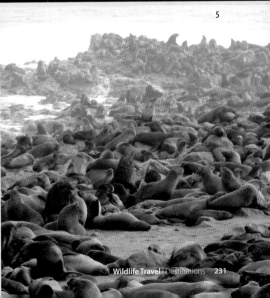

Based in South Africa, **Cedarberg African Travel** (cedarberg-travel.com) is one of the country's leading specialists. Also try **Rainbow Tours** (rainbowtours.co.uk), **Safari Consultants** (safari-consultants.co.uk) and **Bushbaby Travel** (bushbaby.travel).

Several airlines serve South Africa, including **South African Airways** (flysaa.com), **British Airways** (ba.com) and **Virgin Atlantic** (virgin-atlantic.com). **Intercape** (intercape.co.za) connects South Africa by bus to Namibia, Botswana, Malawi, Zimbabwe and Zambia.

South Africa has a wide range of accommodation, from B&B guesthouses to luxury safari lodges. Online directories inclue sa-venues.com. For Fair Trade accredited properties, visit fairtourism.org.za

GMT+2

Visit year round. Winters are mild and dry, summers are hot (especially in the lowveld) with afternoon thunderstorms. Southern right whales can be observed close offshore from July to November, while flowers are at their best during spring (August to September).

Malaria is found only in the lowveld of Mpumalanga and Limpopo and on the Maputaland coast of KwaZulu-Natal.

South African rand (R).

southafrica.net

South African National Parks (sanparks.org).

Leopard, Sabi Sands

Kruger National Park

⭐ Lion, elephant, rhino, leopard, buffalo

For the ultimate South African safari head east to Kruger National Park, a vast reserve stretching 350 km along the border with Mozambique. How you visit depends largely on budget. There are several luxury, all-inclusive camps in game reserves along Kruger's western boundary, but for free-spirited travellers a better (and cheaper) option is to drive into the park, exploring its tarred road circuits and staying at self-catering restcamps. Many, like Olifants, offer excellent facilities such as restaurant, swimming pool and guided game-viewing excursions. Work your way south through Kruger, ticking off some of its 147 mammal species (including the big five) and 500-plus varieties of birds, before continuing through Swaziland and on towards the Greater St Lucia Wetland Park.

Kruger's private game reserves include Sabi Sabi, Londolozi, Singita and Ulusaba – names synonymous in the safari business with exclusive accommodation, outstanding service, fine cuisine and outstanding game-viewing with top-quality guides.

Directions Located in the south of Kruger, approximately 460 km east of Pretoria on sealed roads, Skukuza is the biggest restcamp with the most facilities in the national park.
Getting around Most people drive themselves on the park's 800 km of mostly sealed game-viewing roads. Guided drives and bush walks are also available at most camps.
Seasons Wildlife concentrates around water sources May to October. Birdwatching is best during summer when migrants arrive, while the wildebeest rut takes place March to May.
Things to do Game drives, bush walks.
Places to stay Skukuza Rest Camp (krugerpark.co.za) has a choice of safari tents, cottages and campsites for all budgets, plus facilities ranging from restaurants and swimming pools to an internet café. It is one of a dozen or so standard self-catering restcamps dotted throughout the park. Private camps include Bateleur Bushveld Camp and Plains Camp. The Sabi Sand Private Game Reserve is home to the spectacular properties of Singita (singita.com) and Sabi Sabi (sabisabi.com). See page 242 for Sabi Sabi's Earth Lodge.

Namaqualand

One of the world's greatest floral spectacles, the mass flowering of Namaqualand transforms a vast swathe of semi-arid desert in the Western and Northern Cape Provinces into a petal-patchwork each August and September. The region's showcase reserve, Namaqua National Park has 3,500 plant species – a third of which are found nowhere else. Bulbs, daisies, succulents and grasses carpet the plains, attracting butterflies and nectar-sipping sunbirds. The world's smallest tortoise, the Namaqua speckled padloper, can be found here, along with meerkat, porcupine, klipspringer, aardwolf and the endangered Hartman's Zebra. Goegap Nature Reserve is particularly good for succulents (including quiver trees) and birds like black eagle. The extent of the Namaqualand flowering depends on winter rainfall, but you can see a guaranteed display at the Clanwilliam Wildflower Show. West Coast National Park is also frequently carpeted in spring daisies. **namaqualand.com**

Namibia

Atlantic Ocean

Richtersveld National Park

Goegap Nature Reserve

Namaqualand

Lamberts Bay

Up to 25,000 Cape gannets nest on Bird Island, easily reached by a breakwater. In West Coast National Park, meanwhile, Langebaan Lagoon attracts migrant waders in September.

Great white sharks

Operating from Gansbaai, boat trips visit the fur seal colony at Dyer Island and Geyser Rock where the Shark Alley is patrolled by great white sharks (particularly active hunting during the November seal pupping season). Cage diving with the sharks is also available. **dyer-island-cruises.co.za**

Cederberg Wilderness Area

West Coast National Park

Paarl

Cape Town

Herman

Cape fynbos

Grootbos Nature Reserve is a showcase for the diverse Cape Floral Kingdom, home to 9,250 species of fynbos plants, including proteas, ericas and gladiolus. **grootbos.com**

Kgalagadi Transfrontier Park
Straddling the border between South Africa's Northern Cape Province and Botswana, Kgalagadi Transfrontier Park is a 'thirstland' of dunes and dessicated riverbeds where adventurous tourists can set out from a spattering of restcamps in search of black-maned Kalahari lions. Even more forbidding, Richtersveld Transfrontier National Park links up with Namibia's Fish River Canyon and is only accessible by 4WD vehicle.

Kruger National Park
see page 232

Greater St Lucia Wetland Park
This World Heritage Site ranges from reedbed to coral reef, encompassing several coastal wetlands and a marine reserve. Birdlife is prolific and you can also find buffalo, hippo, black rhino and various antelopes, such as nyala and reedbuck. To the north, in the adjoining Maputaland Marine Reserve, Sodwana Bay is an important rookery for leatherback and loggerhead turtles (October to March), and also attracts migratory humpback whales and whale sharks. The reef diving is superb.

Limpopo

Polokwane

Pilanesberg National Park

Blyde River Canyon Nature Reserve

Botswana

Pretoria

Madikwe Game Reserve
see page 234

Johannesburg

Swaziland

Kalahari Desert

Vereeniging

Klerksdorp

Tswalu Private Desert Reserve

Giant's Castle
The Lammergeyer Hide (open May to September) puts you in an excellent position to watch the mighty bearded vulture, as well as Cape vulture, black eagle, jackal buzzard and lanner falcon.

Hluhluwe-Umfolozi Game Reserve
White rhino, elephant, buffalo

Upington

Kimberley

Augrabies Falls National Park
Klipspringer, springbok rock dassie

Bloemfontein

Richards Bay

Drakensberg

Lesotho

Pietermaritzburg

Thabana Ntlenyana

Durban

Karoo National Park
A remnant of the large herds that once roamed the highveldt of the Great Karoo, springbok, zebra, hartebeest and black wildebeest can still be seen in this national park. The Nuweveld Mountains are a good spot to search for klipspringer and black eagle.

Orange

Wild Coast marine life
Whipping the KwaZulu Natal coast into a foaming frenzy, the sardine run takes place between May and July when vast shoals of baitfish migrate towards South Africa straight onto the menu of whales, sharks, dolphins, seals and seabirds. Boat trips give experienced divers (and brave snorkellers) the opportunity to witness bronze whaler sharks and both common and bottlenose dolphins corralling the sardines into tight bait-balls, bombarded from above by Cape gannets. For more adrenaline-charged marine encounters, Protea Banks near Durban are bristling with copper, dusky, ragged-tooth, thresher, tiger and Zambezi sharks. With strong currents and depths ranging from 30-40 m this is a site for experienced divers only. Nearby Aliwal Shoal hosts congregations of up to 150 ragged-tooth sharks between June and November. sardinerun.net

Indian Ocean

Great Karoo

Samara Private Game Reserve

Kwandwe Private Game Reserve

Shamwari Private Game Reserve

East London

Little Karoo

Oudtshoorn

Grahamstown

George

Knysna

Addo Elephant National Park

Port Elizabeth

De Hoop Nature Reserve
Cape mountain zebra

Tsitsikamma National Park

Private game reserves of the Eastern Cape
The perfect way to round off a trip touring the Winelands and Garden Route, the private game reserves of the Eastern Cape are not only malaria-free (ideal for families with young children), but also boast the big five, excellent accommodation and outstanding opportunities for walking safaris.

Whale watching
Southern right whales migrate close inshore along the Cape coast between July and November, providing one of the world's best land-based cetacean spotting spectacles.

Madikwe Game Reserve

★ Cheetah, wild dog, brown hyena, black rhino, lion

Tucked into a remote corner of South Africa's North West province, the 75,000-ha Madikwe Game was only established in 1991. Prior to that, farmland had a tenacious, yet unproductive, grip on this Kalahari borderland. Not only were cattle degrading the land, but they were doing little to improve livelihoods in an economically depressed region.

When extensive land-use studies suggested that Madikwe would be far more prolific as a wildlife estate, the green light was given to an extraordinary transformation process. A 150-km-long fence was erected around the reserve's perimeter, while its habitats were carefully restored to a blend of Kalahari thornveld and mixed bushveld – a merging of biomes that brought geographically distinct species like impala and springbok side-by-side.

It was the restocking of Madikwe, however, that dominated the headlines. A kind of modern-day Genesis, over 8,000 animals from 25 large mammal species were released into the reserve during Operation Phoenix – the world's largest ever reintroduction programme. The herbivores came first, with 1,175 impala, 770 blue wildebeest and 547 zebra being added in 1992 alone. Hundreds more arrived the following year, along with an ever-growing infantry of buffalo, eland, elephant, gemsbok, giraffe, hartebeest, kudu, waterbuck and both white and black rhino. Then, from 1994 onwards, small numbers of predators were added to the mix, including lion, spotted hyena and African wild dog. With leopard already present on the reserve, Madikwe's big five status was sealed and the tourists started arriving.

Directions Lodges in Madikwe can arrange private air charters to the reserve. Otherwise allow around four hours to drive to Madikwe from Johannesburg. A good option for breaking the journey is to spend a few nights at Pilanesburg National Park.
Getting around Lodges organise game drives and activities.
Seasons Best time to visit is May-September when wildlife congregates near waterholes.
Things to do Game drives.
Places to stay Properties include Jaci's Lodges (madikwe.com, see also page 242), Madikwe Safari Lodge (andbeyond.com) and Thakadu River Camp (thakadurivercamp.com) – a partnership ecotourism project between the reserve and Molatedi Community.
Further information madikwe-game-reserve.co.za, madikwecollection.co.za.

Goegap Nature Reserve

South Africa for free spirits | Two self-drive Cape escapes

East from Cape Town

As soon as you arrive in Cape Town, take a peek at Table Mountain. If it's clear don't waste time in taking the Cableway to the summit. Back at sea level visit the Waterfront's mesmerizing Two Oceans Aquarium. Allow at least one day for exploring the Cape Peninsula. Not to be missed are Chapman's Peak Drive, Kirstenbosch Botanical Gardens, Cape Point and Boulders' penguin colony. The N2 highway whisks you eastwards onto the Garden Route (breaking the journey in the Winelands and at Hermanus for some whalewatching). Stretching from Still Bay to Storms River Mouth, the myriad highlights of the Garden Route include birdwatching at Wilderness, hiking in coastal forests at Tsistsikamma and dolphin spotting in Plettenberg Bay. Round off your trip by driving on beyond Port Elizabeth where Addo Elephant National Park and various private game reserves provide malaria-free, big five game-viewing.

North from Cape Town

It's worth dawdling a few days in West Coast National Park for birdwatching and game viewing on the Postberg peninsula. With its rock art, wildflowers and hiking trails, the Cederberg Wilderness Area is another worthwhile diversion. Continuing north to Namaqualand (ablaze with orange daisies in late August/September), the Goegap Nature Reserve near Springbok is a good place to see weird and wonderful quiver trees and other succulents that have adapted to the region's arid conditions. Travelling west you reach Augrabies Falls National Park where the Orange River froths like cappuccino through a dramatic gorge. You can kayak, mountain bike and track rhino here, using the well-equipped campground and self-catering chalets as a base. From Augrabies, continue west along the verdant corridor of the Orange River to Upington. Those with time and a 4WD vehicle should detour north to take in the remote Kgalagadi Transfrontier Park with its Kalahari lions, gemsbok and desert species.

Cape kaleidoscope – the variety of habitats and wildlife in South Africa's Cape provinces is staggering. Rich seas support large nesting colonies of Cape gannets, including the one shown above at Lambert's Bay. A stroll along the strandline in Tsitsikamma National Park (far left, middle) reveals more marine riches, including mermaid's purses and abalone. Winter rains trigger the mass flowering of daisies in Namaqualand and West Coast National Park (far left, top), while pincushion proteas (far left) are just one of thousands of plant species in the Cape Floral Kingdom. Mammals, meanwhile, range from rhinos to rock hyraxes (left).

Africa | Madagascar

Making tracks | Madagascar

➋ Local operators include **Mada Tours** (madagascar-tour.com) and **Wild Madagascar** (wildmadagascar.com). Numerous overseas operators feature Madagascar. **Rainbow Tours** (rainbowtours.co.uk), **Reef & Rainforest Tours** (reefandrainforest.co.uk) and **Wildlife Worldwide** (wildlifeworldwide.com) can tailormake trips.

✈ **Air France** (airfrance.com) and **Air Madagascar** (airmadagascar.com) have flights to Madagascar from Paris and Marseilles, while **South African Airways** (flysaa.com) flies via Johannesburg. Buses run to most destinations, although distances are huge and road conditions often poor. Internal flights are widely available.

🛏 The various camps and lodges near Madagascar's national parks tend to be simple but comfortable. Some, like Mandrare River Camp in the Ifotaka Community Forest, offer African safari-style camping with beautifully furnished tents, fine dining, excellent local guides and village visits.

🕐 GMT+3

☀ April to November is the driest period, with May, October and November generally the best months for wildlife viewing.

💊 Take precautions against malaria.

💲 Malagasy ariary (Ar).

ⓘ madagascar-tourisme.com

🛈 **Madagascar National Parks** (parcs-madagascar.com).

Masoala National Park & Nosy Mangabe

★ Red-ruffed lemur, helmet vanga, aye-aye, leaf-tailed gecko

Madagascar's largest remaining tract of lowland rainforest can be found on the Masoala peninsula – the only place to see red-ruffed lemur. Covered in epiphytes and orchids, the forest's tree ferns are a good place to look for the helmet vanga with its large blue bill. Nearby Nosy Mangabe island is the best place in Madagascar to spotlight a nocturnal aye-aye.

Seasons Humpback whales can be seen offshore July to August.
Things to do Forest walks, kayaking, snorkelling.
Places to stay The safari-style, beachside Masoala Forest Lodge (masoalaforestlodge.com) has five large tents with palm-thatched roofs, ensuite bathrooms and private decks.

Andasibe-Mantadia National Park

★ Indri, diademed sifaka, black-and-white ruffed lemur

Located near the village of Andasibe and easily accessible, this hilly expanse of rainforest is home to several species of lemur. You are almost guaranteed close views of indri, while the forest trails also provide great opportunities for spotting chameleons, leaf-tailed geckos and giraffe-necked weevils.

Places to stay Vakona Forest Lodge (hotelvakona.com).

Ranomafana National Park

★ Milne-Edward's sifaka, greater and golden bamboo lemurs

A beautiful rainforest reserve with streams and waterfalls, Ranomafana is renowned for its bamboo lemurs. Birdlife is also rewarding, with 36 of the park's 100 or so species endemic to Madagascar.

Places to stay Setam Lodge (setam-madagascar.com).

Berenty Private Reserve

★ Ring-tailed lemur, Verreaux's sifaka, mouse lemurs

An island of natural vegetation in a sea of sisal plantations, Berenty is the place to go for troops of ring-tailed lemur and 'dancing' Verreaux's sifaka. On early morning walks, you will often be accompanied by these charismatic lemurs, while nocturnal forays may reveal mouse and sportive lemurs.

Seasons Visit September to October to see baby lemurs.
Things to do Easy walking trails through gallery forest.
Places to stay Berenty Lodge has comfortable bungalows, a café and restaurant. It supports several conservation projects in the area.

Ifotaka Forest
This community forest is sustainably managed by the Tandroy people. Some areas are harvested for forest products, while others are set aside for ecotourism.

Wild places

1. Montagne d'Ambre National Park – mountain forest.
2. Ankarana Special Reserve – limestone plateau.
3. Marojejy National Park – realm of the rare silky sifaka.
4. Masoala National Park – forest peninsula rich in wildlife.
5. Nosy Mangabe Special Reserve – island of the aye-aye.
6. Andasibe-Mantadia National Park – best place for indri.
7. Tsingy de Bemaraha National Park – limestone pinnacles.
8. Kirindy Forest – dry forest, good place for seeing fosa.
9. Ranomafana National Park – lush, rainforested hills.
10. Andringitra National Park – mountain forest, good treks.
11. Isalo National Park – Sandstone canyons and rare plants.
12. Zombitse National Park – forest full of endemic species.
13. Ifaty Spiny Forest – octopus trees and baobabs.
14. Berenty Private Reserve – famed for its dancing sifakas.
15. Andohahela National Park – spiny forest.

Made in Madagascar – a staggering 80% of Malagasy wildlife occurs nowhere else. From top left: Verreaux's sifaka, Berenty Private Reserve; the lemur-hunting fosa – Madagascar's apex predator; a cryptic leaf-tailed gecko (resting head-down on a tree trunk); the bizarre giraffe-necked weevil; Grandidier's baobabs lining the island's iconic Avenue du Baobab; one of the 150 or so species of chameleon found on Madagascar; greater bamboo lemur, Ranomafana National Park.

Wild nights out | African camps & lodges

Looking for a community-run camp or a chic ecolodge? How about a treehouse or a lakeside camp? Do you want to watch elephants from your private verandah, camp out in the wilderness or play the pampered explorer in 1920s-style luxury? Africa has a breathtaking range of places to stay on safari. Essentially, though, it all boils down to the magic of spending a night in the bush – that multi-sensory experience supercharged by a starlit sky, a crackling fire and the strange, wild orchestra of the night shift.

It doesn't matter whether you muck in on a budget camping safari or splash out on five-star indulgence at a top lodge, the basic feelings of remoteness, atmosphere and intimacy are trademarks of wild nights out in Africa that every discerning traveller can enjoy – regardless of how much they spend.

My first taste of an African safari was a shoestring 10-day jaunt to Kenya's Lake Turkana in the 1980s. Our minibus was so dilapidated that somewhere between Maralal and Baragoi the suspension collapsed. Our food dwindled to a few over-ripe bananas, the driver-guide couldn't tell his dipstick from his dik-dik, and our tents were apparently designed for hobbits. None of the zips worked and, inevitably, I woke one morning to find an army of ants bivouacked in my boots.

But don't let me put you off the budget option. Low-cost camping safaris, in which you take an active role in pitching tents and cooking, are excellent value and great fun – particularly if you are travelling alone. Just be sure to choose a reputable operator and find out exactly what's included.

At the other end of the scale are luxury lodges and tented camps. Generally, the smaller, more intimate and off-the-beaten-track they are, the more you'll pay. As well as lavish furnishings and fine dining you can expect highly trained, experienced guides and few other guests.

Everyone knows what a lodge is, but the term 'tented camp' can sometimes be confusing. Just because it has the words 'tent' and 'camp' in it, don't run away with the notion that staying at one involves bouncing around on an airbed, grappling with multi-jointed tent poles or traipsing half a mile to a hygienically challenged toilet block. 'Tent-house suite' better describes these mini-marquee marvels with their mosquito-netted beds, squishy duvets, rattan chairs and ensuite bathrooms. Modestly screened, but open to the elements (and sometimes the elephants), the latter usually boast flush toilets, showers and hot running water.

There is something almost precocious in the way in which accommodation is crafted in some of Africa's safari destinations. Confronted by wild environments, seasonal rains, remote locations and difficult access, safari operators respond with feather duvets and a silver tea service. The bottom line is that you will rarely leave Africa having stayed somewhere ordinary – whether it's waking in a cramped tent to find your boots full of ants or pulling back the mosquito net to find a fresh pot of Earl Grey beside your four-poster.

What makes a sustainable safari operator?

Responsible safari operators are continually making innovations to ensure their camps and lodges not only leave a minimal footprint on the environment, but actually make a positive impact on wildlife and local communities.

One company that takes its ethical responsibilities seriously is **&beyond** (andbeyond.com). Its ethos, 'Care of the land, care of the wildlife, care of the people' is reflected in numerous sustainable projects at its 35-plus luxury camps and lodges scattered throughout southern and East Africa. At its Bateleur Camp in the Masai Mara, for example, beekeeping is taught (and hives provided) to local Maasai who can then sell the honey back to the lodge. At Grumeti Serengeti Tented Camp, a doctor is employed to assist with staff and local community health, and villagers are trained how to plant vegetable gardens. The green architectural designs of stilted rooms at Xudum Okavango Delta Lodge allow for complete regeneration of the forest floor, while the soft footprint of totally movable camps like Chobe Under Canvas and Serengeti Under Canvas removes the physical impact of a permanent camp.

Another company seeking solutions to protect wildlife and provide education and training for local people, **Wilderness Safaris** (wildernesstrust.com) has supported projects ranging from turtle monitoring in South Africa to rhino relocation in the

Genty does it – low-impact camping in the Serengeti

A mobile tented camp, &Beyond's Serengeti Under Canvas is moved on a regular basis, not only to keep pace with the wildebeest migration, but to minimize its impact on the environment. When the camp moves on, no trace is left.

Confronted by wild environments, seasonal rains, remote locations and difficult access, safari operators respond with feather duvets and a silver tea service

Okavango Delta. One of its key aims is to empower local communities so that they benefit from the wildlife on their doorsteps. A successful project in Zambia – Community Markets for Conservation – links villagers with urban markets through a chain of environmentally smart products. It is a scheme that's helping to convert poachers to carpentry, fish farming and other sustainable rural livelihoods.

In Kenya, meanwhile, Naibosho is one of the latest conservancies in the Greater Mara to provide direct income to individual Maasai landowners – irrespective of the tourism income generated. Covering an area almost half the size of the Masai Mara Game Reserve, the conservancy is a partnership between 500 Maasai landowners and ecotourism operator **Basecamp Explorer** (basecampexplorer. com), which already finances the Koiyaki Guiding School for young Maasai.

Each landowner earns monthly rent based on the size of land they have contributed to the conservancy. Conservancies like Naibosho tackle threats facing the Serengeti-Mara ecosystem, such as human population growth, encroachment from commercial agriculture and privatisation of communal land, by supporting local livelihoods and guaranteeing income to landowners while safeguarding wildlife – including the annual wildebeest migration. The core area of Naibosho (around 20,000 ha) will be dedicated to conservation, while surrounding areas will integrate grazing management, wildlife and human settlements. The conservancy is also good news for Kenya's dwindling lions – around 100 of the big cats (5% of the country's total population) live in the area.

ⓘ See pages 240-243 for a selection of African camps and lodges.

Sleep talking – Africa's stylish safari accommodation

Sossusvlei Desert Lodge, NamibRand Reserve, Namibia (1); Ngerende Island Lodge, Masai Mara, Kenya (2); Lianshulu Lodge, Caprivi Strip, Namibia (3); Jaci's Safari Lodge, Madikwe Game Reserve, South Africa (4); Kiangazi House, Lake Naivasha, Kenya (5); Tangala Private Safari House, Upper Zambezi, Zambia (6); Madikwe Safari Lodge, South Africa (7).

Nhoma Safari Camp
Bushmanland, Namibia

There is no better way to learn about wildlife and survival in the Kalahari than by spending time with the San, or Bushmen. A partnership with the //Nhoq'ma community of Ju/'hoan Bushmen, Nhoma Safari Camp was set up in 1999 by Arno Oosthuysen – a Namibian safari operator who, six years earlier, had built a lodge at Tsumkwe, a tiny settlement 80 km away. Revenue from carefully managed tourism allows the Ju/'hoan to buy food and supplies to supplement their hunter-gatherer lifestyle. Without it, the community would likely have left their ancestral land and moved to settled areas.

Pitched on a dune with far-reaching views over wooded savannah, Nhoma Safari Camp has 10 large tents and a thatched dining area shaded by teak trees. It's a short walk to //Nhoq'ma village where you will learn traditional Bushmen skills such as setting traps, curing antelope hides, making fire and fashioning arrows from stalks of elephant grass. Experiencing village life is fascinating, but it's only by accompanying the Ju/'hoan on a foraging expedition that you truly appreciate their remarkable bush skills. Walks can last several hours and turn into an actual hunt should the opportunity arise. You'll learn how to track game, harvest bushfood (such as Kalahari raisins and mangeti nuts), squeeze moisture from plant tubers, extract honey from wild bee nests and check aardvark burrows for possible food in the form of porcupines or spring hares. Back at the village, you can join in with games and watch mesmerizing healing dances around the communal fire.

Most visitors spend a night or two at Tsumkwe Lodge before transferring to Nhoma Safari Camp. It is a three-hour drive from Grootfontein, the final 200 km to Tsumkwe on a gravel track suitable for 2WD vehicles. Nearby Khaudum National Park offers a strictly 4WD wilderness experience.
tsumkwel.iway.na

Wasa & Luwombwa Lodges
Kasanka National Park, Zambia

Privately run by the Kasanka Trust, Kasanka National Park has two permanent lodges and three campsites. The lakeside Wasa Lodge is a short walk from Fibwe Hide, renowned for its sightings of the rare sitatunga (pictured above) and a roost of one million straw-coloured fruit bats. The lodge has three ensuite rondavels with private verandahs and six simple chalets. Luwombwa Lodge, meanwhile, is well placed for river trips.
kasanka.com

Explorers Camp
Gorongosa National Park, Mozambique

A seasonal tented camp in the heart of the rejuvenated Gorongosa National Park, Explorers offers an authentic bush experience with comfortable safari tents, waterless eco-toilets, open-air showers, dinner under the stars and superb walking in this little-visited area. A series of wilderness fly-camps – the Gorongosa SkyBeds – gets you even closer to nature, enabling you to sleep out in the bush under mosquito nets.
exploregorongosa.com

Satao Elerai Camp
Amboseli, Kenya

This community-owned lodge is an organic masterpiece of twisted acacia branches collected from elephant-damaged trees. Its 14 tented suites have superb views of Mt Kilimanjaro and Amboseli National Park. Located in the Elerai Conservation Area (part of a critical wildlife corridor between Kilimanjaro's forests and Amboseli), the lodge offers Maasai-guided game walks, night drives, balloon safaris and community visits.
sataoelerai.com

1. Nhoma Safari Camp
2. Wasa Lodge
3. Explorer's Camp
4. Satao Elerai Camp
5. Tongabezi
6. Little Vumburu Camp
7. A Tent with a View
8. Bwindi Safari Lodge
9. Kapani Lodge
10. Ngorongoro Crater Lodge
11. Basecamp Masai Mara
12. Jaci's Safari Lodge
13. Earth Lodge
14. Porini Rhino Camp
15. North Island

Tongabezi
Near Livingstone, Zambia

The original romantic retreat on the Upper Zambezi, Tongabezi offers a variety of accommodation options, from the original Tongabezi Lodge, with its sumptuous riverfront cottages and wonderful dining deck, to an exclusive eco-camp a short distance upstream on Sindabezi Island. Tangala House, meanwhile, is a luxurious family home that comes with a safari vehicle and boat, chef, waiters and private guide. Boat trips to Livingstone Island on the lip of Victoria Falls are a must.
tongabezi.com

Little Vimburu Camp
Okavango Delta, Botswana

One of several idyllic camps operated by Wilderness Safaris in the Okavango Delta, Little Vimburu is part of the Okavango Community Trust which brings financial benefit, employment opportunities and skills development to villages on the Delta's northern fringes. Located on a wooded islet, the camp has six beautiful tented suites, a star-gazing deck and a plunge pool overlooking floodplains frequented by wildlife. Walks, game drives and mokoro rides are all available.
wilderness-safaris.com

A Tent with a View
Saadani National Park, Tanzania

Scattered along a pristine stretch of Indian Ocean shoreline, A Tent with a View rolls safari and beach holiday into one. Its six luxurious suites and nine bandas have large, hammock-strewn balconies peeking through coconut plams to the sea. Elephants roam the beach, while nearby Madete Marine Reserve is a green turtle nesting site. Heading inland on foot, by boat or 4WD vehicle, you can see a variety of big game, including lion, buffalo, giraffe and sable.
saadani.com

Bwindi Safari Lodge
Bwindi Impenetrable National Park, Uganda

Sit on the terrace at this ecolodge (with its eight stone bandas, composting toilets and bush showers) and you can hear the exotic calls of primates and birds rising from the canopy of Bwindi's primeval forest. Tracking mountain gorillas is the highlight of a visit here. You can spend several hours hiking through the forest before encountering the great apes – or you might get lucky and find them at one of their favourite haunts by the river below the lodge.
volcanoessafaris.com

Kapani Lodge
South Luangwa National Park, Zambia

The main base for Norman Carr Safaris, Kapani stands beside an old ox-bow lake and has eight suites and a Lagoon House that's suitable for families. The lodge acts as a hub for expertly guided walking safaris deeper into South Luangwa, staying at seasonal bushcamps. From January to March, 'green season' safaris are available to bushcamps accessible only by boat. Kapani can also arrange specialist photographic and birdwatching safaris.
normancarrsafaris.com

Wild nights out | African camps & lodges

Ngorongoro Crater Lodge
Tanzania

One of &Beyond's flagship properties, this wonderfully indulgent lodge has breathtaking views across Ngorongoro Crater. The main building's dramatic façade of red-ochre walls, tiered decks and giant pots full of Maasai spears leads to an interior of Baroque splendour with chandeliers, ceilings inlaid with gold leaf, leather armchairs and vases crammed with red roses. The cottage suites are equally romantic, with Victorian baths, teak-panelled walls, fireplaces and exotic rugs. The cuisine is outstanding and the service second to none (laundry is returned to you – by your personal butler – wrapped in red velvet with a rose on top). Sustainability is given equal attention. Over 30,000 indigenous trees have been planted in the area, lodge rangers take groups of Maasai children on game drives into the Crater, while other community initiatives focus on health and education.
andbeyond.com

Basecamp Explorer
Kenya

Designed to help secure the future of Maasai livelihoods, Basecamp Explorer runs three camps in the Naboisho Conservancy. Basecamp Wilderness has five safari huts set on a spectacular escarpment overlooking the Koiyaki River; Basecamp Masai Mara has 12 spacious and luxurious tents bordering the Masai Mara National Reserve, while Dorobo Fly Camp is a simple bushcamp that's perfectly placed for walking safaris with Maasai guides.
basecampexplorer.com

Jaci's Safari Lodge
Madikwe Game Reserve, South Africa

One of several properties in Madikwe whose main aim is to generate income-earning opportunities for local communities, Jaci's nuzzles like a well-hidden bird's nest in a grove of tamboti trees. Large thatch-and-canvas suites with sunken stone baths and outdoor ensuite showers offer a monkey's eye-view through the trees. The neighbouring Jaci's Tree Lodge has a hide and four-poster 'star bed' overlooking a waterhole.
madikwe.com

Earth Lodge
Sabi Sabi Private Game Reserve, South Africa

Sculpted into the earth, almost entirely concealed from view, Earth Lodge has 12 opulent suites with stylish interiors that celebrate the richness of Africa's mineral wealth. Handmade twig chandeliers with gilded copper, bronze and silver branches are just one of the touches you'll find in this unique property which also boats an outdoor boma and Amani spa. Expert guides and Shangaan trackers lead game drives and bush walks.
sabisabi.com

Porini Rhino Camp
Ol Pejeta Conservancy, Kenya

A 36,400-ha wildlife conservancy between the Aberdares and Mt Kenya, Ol Pejeta is not only a haven for rhino and other big game, but also has a sanctuary for rescued chimpanzees. The six-tent Rhino Camp is tucked away among acacias and is one of four minimal-impact Porini camps located on conservancies in Kenya that are owned by Maasai communities – providing benefits for local people through tourism.
porinisafaricamps.com

North Island
Seychelles

This stunning private island has become world renowned as a sanctuary for both endangered wildlife and discerning travellers. North Island's handcrafted villas offer presidential-style comfort with private plunge pools, marble baths and huge sundecks overlooking gorgeous beaches. A rat eradication programme on the island paved the way for the return of rare species such as the black paradise flycatcher, Seychelles warbler and Seychelles magpie robin.
north-island.com

①

① Meet the marine life
Snorkelling or diving in the Seychelles, you can encounter anything from hawksbill turtles to manta rays and whale sharks.
diveseychelles.com.sc

② Explore a marine park
Marine parks close to Mahé include Ste Anne and Cerf. Much further afield is the World Heritage Site of Aldabra – reached by occasional liveaboards.

③ Island-hop on a yacht
Several companies offer bareboat or skippered yacht charters – a perfect way to explore the archipelago and find deserted coves.
seychelles.travel

④ Go nuts on Praslin
Largely unchanged since prehistoric times, Vallée de Mai is home to the coco de mer palm and endemic black parrots.
unesco.org

⑤ Watch the birdies
White-tailed tropicbirds are common in the Seychelles. You can see them at Bird Island, along with fairy terns and 1.5 million sooty terns.
birdislandseychelles.com

②

③

④

⑤

Asia

The scale of Asia, its vast range of habitats and extremes of climate go a long way to explaining the continent's rich array of life. It is arguably the most varied place on Earth, encompassing landscapes as diverse as the cold deserts of Mongolia, the humid wetlands of Bangladesh, the wind-raked steppes of Central Asia and the sultry rainforests of Borneo and Sumatra. Biodiversity runs riot through this complex framework of ecosystems with India, alone, home to 1,200 species of birds and 340 varieties of mammal. But how, in a continent of around four billion people, has this wealth of wildlife managed to survive?

The answer lies, in part, to the special relationships many Asian cultures and religions share with nature. To Hindus, for example, it is not just the cow that is held sacred, but many wild animals, such as elephants, tigers, monkeys and snakes. Even plants, like the fig tree, are reverred in parts of India.

Asia also has a strong, if relatively young, system of protected areas. Project Tiger, in which reserves were set aside across India to help protect the endangered big cat, was launched as recently as 1972 – about the same time as Nepal created its flagship Royal Chitwan National Park.

The big question is whether these (and other) conservation initiatives and deep-held religious beliefs will be enough to resist modern-day pressures on Asia's wildlife – whether it's the poaching of tigers to supply the trade in Chinese traditional medicine, or the destruction of the orang-utan's native rainforest in Borneo to fuel the worldwide demand for palm oil.

Although indigenous people have long celebrated the diversity of Asia's natural wealth, it is only within the last 150 years or so that scientific expeditions have revealed just how spectacularly diverse its flora and fauna really is. One man in particular – Alfred Wallace – did more than most to shed light on Asia's biodiversity. In 1854, Wallace embarked on a collecting trip to the islands of Malaya, returning eight years later with an astonishing 125,000 specimens – many of them new to science.

Published in 1869, Wallace's account of his travels, *The Malay Archipelago*, not only proved riveting reading (due in no small part to the chapters devoted to popular subjects like the orang-utan and birds of paradise), but it also broke new ground on theories delving into the distribution of animals.

Wallace concluded that the Malay Archipelago represented the frontier between two distinct faunal provinces – an Indo-Malayan one to the east and an Australasian one to the west, and that the two zones could be separated by an imaginary line running between the Philippines, Borneo and Java on one side and Celebes, the Moluccas and New Guinea on the other. The so-called 'Wallace Line' still recognises the explorer's defining contribution to biogeography – but in many ways he should also be remembered as one of the great early exponents of biodiversity.

Off the beaten track | Mongolia

A four-hour drive northeast of Ulaan Baatar takes you across treeless steppes and through larch forests to reach Jalman Meadows where Nomadic Journeys (nomadicjourneys.com) runs a summer camp for just 20 tourists. Based on traditional gers, the camp has composting toilets, solar-powered electricity and leaves little trace when it's packed away at the end of the season. Activities include hiking, horse riding and yak-cart rafting where an inflatable raft is towed upstream by bovine power. Wildlife includes wolf, lynx and brown bear. Another low-impact ger camp, Arburd Sands is located on the Gobi steppes near Zorgol Hairhan Uul, a gigantic rock formation that's home to Argali sheep and Siberian ibex. Here you can camp out in the sands, stake out a wolf hide and ride horses or camels.

Spotted deer, or chital, are always on the alert for predators – especially tigers.

Axis axis
Ranthambhore National Park, India

Chital often associate with langur monkeys. The deer have good eyesight and a keen sense of smell, while troops of langur often post a look-out in the trees, ready to bark a warning should a big cat be seen on the prowl.

The world's largest continent stretches from north of the Arctic Circle to south of the equator. Spanning these extremes are ecosystems ranging from the taiga forests of the Siberian wilderness to the tropical rainforests and coral reefs of Indonesia.

Natural zones

The great conifer woods of Siberia cover a vast area of northeastern Russia – a mantle of spruce and pine in which several species of large mammal thrive, including caribou, moose, brown bear and wolf. Victims of poaching, critically endangered subspecies of tiger and leopard are found in the Amur region of the Russian Far East, while the steppes, deserts and mountains of Central Asia are a refuge for rarities like the Bactrian camel, Przewalski's horse, saiga antelope and snow leopard.

The Himalayan region contains a wealth of habitats, from subtropical foothills to the cold, desert-like Tibetan Plateau. Great rivers like the Indus and Ganges flow across the Indian subcontinent where wildlife-rich forests and wetlands are closely attuned to seasonal changes brought by the monsoon.

Stronghold of the giant panda, the temperate forests of southwest China are botanical treasure chests. It's in the tropical forests and seas of Southeast Asia, however, that biodiversity runs amok. Ancient jungles on the Malay Peninsula support an incredible array of species, while islands like Borneo, Sumatra and the Philippines have high levels of endemism.

Wildlife travel

For all its natural riches, only a handful of countries in Asia excel as wildlife destinations, with experienced local operators, a readily accessible networks of parks and reserves and a good range of places to stay. India, Nepal, Sri Lanka and Malaysia (especially its Bornean states of Sarawak and Sabah) are top of most wildlife travellers' wishlists. All four countries promise spectacular wildlife experiences on well-established circuits. More specialised trips await adventurous travellers in search of bears and whales in Russia's Kamchatka Peninsula, giant pandas in China, Komodo dragons in Indonesia, whale sharks in the Philippines and snow leopards in Kazakhstan.

it's a wild life

Pete Raines | Founder & CEO, Coral Cay Conservation | coralcay.org

⬊ My big five
1. Sogod Bay, Philippines
2. Chagos Marine Protected Area, British Indian Ocean Territory
3. Koh Rong Island, Cambodia
4. Mau Enderit Forest, Kenya
5. Isles of Scilly, United Kingdom

" " Re-supplying by boat a Coral Cay Conservation expedition on a remote island, I stopped to refuel. The boat began rocking as though someone was trying to board. Turning around, I found a large dolphin, leaning in and taking a look. It slipped below, popping up again on the other side. This 'port-starboard dance' continued until I did something really stupid: grabbing a mask and the mooring line, I jumped overboard. Me and the dolphin played and 'chatted' before reality set in – I was alone, in open sea, with just a rope between me and certain death!

Day 1 Arrive Kota Kinabalu, transfer to Mt Kinabalu National Park **Day 2** Explore trails and botanical gardens **Day 3** Search for rafflesia **Day 4** Fly to Sandakan, evening turtle watching on Selingan Island **Day 5** Sepilok Orang-utan Rehabilitation Centre, overnight Sepilok Nature Resort **Day 6** Kinabatangan River **Day 7** Forest walks and boat trips at Sukau Rainforest Lodge **Day 8** Gomantong Caves **Days 9 & 10** Danum Valley, overnight Borneo Rainforest Lodge **Day 11** Fly to Kota Kinabalu
◗ Based on an itinerary from **Reef & Rainforest Tours** (reefandrainforest.co.uk), this trip would cost around £3,400 per person, including flights from the UK, transfers, activities and mostly full-board accommodation.

Wild city | Chéngdu, Sichuan Province, China

Just 10 km north of Chéngdu – economic hub of southwest China and a burgeoning metropolis of 10 million people – the Chengdu Panda Base (panda.org.cn) is one of the few places on earth where the giant panda is thriving. From a founding group of six pandas rescued from the wild in 1987, the centre's captive bred population now stands at over 80 and serves as a genetic reservoir for other breeding programmes around the world. Red panda, golden monkey and other threatened species also find sanctuary in over 200 ha of beautifully landscaped grounds. You can join a three-hour walking tour or 90-minute bus tour (both available in English), during which you'll visit the panda nursery, adult enclosures, veterinary and food-processing facilities as well as Swan Lake – a refuge for wildfowl. There's also an excellent museum. Try to get to the park when it opens at 0800 – the pandas are up and about waiting to be fed at 0900 after which they tend to settle down for a long nap. For a chance to spot wild giant pandas, head to reserves in the remote mountain forests of the Qinling Mountains, north of Chéngdu (see page 251).

Wild places

The Russian Far East reaches its most spectacular in the Kamchatka Peninsula ❶ where an expedition voyage is the best way to see Ring of Fire volcanoes and observe wildlife ranging from brown bear and sea otter to orca and Steller's sea eagle. The Tien Shan Mountains of Kazakhstan ❷ are the haunt of snow leopards, but far easier to see are the spectacular displays of spring flowers (especially wild tulips) and birds such as ibisbill and Himalayan rubythroat. Key locations include Aksu Dzabagly Nature Reserve, easily accessed by overnight train from Almaty. As well as giant pandas (see box, left), wildlife highlights in China ❸ include golden snub-nose monkey and crested ibis – endangered species that can be sought in Shaanxi Province. In Nepal ❹, Chitwan National Park protects one of the few remaining tracts of undisturbed terai, a wildlife-rich region of swamp and sal forest, while Bhutan ❺ is renowned for mountain forests of oak and hemlock, teeming with rare birds. Tigers find refuge in both Nepal and Bhutan, but the national parks and reserves of India ❻ remain the best places to see this majestic big cat. The high mountain valleys of Ladakh ❼ are a stronghold for snow leopard, while Kaziranga National Park in Assam ❽ provides sanctuary for the Great Indian one-horned rhinoceros. Three more Indian rarities – the Asiatic lion, Indian wolf and Asiatic wild ass – can be found in the little-explored region of Gujarat ❾. For its relatively small size, Sri Lanka ❿ boasts a wealth of wildlife, from blue whales and sea turtles to leopards and elephants. In Thailand ⓫ you can explore the tropical rainforest of Khao Sok National Park by elephant-back and snorkel with whale sharks at Ko Tao. Over 130 million years in the making, the ancient rainforest of Taman Negara in Malaysia ⓬ is home to tapir and elephant (best seen at clay licks), highly elusive leopard, tiger and sun bear and over 350 species of birds, including the impressive rhinoceros hornbill. The parks and reserves of Sarawak and Sabah ⓭ provide easy access to tropical forests, coral reefs, turtle-nesting islands, enormous bat-filled caves and the botanical treasure chest of Mt Kinabalu. Sabah's Danum Valley is one of the best places to see wild orang-utans, while Gunung Leuser National Park in northern Sumatra ⓮ is also a good place to find the 'man of the forest'. The world's largest archipelago, Indonesia lies on a biodiversity hotspot with an astonishing range of endemic species – the most famous being the Komodo dragon, found on just five islands off Flores ⓯. An array of unique wildlife can also be found in the Philippines ⓰. The islands of Cebu, Mindanao and Palawan are particularly rewarding for birds such as Philippine eagle, Palawan peacock pheasant and various flowerpeckers. Between February and May, Donsol (on the southern tip of Luzon) is one of the world's best places to see whale sharks. Whale watching in Japan ⓱ is particularly good in the Ogasawara Islands, while Ras Al Hadd in Oman ⓲ is renowned for its humpback whales, dolphins and nesting green turtles.

🪶 African safari specialist **&Beyond** (andbeyond. com) now offers India's first and only wildlife circuit, staying at its four luxury jungle safari lodges in Madhya Pradesh. Other local operators include **Tigerland Safaris** (tigerlandsafaris.com). Of the numerous overseas specialists, **Exodus** (exodus.co.uk), **Naturetrek** (naturetrek.co.uk) and **TransIndus** (transindus. co.uk) have some of the best itineraries.

✈️ Delhi and Mumbai are major hubs, served by national carrier **Air India** (airindia.in) and numerous other airlines. The easiest way to book tickets for **Indian Railways** is online at cleartrip.com. Hiring a car with a driver/guide is also straightforward. Various domestic airlines, such as **SpiceJet** (spicejet.com) and **IndiGo** (goindigo.in) offer low-cost internal flights.

🛏️ Places to stay range from national park restcamps to ecolodges and Rajasthan palaces.

🕐 GMT+5.5 (Delhi)

🌙 Wildlife watching is generally best from October to April when leaves fall and grasses wither (improving visibility) and water sources recede, concentrating animals around waterholes. Monsoon rains usually arrive by mid-June.

➕ Seek medical advice on malaria prevention.

💲 Indian rupee (Rs).

ℹ️ incredibleindia.org

Tiger, Kanha

Gaur, Satpura

Elephants, Periyar

Marsh mugger, Satpura

Kaziranga National Park

★ Indian greater one-horned rhino, Asian elephant

Thick swathes of swamp, elephant grass, reedbed and forest crowd the banks of the Brahmaputra River in this remote wildlife-rich gem. Your chances of sighting a tiger are quite slim, but this is *the* place to view Indian greater one-horned rhinoceros – nearly 80% of the world's population of around 2,500 lives here. Large herds of elephant and buffalo are also present, along with sambar, swamp and hog deer. The birdlife is excellent, with migratory bar-headed geese joining resident pelicans, Brahminy kites and Pallas's fish eagles. The nearby Panabari Forest Reserve is a refuge for the elusive hoolock gibbon, India's only ape.

Directions Located in Assam, Kaziranga is 220 km from Guwahati. **Getting around** 4WD vehicles and elephants. **Seasons** Open November to April; March and April are best. **Things to do** Jeep and elephant-back safaris, observation towers. **Places to stay** Five nearby lodges, including Bonhabi Resort (bonhabiresort.com), a short walk from the park's main entrance, and the more upmarket Diphlu River Lodge (diphluriverlodge.com) with air-conditioned thatched cottages-on-stilts.

Ranthambhore National Park

★ Tiger, sloth bear, wild dog (dhole), spotted deer (chital)

Rajasthan's premier wildlife reserve is famed for its tigers, scenery and history: rolling hills, dry dhok forest and tranquil lakes, crumbling ruins of Moghul temples and an 11th-century hilltop fort. Tiger numbers are not what they used to be, but you still stand a fairly good chance of spotting the big cat. Common species like rhesus macaque, wild boar, sambar and chital are almost guaranteed, and the birdlife is sensational. There are parakeets and peacocks galore, along with other colourful species, such as coppersmith barbet, purple sunbird and golden oriole.

Directions 300 km southeast of Delhi, easily reached by train. **Getting around** Jeep safaris depart morning and afternoon.

Seasons October to June. **Things to do** Jeep safaris. **Places to stay** Wide range of accommodation nearby, including the luxury tented camps like Jungle Niwas (jungleniwas.com) and Ranthambhore Bagh (ranthambhore.com).

Satpura National Park

★ Sloth bear, dhole, blackbuck, marsh mugger, leopard

This little-visited park may not have the most readily seen tigers in India, but it is unique in offering a full safari experience that includes game walks, boat trips, elephant-back rides, birdwatching ambles, nocturnal hides and visits to local communities, as well as jeep safaris. Covering 524 sq km of rugged hills, gouged by monsoonal ravines and cloaked in teak forest, Satpura is also one of India's most beautiful reserves.

During a boat trip on the Tawa Reservoir, you can watch marsh mugger crocodiles, spoonbills, storks and egrets against the hazy backdrop of the Satpura Range. The dry riverbed of the Sonbhadra Valley is a good place to search on foot for signs of tiger and sloth bear, while walking safaris across the plains and woodlands near the park headquarters may lead to encounters with packs of dhole. Blackbuck, chital, langur and wild gaur are common, while leopard are frequently spotted on game drives. Elephant safaris, meanwhile, allow you to track tigers in remote parts of the forest.

Directions Located 180 km southeast of Bhopal in Central India. **Getting around** You enter the park by crossing the Tawa reservoir. **Seasons** October to April. **Things to do** Jeep, elephant-back and walking safaris, boat trips. **Places to stay** Forsyth's Lodge (forsythlodge.com) offers comfortable accommodation just outside Satpura National Park. Its 12 earthen cottages are arranged around a main lodge building with terraces looking towards the hills. There's a swimming pool, cosy lounge and a hide for spotting palm civet, jungle cat and other nocturnal wildlife that frequents the surrounding woodland. The lodge works with park management to recruit and train local people as naturalist guides, jeep drivers and boatmen.

Bandhavgarh National Park
Steeped in history, this former royal hunting reserve in the Vindhyan Hills has an ancient fort perched atop an 800-m-high plateau. Jeep and elephant-back safaris provide a good chance of spotting sambar and spotted deer, langur and rhesus macaque, sloth bear, wild dog (dhole) and leopard. Bandhavgarh also has one of India's highest tiger densities.

Manas National Park
A World Heritage Site extending into Bhutan and encompassing grasslands and forests along the banks of the Manas River in the Himalayan foothills, Manas National Park has endemic golden langur, elephant and exotic birds like great hornbill and red-headed trogon. Thick forest makes tiger sightings difficult, but this is exciting, little-visited territory to explore.

Corbett National Park
see page 52

Keoladeo National Park
Wetland birds

Ranthambhore National Park
see pages 52 & 248

Little Rann of Kutch
Wild Ass Sanctuary

Bandhavgarh National Park
See box above

Chambal Sanctuary
Gharial, Gangetic river dolphin

Kaziranga National Park
see page 248

Satpura National Park
see page 248

Sasangir National Park
Asiatic lion

Pench National Park
See box below

Sunderbans National Park
Spread over 10,000 sq km of the Ganges Delta, the Sunderbans is a gloriously muddy mishmash of tidal waterways, mudflats and mangrove forest. Although it's a stronghold for the Bengal tiger, the swampy nature of the place makes them hard to spot. Boat tours offer a chance to see crocodiles, snakes, spotted deer and various waterbirds.

Tadoba-Andhari Tiger Reserve
You'll see few other tourists in this 625-sq-km reserve of mainly teak and bamboo forest. Up to 40 tigers are estimated to live here, along with leopard, sloth bear, gaur, dhole, plus a few surprises such as striped hyena and jungle cat.

Kanha National Park
Covering an area of 1,945 sq km, Kanha's habitats range from bamboo and sal forest to grassland and rugged plateau. The park is renowned for its swamp deer, but you'll also find spotted, sambar and barking deer, plus four varieties of antelope. Among Kanha's 220 bird species are forest beauties like the Malabar pied hornbill. Stake out grassland areas for a chance to see tigers hunting. Jeep and elephant-back safaris are available.

Pench National Park
Inspiration for Kipling's *Jungle Book*; Pench covers 758 sq km of prime tiger country. The Pench River (a series of pools during the dry season) meanders through hills cloaked in teak forest. Anywhere can be rewarding, but the waterholes are probably your best bet for a tiger encounter. Other wildlife includes gaur, wild boar, spotted and sambar deer, common langur, dhole and leopard.

Periyar National Park
The lush forests in the Cardamom Hills of the Western Ghats are home to elephant, gaur, wild boar, four species of primate (including the endemic lion-tailed macaque), sloth bear, leopard and otter.

Pakistan · Thar Desert · Ludhiana · Himalayas · Nanda Devi · Nepal · Bhutan · Kanchenjunga · Brahmaputra · New Delhi · Agra · Jaipur · Lucknow · Varanasi · Patna · Bangladesh · Burma · Ganges · Bhopal · Jabalpur · Kolkata · Ahmadabad · Narmada · Satpura National Park · Nagpur · Pench National Park · Mumbai · Hyderabad · Western Ghats · Bangalore · Chennai · Andaman Sea · Andaman Islands · Cochin · Madurai · Trivandrum · Sri Lanka · Indian Ocean

Tigers may be India's stars in stripes, but they are not the country's only big cats. As well as a relic population of 300 Asiatic lions in the Sasangir National Park of Gujarat, leopards are widespread. This young male was photographed in Satpura National Park, one of India's lesser-known 'tiger reserves'. Satpura is unusual in that it allows walking safaris – the Sonbhadra Valley (far left) being a prime location for spotting tiger tracks. Other typical wildlife in the park includes spotted deer, sloth bear and langur – seen here feeding on the petals of flame-of-the-forest trees.

Sri Lanka

Better known for cultural highlights like Sigiriya rock fortress and the cave temples of Dambulla, Sri Lanka has also developed a following among wildlife enthusiasts. A birdwatcher's paradise and one of the best places in the world to see leopards and large herds of Asiatic elephant, the island has more recently become a whale-watching hotspot thanks to the relatively recent discovery of a large migratory population of blue whales off the southern coast. Present between the months of December and April, the whales are attracted to deep-water feeding grounds off **Dondra Point**. Responsible whale watching trips can be arranged with Eco Team Sri Lanka (srilankaecotourism.com).

Several stretches of Sri Lankan coast are nesting sites for sea turtles. The most common species, the olive ridley, comes ashore between September and November; leatherbacks nest from April to June, while peak season for green turtles is January to March. One of the best spots for turtle watching is **Bundala** on the south coast where a wetland reserve also attracts a wide range of birds, including greater flamingo and painted stork.

Nearby **Yala National Park** is famed for its high densities of leopard. Early morning and late afternoon game drives provide the best chances of spotting the big cats, along with elephant, chital, sambar, sloth bear and wild boar. West of Yala, **Udawalawe National Park** has some good-sized herds of elephant. However, Sri Lanka's ultimate jumbo offering can be found further north at **Minneriya National Park** where, from June to September, an extraordinary 'gathering of the herds' takes place. Over 300 elephant can sometimes be seen around the receding shores of the Minneriya Tank. For some of Sri Lanka's smaller specialities, head for the **Sinharaja Biosphere Reserve** – the island's last remaining tract of primary lowland rainforest. Guided walks here are sometimes rewarded with sightings of the rare blue-faced leaf monkey, rufous-bellied eagle and Sri Lanka hanging parrot. Sinharaja also has a wonderful variety of butterflies, including blue morphos and bird-wings. Walking conditions are best during the largely leech-free dry season between January and March.

Nepal

A popular haunt of aristocratic hunters in the 19th century, **Chitwan National Park** is now one of Asia's premier wildlife reserves, offering jeep and elephant-back safaris in search of tiger and Asian one-horned rhinoceros. Other wildlife includes spotted deer, leopard, sloth bear, wild boar, rhesus monkey, grey langur, wild dog, marsh crocodile, gharial (or Gangetic crocodile) and freshwater dolphin. Of the 450 bird species that have been recorded in Chitwan, look out for year-round residents like woodpeckers, hornbills and redheaded trogons. Brahminy ducks and bareheaded geese flock here in winter, while summer sees Chitwan's forests bustling with migrant parakeets and paradise flycatchers. The park has a good range of lodges and camps and can be reached by air, road or river.

Also in Nepal's lowlands, **Koshi Tappu Wildlife Reserve i**s a large wetland area that will have keen birdwatchers ticking off a long list of egrets, herons, storks, ibises, gulls, terns and warblers. The rarely visited **Bardia National Park** protects a swathe of forest along the Karnali River, where rafting trips sometimes allow sightings of smooth otter and Ganges river dolphin.

For wildlife travellers, April and May are the best months for trekking in the Himalayas. Rhododendrons are flowering in mountain forests, while alpine meadows are carpeted in gentians and other spring flowers. Trekking from Lukla to the Sherpa capital of Namche Bazaar and on into the heart of **Sagarmatha National Park**, you will also have a good chance of seeing musk deer and Himalayan Thar, as well as high-living birds like the Himalayan Monal, rubythroat and Tibetan snowcock.

China

Although you can see giant pandas at the captive breeding centre near Chéngdu (see page 247), tracking these largely solitary creatures in the wild takes you deep into their mountain forest stronghold where you may also see other rare species, such as golden snub-nosed monkey, Asiatic black bear, golden takin (goat antelope), clouded leopard, crested ibis and various pheasants.

The world's highest density of giant pandas is found in the linked nature reserves of Foping and Laoxiancheng in the **Qinling Mountains**, around 200 km south of Xi'an. Rangers lead you on foot across terrain that is often steep and slippery, aiming for the vegetation zone of umbrella bamboo that forms the major part of the pandas' diet.

Although sightings are never guaranteed, you can increase your chances by visiting the region in late October and November following the first snows. This not only makes finding pandas easier (by following their tracks in the snow) but they also tend to move down from higher elevations in search of food around this time.

Low life and high life

From top: The great gathering of Asiatic elephants in Sri Lanka's Minneriya National Park; portrait of a painted stork, Yala National Park; Asian one-horned rhinoceros, Chitwan National Park, Nepal; Tibetan snowcock at 5,400 m in the Gokyo Valley, Nepal.

Making tracks | Borneo

Local wildlife tour operators include **TYK Adventure Tours** (tykadventuretours.com) and **Wildlife Expeditions** (wildlife-expeditions.com). Also try UK-based **Reef & Rainforest Tours** (reefandrainforest.co.uk).

Malaysia Airlines (malaysiaairlines.com) has connecting flights from Kuala Lumpur to various cities in Sabah and Sarawak – particularly cost effective with a Discover Malaysia Pass. Other carriers serving the region include **Royal Brunei Airlines** (bruneiair.com) and **Singapore Airlines** (singaporeair.com). Air-conditioned buses connect major towns and cities in Malaysian Borneo, although you may need to fly or use river boats to reach remote areas.

Accommodation ranges from jungle lodges to mountain huts. Spending a night at a longhouse is the best way to learn about the customs of the Iban – Sarawak's largest indigenous group.

GMT+8

Dry season is May to October, wet season November to April. Average daily temperatures range from 21-28°C year round.

Seek advice on malaria precautions if visiting remote rural areas.

Ringgit (RM).

sabahtourism.com, sarawaktourism.com

Forest Department (forestry.sarawak.gov.my), **Sabah Parks** (sabahparks.org).

Gunung Mulu National Park

★ Wrinkle-lipped bat, cave swiftlet, hornbills, butterflies

It is only when you stand at the gaping maw of Deer Cave and try to envisage five St Paul's Cathedrals snug inside that the true enormity of Mulu's subterranean wonders strikes you. Deer Cave is the world's largest cave passage – over 4 km long and up to 169 m high and 148 m wide – a fitting backdrop for the nightly exodus of over three million wrinkle-lipped bats.

To reach the cave entrance, trails and boardwalks thread through peat swamp and mixed dipterocarp rainforest where you can spot some of Mulu's 262 species of birds (including all eight of Sarawak's hornbills), 74 types of frog, 281 different butterflies and 458 kinds of ant.

After cowering beneath the pressing tangle of the jungle, walking into Deer Cave is like being swept into outer space; from oppressive humidity to cool vacuum, from impenetrable plantlife to oblivious darkness. Deep in the damp recesses of the cave, where no daylight can penetrate, you hear the ratchet-clicks and whirrs of echo-locating cave swiftlets and bats. Your eyes well from the sting of ammonia as you walk past huge domes of bat guano seething with scavenging hordes of earwigs, cave crickets, spiders, scorpions and centipedes. A fine rain of beetle wings, moth bits and other undigested insect remains settles on your head and arms – a gruesome black pepper of bat dung.

By late afternoon, the bats begin to gather in a vast, swirling vortex at the cave entrance. At regular intervals, large swarms detach themselves from the main group and stream away across the forest canopy in long, dark ribbons, their frenzied wingbeats sounding like distant surf.

....

Directions Fly to Mulu from Miri or take a boat from Kuala Baram.
Getting around Walking and boat travel only. Activities must be arranged through the park headquarters. Guides are mandatory.
Seasons Park open year round; November to June is best. Aim to be at the viewing area in front of Deer Cave by 1700 to witness the bat exodus.
Visitor centres Park headquarters has an discovery centre, canteen, gift shops and various accommodation options.
Things to do Rainforest and cave walks, canopy skywalk, boat trips, adventure caving, treks to the Pinnacles (limestone spikes piercing the rainforest) and to the summit of Gunung Mulu (2,377 m).
Places to stay Royal Mulu Resort (royalmuluresort.com).
Further information mulupark.com

Wild places

1 Just 40 km from Kuching, Bako National Park provides an excellent introduction to Borneo's wildlife. Boardwalks through mangrove forest provide a good vantage from which to spot proboscis monkeys, while night walks in the rainforest might reveal mouse deer or slow loris.
2 Reached by a boardwalk weaving through dense rainforest (keep an eye out for hornbills, bird-wing butterflies and flying lizards), the limestone caves of Niah National Park are home to countless swiftlets and bats.
3 Gunung Mulu National Park protects one of the world's largest cave systems – the setting for a spectacular nightly exodus of some three million bats.
4 A short boat ride from Kota Kinabalu, the five reef-fringed islands of Tunku Abdul Rahman Park are popular with snorkellers and divers. Whales sharks are sometimes seen between November and February.
5 Mt Kinabalu is a botanist's mecca. As well as insectivorous pitcher plants, there are 1,200 varieties of orchids thriving in the mountain's cool, moist climate.
6 Green and hawksbill turtles come ashore year round to nest in Turtle Islands Park, but the best time to visit is between July and October. Pulau Selingan has a turtle hatchery where it's possible to join rangers in their efforts to safeguard the vulnerable clutches from predators.
7 Named after the rivers that flow into mangrove-fringed Sandakan Bay, Kabili-Sepilok Forest Reserve is best known for its orang-utan rehabilitation centre.
8 Gomantong Caves are famous for their colonies of swiftlets, whose nests are sustainably harvested for use in Chinese soup between February and April by locals using a gravity-defying system of rattan ladders, ropes and poles.
9 The Kinabatangan river flows through one of Southeast Asia's richest rainforests. Boat trips allow close views of primates, particularly the proboscis monkey.
10 Danum Valley is home to such rarities as the Sumatran rhinoceros, orang-utan and clouded leopard.
11 Sipadan Island is one of the world's premier dive spots.

Borneo to be wild – a stream courses through tropical rainforest in Sabah's Crocker Range. Ten hectares of Borneo jungle can support a greater diversity of trees than the whole of North America. Top left: Primates include the proboscis monkey. Left: The island's extraordinary biodiversity also encompasses tiny frogs and the world's largest flower, the parasitic rafflesia, which can be seen at Tamunan Rafflesia Reserve, a two-hour drive from Kota Kinabalu.

Danum Valley Conservation Area

★ Orang-utan, Sumatran rhinoceros, clouded leopard

One of Borneo's top wildlife locations, Danum Valley covers 438 sq km of pristine dipterocarp rainforest – home to Sabah's 10 species of primate, including orang-utan. The orange-haired 'man of the forest' often makes an appearance when the durian trees are in fruit. Explore forest trails and stake out the canopy walkway during the early morning and you may also glimpse (or, more likely, see signs of) other rarities like Asian elephant, clouded leopard, flat-headed cat, Sumatran rhino and sun bear. Bearded pig, mouse deer and Bornean red muntjac are more easily spotted, and there are always plenty of hornbills, barbets, broadbills and other birds about. Night walks, meanwhile, shine a light on the secretive nocturnal world of the giant flying squirrel and slow loris.

Directions Fly or travel overland to Lahad Datu, 100 km from Danum.
Getting around Most visitors book packages including activities.
Seasons Year round. March to October is best.
Things to do Forest trails, canopy walkway, night drives, tubing.
Places to stay Borneo Rainforest Lodge – see page 258.

Kabili-Sepilok Forest Reserve

★ Orang-utan, pig-tailed macaque

Although wild orang-utans are sometimes seen in Danum Valley and along the Kinabatangan River, the best place to see them up-close is this 5,666-ha sanctuary near Sandakan. Sepilok is renowned for its rehabilitation centre – a kind of hospital and training camp for orang-utans that have been orphaned by hunting or deforestation. Once nursed to health, young orphans have to be taught all the skills essential to life in the jungle – everything from swinging to eating. A tedious diet of milk and fruit encourages them to forage in the wild and gradually gain independence. Around 80 are now roaming wild in the reserve. Amble slowly along the reserve's boardwalks and trails and you may also see pig-tailed macaques, a variety of birds and abundant insect life.

Directions Buses and taxis run from Sandakan to the reserve.
Getting around A network of trails lead from the visitor centre.
Seasons Year round. The apes emerge for free meals around 1000 or 1500 at feeding platforms in the forest.
Things to do Orang-utan viewing, boardwalk trails.
Places to stay Sepilok Nature Resort (sepilok.com).
Further information orangutan-appeal.org.uk

Mt Kinabalu

Kinabalu National Park

★ Rhododendrons, pitcher plants, orchids, butterflies

At 4,101 m, Mt Kinabalu is the tallest mountain between the Himalayas and New Guinea. Mist-wrapped and shaggy with moss and lichen, its forests seem otherworldly. This is a place where worms grow to the length of your leg, frogs are as tiny as your fingernail and carnivorous pitcher plants feast on insects. The mountain's slopes run riot with 1,200 different orchids, numerous indigenous rhododendrons and the rare, but unforgettable, rafflesia – a parasite devoid of leaf, stem or root that produces a single, whiffy bloom measuring nearly a metre across.

Nature trails probe the forests on Kinabalu's lower slopes, but it's a knee-jarring two-day slog to the summit and back. Allow at least five hours after setting out from the national park headquarters to reach Laban Rata, a hut at 3,272 m where trekkers spend the night before tackling the summit. Well before dawn the following morning, you steal outside and grope your way upwards by torchlight. The forest soon succumbs to the altitude as you scramble across bare slopes of granite using fixed ropes and ladders to scale the steepest sections. The effort is more than worthwhile, however, when you reach the summit in time to witness the remarkable spectacle of Sabah spread beneath you – from the smooth sweep of the South China Sea to the crumpled mantel of the Crocker Range.

Directions 92 km east of Kota Kinabalu, easily reached by bus.
Getting around Porters and guides can be booked at park HQ.
Seasons Year round. If you are planning on climbing Mt Kinabalu, pack good walking boots, waterproof jacket and warm clothing.
Things to do Nature trails, trekking, gallery, mountain garden, nearby Poring Hot Springs and canopy walkway.
Places to stay Accommodation ranges from basic hotels to luxurious chalets. Nepenthes Villas are close to the park headquarters and restaurant.

> Mist-wrapped and shaggy with moss and lichen, Kinabalu's forests seem otherworldly. This is a place where worms grow to the length of your leg, frogs are as tiny as your fingernail and carnivorous pitcher plants feast on insects

Orang-utan >

Pongo pygmaeus
Sabah, Borneo

The rehabilitation centre at the Kabili-Sepilok Forest Reserve is one of the best places in the world for a close encounter with orang-utans – most of which have been orphaned through hunting or deforestation.

South China Sea
Celebes Sea
Pacific Ocean
Medan
Sumatra
Padang
Kalimantan
Manado
Banjarmasin
Sulawesi
Moluccas
Jakarta
Java Sea
Ambon
Surabaya
Banda Sea
Indian Ocean
Java
Lesser Sunda Islands
Denpasar
East Timor
Papua

Making tracks | Indonesia

↻ **Local operators**
Adventure Indonesia (adventureindonesia.com) offer trips ranging from Komodo Island liveaboard cruises and orang-utan safaris to jungle survival courses. International companies with specialist knowledge of Indonesia include **Audley Travel** (audley.co.uk).

✕ Airlines serving major gateways like Jakarta and Denpasar include **Cathay Pacific** (cathaypacific.com) and **Emirates** (emirates.com). Domestic flights in Indonesia are relatively cheap; regular ferries connect Java with Sumatra and Bali, with less frequent services to other islands.

🚌 Wide range available.

🕐 GMT+7 to GMT+9

☀ The rainy season (October to March) can cause trails in some national parks to close.

⑤ Rupiah (Rp).

➕ Seek advice on malaria precautions.

ⓘ indonesia.travel

Komodo National Park

★ Komodo dragon, Timor deer, dugong, sea turtles

Located between Sumbawa and Flores and encompassing the islands of Komodo, Rinca and Padar, as well as several smaller islets, Komodo National Park supports a population of between 3,000 and 5,000 Komodo dragons. The world's largest lizard, Komodo dragons can reach lengths in excess of 3 m and top the scales at 70 kg. They prey mainly on Timor deer and water buffalo using their toxic saliva to deliver a fatal bite. Indonesian spitting cobra, Russell's pit viper and green tree viper are also found in the park, along with long-tailed macaque, palm civet, the endemic Rinca rat and orange-footed scrub fowl. In contrast to the dry woodland and scrub found on the islands, the marine environment is extremely rich and diverse, with coral reefs, mangroves and seagrass beds. Dugong, manta ray and several species of cetacean and sea turtle have been recorded here.

Directions The national park can be accessed by boat from either Labuan Bajo in the west of Flores or Bima in eastern Sumbawa. Both towns are served by flights and ferries from Bali. You can also reach Komodo on a more leisurely liveaboard cruise.
Getting around Local rangers lead guided walks in search of dragons from one of two park entry points: Loh Liang on Komodo Island or Loh Buaya on Rinca Island. Groups are limited to a maximum of 10 people.
Seasons Dry season is April to November. Dragon mating season is July to August, with nesting from September to November.
Visitor centres Interpretation boards at Loh Liang.
Things to do Walking safari, diving, snorkelling, boat trips.
Places to stay Hotels in Labuan Bajo and Bima.
Further information komodonationalpark.org

Wild places

❶ Gunung Leuser National Park, Sumatra, is an important wilderness for rainforest wildlife, including orang-utan, elephant, rhino and tiger. The rhinoceros hornbill is top of most birdwatchers' must-see lists.
❷ Ujung Kulon National Park, Java, is a stronghold of the Javan rhinoceros.
❸ Around 1,800 sq km of rainforest in Central Kalimantan is protected in Bukit Baka-Bukit Raya National Park, home to orang-utan, clouded leopard and sun bear.
❹ Bali Barat National Park, Bali, protects the endangered Bali starling.
❺ Komodo National Park was established in 1980.
❻ Bunaken National Park, Sulawesi, and the Raja Ampat Islands of Papua ❼ are both renowned for their exceptionally rich coral reefs. Lombok ❽ also has great marine life, particularly at Blongas Bay (hammerhead sharks) and the Gili Islands (turtles).

Biodiversity hotspot – Wallacea covers the islands of central Indonesia, including Sulawesi, the Moluccas (or Spice Islands) and the Lesser Sundas. This region has been identified by Conservation International as one of the world's 34 biodiversity hotspots (biodiversityhotspots.org) and is second only to the tropical Andes in terms of bird endemism. An adjacent hotspot, Sundaland, is separated by Wallace's Line (see page 245).
Left: Unique species in Wallacea include the Celebes crested macaque, Sulawesi hornbill and Komodo dragon.

Wild nights out | Ecolodges & camps in Asia

Sukau Rainforest Lodge
Kinabatangan River, Sabah

Built in the style of a Malay longhouse, this 20-room ecolodge has viewing platforms and decks overlooking the Kinabatangan River, as well as a network of rainforest boardwalks (complete with elephant crossing points). The lodge supports local community projects, participates in a tree-planting programme and uses tour boats equipped with silent, electric motors in order to minimize disturbance to wildlife.
sukau.com

Tabin Wildlife Resort
Tabin Wildlife Reserve, Sabah

At 123,000 ha, Tabin is the largest wildlife reserve in Malaysia and this wonderful ecoresort currently offers its only accommodation. A cluster of 20 timber chalets tucked into jungle beside the Lipad River (southeast of Sandakan) Tabin Wildlife Resort is an excellent spot for tracking orang-utans in the wild. A network of trails can also be used for night walks, birdwatching (Tabin boasts 260 species) and visiting nearby waterfalls and mineral-rich 'mud volcanoes'.
tabinwildlife.com.my

Borneo Rainforest Lodge
Danum Valley, Sabah

Occupying a magnificent setting next to the Danum River in Sabah's largest area of protected lowland rainforest, this comfortable lodge has chalets built on stilts and balconies looking straight out onto pristine jungle. Boardwalks and a passive ventilation system (rather than air con) help to reduce environmental impact. The lodge runs a variety of activities, including night walks, and has a spectacular, 300-m-long canopy walkway.
borneonaturetours.com

Banjaar Tola Kanha Tented Camp
Kanha National Park, Madhya Pradesh, India

Tucked into indigenous sal forest right beside the Banjaar River and looking across to the lush woodland and grassy meadows of Kanha National Park, the two intimate camps of Banjaar Tola Kanha each have nine tented suites, designed with a light footprint to protect the sensitive riverine environment. Each of the contemporary suites features bamboo floors, canvas roof and walls, and glass doors leading onto a riverside veranda. Both camps have a spacious open-air dining area and library. Activities include twice-daily jungle drives with expert naturalists, guided nature walks, birdwatching and tiger viewing from elephant back in Kanha National Park. Banjaar Tola Kanha is one of four luxury camps operated by &Beyond in Madhya Pradesh – the others are located near Bandhavgarh, Panna and Pench National Parks.
andbeyond.com

Sipadan Kapalai Dive Resort
Sabah, Eastern Malaysia

Rising from the Celebes Sea on wooden stilts, like a rustic Atlantis, this stunning resort is based on a traditional Bajau fishing village. Consisting of 59 thatched chalets connected by boardwalks stretching across a shallow reef flat, Kapalai offers superb snorkelling and diving (including PADI courses). It's renowned for colourful macro life, such as nudibranchs and mandarin fish. Best of all, the diving mecca of Sipadan (see page 48) is just a 15-minute boat ride away.
sipadan-kapalai.com

Kings Lodge
Bandhavgarh National Park, India

Designed to blend into its surroundings, Kings Lodge has 18 rural-style cottages (some on stilts) with large verandahs overlooking sal forest and grassland. Added touches include an eco-sensitive waste disposal system and environmentally friendly swimming pool filtration. Located 10 minutes from Bandhavgarh National Park, the lodge offers jeep and elephant-back safaris, as well as cycling, wilderness walks and village visits and workshops outside the park.
kingslodge.in

Shergarh Tented Camp
Kanha National Park, India

With just six tents (under roofs of locally made clay tiles), Shergarh Tented Camp is a model of responsible tourism. As well as regenerating native forest on its home patch, the small, low-impact camp produces homegrown vegetables, runs effective waste recycling and water conservation schemes and works closely with villagers to provide employment opportunities and utilise local skills, such as carpentry. Activities outside Kanha National Park include cycle rides and forest walks.
shergarh.com

Australasia

Australia, New Zealand and New Guinea are ancient arks, carrying the descendants of Gondwana, the great supercontinent that began to break up and drift south some 200 million years ago. Isolated over millennia, plants like the endemic Araucaria pines of New Caledonia are relics of that prehistoric age, while monotremes, marsupials and ratites (flightless birds like the kiwi and cassowary) also have Gondwanan ancestry.

When exactly the ancestors of indigenous Australians arrived is still a matter of debate. Lower sea levels some 50,000 years ago gave rise to extended regions of dry land across much of Southeast Asia, which would certainly have brought Australia and New Guinea within range of humans paddling canoes.

Following their arrival, the Australian Aborigines evolved a rich diversity of cultures and customs which is still deeply entwined with the land and its wildlife. Clan members share a totemic ancestor who they believe created the landscape, leaving its creative essence at certain significant sites. It is these links to nature that the Aborigines emphasise when celebrating the creation period – or Dreaming. Walk westwards from Alice Springs, for example, and you follow the Arrernte spiritual track or 'songline' known as Caterpillar Dreaming – and looking at the crumpled hills of the MacDonnell Ranges you can clearly envisage a line of caterpillars marching across the landscape.

This rich cultural complexity is most vividly portrayed in the symbolic designs of Aboriginal art. With the arrival of Europeans, however, came an Austrian artist who would provide the first scientific illustrations of Australia's fascinating flora and fauna.

Ferdinand Bauer is now regarded as one of the greatest natural history artists that ever lived. Assigned to the 30-m sloop *Investigator*, under the command of Matthew Flinders, Bauer joined naturalist Robert Brown on a survey of the Australian coast.

Setting sail from England in July 1801, they reached Cape Leeuwin in south-western Australia five months later. Within a few days, the expedition had collected some 500 plant species, almost all of them new to science. Surveys of southern Australia, the Blue Mountains, Great Barrier Reef, Cape York, the Gulf of Carpentaria and Arnhem Land followed, with Bauer amassing a spectacular portfolio of drawings.

By the time the *Investigator* returned to Liverpool in 1805, her hold contained a collection of around 2,000 sketches. Among them were gloriously detailed studies of cycads and banksias, vivid portraits of reef fish and meticulous illustrations of wallabies and wombats. Perhaps most extraordinary of all, though, was an anatomical study of a duck-billed platypus – a creature that Joseph Banks, President of the Royal Society, had questioned the very existence of, until he saw Bauer's artwork (backed up by a preserved specimen). The treasure chest of Australia's unique plants and animals had been thrown open – and its contents continue to delight and inspire visitors today.

Birds in paradise | Coral cays of the Great Barrier Reef

Although Heron Island, one of the Capricorn Group of coral cays east of Gladstone, consists of little more than a single square kilometre of land, it supports a population of over 100,000 birds during peak breeding season. Every octopus bush and pisonia tree is host to numerous black noddy nests, while the ground is riddled with the burrows of wedge-tailed shearwaters. Many coral islands, which are either bare sand or covered with low-lying grasses, are inundated with thousands of ground-nesting birds during the summer. Around 10,000 pairs of sooty terns nest on Michaelmas Cay, 40 km northeast of Cairns, along with common noddy, crested tern and lesser crested tern. Other birds recorded on the island include brown booby, lesser frigatebird, silver gull, bridled tern, black-naped tern, reef heron and roseate tern.

Finke Gorge (left) in the MacDonnell Ranges near Alice Springs. Reef heron (above) taking flight from its roost on a Great Barrier Reef coral cay

Australasia | Wildlife highlights

In biogeographic terms Australasia includes Australia, New Guinea and the easternmost islands of Indonesia, but for the purposes of this book it extends to cover the wider region of Oceania, incorporating New Zealand and the islands of the southwest Pacific.

Natural zones

Vulture-shaped New Guinea squats just below the equator, its highlands smothered in tropical rainforest that's home to many endemic species, including birds of paradise and tree kangaroos. The island's reefs are part of the so-called Coral Triangle, an area of exceptional biodiversity

The tropics rub off on Australia's Top End where the Cape York forests and Kakadu wetlands support a wealth of flora and fauna. Nowhere is nature more exuberant in Australia, though, than the Great Barrier Reef – a vast ecosystem of coral reefs and islands covering an area of nearly 350,000 sq km.

The temperate forests and heathlands of southeastern Australia and Tasmania support some of the continent's iconic animals, such as koalas and wombats, while the deserts of the Australian Outback have their own unique cast of arid-adapted species, from lizards like the thorny devil and bearded dragon to rock wallabies, bandicoots and other marsupials.

Native kauri forests, sub-alpine grasslands, rugged coastlines and offshore islands provide refuges for New Zealand's endemic wildlife, which includes the kakapo, a flightless and nocturnal parrot. A relative of the rails and cranes the kagu is endemic to New Caledonia, while Lord Howe Island is an important nesting site for the Providence petrel – one of many species in Australasia vulnerable to predation by introduced rats and stoats.

Wildlife travel

With an impressive range of national parks and reserves, a strong conservation ethic and superb local guides, Australia and New Zealand make excellent wildlife travel destinations. Everywhere you go, you will find responsible tour operators, excellent facilities and a range of places to stay – from wilderness lodges in the Southern Alps to Aborigine-owned safari camps in the Outback.

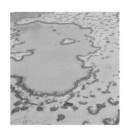

Heart Reef – just one small, perfectly formed part of Queensland's 2,300-km-long Great Barrier Reef

The planet's largest World Heritage Site, the Great Barrier Reef is home to around 360 species of hard coral, over 1,500 varieties of fish, up to 8,000 types of mollusc, six species of sea turtle, 17 species of sea snake, 30 species of cetacean and 22 species of seabird.

The tropics rub off on Australia's Top End where the Cape York forests and Kakadu wetlands support a wealth of flora and fauna. Nowhere is nature more exuberant in Australia, though, than the Great Barrier Reef

Wild ways | Two weeks exploring Western Australia

Days 1-2 Perth **Day 3** Drive Perth to Geraldton via the Pinnacles of Nambung National Park **Day 4** Drive to Kalbarri National Park, famed for its spring wildflowers **Day 5** Drive to Monkey Mia, Shark Bay – home of dugongs and bottlenose dolphins **Day 6** Monkey Mia **Day 7** Drive to Carnarvon **Day 8** Drive to Coral Bay – gateway to the Ningaloo Reef **Day 9** Snorkel with manta rays and whale sharks **Day 10** Drive to Karljini National Park **Days 11-12** Explore the wildlife of gorges and waterholes in Karljini **Day 13** Drive to Broome **Day 14** Venture further to either Cape Leveque or Purnululu National Park

🔁 Based on an itinerary from **Discover the World** (discover-the-world.co.uk), this trip would cost around £2,000 per person, including accommodation, car rental and some meals and activities. Other Australian specialists include **Bridge & Wickers** (bridgeandwickers.co.uk).

Wild city | Brisbane, Queensland

As dusk falls, thousands of bats take to the skies over Brisbane, but fear not – these are fruit-nibblers, not blood-suckers. There are flying fox roosts (or camps) throughout the city, but one of the largest and best known is on Indooroopilly Island, 6 km from Brisbane's Central Business District. Batty boat trips operated by the Wildlife Preservation Society of Queensland (wildlife.org. au) depart for the island from Mowbray Park on the banks of the Brisbane River. Each cruise lasts around four hours, during which time experts will help you identify the black flying fox (the largest species with wingspans of up to 1.2 m), grey-headed and little red flying fox. For a more intimate encounter with Brisbane's fruit bats (and other indigenous critters), Lone Pine Koala Sanctuary (koala. net) can be reached by boat or bus from the city centre. D'Aguilar National Park (epa.qld.gov.au), a mosaic of eucalypt woodland and subtropical rainforest is around 15 minutes' drive from downtown Brisbane.

Pick of the paddles | Top places to kayak on the wild side

With jaw-dropping scenery, abundant wildlife and a proven pedigree in paddling, New Zealand is hard to beat as an all-round sea kayaking destination. You'll find calm, warm-weather options (particularly in North Island), as well as white-knuckle paddles in more extreme locations like Fiordland. There is also an excellent range of trips available, from gentle, half-day outings to wilderness expeditions lasting a week or more.

North Island's watery playground, the Bay of Islands offers everything from game fishing and scuba diving to swimming with dolphins. It is also a perfect place for sea kayaking with some 150 islands to explore and a climate that won't make you shudder at the prospect of getting wet. Nip across Cook Strait and you have a choice of two kayaking hotspots at the northern tip of South Island. Base yourself at Picton or Havelock for forays into the labyrinth of bays and inlets comprising the Malborough Sounds and head to Marahau or Totaranui, gateways to Abel Tasman National Park with its sandy beaches and forest-fringed estuaries. Fiordland is a mecca to sea kayakers with slightly more challenging paddling in Milford and Doubtful Sounds, while Paterson Inlet on Stewart Island promises hardy souls close encounters with marine life and a chance to visit some of New Zealand's most ancient and intact forests. Remember to take a pair of waterproof binoculars with you – New Zealand has an extraordinary range of seabirds, including penguins and albatrosses.

Boasting a diverse range of coastal scenery, from coral islands and kelp-fringed estuaries to vast bays covered with seagrass meadows, Australia's prime kayaking locations include Queensland's Whitsunday Islands, Tasmania and the Ningaloo Reef.

If your idea of sea kayaking is to be able to occasionally flop overboard into warm, azure waters before drying off on a tropical island beach then make for Fiji. A paddle in paradise is a laid-back affair with plenty of time for other activities like snorkelling, visiting local villages and playing the castaway on remote desert islands. The Yasawas, a chain of 16 volcanic islands to the northwest of Viti Levu, is one of Fiji's most popular kayaking destinations. Allow at least a week for paddling between three or four of the islands.

Fiordland, New Zealand

Lush forests, sandy beaches and turquoise lagoons vie for attention along Abel Tasman's crinkle-cut coast – one of New Zealand's top kayaking locations

Making tracks | Australia

Numerous operators in Australia offer wildlife tours. **Ecotourism Australia** (ecotourism.org.au) lists tours, attractions and accommodation accredited under the ECO Certification Program. Overseas operators with expertise in Australian wildlife itineraries include **Bridge & Wickers** (bridgeandwickers.co.uk) and **Discover the World** (discover-the-world.co.uk). National carrier **Qantas** (qantas.com.au) has an extensive global network, while other airlines include **Emirates** (emirates.com) and **Air New Zealand** (airnewzealand.com). Australia has some superb ecolodges and safari-style camps, often run in close partnership with local Aboriginal groups (see pages 274–277). You will also find excellent value B&Bs, campsites and hostels. Motorhomes are another popular option. GMT+8 (West), GMT+10 (East) The southern half of the country is best from October to April, while the more tropical north is less humid and wet from May to September. The coolest months for the Outback are from April to September. Box jellyfish and the Irukandji jellyfish are present in tropical waters of northern Australia between October and June. Australian dollar (A$). australia.com **Parks Australia** (environment.gov.au/parks).

Kakadu National Park

★ Magpie goose, brolga, saltwater crocodile, sugar glider
Australia's wetland wonder, Kakadu undergoes dramatic seasonal changes, with six main phases identified by the indigenous Bininj-Mungguy.

From December to March, *Gudjewg* is the main wet season. Heavy rain creates widespread flooding, magpie geese disperse to nest in sedgelands, while reptiles and mammals seek refuge on islands or in trees. In April, windy conditions flatten lush swathes of spear grass in the so-called *Banggerreng* or 'Knock 'em down' season. Floodwaters recede and many birds and mammals have young. Humidity levels drop during *Yegge* from May to June. Early morning mists drift across the plains, while waterlilies carpet the billabongs. This is traditionally the time when the Bininj-Mungguy start burning the land to encourage new growth for grazing animals. Birds of prey patrol the fire lines as insects and small animals flee the flames. From June to August, *Wurrgeng* is a cool season when night-time temperatures can drop to 17°C. The floodplains continue to dry out, forcing huge flocks of waterbirds to crowd the shrinking billabongs. Hot dry weather occurs during the *Gurrung* from mid-August to mid-October. The arrival of white-breasted wood swallows heralds the pre-monsoon season of *Gunumeleng* (October to December) when thunderstorms begin to green the land and streams flow once more.

Directions 250 km east of Darwin, Kakadu can be reached by car or coach tour, although seasonal flooding may close some roads.
Getting around Guided tours are availabe (see below).
Seasons Park open year round. See above for seasonal variations.
Visitor centres Bowali Visitor Centre and Warradjan Aboriginal Cultural Centre, both open daily.
Things to do 4WD safaris, boat trips, Aboriginal rock art tours, scenic flights, bush walks, fishing. Self-guided trails, such as the 4-km Bubba Wetland Walk from the Muirella park camping area, are also possible. Tours are available from Animal Tracks Safari (animaltracks.com.au), Gagudju Adventure Tours (gagudju-dreaming.com) and Kakadu Culture Camp (kakaduculturecamp.com).
Places to stay Located 5 km from Bowali Visitor Centre, Jabiru has accommodation, including the Gagudju Crocodile Holiday Inn (gagudju-dreaming.com), Kakadu Lodge (auroraresorts.com.au) and Lakeview Park (lakeviewkakadu.com.au), plus facilities ranging from a service station and supermarket to travel agency and pharmacy. The Aurora Kakadu Resort (auroraresorts.com.au) is located in the South Alligator River area, while Gagudju Cooinda Lodge is situated near Yellow Waters Billabong. Camping is also possible.
Further information environment.gov.au/parks/kakadu

Brolgas in flight

Grus rubicunda
Kakadu National Park

Kakadu | Wildlife

Many of Kakadu's mammals are either shy or nocturnal: sugar gliders and northern quolls hide during the day in tree hollows, while bandicoots shelter in logs. Wallabies and wallaroos are more readily seen and dingoes can be heard howling at night. Flying foxes roost in large colonies in mangroves and paperbark forests, dispersing at night to feed on fruit and nectar. Kakadu supports over 280 bird species, the most conspicuous being dry-season flocks of magpie geese, whistling ducks and other waterbirds. Brolgas, jabirus and egrets pace the shallows, while comb-crested jacanas tiptoe across lily pads. Woodlands are home to kookaburras, lorikeets and honeyeaters. The national park's 117 reptile species range from saltwater and freshwater crocodiles to pythons, goannas and the bizarre frill-necked lizard.

Indian Ocean

Exmouth

Ningaloo Marine Park
see pages 50–51

Shark Bay
Dugong, bottlenose dolphin, turtles, seabirds

Geraldton

Perth

Margaret River
Albany

Rottnest Island
A popular day trip from Perth, Rottnest island is a refuge for the quokka, a small species of wallaby endemic to Western Australia. Rock parrots and red-capped robins can also be seen, along with various waterbirds on the island's beaches and wetlands.

Timor Sea

Darwin

Kakadu National Park
see left

Arnhem Land

Litchfield National Park
Woodland-covered plateau

Katherine

Gulf of Carpentaria

Cape York Peninsula

Daintree National Park
The rainforest-cloaked mountains of Daintree are a refuge for the rare Bennett's tree kangaroo. Easier to spot are the large saltwater crocodiles of the Daintree River, and Ulysses butterflies at Mossman Gorge (see page 269).

Kimberley Plateau

Kununurra

The Kimberley
From mangroves and tropical savannah to arid plateaux and rainforest-choked gorges, the Kimberley's diverse range of habitats is reflected in its wonderful array of birds. Visit the Broome Bird Observatory between September and April and you can witness up to a million migrant and resident waders on the mudflats of Roebuck Bay. Freshwater wetlands, such as Lake Eda, attract magpie geese and other waterfowl, while grass finches and parrots can be seen around waterholes in the Kununurra region. Other typical Outback wildlife in the Kimberley includes euro, rock wallaby, dingo and frill-necked lizard, while the coast is a nesting site for the green turtle.

Broome

Port Douglas
Cairns

Great Barrier Reef Marine Park see page 268

Coral Sea

Townsville

Eungella National Park
Platypus

Great Sandy Desert

MacDonnell Ranges

Alice Springs

West MacDonnell National Park
Stretching west from Alice Springs, this arid mountain range is steeped in Aboriginal Dreamtime lore. The long-distance Larapinta Trail (see page 268) links a series of dramatic gorges where relict cycad palms and rock wallabies can be found. Birdlife is prolific and includes cockatoos, finches and grasswrens.

Uluru

Uluru-Kata Tjuta National Park
Desert birds and reptiles

Simpson Desert

Fraser Island
Around 120 km in length, the world's largest sand island is covered in a mixture of healthland, eucalypt forest, subtropical rainforest and mangroves. The purest surviving strain of dingo can be found here, while humpback whales enter Hervey Bay between July and October.

Rockhampton

Hervey Bay

Great Victoria Desert

Lake Eyre

Brisbane

Kalgoorlie

Nullarbor Plain

Flinders Range

Darling

Great Dividing Range

Lamington National Park see page 268

Great Australian Bight

Port Augusta

Warrumbungle National Park
Echidna, koala, kangaroo

Fitzgerald River NP
Humpback and southern right whale, fur seal, sea lion, seabirds

Port Lincoln

Kangaroo Island
see page 268

Adelaide

Royal National Park
Lyrebird, wallaby

Newcastle

Sydney

Wollongong

Canberra

Coorong National Park
Lagoon breeding grounds for waterbirds

Murray

Tasmania
Almost a third of this rugged, forested island is protected in national parks and reserves. Cradle Mountain-Lake St Clair National Park is one of the best places in Australia to see mammals – Bennett's wallabies and pademelons can be seen during the day around the visitor centre, while Tasmanian devils, quolls and eastern pygmy possum emerge at dusk. Sit quietly at Echo Point and you might even spot a platypus. Asbestos Range, Freycinet and Maria Island National Parks also promise sightings of wallabies, wombats and possums, along with numerous coastal birds. For the best marine life, however, head to Bruny Island where albatrosses, gannets, sea eagles, penguins, dolphins and fur seals guarantee a riveting boat trip. The snorkelling trail at Tinderbox Marine Reserve trains your gaze on pipefish and leafy sea dragons. parks.tas.gov.au

Geelong

Melbourne

Wilsons Promontory

Bass Strait

Flinders Is

Phillip Island
A steady parade of little penguins (the world's smallest at just 33 cm in height) can be witnessed each dusk on Phillip Island as they head from the sea to their nesting burrows. Seal Rocks has a colony of several thousand fur seals, while short-tailed shearwaters nest at Cape Woolamai between October and May. penguins.org.au

Cradle Mt-Lake St Clair National Park

Tasmania

Hobart

Wet and wild – Kakadu National Park is located in Australia's tropical north where a cycle of wet and dry seasons causes wetlands like the Yellow Waters Billabong to contract and expand.
Far left: Red ochre cliffs of the Arnhem Land escarpment near Jim Jim Falls. Top left: Magpie geese breed in their thousands in Kakadu National Park. Left: Frill-necked lizard, saltwater crocodile and pink galah.

Koala

Echidna

Crimson rosella

Kangaroo Island

★ Fur seal, sea lion, koala, grey kangaroo, echidna, pelican

Australia's third largest island is a veritable ark of native wildlife. Not only is a third of its land protected in national parks and reserves, but there are no predatory dingoes or foxes to prey on its koalas, echidnas, bandicoots, possums and endemic subspecies of Tammar wallaby and western grey kangaroo. Flinders Chase National Park at the western end of the island is one of the best places to observe Kangaroo Island's abundant wildlife. Koalas are common in the manna gum trees near the park headquarters, while platypuses are sometimes seen at Rocky River Waterhole. The Admiral's Arch area is a popular haul-out for around 6,000 New Zealand fur seals, while Seal Bay has a colony of 600 Australian sea lions. Don a mask and snorkel for underwater encounters with these graceful marine mammals, and keep an eye out for well-camouflaged leafy sea dragons. During winter, southern right whales are sighted off the island, while seabirds like gannets, terns and shearwaters are regularly seen along the coast. Other top ticks include pelican, white-bellied sea eagle, wedge-tailed eagle, glossy black cockatoo, little penguin and Cape Barren goose.

Directions Around 100 km southwest of Adelaide, Kangaroo Island is reached by Sealink ferry (sealink.com.au) from Cape Jervis.
Getting around Self drive or join a guided tour.
Seasons Year round.
Visitor centres Kingscote Visitor Centre, open daily.
Things to do Guided tours, walks, kayaking, snorkelling, diving.
Places to stay Wide range, from luxury lodges to campsites.
Further information tourkangarooisland.com.au

Lamington National Park

★ Bowerbirds, fruit doves, parrots, noisy pitta, pademelons

Subtropical rainforest merges with rare fragments of moss-cloaked Antarctic beech forest in this highland reserve in southern Queensland. Although red-necked pademelons are often seen at dawn and dusk on forest paths and around campgrounds, birds are the main attraction at Lamington. You only have to visit the bird-feeding area at O'Reilly's Rainforest Retreat to get an idea of the diversity of species found here. King parrot, crimson rosella, rainbow lorikeet, Australian brush-turkey and regent bowerbird are easily seen, but you will have to work harder – listening for calls – to identify more elusive forest species, such as Albert's lyrebird, eastern whipbird, green catbird and paradise riflebird. Night walks in the forest might reveal the eyeshine of the well-camouflaged marbled frogmouth and, if you're extremely lucky, you could see a greater glider take flight, its 'gliding membranes' stretched taut between wrist and ankle.

Directions Two-hour drive south of Brisbane.
Getting around Easily accessible by road.
Seasons Year round.
Things to do Guided tours, hiking, birdwatching.
Places to stay Accommodation at O'Reilly's Rainforest Retreat (oreillys.com.au) ranges from simple Garden View rooms to luxurious Canopy Suites. Facilities include a cosy lounge and library, plunge pool, spa and a Discovery program featuring 4WD tours, rainforest hikes, tree-top walkway, glow worm walks, evening spotlighting and zip-lining.
Further information derm.qld.gov.au/parks/lamington/index

Walkabout | Three of the best wildlife hikes in the Outback

Larapinta Trail West MacDonnell Ranges, 223 km from Alice Springs to Mt Sonder. Takes 14 days, although shorter hikes and day walks are possible. Challenging wilderness hiking (with or without a guide), desert wildlife, Aboriginal bushlore and superb scenery. Best from April to October.
Tabletop Track Litchfield National Park, 39-km, three- to five-day trail through woodlands to creeks and waterfalls. Usually closed at the end of September for the wet season.
Giles Track Watarrka National Park, Kings Canyon to Kathleen Springs; two days in spectacular canyon scenery.

Great Barrier Reef | Logistics

A chain of 2,600 reefs and 300 coral cays stretching over 2,300 km along the Queensland coast, the Great Barrier Reef can be reached by helicopter, plane or boat from several towns, including Cairns, Townsville, Port Douglas and Airlie Beach. Day trips are available to coral cays or floating pontoons on the outer reef, while accommodation is available on various islands. Open daily, **Reef HQ** (reefhq.com.au) in Townsville provides an excellent introduction to this spectacularly diverse ecosystem. Nesting season for sea turtles is November to February, while corals spawn after the full moon in November. Ecocertified operators listed by the **Great Barrier Reef Marine Park Authority** (gbrmpa.gov.au) include: Adrenalin Dive (adrenalindive.com.au), Big Cat Green Island Reef Cruises (greenisland.com.au), Cairns Dive Centre (cairnsdive.com.au), Coral Princess Cruises (coralprincess.com.au), Deep Sea Divers Den (diversden.com.au), Fantasea Cruises (fantasea.com.au), Great Adventures Cruises (greatadventures.com.au), Lady Elliot Island Eco Retreat (ladyelliot.com.au), Lizard Island Resort (lizardisland.com.au), Magnetic Island Sea Kayaks (seakayak.com.au/), Mike Ball Dive Expeditions (mikeball.com), Pro Dive Cairns (prodivecairns.com), Quicksilver (quicksilver-cruises.com) and Wavelength (wavelength.com.au).

① Get out to the GBR
With their stunning reefs, bird-filled forests and turtle-nesting beaches, coral cays like Heron Island make a superb wildlife holiday base. **heronisland.com**

② Watch humpbacks
Hervey Bay Whale Watch runs trips to see humpback whales between mid-July and early November. **herveybaywhalewatch. com.au**

③ Discover the rainforest
Walks in Mossman Gorge with Aboriginal guides shine a light on the wildlife and cultural heritage of the Daintree rainforest. **yalanji.com.au**

④ See what lies beneath
Numerous operators offer diving and snorkelling trips on the Great Barrier Reef – home to over 2,000 species of fish, including the Napolean wrasse.

⑤ Explore the far north
Tropical Queensland at its wildest and most lush, Cape York Peninsula supports abundant rainforest birds, including the cassowary. **kirrama.com.au**

①

②

③

④

⑤

Australasia | New Zealand

Cape Reinga
Seabirds, migratory waders in March

Bay of Islands
Boat trips to see whales, dolphins, seals, penguins; swimming with dolphins

Waipoua Forest
Enormous kauri trees erupt through tree ferns like arboreal exclamation marks in this ancient and mysterious forest, deeply rooted in Aboriginal lore. On guided night walks, you'll hear the mournful calls of morepork owls and shrill cries of kiwis, while giant carnivorous land snails prowl the boardwalks.
footprintswaipoua.com

Coromandel Peninsula
Wading birds on estuaries, kiwis in native forest

Auckland

Hamilton

Rotorua

Abel Tasman National Park
One of New Zealand's 14 national parks, Abel Tasman's beautiful coast is popular with sea kayakers (see page 263). Bellbirds and tui are common in the forests, while the pukeko (or swamp hen) is found near estuaries. Tonga Island Marine Reserve has a seal colony and is a good spot for snorkelling.
doc.govt.nz

Tasman Sea

North Island

Mt Ruapehu

Napier

Cape Kidnappers
World's largest, most accessible mainland gannet colony

Palmerston North

Nelson

Blenheim

Wellington

Pacific Ocean

South Island

Greymouth

Kaikoura
One of the world's best marine wildlife destinations, Kaikoura is famed for its resident population of sperm whales feeding relatively close offshore on the edge of the continental shelf. On a typical boat trip you will also see large pods of dusky dolphin, New Zealand fur seal and, depending on the season, migratory humpback, pilot, blue and southern right whales. Orca, Hector's dolphin and up to 13 species of albatross are also found here.
whalewatch.co.nz, albatrossencounter.co.nz

Aoraki (Mt Cook)

Southern Alps

Fiordland National Park
Crested penguin, kiwi, takahe

Christchurch

Arthur's Pass National Park
Great spotted kiwi, kea

Timaru

Queenstown

Invercargill

Dunedin

Catlins Coast
Fur seal, sea lion, Hector's dolphin, sooty shearwater

Otago Peninsula
The only mainland breeding albatross colony in the southern hemisphere, the royal albatrosses at Taiaroa Head are a highlight of a visit to the Otago Peninsula. An observatory offers excellent views of the courtship and nesting behaviour of these magnificent birds, which can have a wingspan of up to 3 m. Elm Wildlife Tours (elmwildlifetours.co.nz) run small-group trips in search of the Otago's other wildlife, which includes the rare yellow-eyed penguin, little (blue) penguin, Hooker's sea lion, New Zealand fur seal, Stewart Island shag and a wide variety of waders and shorebirds.
albatross.org.nz

Stewart Island
Some of New Zealand's rarest native birds find sanctuary on Stewart Island. Ruggedy Range offers hiking, kayaking and birdwatching tours, with a chance to spot South Island saddleback, Stewart Island robin, kaka, tui and yellowhead in the pristine podocarp forest of Ulva Island; sooty shearwater and blue penguin at Ackers Point, albatrosses in Paterson Inlet and Stewart Island Tokoeka – a variety of kiwi – at Mason Bay.
ruggedyrange.com

Albatross tug-of-war – Kaikoura attracts New Zealand's largest concentration and variety of seabirds, including 13 species of albatross, 14 varieties of petrel and seven types of shearwater. Among the 'great albatrosses' are wandering, Antipodean, Gibson's, northern royal and southern royal. The smaller albatrosses – or mollymawks – include the black-browed, shown here fighting for scraps from fishing boats. Top left: Sperm whale diving. Left: kelp gulls, dusky dolphin, New Zealand fur seal.

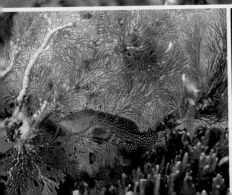

Show time – a male Raggiana bird of paradise displays to a prospective mate in Papua New Guinea's Varirata National Park. Far left: Victoria crowned pigeon. Top left: Crocodile fish. Left: Papua New Guinea's coral reefs are some of the most biodiverse and pristine in the world. Spotted cuscus photographed at night in lowland rainforest. Country Tours (countrytours.com.pg) organise birdwatching trips in Papua New Guinea, while diving and snorkelling can be arranged at Kabaira Beach Hideaway (kabairabeachhideaway. com). For further information, contact Papua New Guinea Tourism (pngtourism.org.pg).

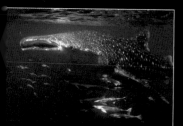

Sal Salis
**Cape Range National Park,
Western Australia**

A little bit of bush luxury, this exclusive, wilderness dune camp has nine spacious safari tents just metres from the Ningaloo shore, renowned for its annual gathering of whale sharks (see page 50). Designed to create a minimal environmental footprint on the coastal scrub of Cape Range National Park, Sal Salis uses solar-generated power, composting toilets, native herb soaps and ecologically sound shampoo. Each tent has uninterrupted views across the Indian Ocean. Hawksbill, green and loggerhead turtles are seen daily in front of the camp, while snorkellers only have to drift a few metres offshore to find huge staghorn coral formations, sponge gardens and sea anemones squirming with clownfish.

The camp's sea kayaks provide easy access to the fringing Ningaloo Reef; boat trips in search of whale sharks, manta rays, humpback whales and dolphins are also available. A short walk from the camp, the middens and rock shelters of Mandu Mandu Gorge provide a fascinating glimpse into the region's archaeology. Guided walks or cruises can also be taken along Yardie Creek, where the gorge walls are inhabited by black-footed rock wallabies. Wildlife frequently seen around camp, meanwhile, includes red kangaroo, wallaroo, Gould's goanna and a variety of birds, from emus to reef herons. **salsalis.com**

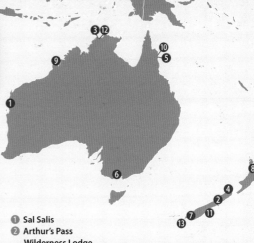

Arthur's Pass Wilderness Lodge, Southern Alps, South Island, New Zealand

Tucked into beech forest on its own 3,000-ha nature reserve and Merino sheep farm, this idyllic lodge has 20 mountain view rooms and four luxurious lodges. A programme of guided nature walks, canoeing and stargazing is available, as well as farm activities, such as sheep mustering. Arthur's Pass National Park is nearby, while a sister property on Lake Moeraki, Fiordland, is well placed for quests in search of crested penguins.
wildernesslodge.co.nz

Bamurru Plains Near Kakadu National Park, Northern Territory

Located on the Mary River floodplains just to the west of Kakadu National Park, this luxurious bush camp has nine supremely comfortable safari-style suites built on raised platforms overlooking savannah teeming with magpie geese – one of 236 bird species found here. As well as 4WD safaris and river cruises (April to October), Bamburru offers airboat tours and scenic helicopter flights, plus visits to Aboriginal rock art sites.
bamurruplains.com

1. Sal Salis
2. Arthur's Pass Wilderness Lodge
3. Bamurru Plains
4. The Resurgence
5. Thala Beach Lodge
6. Great Ocean Ecolodge
7. Fiordland Lodge
8. Manawa Ridge
9. Kooljaman at Cape Leveque
10. Daintree Ecolodge
11. Kaimata Retreat
12. Wildman Wilderness Lodge
13. Stewart Island Lodge

The Resurgence, Nelson, North Island, New Zealand

A luxury ecolodge in the Riwaka Valley, this homely property nestles in 20 ha of bush, where 5 km of walking trails provide an ideal opportunity for spotting birds such as kea, morepork and fantail. The owners of the lodge grow their own organic vegetables and plant native trees to restore local habitat. Sea kayaking, day hikes and sailing are available at nearby Abel Tasman National Park, while Kahurangi National Park offers mountain and forest walks.
resurgence.co.nz

Thala Beach Lodge Port Douglas, Queensland

For total immersion in the Queensland tropics, this stunning lodge enjoys a triple whammy of World Heritage-listed rainforest, Great Barrier Reef and sandy beaches. Relaxing on the verandah of your bungalow, you can watch butterflies, sugargliders and birds, while nearby Port Douglas is the stepping-off point for trips to the Great Barrier Reef. Thala Beach Lodge has been awarded the highest ecotourism accreditation for its sustainability and contribution to conservation.
thalabeach.com.au

Great Ocean Ecolodge Apollo Bay, Victoria

With all profits reinvested into wildlife conservation, this exemplary ecolodge is entirely solar powered and ecologically responsible. Located just off the Great Ocean Road and Great Ocean Walk, the five-room guesthouse has lawns grazed by wild kangaroos. During your visit, naturalists will lead you on twilight bush walks in search of koalas and other indigenous wildlife. You will also gain an insight into the work of the Cape Otway Centre for Conservation Ecology.
greatoceanecolodge.com

Fiordland Lodge, Te Anau, South Island, New Zealand

An excellent base for exploring the mountains, forests and lakes of Fiordland National Park, this exclusive 10-room lodge (with an additional two self-contained loft-style cabins) organises privately guided hiking, birdwatching and fishing trips, as well as cruises on Milford Sound and visits to the Glowworm Caves. There are wonderful views of Lake Te Anau from the lodge's timber-framed lounge with its cosy open fire and soaring log trusses. The cuisine is also superb.
fiordlandlodge.co.nz

Manawa Ridge
Coromandel Peninsula, North Island,
New Zealand

Handmade by owners Carla and Willem van de Veen using recycled timbers and energy efficient mud-brick and straw-bale walls, Manawa Ridge is located the historic gold-mining town of Waihi and has a solid, organic feel. Part of a 100-ha farm, the three-suite property enjoys panoramic views across the forests and hill country of the Coromandel Peninsula and beyond towards the Pacific coast. Highlights of this beautiful region include kayaking in Tairua's sheltered harbour, shell-seeking along Ocean Beach and gently poaching yourself at Hot Water Beach. During low tide, superheated water bubbles up through the sand at one end of this crescent-shaped bay – simply scoop up a dam, temper with a little seawater and you have an instant geothermal spa pool. Guided ecotours with Kiwi Dundee Adventures (kiwidundee.co.nz) are also highly recommended. Accompanied by expert local naturalists, you'll track down some of New Zealand's indigenous forest birds, poke around in old gold mineshafts twinkling with glow worms, and learn about the different uses pioneer settlers found for plants – dried manuku leaves for tea, crushed komeroa leaves for soap and kauri trunks for ships' masts.
manawaridge.co.nz

Kooljaman at Cape Leveque, Dampier Peninsula, Western Australia

Located 220 km north of Broome, this Aboriginal-owned wilderness camp has 14 large, beachfront safari tents, two bush lodges, plus a choice of tin-roof cabins and beach shelters. Local guides teach traditional fishing and mudcrabbing methods and show you how to make spears and forage for bush tucker; there's also snorkelling and glass-bottom boating. Humpback whales can be seen offshore from mid-July to October.
kooljaman.com.au

Daintree Ecolodge Queensland

With just 15 treehouses (some with private jacuzzis) carefully slipped into the ancient Daintree rainforest of northern Queensland, this award-winning ecolodge combines environmental sensitivity with ultimate pampering. Its spa is world-renowned, but there are plenty of activities available, from Aboriginal-guided rainforest walks, river cruises, sea kayaking and mountain biking to ziplining through the canopy with views over Cape Tribulation.
daintree-ecolodge.com.au

Kaimata Retreat, Dunedin, South Island, New Zealand

Perched above Papanui Inlet on the Otago Peninsula, this cosy, lodge-style getaway has just three rooms – all with views across the bay where seals and shorebirds can be observed. Kaimata also offers expert-guided birdwatching and wildlife photography tours, as well as three-hour trips with a local farmer who manages his land to benefit pupping sea lions and nesting yellow-eyed and little blue penguins (breeding from September to March).
kaimatanz.com

Wildman Wilderness Lodge Near Kakadu National Park, Northern Territory

Comprising 10 cabins and 15 chic safari tents built on raised decks to preserve the environment of the Mary River floodplains, Wildman provides a stylish base from which to explore Kakadu. Local Aboriginal guides conduct birdwatching and crocodile-spotting billabong tours, while 4WD safaris explore paper bark forests, and pandanus swamps in search of sea eagles, brolga and magpie geese.
wildmanwildernesslodge. com.au

Ancient podocarp forest, Ulva Island (Paterson Inlet, Stewart Island, New Zealand)

Stewart Island Lodge New Zealand

A friendly B&B deep in bush that's full of native birds, Stewart Island Lodge has views across Halfmoon Bay and makes a superb base for exploring this southern outpost. Birdwatchers will find kakas, wekas, tuis and other avian rarities in the moss-clad splendour of Ulva Island's pristine forests, while midnight expeditions to Ocean Beach are often rewarded with a glimpse of Stewart Island kiwis foraging along the strandline. Offshore, albatrosses and dolphins can all be seen.
stewartislandlodge.co.nz

Polar regions

A wilderness the size of a continent, frozen yet miraculously alive with seabirds, seals and whales, Antarctica tops the wishlist of many wildlife travellers.

There are few things more quietly exhilarating than crouching next to a colony of inquisitive, trusting penguins. It might be a few hundred gentoos on a sandy beach in the Falkland Islands, a couple of thousand chinstraps in an ice-wreathed bay on the Antarctic Peninsula or 250,000 king penguins on Salisbury Plain, South Georgia. The air surrounding you reverberates to the constant hubbub of penguin babble, but most human visitors respond with nothing but silent wonder.

It's a natural reaction in a place where the sheer scale of the scenery and super-abundance of wildlife instils a sense of reverence to all who venture there. Embarking on an expedition voyage to Antarctica or sub-Antarctic islands like South Georgia, you are not only following in the wake of famous polar explorers like Scott and Shackleton, but also bearing the responsibility of visiting one of the last remaining wildernesses on earth.

Responsible travellers choose Antarctic cruises that are small-scale and conducted by members of the International Association of Antarctica Tour Operators (iaato.org) which abide by a stringent code of conduct to minimize environmental impact.

The same applies to the Arctic, where the Association of Arctic Expedition Cruise Operators (aeco.no) ensures that its members are as gentle on the environment as possible.

Although the Arctic has a similar animal magnetism as Antarctica (who wouldn't want to see a polar bear prowling the pack ice, a quivering mass of walrus or a pod of beluga coursing through frigid seas), it differs from the south in having a strong, deeply rooted human presence. Experiencing the Arctic in the company of an Inuit guide, for example, you will not only learn about indigenous culture, but develop a strong sense of respect for these hardy, versatile people and their traditional bonds to land, ice, sea and wildlife.

Cool kayaking | Where to paddle at the Poles

Travelling by sea kayak in the High Arctic enables you to experience one of the world's least visited places and explore a truly wild frontier with minimum impact on the environment. During the brief Arctic summer, when the sun never sets and temperatures creep to 18°C, the fiordland of northern Ellesmere Island frees itself of enough ice to allow access to kayakers. Paddling between icebergs with a backdrop of high peaks and tidewater glaciers, this extraordinary 'top-of-the-world' experience is embellished by sightings of walrus, muskox and narwhal, as well as fascinating insights into Inuit culture and prehistory. You can also paddle in Antarctica. Some cruises to the great white continent now include sea kayaking as an exciting optional extra.

Blue icebergs

Greenland

Emperor penguin *Aptenodytes forsteri*	**King penguin** *Aptenodytes patagonicus*	**Gentoo penguin** *Pygoscelis papua*	**Adélie penguin** *Pygoscelis adeliae*	**Chinstrap penguin** *Pygoscelis antarcticus*	**Macaroni penguin** *Eudyptes chrysolophus*	**Rockhopper penguin** *Eudyptes chrysocome*

Scale markings: 110 cm, 100 cm, 90 cm, 80 cm, 70 cm, 60 cm, 50 cm, 40 cm, 30 cm, 20 cm, 10 cm

On a continent covered in ice up to 4,200 m in depth, it's not surprising that most life clings to the edge of Antarctica. What is surprising, though, are the huge numbers of seabirds, seals and whales that crowd its shores. Unlike the Arctic (an ocean surrounded by continents), the Antarctic is encircled by sea (the Southern Ocean) where winds and currents create ideal conditions for the proliferation of plankton. It is this cornerstone of the Antarctic food web that sustains everything from krill-feeding humpback whales to penguin-hunting leopard seals.

Natural zones

Only in summer when Antarctica lifts her snowy skirts slightly to reveal a few rocky shores and headlands are the penguins, petrels and elephant seals able to claim their breeding grounds – with the notable exception of the emperor penguin which breeds on sea ice. Any islands within, or close to, the Antarctic Convergence (where warm surface currents mix with colder waters moving north from Antarctica) are also prime territory for seabird and seal colonies. Indeed, South Georgia and Macquarie Island are probably two of the most wildlife-rich locations anywhere on earth.

The Arctic food chain is also partly founded on plankton, but it is sustained not by the turbulent mixing of warm and cold waters, but by the spring melting of pack ice. This leaves behind a nutrient-rich layer of fresh water on the sea's surface, which, with lengthening days of sunlight, triggers a bloom of phytoplankton. On land, partial thawing of the permafrost creates pools in which mosquitoes can breed, providing a valuable source of food for migratory birds like buntings, larks, pharalopes and plovers. The tundra also unleashes a flush of plant growth, grazed by millions of geese, while saxifrages and other alpine species seize the brief summer to flower and set seed. Arctic fox, wolf and polar bear roam tundra, shore and sea ice; cliffs host enormous colonies of auks, fulmars, guillemots, kittiwakes and puffins, while beluga, narwhal and bowhead whales follow leads in the pack ice to reach seasonal feeding and breeding grounds.

Penguin ID parade

Only seven of the world's 17 (some experts claim there are 18) species of penguin are truly Antarctic. The Magellanic penguin, for example, is restricted to Patagonia and the Falkland Islands, while the Galápagos penguin has the distinction of being the only member of the family to stray into the northern hemisphere. Highly sociable birds, penguins form huge breeding colonies in Antarctica and the sub-Antarctic islands, sometimes climbing steep cliffs or walking for days across pack ice to reach their rookeries.

Wildlife travel

Antarctica is only accessible during the austral summer months of November to March, when temperatures range from -5°C to 5°C. Ships depart from Ushuaia, Christchurch, Hobart and Cape Town. There are three main Antarctic voyage routes: crossing Drake Passage to the South Shetland Islands and Antarctic Peninsula; looping east via the Falklands and South Georgia to the Weddell Sea and Antarctic Peninsula, or heading south to New Zealand's sub-Antarctic Islands and the Ross Sea. You can also fly from Punta Arenas direct to the interior of Antarctica where a camp at Patriot Hills provides a staging post for a further flight to the South Pole.

Arctic regions are best visited between June and September when sea ice retreats sufficiently to allow access to ships exploring the coasts of Svalbard, Greenland and the Canadian Arctic. Icebreaker voyages also bring the North Pole within reach, while those with the time (and money) can embark on two-month circumnavigations of the Arctic Ocean. Expedition voyages, however, are not the only ways to explore the region. Land-based trips in Svalbard and Greenland can be equally rewarding. Sea kayaking trips along the coast of Baffin Island are also available, while Hudson Bay plays host to polar bears in October and November.

Wild ways | Three weeks exploring Antarctica

Day 1 Overnight Ushuaia **Day 2** Board ship and sail along Beagle Channel **Day 3** Sail east towards the Falkland Islands **Days 4-5** Falkland Islands **Days 6-8** At sea sailing towards South Georgia **Days 9-11** Exploring South Georgia **Day 12** At sea sailing towards South Orkney Islands **Day 13** South Orkney Islands or Elephant Island **Day 14** At sea sailing south to Antarctica **Days 15-17** Antarctic Peninsula **Days 18-19** Sailing north across Drake Passage **Day 20** Disembark in Ushuaia

⌕ Based on an itinerary from **Exodus** (exodus.co.uk) in partnership with **Quark Expeditions** (quarkexpeditions.com), this trip would cost from around £6,130 per person sharing a triple cabin on the *Vavilov* or *Ioffe*, excluding international flights to Ushuaia. Other major operators offering polar voyages include **Discover the World** (discover-the-world.co.uk) and **Oceans Worldwide** (oceansworldwide.co.uk).

Porpoising gentoo penguins

Pygoscelis papua
Sea Lion Island, Falklands

Upright, slow and awkward on land, penguins are transformed into fast, graceful swimmers the moment they hit the water. Their speed and agility enables them to pursue fish and squid.

Polar regions | Voyages

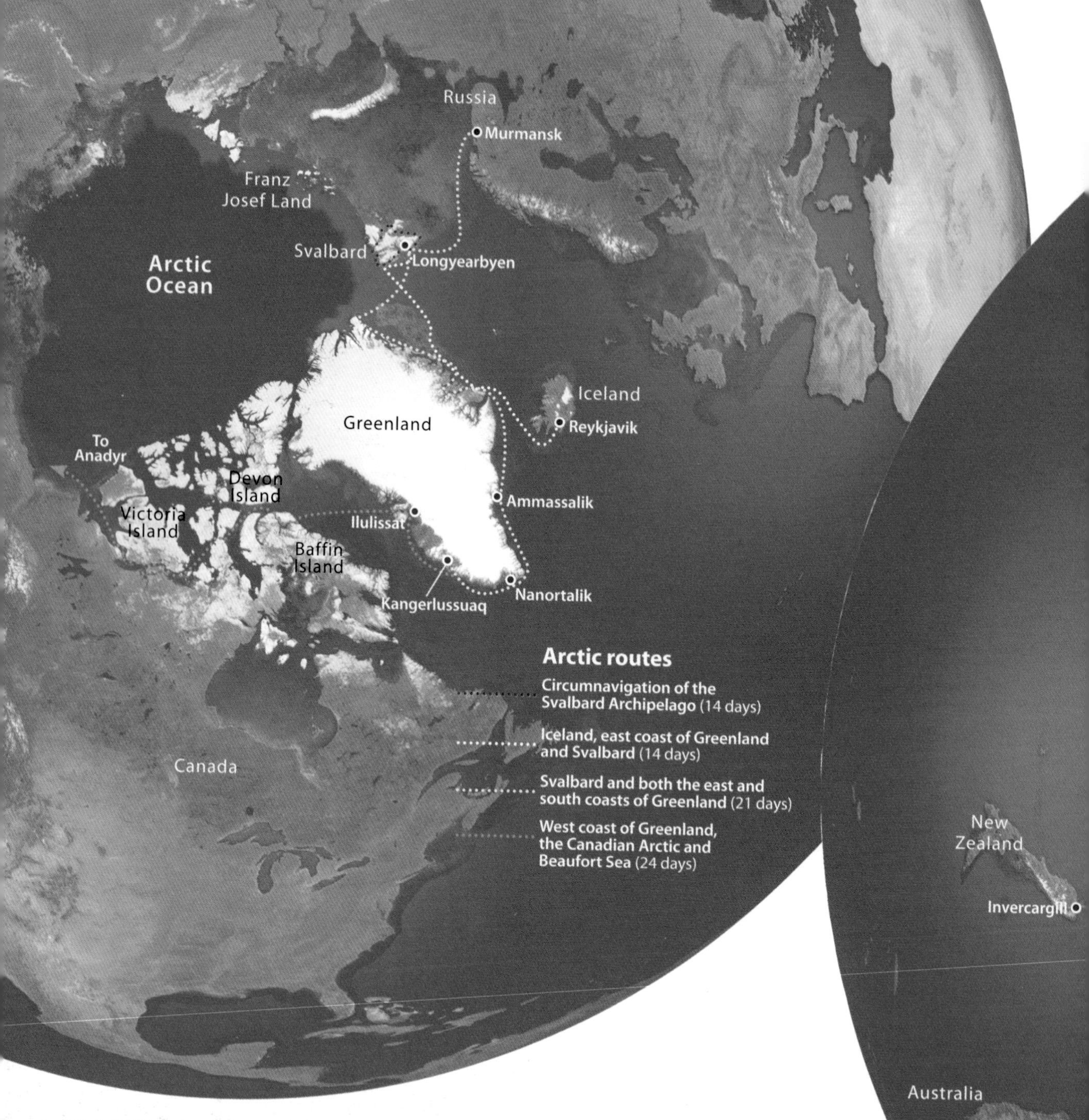

Russia

Murmansk

Franz
Josef Land

Svalbard

Longyearbyen

**Arctic
Ocean**

Iceland

Reykjavik

Greenland

To
Anadyr

Devon
Island

Ammassalik

Victoria
Island

Ilulissat

Baffin
Island

Kangerlussuaq

Nanortalik

Arctic routes

Circumnavigation of the
Svalbard Archipelago (14 days)

Iceland, east coast of Greenland
and Svalbard (14 days)

Svalbard and both the east and
south coasts of Greenland (21 days)

West coast of Greenland,
the Canadian Arctic and
Beaufort Sea (24 days)

Canada

New
Zealand

Invercargill

Australia

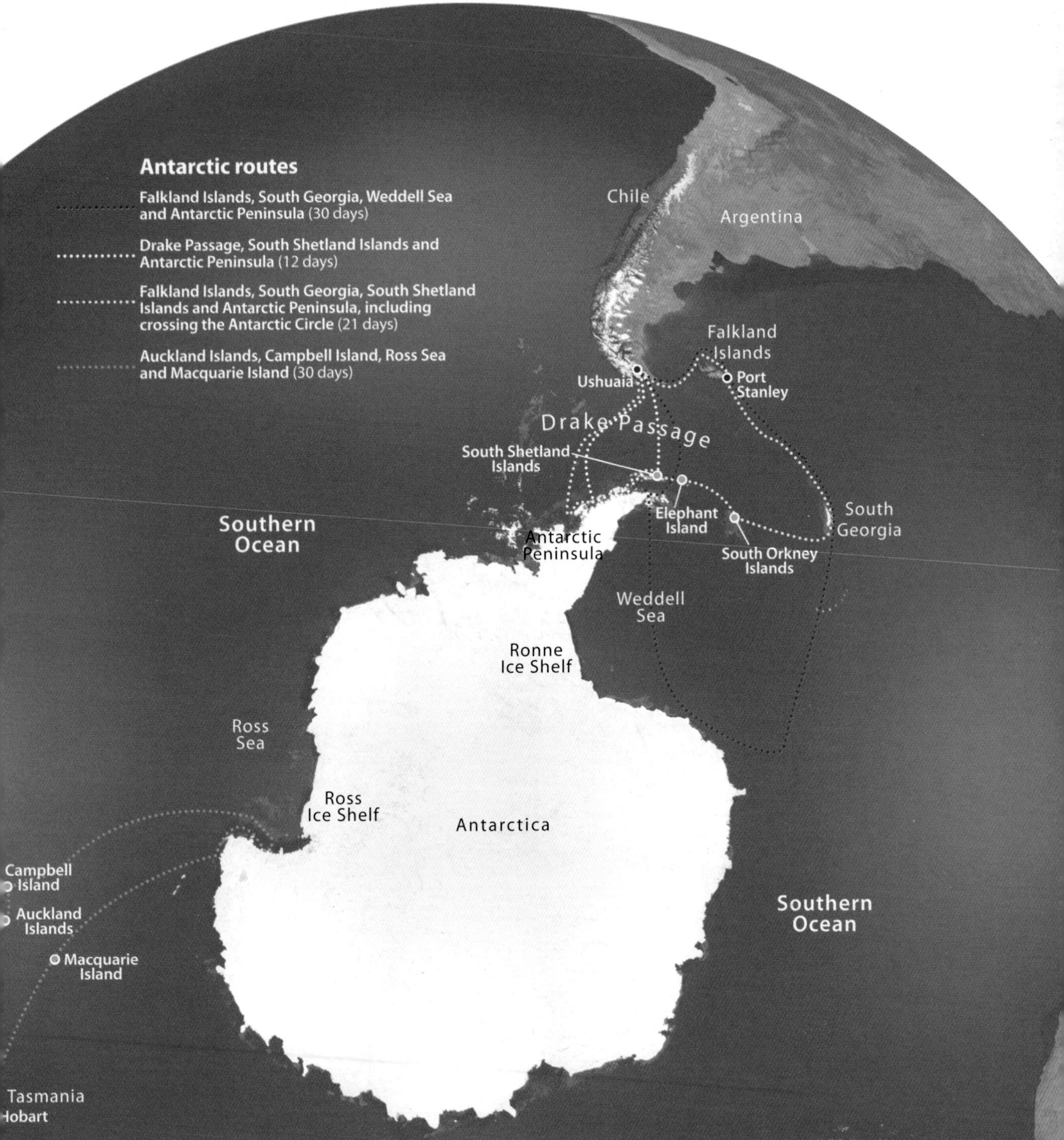

Antarctic routes

········· Falkland Islands, South Georgia, Weddell Sea
and Antarctic Peninsula (30 days)

·········· Drake Passage, South Shetland Islands and
Antarctic Peninsula (12 days)

·········· Falkland Islands, South Georgia, South Shetland
Islands and Antarctic Peninsula, including
crossing the Antarctic Circle (21 days)

·········· Auckland Islands, Campbell Island, Ross Sea
and Macquarie Island (30 days)

Chile

Argentina

Falkland
Islands

Ushuaia   ○ Port
Stanley

Drake Passage

South Shetland
Islands

Elephant
Island

South
Georgia

South Orkney
Islands

Southern
Ocean

Antarctic
Peninsula

Weddell
Sea

Ronne
Ice Shelf

Ross
Sea

Ross
Ice Shelf

Antarctica

Campbell
Island

Auckland
Islands

Macquarie
Island

Southern
Ocean

Tasmania
Hobart

Polar regions | Arctic

Svalbard | Kingdom of the ice bear

Longyearbyen on the island of Spitsbergen is the departure point for voyages in the breathtaking Svalbard archipelago (see also pages 120-121). Riven by deep fjords, with huge glaciers squatting beneath snow-capped peaks, this Arctic gem is the realm of polar bear, walrus, Svalbard reindeer, Arctic fox and prolific birdlife.

The peak time for polar bear watching is late July to early August when pack ice has retreated enough to allow ships access to prime bear habitat along the northern and eastern coasts. Seabird breeding activity, however, reaches its peak by late June or early July.

Key wildlife sites

Spitsbergen's southernmost fjord, **Horsund** is ringed by jagged peaks, including 1,431-m Hornsundtind. Ice shelves at the foot of several glaciers here are good places to look for seals and polar bears. Further north along Spitsbergen's west coast, **Bellsund** splits into two fjords and has dramatic seabird cliffs. Just beyond the entrance to Isfjorden, the island of **Prins Karls Forland** is a favoured haul-out for walrus. In **Kongsfjorden**, Ny Alesund research centre has nesting pink-footed geese and Arctic terns, while the cliffs above Fjortende Julibukta bay in nearby **Krossfjorden** are teeming with fulmars, kittiwakes and Brünnich's guillemots, with pink-footed geese nesting on the slopes below. Arctic foxes also den in this area. **Liefdefjorden**, near the tip of Spitsbergen, has a spectacular tidewater glacier. Ice shelves and islets in the area are popular hunting grounds for polar bears. The island of **Nordaustlandet** – second largest in Svalbard – is also prime territory for polar bears, while smaller **Lagoya** has high concentrations of walrus. Sailing into Hinlopen Strait between Spitsbergen and Nordaustlandet brings the guillemot colony at **Alkefjellet** within reach. If ice conditions permit, you may also be able to reach the islands of **Barentsoya** and **Edgeoya**, deep in the heart of ice bear territory.

Take care not to disturb ground-nesting birds in Svalbard. Geese are particularly prone to abandoning their nests, leaving clutches vulnerable to predation from Arctic foxes and glaucous gulls.

Polar bear Around 3,000, including Franz Josef. Most often seen in northern and eastern parts of Svalbard, but can be found anywhere that seals are hauled out on sea ice.
Arctic fox Numbers unknown, but widespread in Svalbard, often seen near bird cliffs feeding on eggs and chicks.
Svalbard reindeer Estimated at 10,000. Often seen beneath seabird cliffs, feeding on vegetation. Common in Reindalen Valley and on the islands of Edgeoya and Barentsoya.
Walrus Around 2,500. Groups often encountered hauled out on pebbly beaches or ice floes.
Ringed seal Approximately 100,000. Occasionally seen on drift ice in fjords, but generally move north to the permanent pack ice.
Bearded seal Several thousand. Individuals often spotted on floating ice in fjords.
Harbour seal Around 1,000. Found mainly around Prins Karls Forland.
Bowhead whale Extremely rare, numbers unknown. The bowhead is the only species of baleen whale to remain in Arctic waters year round.
Beluga Numbers unknown. Frequently seen in coastal areas, often near glaciers.
Narwhal Numbers unknown. Most often spotted in the fjords of Nordaustlandet and in the strait of Hinlopenstretet.
Other cetaceans sighted in Svalbard waters include blue, fin, humpback, minke, sperm, northern bottlenose and pilot whales, plus orca and white-beaked dolphin.

Pink-footed goose Over 50,000. Nests in tundra areas throughout Spitsbergen.
Barnacle goose Around 30,000. Breeds on islands along the west coast of Spitsbergen and in the Tusenoyane islands.
Brent goose Estimated at 7,500 (including East Greenland). Most of the Svalbard population of brent geese breeds on the islands of Tusenoyane.
Common eider 17,000 pairs. Nests throughout Svalbard.
Red-throated diver Nests on tundra lakes and ponds.
Northern fulmar Common companion on expedition voyages. Nests on cliffs throughout the archipelago.
Common & Brünnich's guillemot Several million pairs in around 150 breeding colonies. Nests on sea cliffs in southeastern Spitsbergen, Hopen and Bjornoya.
Little auk Several million pairs in over 200 colonies. Widespread in Svalbard.
Other seabirds include Arctic skua, Arctic tern, Atlantic puffin, black-legged kittiwake, glaucous gull and Ivory gull; migrant waders include dunlin, grey phalarope, purple sandpiper, ringed plover and sanderling. Migratory snow buntings are the only songbirds found on Svalbard. The Svalbard rock ptarmigan is present year round.

Ice patrol – polar bears use their keen sense of smell to detect seals, including pups hidden beneath the snow. Left: Little auks nest in large, noisy seacliff colonies in Svalbard where Arctic foxes are continually on the prowl for eggs and chicks. Arctic terns also breed in the archipelago, vigorously defending their nests by dive-bombing intruders – including humans that unwittingly wander too close.

Falkland Islands & South Georgia
See pages 288 to 291.

Drake Passage

Also known as 'Drake Lake' or 'Drake Shake' depending on the sea conditions you experience, the notorious passage between Cape Horn and the Antarctic Peninsula takes around two days to navigate. You won't get a better opportunity to break in your sea legs or test your seabird identification skills as you attempt to track the wheeling flight of albatrosses and petrels from the pitching deck of a ship. Albatrosses commonly sighted include wandering, northern and southern royal, grey-headed and light-mantled. Southern giant petrel can also be seen, along with smaller members of the tube-nosed seabird family, such as southern fulmar, cape petrel and Wilson's storm petrel. Keep scanning the horizon for whale blows. From around mid-December onwards, Drake Passage will be heaving with humpbacks, lured south by the promise of summer krill blooms. Orcas are also commonly sighted, along with fin whale and hourglass dolphin. The southern bottlenose whale is decidedly rarer – as are other species of beaked whale. As you voyage south across Drake Passage, you enter the Antarctic Convergence, where warmer sub-Antarctic currents meet polar waters. Birds like the Antarctic prion start to be seen – heralds of the great white continent that lies just over the horizon.

South Shetland Islands

Located about 120 km north of the Antarctic Peninsula, the mountainous, glacier-covered South Shetlands include **Elephant Island**, where Shackleton and his crew were stranded for 135 days in 1915. The South Shetland Islands are renowned for their large colonies of chinstrap, gentoo and Adélie penguins, southern elephant seals and fur seals. Largest of the South Shetlands, **King George Island** (site of several scientific bases) is also a good place to see Antarctic tern, blue-eyed shag and southern giant petrel. The flooded caldera of **Deception Island**, accessed by a 230-m wide entrance known as Neptunes Bellows, has several chinstrap penguin rookeries, while **Livingston Island** supports breeding populations of both chinstraps and gentoos.

Antarctic Peninsula

Sailing from the South Shetland Islands, expedition ships navigate Bransfield Strait to reach the Antarctic Peninsula, a magnificent polar wilderness of ice-clad peaks rearing above channels strewn with colossal, blue-tinted icebergs. Two of the most spectacular areas are the **Lemaire Channel** and **Paradise Harbour** where you can witness the full cast of Antarctic wildlife – from minke whales, crabeater seals and orcas to penguins, petrels and sheathbills – against a dramatic backdrop of sheer cliffs, calving glaciers and snow fields. If conditions allow, this is a wonderful area to explore by sea kayak, nosing about in sheltered bays, drifting warily past leopard seals lounging on ice floes or paddling alongside humpback whales. Some voyages also offer camping and cross-country skiing.

Weddell Sea & South Orkney Islands

Sailing along the west coast of the Antarctic Peninsula, some expedition voyages attempt to cross the Polar Circle before retreating north. Other itineraries probe the peninsula's eastern shores, edging through 'iceberg alley' into the Weddell Sea. Popular landing sites here include **Paulet Island** (Adélie penguin, blue-eyed shag, sheathbill) and **Half Moon Island** where chinstrap, gentoo and macaroni penguins can be found along with elephant seals, cape pigeons and southern giant petrels. Icebreaker ships (with the extended reach of their helicopters) can get you to **Snow Hill Island** – site of Antarctica's northernmost emperor penguin colony.

Sometimes included on cruises that voyage clockwise from the Falklands and South Georgia to the Antarctic Peninsula, the wild and windy South Orkneys are difficult to land on – but promise fabulous birdlife if the weather is on your side.

Ross Sea & Ross Ice Shelf

Accessible only to icebreakers like the Kapitan Khlebnikov (returning to full-time research duties in 2012), voyages to the Ross Sea and Ross Ice Shelf include visits to Scott's Discovery and Terra Nova huts, as well as Shackleton's hut at Cape Royds and the impressive colony of Adélie penguins at Cape Adare. Onboard helicopters, meanwhile, bring the 'Dry Valleys' of the Antarctic interior within range.

Royal penguin

Under Down Under

Usually incorporated as stopovers enroute to the Ross Sea, the sub-Antarctic Islands of New Zealand also make an extremely rewarding voyage in their own right. Departing Invercargill, expedition ships skirt Stewart Island before pushing on southwards towards **Snares Island**. Although landings are forbidden here, zodiac rides give a vivid impression of the scale of Snares' seabird colonies, which include millions of sooty shearwaters and 30,000 pairs of the endemic Snares Island penguin. Continuing south, the **Auckland Islands** are a breeding ground for yellow-eyed penguin, several species of albatross and most of the world's Hooker's sea lions. **Macquarie Island**, meanwhile, has the only breeding population of the royal penguin – 850,000 pairs of them nesting alongside gentoos, kings and rockhoppers. Add to that around 100,000 elephant seals and you have one of the greatest concentrations of wildlife anywhere in the world. An impressive finale to this Antipodean sub-Antarctic voyage, **Campbell Island** is home to 7,500 pairs of southern royal albatross.

Going with the floe – chinstrap penguins hitch a ride on an iceberg. Left: Adélie penguins march towards the sea to embark on a fishing trip. Food is often on the mind of the leopard seal, a voracious hunter of penguins and other seals which can reach lengths of nearly 3 m and weigh up to 400 kg.

Making tracks | Falklands

Wildlife tours are available from **Falkland Islands Holidays** (falklandislandsholidays.com).

LAN (lan.com) flies to Santiago, with onward flights to Mount Pleasant via Punta Arenas. Direct **MoD** flights from RAF Brize Norton, UK, take 18 hours. The **Falkland Islands Government Air Service** runs light aircraft between most islands. Cruise ship operators visit the islands.

Stanley's **Malvina House Hotel** (malvinahousehotel.com) has comfortable rooms and excellent food. **Carcass Island** (contact via tourist board) has a cosy, welcoming farmhouse, full of character and sheltered by an exotic garden. Superb walks, Land Rover tours and delicious home cooking. **Sea Lion Lodge** (sealionisland.com) is a smart single-storey lodge overlooking gentoo penguin rookeries. **Saunders Island** has self-catering cottages, plus a cabin with bunk beds on the wildlife-rich Neck.

GMT-4 (FI winter), GMT-3 (FI summer)

Summer (October to March) has long daylight hours, lots of sunshine and an average temperature of 15°C. Several species of wildlife return to the islands to breed in September.

Observe minefield warning signs.

Falklands Pound (FK£)

visitorfalklands.com

Falklands Conservation (falklandsconservation.com).

Falklands | Wildlife highlights

Bluff Cove Few beaches are more remote, but don't expect to have Bluff Cove all to yourself. Some 3,000 gentoo penguins (and a small colony of kings) stake out the powder-white sands of this pristine bay, pacing well-trammelled 'highways' between their raucous rookeries and the South Atlantic surf. To reach this penguin paradise join a 4WD tour from Stanley. Sit quietly on the beach and the curious gentoos will waddle right up to you (the kings tend to remain aloof). Magellanic penguins and sea lions frequently surf onto the scene, but you can always escape the crowds at Bluff Cove's Sea Cabbage Café. You won't find a better cream tea within 7,000 miles. Don't miss the new Bluff Cove Museum (falklandpenguins.com) at the Sea Cabbage Café to discover how people, as well as penguins, fare in this far-flung outpost.

Sparrow Cove & Kidney Cove Join a Land Rover safari from Stanley with local farmer Adrian Lowe to visit this wild stretch of coastline that became the resting place of Brunel's *SS Great Britain*. Four species of penguin breed here (gentoo, king, Magellanic and rockhopper).

Volunteer Point Home to the largest king penguin colony in the Falklands (around 500 pairs), Volunteer Point on East Falkland also has rookeries of gentoo and Magellanic penguins.

Carcass & West Point Islands A pick-up point for boat trips to West Point Island (see opposite), Carcass also boasts superb wildlife. Gentoo and Magellanic penguins can be found at Leopard Beach, while striated caracaras and various small birds (such as Cobb's wren) are common around the McGill's settlement. Keep an eye out for Commerson's dolphins offshore.

Pebble Island Named after the agate pebbles found on its beaches, this 31 km-long island is a gem for birdwatchers. Not only do gentoo, macaroni, Magellanic and rockhopper penguins breed here in good

numbers, but there are also large colonies of king cormorants. The ponds on the eastern side of the island, meanwhile, are a magnet to waterfowl and waders.

Saunders Island Another birding paradise, Saunders has large numbers of penguin, cormorant and black-browed albatross. Head to The Neck for the greatest concentrations.

Sea Lion Island Lying 16 km south of East Falkland, Sea Lion Island is like a sub-Antarctic Galápagos. The 9-sq-km island is home to a fabulous array of birds, including 6,000 gentoo penguins, 1,000 rockhoppers and a smaller population of Magellanic penguins. A large colony of king cormorants can be found on dramatic cliffs on the south side of the island, while a special hide provides views of around 20 pairs of giant petrel (highly vulnerable to disturbance) nesting behind a beach in the north. A chain of freshwater ponds attracts Chiloe wigeon, crested duck, speckled and silver teal, silvery grebe and a variety of waders, such as rufous-chested dotterel and two-banded plover. The surrounding grassy areas are a good place to look for Magellanic snipe, crested caracara, ruddy-headed goose and endemic Cobb's wren.

Around 2,000 elephant seals haul out on the beaches of Sea Lion Island, pupping between October and November. Orca have been observed hunting elephant seal pups in large tidal pools on the island's southeastern coast. Sea lions can be seen at the base of cliffs from viewpoints around the island, while Peale's dolphin are sometimes seen offshore.

Sea Lion island

66 99 West Point Island condensed from the mist, 380 m-high seacliffs looming above our bright yellow trawler. The base of the cliffs was worn smooth in places where rockhopper penguins had scrabbled from the sea to begin their Herculean ascents to clifftop rookeries, mingling with over 14,500 pairs of black-browed albatross.

William Gray

From the boat landing at Napier's House, it is a 2-km walk across West Point Island to the Devil's Nose where a large colony of black-browed albatrosses and rockhopper penguins nest among boulders in the tussac grass. Top left: Ruddy-headed goose. Left: Striated caracara, Magellanic snipe and flightless steamer duck with brood.

South Georgia | Sub-Antarctic Serengeti

A ravaged scimitar of land over 2,000 km east of Tierra del Fuego, South Georgia defies the brutal storms of the Southern Ocean, its mountainous backbone shielding bays along the island's north coast where one of the world's greatest annual gatherings of seabirds takes place.

No less than 60 million birds are thought to breed on this wild, uninhabited and strikingly beautiful island. Wandering albatross hunker down on clifftop nests, Antarctic shags stake out rocky shores, and storm petrels seek gaps and crevices in screes in which to lay their eggs.

Southern elephant seals and Antarctic fur seals commandeer beaches, littering the strandline in vast, twitching hordes, but nothing can upstage the birds on South Georgia – and there is one species in particular that steals the show. King penguins breed in such numbers on the island that their massed ranks transform entire bays into a monochromatic mêlée of sleek black-and-white bodies, speckled with the bright orange flashes of their ear patches and the shaggy brown coats of chicks. As biennial breeders, king penguin rookeries are in constant use. Birds incubating eggs can be found alongside crèches of 12-month-old chicks, making it possible to witness almost every stage of rearing young.

Key wildlife sites

A 3-km stretch of dark sand, **St Andrews Bay** is backed by a glacial outwash plain, meltwater streams flowing from the Cook, Heaney and Buxton Glaciers past large breeding colonies of king penguin and elephant seal. Light-mantled sooty albatross, white-chinned petrel, snowy sheathbill, brown skua and Antarctic tern also nest in the area. At **Cooper Bay**, cobbled coves indent a shoreline of low cliffs, wave-cut platforms and scree slopes to form ideal breeding conditions for macaroni penguins. Fur seals haul out here, while the South Georgia pipit (the island's only endemic land bird) can be seen among lichen-covered boulders. Located 20 km north of Cape Vahsel, **Gold Harbour** is ringed by spectacular hanging glaciers and cliffs and has a pool-studded glacial outwash plain where a large king penguin rookery can be found. Another superb site for king penguins, **Salisbury Plain** lies between the Grace and Lucas Glaciers and is also a good place to see elephant seals and fur seals, as well as gentoo penguin, light-mantled sooty albatross, snowy sheathbill, kelp gull and giant petrel. Marking the southern entrance of King Haakon Bay, **Cape Rosa** has nesting colonies of wandering albatross and various burrow-nesting petrels. A cave in one of the shoreline coves was used as a shelter by Shackleton's expedition. The last section of the route taken across South Georgia by Shackleton, Crean and Worsley in 1914 can be traced on a 5.5-km hike across the mountain pass between **Fortuna Bay** and **Stromness Harbour**. Breeding birds in the area include light-mantled sooty albatross, southern giant petrel, white-chinned petrel and Wilson's storm petrel. King penguin, gentoo penguin and elephant seals can be seen in Fortuna Bay.

Of the 81 species of birds recorded in South Georgia, 27 are breeding seabirds. The island is home to around half of the world's population of macaroni penguins, grey-headed albatrosses, northern giant petrels, white-chinned petrels and Antarctic prions, the most numerous seabird on South Georgia. Breeding birds (in taxonomic order) include:

Macaroni penguin 2 million pairs
King penguin 400,000 pairs
Gentoo penguin 100,000 pairs
Chinstrap penguin 6,000 pairs
Wandering albatross 4,000 pairs
Grey-headed albatross 80,000 pairs
Light-mantled sooty albatross 5,000-8,000 pairs
Black-browed albatross 100,000 pairs
Antarctic prion 22 million pairs
White-chinned petrel 2 million pairs
South giant petrel 5,000 pairs
Northern giant petrel 3,000 pairs
Blue petrel 70,000 pairs
Cape petrel 10,000 pairs
Snow petrel 3,000 pairs
Fairy prion 1,000 pairs
Wilson storm petrel 600,000 pairs
Black-bellied storm petrel 10,000 pairs
South Georgia diving petrel 50,000 pairs
Diving petrel 4 million pairs
South Georgia shag 7,500 pairs
Brown skua 2,000 pairs
Kelp gull 2,000 pairs
Antarctic tern 10,000 pairs
Yellow-billed sheathbill 2,000 pairs
South Georgia pintail duck 1,000 pairs
Speckled teal 10 pairs
South Georgia pipit 3,000 to 4,000 pairs

Wandering albatross

Grytviken

Vital statistics

Co-ordinates 35°47' to 38°01' west and 53°58' to 54°53' south.
Size 170 km in length and 2 to 40 km in width.
Height 11 peaks exceed 2,000 m, with Mount Paget the highest at 2,934 m.
Seasons Glaciers, ice caps and snowfields cover about 75% of the island during the austral summer (November to January), while a blanket of snow reaches to the sea in winter (July to September).
Nearest town Port Stanley in the Falklands is 1,390 km to the west.
Population During the whaling period in the early 1900s, around 2,000 people lived on the island. Now there are only two British Antarctic Research Stations (Bird Island and King Edward Point), staffed by government officers and museum curators during the summer.
Historic interest Sir Ernest Shackleton's Grave is located in the small cemetery at Grytviken near the remains of the old whaling station. The **South Georgia Museum** (sgmuseum.gs) illustrates various aspects of the island's history and natural history and is managed by the **South Georgia Heritage Trust** (sght.org).
Further info sgisland.gs

Right royal gathering – the king penguin colonies on South Georgia are one of the wildlife wonders of the world. Following a typically raucous courtship period, eggs are usually laid in late November, with males and females sharing incubation duty. Chicks hatch after about 54 days and moult into their fluffy down coats at around the age of six weeks. Soon after, they join communal crèches, allowing their parents to go fishing.

The *Noorderlicht* entering Magdalena Fjord in Svalbard. See page 120 for a description of a voyage onboard this beautiful Arctic schooner.

Akademik Sergey Vavilov

Type Built in the 1980s for the Russian Academy of Science, this ship was designed for hydro-acoustic research and is, therefore, extremely quiet and stable. The hull is ice-strengthened.
Length 117 m
Berths 107 passengers in twin or triple cabins, all with windows; either ensuite or with shared bathroom.
Facilities Dining room, lounge, bar, library, clinic, sauna, plunge pool.
Crew 53, including doctor and expedition staff.
Destinations Antarctica, Spitsbergen, Greenland.
quarkexpeditions.com

Ocean Nova

Type This Scandinavian-designed ship has a shallow draft, good manoeuvrabilty and an ice-strengthened hull, allowing it to navigate close to shore and traverse pack ice. Kayaking and camping options available.
Length 73 m
Berths 73 passengers in outside, ensuite cabins; some single cabins.
Facilities Glass-enclosed observation lounge, dining room, bar, library.
Crew 38, including doctor.
Destinations Antarctic Peninsula, South Shetlands, Falklands, South Georgia.
quarkexpeditions.com

Clipper Adventurer

Type An elegant vessel built in 1975 and refitted in 1998, the *Clipper Adventurer* is renowned for its high levels of comfort and fine dining. Ice-strengthened hull and cruising speed of 12 knots.
Length 101 m
Berths 122 in 61 ensuite cabins with exterior views.
Facilities Window-lined dining room, lounge, presentation room, two bars, gift shop, polar library, exercise room.
Crew 72, including doctor and expert naturalist guides.
Destinations South Shetland Islands, Antarctic Peninsula
quarkexpeditions.com

Noorderlicht

Type Steel-hulled, twin-masted schooner with 550-sq-m sail area.
Length 46 m
Berths 20 passengers in 10 twin cabins with bunkbeds; five showers and four toilets for communal use.
Facilities Saloon, zodiacs.
Crew Five crew, including expedition leader.
Destinations Svalbard archipelago. Sailing season is usually late May to September, during which time the ship attempts to circumnavigate Spitsbergen (ice permitting), with midsummer cruises taking place under the midnight sun. In October, the *Noorderlicht* often sails to the Lofoten Islands in search of orca, returning to Svalbard in December where she is ice-bound in Tempelfjorden and can be visited by dog sleigh or snowmobile. This is an excellent time to witness the Aurora Borealis.
noorderlicht.nu

50 Years of Victory

Type The world's largest, most powerful and sophisticated icebreaker, *50 Years of Victory* is driven by two nuclear reactors generating 75,000 horsepower. The ship is designed to break through ice up to 3 m thick and cruise at over 24 knots.
Length 159 m
Berths 128 passengers in 66 ensuite cabins and suites, all with exterior views.
Facilities Helicopter for aerial sightseeing, dining room, aft saloon for presentations, bar, polar library, lounge, gym, saunas, massage room, small swimming pool.
Crew 140, including doctor, expedition staff and expert naturalist guides.
Destinations The *Victory* operates one departure each year to the North Pole. The 15-day voyage from Murmansk includes an exploration of Franz Josef Land (renowned for its polar bears and seabirds) and the use of the ship's MI8 helicopter for exploring the pack ice.
quarkexpeditions.com

Directory & Index

PIONEERING TRAVEL
TO LATIN AMERICA
SINCE 1980

Whether it's a tailor-made escape or a small group tour, we know the places you'll love. ONLY LATIN AMERICA SINCE 1980

www.journeylatinamerica.co.uk ☎ 020 8622 8464

JOURNEY
LATIN
AMERICA

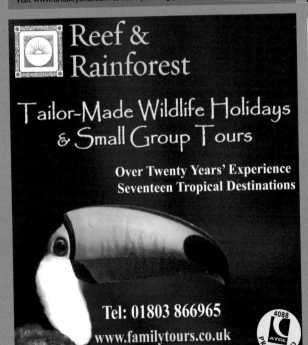
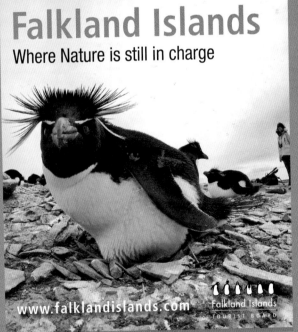

Index

*Numbers in **bold** refer to photos*

50 years of Victory **293**

A

&Beyond 28, 64, **65**, 238
aardvark 61
Abel Tasman NP **263**, 270
Abisko NP 202, **204-205**
Abrolhos MNP 170
Abruzzo NP 198
Abu Camp 47
Acadia NP 148
accommodation 18-19
adder
  puff **43**
Addo Elephant NP 57, 234
Admiralty Island NM 141
Adventure Company 26
African Conservation
  Experience 130
African wild dog 60, **61**, 216,
  222, 226, 228, 234
AfriCat Foundation 230
Akademik Sergey Vavilov **293**
Akagera NP 221
Aksu Dzabagly NR 247
Alaska 8, 23, 67, 92, 93, 99,
  100, 105, 114, 126, 135,
  140-143
Alaska Adventures 93
Alaska Chilkat Bald Eagle
  Preserve 141
albatross 286, 290
  black-browed **36, 37, 271,**
  288-289
  wandering **290**
  waved **118, 176, 174**
Alfred Wallace 245
Algonquin PP 154
alligator
  American **13**, 150
Allpahuayo-Mishana Res 160
Alps 88, 189, 192
altitude sickness 40
Amanda Marks **84**
Amangani **157**
Amazonas 168
Amazon rainforest 160, 170,
  172
Amazon River 114
Amboseli NP 212
anaconda 168, 169, 170, 180
Andalucía 195
Andes 160
Andisabe-Mantadia NP 74, 236
Andy Rouse **67**
Angel Falls **168**
angelfish, French **48**

Ånns Jön Wetlands 202
Antarctica 8, 22, 23, 46, 101,
  115, **116-117**, 126, **181**, 279,
  280-281, 283, 286-291, **293**
  voyages 283
Antarctic Peninsula 115, 286
anteater
  giant 168, 169
antelope 222, 226 see also
  individual species
Appalachian Mountains 139
Arabuko Sokoke FR 213
Arapaho NWR 145
Araras Ecolodge **185**
Archipelago NP 202
Arctic 114, 278-282, 284-285,
  292
  voyages 282
Arctic Expedition Cruise
  Operators 279
Arctic NWR 141
Argentina 23, 47, 100, 161, 180
armadillo 168
  hairy **183**
Arthur's Pass Wilderness
  Lodge **275**
artwork **38-39**
Asbyrgi 203
Auckland Islands 286
Augrabies Falls NP 234
auk, little **284**
Aulavik NP 153
Australia 23, 46, 47, 50-51,
  101, 105, 115, 127, 260-269
Awash NP 221
aye-aye 76, **77**, 236
  see also lemur
Azores 101, 105, 197

B

baboon
  gelada **58**, 74, 221
  olive **76**
Badlands NP 145
Baffin Island 22
Bahamas **17**, 110-111
Baja California 8, 22, 100, 106-
  109, **107, 109**, 114, 161, 185
Bako NP 75, 252
Balearic Islands 195
Bali 256
Bali Barat NP 256
Bamurru Plains **275**
Banc D'Arguin 209, 210
Bandhavgarh NP 249, 259
bandicoot 264
Banff NP 139, 153
Bangladesh 116

Bangweulu Wetlands 22,
  58, 63, 223
Banjaar Tola Tented Camp **258**
Bardia NP 251
Barra del Colorado WR 167
barracuda **48**
Basecamp Explorer 239, **242**
Bass Rock 190
bat
  fruit **262**
  Mexican free-tailed 145
  straw-coloured fruit 222, 241
  wrinkle-lipped 252
Bay Islands **165**
Bay of Biscay 105, 116, 189
Bay of Fundy 100, 139, 154
Bay of Islands 263
Bazaruto Archipelago 226
Beagle Channel 181
bear
  American black 91, **93,**
  150, 153
  Andean spectacled 92
  Asiatic black 91
  brown 23, 91, **93**, 142
  grizzly 67, **90**, 91, 140, 146,
  147, 153, **156**, 195, 198,
  200, 202
  Kodiak 91
  polar 23, **43**, 91, **93**, 94,
  95, 138, 153, 154, 284, **285**
  safety 93
  sloth **93**, 249, 251
  sun 92, 254, 256
  watching 90-97, 202, 135,
  156, 157, 202
bee-eater
  carmine 23, 224, **227**
  red-throated **211**
  white-fronted 224
beetle, dung **229**
Belarus 189
Belize 48, 74, 78, 161, 164
Belize Barrier Reef **48**, 164
Bellavista Cloud Forest 46,
  172, **185**
Bempton Cliffs 187
Berenty PR 75, 79, 236
Bhutan 247
Bialowieza Forest 188, 189,
  200, **201**
Big Bend NP 144
Big Cypress NP 151
Bill & Knowdla Keefe's Bimini
  Undersea 110
Bimini 110
binoculars **32-33**
biodiversity 12-13, 257

Biosphere Expeditions 86,
  88, 130
Bird Island 243
bird of paradise
  Raggiana **273**
birdwatching 46, 63, 148, 151,
  165, 167, 172, 184, 185, 193,
  194, 210, 211, 223, 270
Biscayne NP 151
bishop, northern red **211**
bison 145, **146-147**
  European **201**
  bites 40
  blackbuck 248
  bleeding 40
  blisters 40
Bluff Cove **288**
boat trips 104, 150, 152, 165,
  181, 194, 216
bobcat 146
Bolivia 161, 180
Bonito NP **165**
bonobo **75**
booby
  blue-footed **15**, 172, 176
  Nazca **175**, 172, 176
  red-footed 172
Borneo 48, 49, 75, 79, 252-255
Borneo Rainforest Lodge
  79, **259**
Bosque del Apache 67
Botswana 22, 23, 47, 58, 63,
  124, 135, 209, 228-229
Braulio Carrilio NP 167
Brazil 73, 78, 161, 170-171
Brian Jackman **102**
Bridge & Wickers 26
Brisbane 262
Britain 39, 116, 190-191
British Columbia 92, 93, 100,
  114, 138
British Trust for Conservation
  Volunteers 130
brolga **264**
Brooks Falls Lodge 93
Brooks Range 126
Bruce Pearson **39**
buffalo
  Cape **58, 61**, 212, 217, 221,
  223, 224, 228
Buhoma Lodge 78
Bukit Baka-Bukit Raya NP 256
Bukit Lawang Cottages 79
Bulgaria 200
Bunaken NP 256
Bundala 251
burns 40
Busanga Plains 222

bushbaby 76, **77**
Bushmen **58**
bustard
  Denham's 223
  great **196**
  kori 216
  little 192
butterfly **229**, 198, 251
  monarch **13, 49**, 163
buzzard, honey 195
Bwindi Impenetrable NP
  74, 221
Bwindi Safari Lodge 78, **241**

C

Cabot Trail 154
Cachalote **177**
Cahuita NP 167
caiman **8**, 169, **171**, 178
Cairngorms NP 190, **191**
California 100, 105
Camargue 189, 192
camel safaris 47
Campbell Island 115, 286
camping 17, 205
  fly 58
  responsible 205
Canada 23, 92, 93, 94, 100,
  114, 138, 139
  Arctic 114
Canaima NP 168
Canary Islands 101, 197
canoeing 17, 148, 150, 154,
  165, 202, 224, 225, 228
Cap Tourmente NWA 154
Cape Byron 105
Cape Canaveral National
  Seashore 151
Cape Cross **231**
Cape Floral Kingdom 208, 209
Cape Horn 181
Cape Rosa 290
Cape York 262
Capri Strip 230
capuchin 74, **166**
capybara 168, 169, 170, **171**
caracara
  crested 162
  striated **36, 37, 288**
carbon offset 16
Carcass Island 288
Caribbean 100, 114, 161, 164
caribou 138, 140, 153, 154
Carlsbad Caverns NP 145
Carpathians 88, 92, 189, 200
cassowary **269**
Cathedral Mountain Lodge
  157

Cathy Iturralde Dillon **117**
Cayman Islands 164
Central Kalahari GR 228
Cévennes NP 192
Chalalán Ecolodge **185**
chameleon 236, **237**
  flap-neck **10**
  Rwenzori **81**
chamois 193, **199,** 200
Chang Tang reserve 127
Channel Islands NP 145
Charles Darwin 130, 159
  Research Station 173
cheetah **6, 8,** 60, **61,** 212, 221, 222, 230
Chéngdu 247
  Panda Base 247
Chilcotin Mountains 47
Chile 100, 127
Chiloé Island 100, 161, 180
Chimfunshi 222
chimpanzee 74, **77,** 82-85, **83,** 216, 217, 221, 222
China 127, 247, 251
Chitwan NP 245, 247, 251
Chobe NP 228
cholera 41
chough, alpine **198**
Chris Breen **224**
Chris McIntyre **208**
Chumbe Island **18-19**
Churchill 23, 92, 93, 94-95, 139, 153
Ciénaga de Zapata NP 164
CITES 16
Clipper Adventurer **293**
clothing **30-31**
cloud forest 159
Clouds Mountain Gorilla Lodge 78
cockatoo, black 268
cock-of-the-rock **32,** 159, 169, **179**
Cockscombe Basin Wildlife Sanctuary 164
Cocos Island NP 167
Colca Canyon 178
colobus 74, 213, 217, 221
  black and white **77**
Community Baboon Sanctuary 74, 78
condor
  Andean **47, 158**
  California 144
Congo 74, 78
Congo Basin 208, 209
Conservation trips 128-131
Cook Strait 116

Cooper Bay 290
coot **38**
Copper Canyon 163
Coral Bay Adventures 50
Coral Cay Conservation **128,** 130, 246
coral reefs 12-13, **16,** 151, 216, 217, 256, **257, 272**
Corbett NP 52-55
Corcovado NP 23, 74, 166, 184
Corkscrew Swamp Sanctuary 150
Cormorant
  flightless 173, **175**
  king **181**
Coromandel Peninsula 276
Corsica 193
Costa Rica 8, 74, 78, 161, 166-167
Coto Doñana 22, 23, 189, 194
Cotopaxi NP 172
coyote 146
crab
  horseshoe 149
  grapsid **38**
  sally lightfoot 172
crane 23, 193, 200
  crowned 212, 216, **220,** 223
  sandhill 145, 146
  wattled 70, **71,** 223
Cree Village Ecolodge **157**
Crete 189
Cristalino Jungle Lodge 78
Croatia 200
Crocker Range **253**
crocodile
  Cuban 164
  gharial 251
  Nile **43,** 221, 223
  marsh mugger **248**
  saltwater **267**
Crooked Tree Wildlife Sanctuary 164
Crystal River NWR 48, 151
Cuero y Salado **165**
Cuevo del Guacharo 168
cuscus, spotted **273**

D
Daintree NP 265
Daintree Ecolodge **277**
Damaraland 58, 209, 230
dangerous animals 40, **43**
Dan Martin 188
Danube Delta 22, 189, 200
Danum Valley 247, 252, 254, 259
Darién Gap NP 161, 164

darter, African **211**
dassie, rock **235**
Deception Island 286
Death Valley NP 145
deer
  key 151
  marsh 170
  mule 146, 153
  red **191,** 198, 200
  sambar 248
  spotted **244,** 248, 251
  white-tailed 146
Deer Cave **49,** 252
Delaware Bay 149
DRC 75
Denali NP 22, 140, **141, 143**
Derrick Nabaala **25**
diarrhoea 42
dik-dik
  Kirk's **61**
dingo 264, 265
diptheria 41
diver
  red-throated **203,** 284
diving 165
dog sledding 47
Dolomites 198
dolphin 17, 101, 162, 202, 210, 286
  bottlenose 101, 213
  Commerson's 288
  common 194
  dusky 101, 270, **271**
  Hector's 270
  river 101, 168, 170, 178, 180, 251
  spotted **17,** 101, 110-111, **111**
  swimming with 17
Dominica 100
Dominican Republic 100, 164
Dondra Point 251
Discover the World 26
diseases 40, 41
Dive Worldwide 50
diving 16, 213
dragonfly **69,** 193
  southern darter **49**
Drakensberg 233
Drake Passage 286
Dreamtime 261
duck 193, 202
  eider 202, 284
  flightless steamer **289**
duiker, common 222

E
eagle
  African fish 223, 224
  bald **8,** 145, 146
  black 223
  Bonelli's 195
  booted 195
  golden 153, 192, 193, 195, 198
  harpy 164, **169**
  white-tailed (sea) 189, **191,** 200, 202
Earth Lodge **242**
Earthwatch 130, **131**
Eastern Arc Mountains 207
echidna **268**
Ecocamp Patagonia **185**
Ecosummer Expeditions 108
Ecuador 23, 46, 100, 114, 161, 172
  see also Galápagos Islands
egret
  great white **46**
eland **61,** 222, 230
elephant
  African **43, 60, 61, 212, 214-215,** 216, 217, 221, 223, 224, **225,** 226, 228, 229, 230
  forest **210**
  Indian (Asian) **55, 248, 251,** 254
  safaris **47,** 52-55, **55**
Elephant Island 286
elephant seal **36,** 180, **183,** 286, 290
elephant shrew 207
Elena Guesthouse 93
elk 144, 146, **147**
Elk Island NP 153
Ellesmere Island 279
El Ray NP 180
Emas NP 170
equipment **30-31**
Estonia 189, 200
Ethiopia 58, 74, 209, 221
Etosha NP 58, 230
Everglades NP **17,** 23, 46, 139, 150
Exodus 26, 281
Expert Africa 29
Explore 26
Extremadura 39, 195, **196**
eye injury 42

F
falcon, Eleonora's 195
Falkland Islands 46, 114, 132-133, 288-289
Färnebofjärden NP 202
Fathom Five NMP 154
Ferdinand Bauer 261
field guides **33, 105**
Fiji 115, 263
finch, Darwin's 172
Finch Bay Eco Hotel **177**
Finke Gorge **260**
Finland 22, 47, 92, 93, 189, 202
Fiordland NP **263**
Fiordland Lodge **275**
first aid 40
first aid kit 41
flamingo
  greater 164, **192,** 230
  lesser **46**
Florida 23, 48, 150-151
Florida Keys 151
Fortuna Bay 290
fosa **237**
fox
  Arctic 284, **285**
  bat-eared **61,** 216
fractures 42
France 49, 192-193
Fraser Island 265
frigatebird
  great 172, **8, 175**
frog **253**
  poison dart **43**
  red-eyed tree **166**
Frontier 130
frostbite 42
fulmar 284
fynbos 232

G
Gabon 74, 78, 209, 210
galah **267**
Galápagos Islands 8, 22, 23, **44-45,** 49, 67, **112,** 113, 114, 122-123, 172-177
  calendar 176
gallinule, purple 194
Gambia 209, 210, 211
gannet 187, **190**
  Cape 232, 233, **235**
Gansbaii 48
Gargano Peninsula 198
Gates of the Arctic NP 139, 141
gaur **248**
gecko, leaf-tailed 236, **237**

Index

gemsbok 228, **229**
Georgetown 169
gerenuk **61**, 212, 213
Ghana 210
gibbon 75, 248
  white-handed **77**
Gibraltar 74, 189, 195
Giles Track 268
giraffe **61**, 217
  reticulated **58**
  Rothschild's 213, 221
  Thornicroft's 224
Glacier Bay NP 114, 140
godwit
  bar-tailed **210**
  marbled **109**
Goegap NR **234**
Gold Harbour 290
Gomantong Caves 252
Gombe Stream NP 74, 217
Gonarezhou NP 226
goose 284
  magpie **266**
  nene 137
  pink-footed 187, 284
  pygmy 223
  red-breasted 200
  ruddy-headed **288**
  snow 153, 154
Gorongosa NP 58, 226, **241**
gorilla 76
  lowland 74, **77**, 210
  mountain **8, 14**, 23, 67, **72**, 74, **77, 79**, 80, **81, 221**
Grand Canyon NP 144, **144**
Grand Teton NP 139
Gran Paradiso NP 189, 198, **199**
Grassholm 190
Grasslands NP 153
Great Barrier Reef 23, 46, 261, **262**, 268, **269**
Great Bear Lodge 93
Great Bear Rainforest 91, 92, 93, 114, 153
Great Canadian Travel Co 94, 139
Greater St Lucia Wetland Park 233
Great Migration 58, 64-67, **65, 66-67, 218-219**
Great Ocean Ecolodge **275**
Great Rift Valley 46, 63, 208, 209, 213
Great Smoky Mountains NP 92, 148
Greece 101
Greenland 100, 114, **278**

Greystoke Camp 78
Guanacaste NP 167
guanaco **180**
Guatemala 161
guillemot 284
gull
  Audouin's 198
  kelp **270**
  swallow-tailed 172, 176
Gunung Leuser NP 75, 247, 256
Gunung Mulu NP 49, 252
Guyana 22, 161, 169
Gwaii Haanas NP 153

H

Half Moon Island 286
Haliburton Forest 154
hartebeest 233
Hawaii 100
Hawaii Volcanoes NP 137
Hawaiian Islands Humpback Whale NMS 137
hawk, Galápagos 172, 176
Hawk Mountain Sanctuary 149
HawkWatch 148
heat exhuastion 42
heat stroke 42
helmet vanga 236
Hemis National Park 86
Henir Pittier NP 168
hepatitis 41
Hermaness NNR **186**
Hermanus 105
heron 200
  boat-billed **165**
  goliath **58**
  great whitelittle blue **150**
  lava **175**
  reef **261**
  yellow-crowned night 172
Heron Island 46, 261, **269**
Hervey Bay 101
hiking 16, 150, 152, 154, 184
Himalayas 22, 23, 246
hippopotamus **8, 38, 58, 61, 227**
hoatzin 178, **179**
Honduras 113, 165, **165**
hoopoe **196**
hornbill
  black and white casqued 221
  rhinoceros 256, **259**
  Sulawesi **257**
horse riding 47, 168, 170
hot-air ballooning 58, 212, **231**
Hortobágy NP 23, 200
Horton Plains NP 75

Huaorani Ecolodge **185**
Huascarán NP 178
Hudson Bay 100
hummingbird 166, 172
  booted racket-tail 160
  buff-tailed coronet **46**
  Lucifer 144
  Xantu's 162
Hungary 23, 189
Hwange NP 226
hyena
  brown **61**, 208
  spotted 212, 216, 222, 223, 226
hypothermia 42

I

ibex **199**
ibis
  crested 251
  glossy 200
  scarlet 164
Iceland 22, 23, 100, 189, 203
iguana
  land 172, 176
  marine **112, 123**, 159, 172 **174,** 176
Iguazú Falls 170, 180
impala 234
India 8, 22, 23, 47, 52-55, 75, 92, 135, 247, 248-250
Indian Ocean 115
Indonesia 75, 79, 115, 247, 256-257 see also Sumatra and other islands
Inside Passage 105, 114, 116, 139, 142
Iquitos 160
Ireland 189
Isabela II **118-119, 177**
Island Roamer 93
Isles of Scilly 116
Isle Royale NP 149
International Association of Antarctic Tour Operators 118, 279
Italy 101, 198-199
Iwokrama Forest 169, 185
  Lodge **185**

J

Jaci's Safari Lodge **242**
Jackson Looseyia **25**
Jacques Cousteau 113
jaguar 164, 167, 169, 170, **171,** 180
Japan 75, 101, 105, 247
Japanese encephalitis 41

Jasper NP 139, 152
Java 256
jellyfish
  box **43**
  Mastigias **48**
John Muir 137
Johnstone Strait 100, 139, 152
Jonathan & Angie Scott 135
Jigokudani Monkey Park 75
journal 39
Journey Latin America 26, 161

K

Kabili-Sepilok Reserve 75, 252, 254
Kafue NP 222
Kakadu NP 22, 262, 264, **266-267,** 277
Kakamega FR 213
Kaikoura 101, 270, **271**
Kaieteur NP 169
Kaimata Retreat **277**
Kalahari 22, 58, 208, 209, 228, 229
Kalimantan 75, 256
Kamchatka 92, 115, 247
Kangaroo Island 268
Kanha NP 249, 259
Kantishna Roadhouse 93
Kaokoland 209
kangaroo 268
Kapani Lodge **241**
KarmaQuest 86
Karoo 233
Kasanka NP 58, 222, **241**
Katavi NP 217
Kate Humble 3
Katmai NP 92, 135, 139, 142
katydid **179**
Kaziranga NP 47, 247, 248
Kenai Fjords NP 139, 142
Kenya 46, 58, 59, 63, 135, 212-213
Kgalagadi TP 22, 233
Khao Sok NP 247
Koshi Tappu WR 251
Kibale Forest NP 74, 221
Kidepo NP 221
Kimberley, The 115, 265
Kinabalu NP 254
Kinabatangan River 252, 259
Kinabatangan Riverside Lodge 79
kingfisher 224
  malachite **211**
King George Island 286
Kings Lodge **259**
Kingstone Mountain NP 92

Kisite Mpunguti MP 213
kiwi 270
klipspringer 232
Kluane NP 153
Knight Inlet Lodge 93, **156**
koala **268**
kob, Ugandan 221
Kodiak Archipelago 92
Kodiak NWR 141
Komodo dragon 247, **257**
Komodo Island 115
Komodo NP 256
Kooljaman at Cape Leveque **277**
Kruger NP 58, 63, 232
kudu 230
Kuyimá Ecolodge **185**
Kwando River 228
KwaZulu Natal 22

L

La Brenne 49, 193
Ladakh 22, 247
Laikipia Plateau 58, 213
Lake Baringo 213
Lake Bogoria 213
Lake Clarke NP 141
Lake Manyara NP 217
Lake Myvatn 22, 189, 203
Lake Naivasha 213
Lake Nakuru 213
Lake Nyasa (Malawi) 226
Lake Tanganyika 209
Lake Turkana 213
Lamington NP 268
Lamberts Bay 232
lammergeier 193, 195, 221, 233
langur 75, **77, 250**
Lanin NP 47
Lapa Ríos Ecolodge **184**
La Pinta **177**
Larapinta Trail 268
Las Baulas NMP 167
Latrabjarg 203
Lauca NP 180
Laurentide WR 92
lechwe 223, 224
Lemaire Channel 286
lemur 74-75 see also aye-aye
  indri 77, 236
  golden bamboo 75, 236
  greater bamboo **237**
  mouse 49
  ring-tailed **14**, 75, **77**, 236
  ruffed **58**, 236
  Verreaux's sifaka 74, **77, 237**

leopard **58**, 60, **61, 135,** 216, 223, **232**
  clouded 254
  Indian 249, **250**
  snow 86-87, **87,** 247
Les Ecrins NP 192
Limpopo TP 226
Linyanti Marshes 228
lion **56,** 60, **61, 65, 206,** 212, 217, **220,** 221, 222, 223, **226,** 228, 229, 234
  Asiatic 247
lionfish **14**
Little Vimbura Camp **241**
Liuwa Plain NP 222
Livingston Island 286
lizard
  basilisk 166
  frill-necked 265, **266**
Loango NP 78, 210
Lochinvar NP 223
Lofoten Islands 189, 202
Lola ya Bonobo Sanctuary 75
Lombok 256
Lopé NP 74, 210
Lord Howe Island 262
loris 75, 76, 254
Los Llanos wetlands 168
Los Quetzales NP 167
Lower Zambezi NP 224
Luangwa Valley 39, 58, 208, 209, 227
Luzon 247
lynx 146, 153
  Iberian **194,** 195

M
macaque **77,** 248
  Barbary 74
  Celebes crested **256**
  Japanese **75**
  lion-tailed 74
macaw
  blue and yellow **178**
  scarlet **46,** 166
MacDonnell Ranges 127
Macquarie Island 115, 286
Madagascar 14, 22, 23, 49, 58, 74-75, 79, 101, 208, 209, 236-237
Madidi NP 180, 185
Madikwe GR 234
Mafia Island MP 217
magpie, azure-winged 194
Mahale Mountains NP 74, 216
Makgadikgadi Pans 127, 228
malaria 41
Malawi 226

Malaysia 75 *see also* Sabah and Sarawak
Malborough Sounds 263
Maldives 48
Mali 210
Mamiraua Sustainable Development Reserve 74
Mana Pools NP 58, 225, 226
Manas NP 249
manatee **48,** 151, 164, 168, 170
Manawa Ridge **276**
mandrill **77**
manta ray **48,** 167
Manu Biosphere Reserve 8, **32,** 46, 73, 126, 159, 178, **179,** 185
Manú Wildlife Centre **185**
Manuel Antonio NP 167
Mark Carwardine **162**
marmoset 74
marmot 193
Martinselkoosen Nature Reserve 92, 93, 202
Masai Mara NR 8, 65-67, **65-67,** 135, 212, 218-219, **220**
Mashatu Game Reserve 60
Masoala NP 236
Matusadona NP 226
Mauritania 209, 210
Mawamba Lodge 78
Mbeli Bai Camp 78
meerkat **61**
Mentawai Islands 75
Mercado NP 180
Mercantour NP 192
Mer d'Iroise 193
Metropolitan Touring 122
Mexico 22, 49, 100, 106-109, 114, 162-163
  monarch butterfly sanctuaries 163
Michaelmus Cay 261
Micronesia 48
Mingan Archipelago NP 154
Minneriya NP 251
mockingbird, Galápagos **175,** 172
Mongolia 245
monkey 76, 213
  howler **74, 77,** 170
  golden **74, 76,** 80, **81**
  proboscis 75, **77, 253**
  spider 74, **77,** 166, 180
  squirrel 74, 166
  snub-nosed 75, 247, 251
Montagne D'Ambre NP 74
Monterey Bay 100, 145

Monteverde Cloud Forest Reserve 166
moose **43,** 140, 146, 152, 153, 202
Morocco 209
Mosi-oa-Tunya NP 223
mosquito 43
Mosquito Coast 113, **165**
Mossman Gorge **269**
mountain lion 144, 152
Mt Kilimanjaro 217
Mt Kinabalu 252 *see also* Kinabalu NP
Mozambique 58, 209, 226
Mulu NP (*see* Gunung Mulu NP)
Mundulea NR 230
Murchison Falls NP 221

N
Nairobi 209
Namaqualand 23, **49,** 232, **234**
Namibia 58, 59, 127, 209, 230-231
  Valley of 10,000 Dunes **17**
Namib Desert 209, 230, **231**
Namib-Naukluft NP 230
NamibRand Reserve **231**
National Audubon Society 137, 150
Nepal 247, 251
Netherlands 189
New Caledonia 262
New England 100
New Forest 190
New Guinea 262 *see also* Papua New Guinea
New Mexico 67
New Zealand 22, 101, 115, 116, 127, 262, 270-271
  Sub-Antarctic Islands 115, 286
Ngama Island 78
Ngorongoro CA 216, **220**
Ngorongoro Crater Lodge **242**
Nhoma Safari Camp **240**
Niah 252
nightjar, long-tailed **211**
Ningaloo Reef 8, 22, 50-51, **51, 274**
noddy
  black **46**
Norderlicht 120-121, **121, 292**
Norfolk 39, 190
North Island **242**
North Luangwa 223
Norway 101, 115, 202
notebooks 39
Nouabalé-Ndoki NP 74, 127

Nullabor 105
Nxai Pans 228
Nyika NP 226
Nyungwe NP 74, 221

O
Ocean Nova **293**
Oceans Worldwide 120
ocelot 168, 180
off-road driving 17
Ogasawara Islands 247
oilbird 168
Okavango Delta 8, 22, 23, 47, **58,** 63, 68-71, **69, 71,** 135, 208, 209, 229
Okonjima 230
Olympic NP 96-97, **97,** 127, 139
Oman 247
Operation Wallacea 131
orang-utan 75, 76, **77, 79,** 254, **255**
orca 23, 100, 101, **102-103,** 152, 153, 194, 286
Orinoco Delta 168
Orkney Islands 46
osprey **150,** 189
Otago Peninsula 14, 270, 277
otter 150, 151, 166, 168, **191**
  giant river 169, 170, 178, 180
owl 202, 222
  great grey **202**
  short-eared **175**

P
Pacaya Samira NR 178
Pachira Lodge 78
Pacific Rim NP 152
Pacific Whale Watch Association 138
Palau 48
Pamir Mountains 127
pampas 160
Panama 161
panda
  giant 91, **247,** 251
Pantanal 8, 22, 160, 170, **171,** 185
panther, Florida 151
Papua New Guinea 115, 272-273
Paracas NR 178
Paradise Bay **116-117,** 286
parakeet
  austral 181
parrot 224, 268
  festive 169
  thick-billed 163

Patagonia 127, 160, 161
Paulet Island 286
Pebble Island 288
pelican 200
  brown **1**
  white **200**
Pembrokeshire 190
Pench NP 249
penguin 286, 290
  Adélie **280, 287**
  chinstrap **280, 287**
  emperor **280**
  Galápagos 172, **175,** 176
  gentoo **36, 37, 46, 132-133, 280, 281,** 288
  king **8, 13, 280,** 288, 290, **291**
  little 265, 268, 270
  macaroni **280**
  Magellanic 180, **183,** 288
  rockhopper **37, 280,** 288, **289**
  Snares Island 286
  yellow-eyed 270
Periyar NP 75, 249
Peru 46, 73, 126, 178-179
Pete Raines **246**
Peter Scott 187
Petkeljärvi NP 202
petrel 286, 288
Philippines 115, 247
Phillip Island 265
photography **34-37,** 63
  equipment **34-36**
  technique **36-37,** 79, 104
pigeon
  Victoria crowned **272**
Picos de Europa 189, 195
Platte River 145
platypus 265, 268
plover
  Egyptian **211**
Poco das Antas Biological Reserve 74
Poland 188
polio 41
porcupine 153, 232
Porini Rhino Camp **242**
possum 265
Primate Lodge 78
primate watching 72-85
pronghorn antelope 145, 146, 153
protea, pincushion **235**
Provence 198
ptarmigan
  rock **121**
  willow **142**

Index

puku **227**
puffin
  Atlantic **46, 190, 203**
Punta Sal NP **165**
Pyrenees 193, 195

Q

Qinling Mountains 22, 251
Quark Expeditions 281
Quebec 92, 105
Queen Elizabeth NP 221
Queensland 269
Quetzal, resplendent **166,** 167
Quirimbas 226
Quirpon Lighthouse Inn **157**
quokka 264

R

rabies 41
rafflesia **253**
Rainbow Tours 27
Raja Ampat Islands 256
Raleigh International 131
Ralph Bousfield **25**
Ramsey Island 190
Ranomafana NP 75, 236
Ranthambhore NP 54, 135,
  248
Red Sea 209
redwood, coast 144
Redwood NP 139, 144
reedbuck 221, 233
Reef & Rainforest Tours 27
reindeer, Svalbard **121,** 280
Resurgence, The **275**
rhinoceros 248, 254, 256
  black 60, **61,** 212, 216, 223,
    230
  Indian one-horned **47,**
    247, **251**
  white 60, 223, **225**
Rhodope Mountains 200
Richard Knocker **208**
Río Plátano **165**
Robson Bight Ecological
  Reserve 152
Rocky Mountain NP 139, 144
roller
  Abyssinian **211**
  lilac-breasted **220**
Romania 22, 92, 93, 200
rosella, crimson **268**
Ross Sea 115, 286
Rottnest Island 264
RSPB 187
responsible travel 14-17
Ruaha NP 209, 217
Rupununi Savannah 169

Russia 92, 247
Rwanda 23, 67, 74, 78, 80-81,
  209, 221

S

Sabah 48, 75, 78, 79, 247,
  252-255
Sabinyo Silverback Lodge 78,
  80, **81**
sable **61**
Sadie Cove **157**
safaris 57-63
  accommodation 238-243
  family 63
  walking 49, 58, 68-71, **71,**
    226
Sagarmatha NP 251
Sagitta **177**
Saguenay-St Lawrence MP
  154
Sahara 208
sailing 17, **243**
Sajama NP 180
salamander 148
Salisbury Plain 290
Sal Salis **274**
Samba **177**
Samburu NR 213
St Andrews Bay 290
St Kilda 46, 190
St Lawrence River 100, 139
San Ignacio Lagoon 163
Santa Cruz **177**
Sarawak 49, 75, 247, 252-254
sardine run 233
Sardinia 198
Satao Camp 214, **241**
Satpura NP 8, 248, **250**
Saunders Island 288
saxifrage **121**
Scotland 101, 127, 188
Scottish Hebrides 105, 115,
  116, 189, 190, **191**
seabird identification 117
sea kayaking 104, 106-109,
  109, 152, 162, 184, 189,
  263, 279
seal 190, 210, 284
  bearded **121,** 284
  fur 172, **231,** 268, **271,** 290
  harbour 140, 284
  leopard **287**
  see also elephant seal and
    walrus
sea lion 268, 288
  Californian **2, 109,** 162
  Galápagos **44-45, 49,** 172,
    174

Steller's 140, 144
Sea Lion Island **288**
Sea of Cortez 100, 114, 162
sea otter 140
Selous GR 58, 209, 216
Semliki Forest 221
Senegal 209, 210
Sepilok see Kabili-Sepilok
  Reserve
Sepilok Nature Resort **78,** 79
Serengeti NP 8, 22, 64-67,
  65, 127, 216, 218-219
serval **61**
Seychelles 209, **243**
Shabani Omary **60**
shark
  basking 7, 190, 193
  bronze whaler 233
  great white **48,** 232
  ragged tooth 233
  whale 50-51, **51, 165,** 176,
    213, 233, **274**
shearwater
  Cory's **197**
  Manx 190
  sooty 286
sheep
  bighorn **47,** 146, 153
  Dall 140, **143,** 153
Shenandoah NP 149
Shergarh Tented Camp **259**
Shetland Islands 46, **186,** 188
shock 42
Sian Ka'an Ecological Res 163
Sibillini NP 198
Sierra Club 137
Sierra de Guara 195
Sierra Nevada de Mérida
  NP 168
Simien Mountains 58, 74,
  209, 221
Simon King **188**
Simpson Desert 47
Sinharaja BR 251
Sipadan Island 48, 252, 259
Sipidan Kapalai Dive Resort
  259
Sitka spruce **96**
Skagit River 145
Skjalfandi Bay 189
Skeleton Coast 127, 230
Skeleton Coast Safaris **231**
skimmer
  black **150**
Skockholm Island 190
Skomer Island 190
sloth, three-toed 178
Snares Island 115, 286

Snettisham RSPB reserve 187
snipe, Magellanic **289**
snorkelling 16, 50-51, 162,
  172, 213, **243,** 265
snowcock, Tibetan **251**
Snowdonia NP 190
Snow Hill Island 286
Snow Leopard Conservancy 86
Sossusvlei **231**
South Africa 23, 48, 49, 58,
  59, 63, 101, 105, 232-235
South Georgia (Antarctica)
  22, 23, 39, 114, 135, 290-291
South Luangwa 8, 22, 63,
  224,226
  see also Luangwa Valley
South Orkney islands 286
South Shetland Islands 286
Spain 39, 116, 194-195
spider
  baboon **48**
  black widow **43**
Sparrow Cove 288
Spirit Bear Lodge 93, **157**
Sri Lanka 75, 101, 247, 251
Steppes Discovery 27
Stewart Island 263, 270
Stewart Island Lodge **277**
stings 42
Stockholm 189
stork
  painted **251**
  saddlebilled **71**
  white 194, **196**
  wood 150, **150**
storm petrel **117**
  white-vented 117
Strait of Magellan 181
Stromness Harbour 290
Stuff your rucksack 15
Sukau Rainforest Lodge 259
Sulawesi 256
Sumatra 75, 79
Sumbu NP 223
sunburn 42
Sunderbans 116, 249
Svalbard **17,** 22, 23, 39, 67,
  92, 93, 115, 120-121, **121,**
  127, 284-285
Sweden 189, 202

T

Tabin Wildlife Resort **259**
Tabletop Track 268
Tadoba-Andhari Tiger Res 249
Tajikstan 127
Tallgrass Prairie Reserve 139,
  149

Taman Negara NP 75, 247
tamarin 74
  golden lion 74, **77**
Tambopata NR 178
Tanjung Puting NP 75
Tanzania 22, 23, 46, 58, 59,
  63, 74, 78, 127, 209, 216-217
tapir 170, 180
  Baird's 164, 166
Tapir Mountain Reserve 164
Tarangire NP 217
tarsier **77**
Tasmania 262, 265
Tasmanian devil 265
Tent with a View **241**
tern
  Arctic **285**
  royal **211**
  sooty 261
tetanus 41
Thailand 247
Thala Beach Lodge **275**
Tien Shan Mountains 247
Tierra del Fuego 114, 161, **181**
tiger **8,** 52-55, **53, 55,** 247, **248**
Tonga 101, 105
Tongabezi **241**
topi 212
Toro-Semliki GR 82-85
Torres del Paine NP 161, 180,
  182, 185
tortoise
  giant Galápagos **173**
Tortuguero NP 166
toucan
  keel-billed **166**
Transylvanian Wolf 188
travel oeprators 26-29
Tribes Travel 28
Trinidad & Tobago 161, 164
tropicbird
  red-billed 172
  white-tailed **243**
Tsavo NP, East & West 212, 214
Tsumkwe 58
Tundra Lodge 93
Tunku Abdul Rahman Park 252
turtle 162, 251, 210
  green 166, 173, 176, 251,
    252, 265
  hawksbill 166, **243**
  leatherback 166, 167, 233,
    251
  loggerhead 166, 233
  olive ridley 251
Turtle Islands Park 252
Tweedsmuir Park Lodge 93,
  157

Photography credits

typhoid 41

U
uakari 74, **77**
Uakari Lodge 78
Udawalawe NP 251
Uganda 74, 78, 82-85, 221
Ujung Kulon NP 256
Ulva Island **277**
Undiscovered Alps 88
USA 47, 48, 67, 88, 92, 93, 100, 114, 116, 126, 135, 136-151

V
vaccinations 41
Vakona Forest Lodge 79
Valdés Peninsula 100, 161, 180
Vallée de Mai **243**
Vancouver Island 22
Valdés Peninsula 22, 23
Vanoise NP 198
Varanger Fjord 189, 202
Venezuela 161, 168
Victoria (BC) 138
Victoria Falls **225**
Virunga Lodge 78
Volanteer Point 288
Volcanoes NP 8, 14, 74, 80-81, 221
Voyageurs NP 139, 148
vulture **65,** 192, 194, 195
 see also lammergeier

W
Waipoua Forest 270
walking safari *see* safaris
wallaby 264, 265
Wallacea 257
wallcreeper 193, 200
walrus **121,** 284
Wapusk NP 153
warthog **61**
water (drinking) 42
waterbuck 221
Weddell Sea 286
weevil, giraffe-necked 236, **237**
Western Australia 262
West MacDonnell NP 265
West Point Island 288, **289**
whale
 beluga 100, **103,** 153, 284
 blue 100, 101, **103,** 162, 251
 bowhead 284
 Bryde's 100, 101, 162
 fin 100, 101, **103,** 154, 162

grey 100, **102, 103,** 106-109, **109,** 144, **162**
humpback 23, **98,** 99, 100-101, **103, 104, 105,** 137, 140, 153, 154, 162, 167, 176, 210, 233, 265, **269,** 286
killer (*see* orca)
migration 99
minke 100, 101, **103,** 154, 162, **203**
narwhal 284
northern right 100, 154
pilot 100, 101, **103,** 197
southern right 23, 101, **103,** 180, **183,** 268
sperm 100, 101, **102, 103,** 162, 194, 197, 202, 270
swimming with 105
whale watching 98-111, 137, 148, 152, 154, 162, 184, 185, 191, 194, 197, 203, 233, 234, 251, 265, 286, 269
 code of conduct 105
Wild Ambitions 28
Wild Coast 233
wild dog (dhole) 249
wildebeest 23, **58, 65, 66-67,** 212, 216, **218,** 228, 230
 blue 234
 Cookson's 224
 see also Great Migration
Wilderness Safaris 238
wilderness travel 17, 124-127
Wilderness Travel 28
 code of conduct 126
Wildfowl & Wetlands Trust 187
Wildland Adventures 28
Wildlife & Wilderness 29
wildlife cruises 112-125
 code of conduct 116
wildlife trade 15
Wildlife Trails 29
Wildman Wilderness Lodge **277**
Wildwings 29
Wildlife Worldwide 27, 139
Wild Side 88
Wild Sweden 88
wolf 88, **89,** 140, **143,** 146, 149, 153, 195, 198, 202
 Ethiopian 221
wolverine 146
wombat 265
woodpecker 200
 black 198
 blood-coloured 169
 gila 162

Magellanic 181
 middle-spotted **201**
World Primate Safaris 29
WWF Travel 28
Wrangell-St Elias NP 141
wrasse, Napolean **269**

Y
Yala NP 251
Yasuní BR 185
yellow fever 41
Yellowstone NP 88, 137, 139, 146, 157
Yellow Waters Billabong **267**
Yosemite Lodge at the Falls **157**
Yosemite NP **136,** 137, 139, 146
Yucatan Peninsula 161

Z
Zambezi River 208, 223, **225**
Zambia 22, 39, 58, 63, 222-227
 green season 23
zebra 64, 216, 217, 221, 228, 233, 234
 Grevy's **61**
 mountain 232
 plains **220**
Zimbabwe 58, 226

Photography credits

William Gray (author)
1, 4, 5, 6-7, 8, 10-11, 13, 14, 17, 18-19, 32, 33, 34-35, 36, 37, 38, 46, 47, 48, 49 (1, 4, 6, 7), 51 (top & bottom), 55, 56, 58, 60, 61, 62, 63, 65, 69, 71, 72 76, 77 (macaque, colobus, langur, orang, mountain gorilla), 78, 79, 81, 84-85, 93 (polar bears), 95, 97, 107, 109, 111 (bottom), 112, 117, 119, 121, 123, 124, 128, 132-133, 136, 138, 143 (ptarmigan), 144, 150, 152, 155, 158, 160, 164, 165 (1, 3, 5), 172, 173, 174, 175, 176, 179 (top, bottom left), 181 (1, 3, 4), 183 (penguins, seals), 186, 190, 191 (Cairngorms, Mull), 196 (landscape, storks), 197 (waterfall), 203 (3, 4, 5), 206, 212, 214-215, 216, 218, 220, 221, 225, 227, 229 (top), 231 (1, 2, 3, 4), 234, 235, 238, 239, 240, 242 (Ngorongoro), 243 (2, 3, 4, 5), 244, 246, 248, 250, 251 (snowcock), 253 (forest, rafflesia), 255, 260, 262 (reef), 263 (Fiordland), 270-271, 277 (Ulva Island), 278, 281, 288, 289, 292-293, 303, inside back cover, back cover

Andy Rouse
Front cover, 66-67

Jonathan & Angie Scott
135

Naturepl
77 (aye-aye/Lynn Stone), 86-87 (snow leopard/Francois Savigny), 88-89 (wolf/Wonders of Europe), 90 (grizzly bear/Eric Baccega), 102 (orca/Mark Carwardine), 162 (grey whale/Mark Carwardine), 182 (Torres del Paine/Oriol Alamany), 182 (armadillo/Daniel Gomez), 269 (Heron Island/Roberto RInaldi), 273 (bird of paradise/Phil Savoie), 273 (reef/David Hall), 273 (cuscus/Phil Chapman)

Shutterstock
2, 12, 13, 15, 16, 40, 43, 47 (4, 5), 48 (1-6), 49 (2, 3), 51 (middle), 53, 55 (top & centre bottom), 58 (1), 59, 61 (wild dog, serval, Grevy's zebra), 74, 75, 77, 83, 92, 93 (black, brown, sloth bear), 98, 100-101, 102, 103, 104, 105, 111 (top), 114, 115, 116-117 (top), 126-127, 137, 143, 147, 148, 165 (2, 4), 166, 168, 169, 171, 178, 179, (bottom centre & right), 180, 181 (2, 5), 183 (whale), 189, 191 (otter, deer, eagle), 192, 194, 196 (bustard, hoopoe), 197 (shearwater), 198, 199, 200, 201, 202, 203 (1, 2), 204-205, 210, 211, 224, 228, 229 (gemsbok), 231 (5), 232, 237, 241 (sitatunga), 242 (rhino), 243 (1), 247, 251, 253 (monkeys, frog), 254, 256-257, 259 (hornbill, Kapalai), 262 (bats), 263 (Abel Tasman), 264, 266-267, 268, 269 (2, 3, 4, 5), 272 (pigeon, crocodile fish), 277 (Cape Leveque), 280, 285, 286, 287, 290, 291

Others
Earthwatch 131, Africa's Eden 210 (elephants), Norman Carr Safaris 226

With thanks to 'Guiding stars' and 'It's a wild life' contributors for portrait photographs, and to accommodation providers for images of lodges, camps, resorts and ships in 'Wild Nights Out'.

Maps and globes:
Shutterstock

Publishing credits & acknowledgements

Acknowledgements

This book is the culmination of more than 25 years of research, involving dozens of trips to every corner of the world in search of wildlife and wild places. I feel immensely privileged to have had the opportunity to channel my passion for nature, travel and conservation into such a project, but none of it would have been possible without the enthusiasm, support and encouragement of countless organisations and individuals.

Top of the list must be my wife, Sally – the best travelling companion (and tripod carrier) anyone could wish for! To have shared with her many of the wildlife experiences recounted in *Wildlife Travel* has been one of the most pleasurable aspects of researching the book. The same goes for my children, Joe and Ellie who have accompanied us on many trips.

I must also say a big thank you to family and friends for their help, advice and motivation during the writing and design of this book; particularly to the Rippons for supplying cups of tea and large wedges of homemade cake at critical 'low-sugar/ low inspiration' points.

Ultimately, I owe a huge debt of thanks to the writers, photographers, artists, film-makers, TV presenters, travel specialists and conservationists that have been a source of inspiration to me for as long as I can remember. I'm delighted that several of them agreed to contribute quotes for *Wildlife Travel* (see inside front cover) and my thanks go to Amanda Marks, Andy Rouse, Brian Jackman, Bruce Pearson, Chris Breen, Chris McIntyre, Jonathan and Angela Scott, Mark Carwardine, Pete Raines and Simon King. I am also extremely grateful to Kate Humble for supplying the book's foreword.

Far too numerous to list in detail, I am also indebted to the numerous travel operators and tourist boards that have supplied invaluable information and practical support for the research of *Wildlife Travel*. I'm particularly grateful to &Beyond, Discover the World, Expert Africa, Falklands Tourism, Journey Latin America, Reef & Rainforest Tours and Wildlife Worldwide, all of which are featured in the directory on pages 294-297.

Thanks, also, to *Wanderlust* magazine, *The Sunday Times*, *Sunday Telegraph*, *Travel Africa* and other newspapers and magazines for supporting my obsession with wildlife travel.

Finally, my thanks go to the team at Footprint for allowing me the freedom to write, photograph and design *Wildlife Travel* – and for letting me take much longer to do it than I should have done!

William Gray

Footprint credits

Project Editor: Alan Murphy
Layout & design: William Gray
Picture Editor: William Gray
Proofreader: Jo Williams

Managing Director: Andy Riddle
Publisher: Alan Murphy
Commercial Director: Patrick Dawson
Editorial: Felicity Laughton, Nicola Gibbs Jo Williams
Digital: Tom Mellors
Marketing: Liz Harper
Sales: Di McEntee
Advertising: Renu Sibal
Finance & administration: Elizabeth Taylor

Photography

All images © William Gray/william-gray.co.uk unless otherwise credited on page 303

Print

Manufactured in India by Replika Press Pvt Ltd

Publishing information

Footprint Wildlife Travel, 1st edition
© Footprint Handbooks Ltd, October 2011

ISBN 978-1-907263-48-4
CIP DATA: A catalogue record for this book is available from the British Library.

® Footprint Handbooks and the Footprint mark are a registered trademark of Footprint Handbooks Ltd.

Published by Footprint

6 Riverside Court, Lower Bristol Road
Bath BA2 3DZ, UK
T +44 (0)1225 469141
F +44 (0)1225 469461
footprinttravelguides.com

Distributed in the USA by
Globe Pequot Press, Guilford, Connecticut